Computer-
Communication
Network
Design and Analysis

Computer-
Communication
Network
Design and Analysis

IIIIIIIIIIIIIIIIIIIIIIIIIIIIIIIIIIIIIIIIIIIIIIIIIIIIIIIIIIIIIIIIIIIIIIIIIIIIIIIIIIIIIIIIIIIIIIIIIIIIIIIIIIIIIIIIIIIIIIIIIIIIIII

MISCHA SCHWARTZ

Department of Electrical Engineering and Computer Science
Columbia University
New York, New York

PRENTICE-HALL, INC., Englewood Cliffs, New Jersey   07632

Library of Congress Cataloging in Publication Data

Schwartz, Mischa (date)
    Computer-communication network design and
analysis.

    Bibliography: p.
    1. Data transmission systems. 2. Computer
networks. I. Title.
TK5105.S38   621.38   76-54691
ISBN 0-13-165134-X

10 9 8

Printed in the United States of America

PRENTICE-HALL INTERNATIONAL, INC., *London*
PRENTICE-HALL OF AUSTRALIA PTY. LIMITED, *Sydney*
PRENTICE-HALL OF CANADA, LTD., *Toronto*
PRENTICE-HALL OF INDIA PRIVATE LIMITED, *New Delhi*
PRENTICE-HALL OF JAPAN, INC., *Tokyo*
PRENTICE-HALL OF SOUTHEAST ASIA PTE. LTD., *Singapore*
WHITEHALL BOOKS LIMITED, *Wellington, New Zealand*

To Liz and David

Contents

Preface   *ix*

1   Overview and Introduction   *1*

2   Examples of Networks   *13*

3   Capacity Assignment in Networks   *58*

4   Capacity Assignment in
Distributed Network   *71*

5   Centralized Networks:
Time Delay—Cost Trade-offs   *85*

6   Elements of Queueing Theory   *103*

7   Concentration and Buffering
in Store-and-Forward Networks   *135*

8   Concentration: Finite Buffers,
Dynamic Buffering, Block Storage   *154*

9   Centralized Network Design:
     Multipoint Connections   *171*

10   Network Design Algorithms   *193*

11   Routing and Flow Control   *212*

12   Polling in Networks   *262*

13   Random Access Techniques   *286*

14   Line Control Procedures   *321*

     Appendix:
     Elements of Point-to-Point
     Data Communication   *340*

     References   *348*

     Index   *358*

Preface

This book is an outgrowth of notes developed while teaching courses on computer–communications over the past five years at the graduate level at both Columbia University and the Polytechnic Institute of Brooklyn, as well as to groups of practicing engineers, systems analysts, and programmers as part of a variety of continuing professional courses and programs. Portions of the material have been taught as well at the advanced undergraduate level as part of a course on data communication. The author has been particularly fortunate in having such a broad group of individuals with whom to interact. Answering, or attempting to answer, innumerable provocative questions from graduate students, engineers, computer scientists, and colleagues has been a truly gratifying learning experience for him. He can only hope that the participants in these courses learned as much as he did and that the experience and insight gained from these many discussions, with novice and expert alike, are reflected in the presentations in this book.

As noted in the first, introductory, chapter the field of computer–communication networks is a particularly broad one and covers many areas, from computer and communication processor hardware and software design to large-scale network layout. There are fascinating problems involving routing, flow, and congestion control that are just beginning to be studied. Problems of computer–to–computer protocol, problems related to integrated voice-and-data networks, to interconnection of large national networks, to the integration of many diverse data sources and computers into one or more smoothly–operating networks, just to select a few, are under intensive study.

The field is diverse and developing rapidly, and it is with some humility that an author must approach the task of writing a textbook for this field.

For pedagogic reasons and because of personal interest and background, the author has chosen to focus principally on the communications network itself in this broad field. He has attempted to seek out and present those topics of network design and analysis that appear to be of lasting interest and usefulness, and that lend themselves to quantitative treatment. It is the author's considered opinion that hard thinking about a subject—the ability to ask appropriate and penetrating questions—is best developed through exposure, where possible, to modeling and analysis. Extremely important topics that may not lend themselves as readily to a quantitative approach, for example, critical questions of software design, are raised in Chap. 2 on examples of real operating networks, and in many of the references listed throughout the book. The author views this book as an introductory one in the area and urges the serious reader and student to actively study the literature cited for the full treatment of many of the topics covered or just barely touched on.

To make the book as useful and interesting as possible, design examples, design tables, and curves, are included throughout the book. Where possible different analysis and design approaches are compared. In addition to the detailed description of the four operating networks appearing in Chap. 2, which is used both to motivate the rest of the book and to point out different design solutions for similar problems, other examples of operating networks or systems are cited in various places throughout the book.

Except for some prior knowledge of elementary probability theory there is no specific background information required for understanding and following the material of the book. Some knowledge of point-to-point digital communication techniques would be useful but for those readers lacking this background the appendix and Chap. 2 should provide ample introduction to both the terminology and technology of the field. The book should prove useful for courses in either engineering or computer science curricula, for in-plant programs for practicing engineers, systems analysts, and programmers, and for self-study by interested individuals. The problems at the end of the chapters serve as an integral part of the book and should be studied by serious readers. They extend some of the material in the text, provide examples of material discussed, and suggest interesting applications.

It is always difficult to provide appropriate acknowledgements to individuals and organizations in books such as this one, covering a variety of topics in a broad area. It is particularly difficult in this case because of the literally hundreds of contacts made through many course presentations, lectures, seminars, conference discussions, and research involvement, all carried out during the preparation of the book. The author would like to single out, however, the National Science Foundation of the United States for its support of his research activities and those of his students in the area over the past few years. Active involvement in the area, plus teaching about it, obviously provide the best way of learning about a subject. The author is particularly thankful to Mr. Elias Schutzman, Project Director with NSF, for his unfailing enthusiasm and guidance.

Professors R. L. Pickholtz of George Washington University and R. R. Boorstyn of the Polytechnic Institute of New York, friends and former colleagues, cooperated in much of the research, teaching, and lecturing over the years, and the author is grateful for their advice, criticism, and support. Particular thanks are due to Mr. Chris Brook of GE, Mr. LaRoy Tymes of Tymshare, Inc., and Dr. John McQuillan of BBN for sharing with the author their knowledge of the individual networks described in Chap. 2, and for uncomplainingly answering many questions and helping him improve his knowledge in the process.

MISCHA SCHWARTZ

Overview

and

Introduction

1

Data networks of various kinds are currently in existence or in the process of being set up. These include large-scale computer networks (e.g., the ARPA network, the French Cyclades network) and the multipurpose data networks set up or proposed by the British Post Office, the trans-Canada Telephone System, DATRAN,* and ATT among others, airline reservation systems, medical data networks, banking networks, educational networks, corporate communication networks, information service networks, and so on. The number is endless and growing rapidly.

In this book we propose to present, in a quantitative way where possible, aspects of network design that are broadly applicable to most of these networks. These include questions related to entry of messages into the networks and the combining of messages from a multiplicity of terminals located in one contiguous geographic area, as well as the global question of routing the message streams to a multiplicity of remote locations. The field is new, and an understanding of many network design problems and their solutions is just beginning to develop. We propose to raise some of the design questions in detail and to outline various approaches for handling them. We shall do this where possible in the context of some existing networks.

Two kinds of networks are either in existence or under development (some networks under development may involve a composite of both types):

*The DATRAN Network ceased operation for financial reasons in August 1976. Its use of line-switched technology was, however, at the state of the art and the references listed in this book provide valuable insight into that technology.

1. *Line-switched type*, analogous to the telephone (voice) network. Here calls and message routing are set up prior to commencement of message transmission. Once a complete circuit or route is established, the message is ready for transmission. Call set-up time plays a critical role in assessing the performance of networks of this type. The DATRAN network is a prominent example of a line-switched data network.

2. *Message- or packet-switched type.* Here a message (either in complete form or in shorter packets) works its way through the network, from link to link, queueing at specific nodal points. Small computers (generally mini-computers and, increasingly, microcomputers) located at message concentration and routing points perform the necessary message coding for entry into the network, carry out message combining and buffering, routing to the next destination, etc. These computers are variously called *programmable* or *remote concentrators*. These networks introduce buffering or queueing delay, and thus delay time or response time plays a critical role in their design.

In this book we shall focus primarily on message-switched networks, hence the use of the words *computer-communication networks*. The programmable concentrator provides a flexibility and capability for growth or change not otherwise possible. The reader is referred to a series of papers on the DATRAN network to provide the contrast with the message- or packet-switched networks discussed in this book.* (Some of these papers are mentioned in footnotes at the end of the introductory section of Chap. 2.)

Two general categories of networks are often distinguished: terminal-oriented networks, those used to transmit various types of low-speed data; and computer networks, a relatively recent development in which computers are interconnected into one network to provide more computer power than might otherwise be possible, to distribute computational loads more efficiently, and to provide a sharing of computational facilities. The ARPA network, to be discussed in detail in the next chapter, is the largest such network in existence. Smaller networks are in existence or under development in the United States, France, Canada, England, and Europe. Most existing networks are of the terminal-oriented type. Some examples will be discussed in the chapter following.

In most cases, the principles of network design are the same for both types of networks. Increasingly, however, networks are being called upon to handle a mix of data. These may vary in speed from 10 characters/sec teletype to 50 kbits/sec (kbps) computer printout; the messages transmitted may be short, as is commonly the case for inquiry messages in many inquiry-response systems, or they may be very long, as with data transmission

---

*Series of papers on the DATRAN network, *Proc. IEEE National Telecommunications Conference*, New Orleans, Dec. 1975.

involving file transfer. They may include voice data as well. The design of networks handling messages with a variety of speeds, lengths, and rates of arrival is an area of great interest. This broad range of possible message statistics represents one fundamental distinction between data networks and the ubiquitous telephone networks transmitting primarily voice information. In this latter case, messages average 3 minutes long, and information bandwidths are limited at the entry to the network to less than 4 kilohertz (kHz).

This question of broad range of data rates, message lengths, and message arrival rates to be considered leads to the concept of integrated networks incorporating both a message-switched and a line-switched capability. For example, if the message to be transmitted is very long, it may be more cost-effective to transmit it over a dedicated path as is the case with line switching. Only if the messages are relatively short and infrequently occurring does it pay to use a message-switched facility, with messages from different users being combined to share the cost of transmission. Modern time-switching and time-multiplexing technology allows both modes of operation to be incorporated in one system.*

What are the specific design questions to be considered in detail in this book? We have already mentioned the two categories of *global* and *local* design questions. Under the global category we include questions relating to the design (in some optimum or cost-valid sense) of the overall network:

1. *Topological design.* Given the geographical location of terminals and other message sources, as well as their expected traffic characteristics, where shall the concentration and switching points (the network nodes) be located? How should they be connected? What form should the network take—star, tree, loop, mesh, etc.? How many links (trunks or connections between nodes) are needed?

2. *Line capacity allocation.* What size trunks, in units of data capacity (bits/sec (bps)), shall be used throughout the network?

3. *Routing procedures.* How do different routing algorithms compare? Should there be local or centralized routing control? How often should routing information and/or routing control be updated? How shall this be done? What are the significant parameters in determining routing?

---

*See, for example: N. Shimasaki and T. Kohashi, "A Compatible Multiplexing Technique for Anisochronous and Isochronous Digital Data Traffic," *Data Networks: Analysis and Design, Third Data Communications Symposium*, St. Petersburg, Fla., Nov. 1973, pp. 59–67; K. Kummerle, "Multiplexor Performance for Integrated Line- and Packet-Switched Traffic," *Proc. 1974 International Conference on Computer-Communications*, Stockholm, Sweden; M. J. Fischer and T. C. Harris, "A Model for Evaluating the Performance of an Integrated Circuit- and Packet-Switched Multiplex Structure," *IEEE Trans. on Communications,* **COM-24**, no. 2, Feb. 1976, 195-202.

4. *Flow control procedures.* How does one ensure smooth traffic flow throughout the network? How are bottlenecks and deadlocks to be prevented? How can one prevent any one customer, data source, or node from tying up the network?

Performance criteria used in answering these questions include:

1. Specified response time, normally in a probabilistic sense (e.g., less than 1 sec, 95% of the time), average for the network, average on any link, maximum from any point to a central computer (CPU) or processor, etc.

2. Specified costs *or* specified (say, minimum) response time for a given cost, *or* minimum cost design for a given response time.

3. Maximum or specified reliability.

Examples of different network topologies are shown in Fig. 1-1.

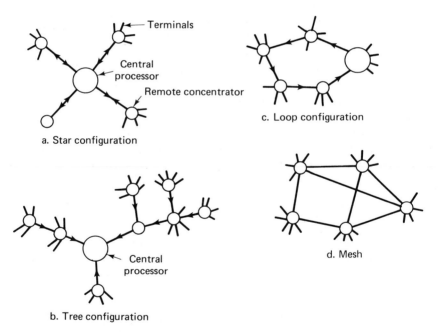

Fig. 1-1. Different topological configurations.

Under the local category we include such questions as: which message concentration or combining (multiplexing) schemes are to be used? How many message sources, and of what type, can reasonably be combined at one concentration point? Shall the multiplexing scheme be synchronous or asynchronous? What are the trade-offs? How do various access techniques such as polling or random access compare? What buffer sizes are needed and what buffer loading strategies should be used to ensure desired response times and/or specified probabilities of buffer overflow?

In answering these and related questions, we shall have to specify message length and traffic statistics and to develop simplified models for the concentration, store, and forward operations.

A simple example serves to put these and other questions in context. Say terminals in each of 7 eastern U.S. cities* are to be connected to a central computer facility located in Washington, D.C. We assume inbound traffic only (user to computer), for simplicity. (Communications between the various terminals are thus ruled out in this rudimentary example.) Each of the terminals contains a teletypewriter (TTY) transmitting at a nominal rate of 10 char./sec, or 80 bps, with an 8-bit character code. Each TTY is assumed active, transmitting on the average one message every 30 sec. The average message is assumed 15 characters (120 bits) long. The 7 cities and number of TTY terminals in each to be connected to the central computer are as follows:

1. Chicago, Ill.   10 terminals
2. Detroit, Mich.   9 terminals
3. Charlotte, N.C.   4 terminals
4. Miami, Fla.   6 terminals
5. New Orleans, La.   6 terminals
6. New York, N.Y.   12 terminals
7. Tallahassee, Fla.   4 terminals

A sketch appears in Fig. 1-2.

How are the terminals in each city to be connected, concentrated, or multiplexed? It is obviously too expensive to run separate lines from each terminal to the central computer (CPU). We are thus faced with the local multiplexing question. One approach might be to use multiplexing concentrators, operating in either the time-division multiplex (TDM) or frequency-division multiplex (FDM) modes. These are essentially *synchronous* devices. This approach is cheaper than the programmable concentrator one (especially for this rather artificial example with relatively few terminals in the network) but statistically inefficient.

As an example, if TDM is used, each of the terminals in a group. e.g., the 10 terminals in Chicago, is allocated a dedicated time slot, even when no

*This example is based on one presented in D. R. Doll, "*Efficient Allocation of Resources in Centralized Computer-Communication Network Design,*" University of Michigan, Systems Engineering Laboratory, Nov. 1969.

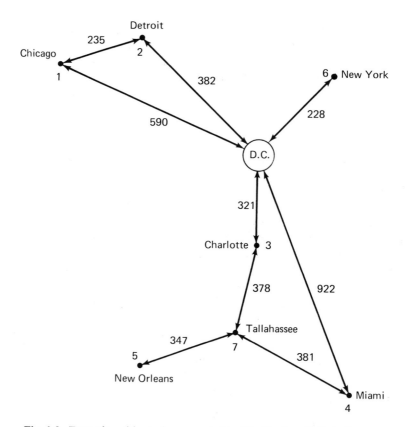

Fig. 1-2. Example—cities to be connected to Washington, D.C. (mileages shown).

messages are present. Ten TTYs each transmitting at a 10 char./sec (80 bps) rate would, when time-division multiplexed, require at least an 800 bps line.

Assume *asynchronous* or statistical multiplexing is now used. The 10 TTYs are first merged into a buffer, the *output* now being taken out at a synchronous rate. Since each TTY produces, on the average, one message every 30 sec, a group of 10 would provide, on the average, one message every 3 sec. With an average assumed message length of 120 bits (15 char.), the average input rate to the buffer is then 40 bps. The output must, therefore, have at least this capacity to prevent messages from building up indefinitely in the buffer. The asynchronous approach takes advantage of the burst nature of typical messages, using a buffer to smooth out the message flow.

Programmable concentrators, using minicomputers or microcomputers, can be readily programmed to provide statistical multiplexing. Their storage capability provides the necessary buffering, and they may be used to carry out a limited amount of processing, bookkeeping, addressing, message format conversion, etc. Their flexibility allows a variety of input terminals to access the network; the number of input terminals connected may be readily changed, different types of scanning may be used, etc. (Scanning or polling techniques include hub polling, roll-call polling, nested polling, as well as others.) The use of programmable concentrators seems to be increasing rapidly, and we shall stress these devices in this book.

Note that we have used *average* statistics for calculation purposes above. In the actual design of the multiplexing or concentrating system, having more detailed message and traffic statistics would be desirable as well. The size of the buffer and its effect on message blocking probability, as well as message time delay due to buffering, depend on these statistics. One simple model is to assume Poisson message arrivals, with exponentially-distributed message lengths. Experimental data indicate that in some situations the Poisson arrival rate model is valid, but that geometrically-distributed message lengths (in keeping with the *discreteness* of the message lengths) may be a more appropriate model.* (For long message lengths, the exponential and geometric distributions are essentially the same.) Some analyses have assumed other forms of statistics. We shall compare several of these approaches later, in focusing on buffer design, to ensure a specified blocking probability, and shall look in particular to see how sensitive the design results are to the message statistics assumed.

With the concentration strategy taken care of, we now focus on the global design of the network. In the particular example in question (Fig. 1-2), how shall the network be organized to provide the necessary connections between each of the cities and the CPU in Washington? Shall a star configuration be used, as shown in Fig. 1-3a, a tree network as in Fig. 1-3b, or two loops as in Fig. 1-3c? All three structures, and many others as well, appear in current computer-communication networks.

The appropriate network topology depends on the choice of criteria for network performance. For example, in calculations we shall outline in a later chapter, the tree structure in Fig. 1-3b turns out to be the best of the three in the sense of the lowest communications cost for a specified tolerable maximum time delay. (This assumes as a crude approximation that the cost of each concentrator is the same, independent of the number of incoming lines connected to it. The cost is then the cost of the trunks connecting the various cities and depends, of course, on the cost figures assumed.) Another performance criterion we shall discuss in detail will be minimum average time delay for a fixed cost.

---

*See, for example, E. Fuchs and P. E. Jackson, "Estimates of Distributions of Random Variables for Certain Computer-Communication Traffic Models," *Communications of the ACM*, **13**, no. 12, Dec. 1970, 752–57.

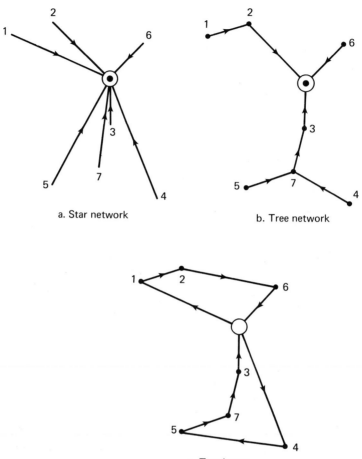

a. Star network

b. Tree network

c. Two loops

Fig. 1-3. Different network topologies, example of Fig. 1-2.

Related to the question of desired network topology, although often considered independent of it, is the appropriate allocation of data-carrying capacity on each link of the network. Essentially, how many bps in capacity is required on each link? This depends again on the particular performance criterion adopted, e.g., minimum average message time delay for a specified (fixed) cost, as well as on the message statistics and buffer assignments assumed at each network node that result in the time delay incurred. In complex networks (even those as simple as the ones in Fig. 1-3) all the design questions are interrelated: buffer allocation, topology, capacity assignments. One of the prime purposes of this book will be to try to develop a systematic approach to network design: Which design questions can be decoupled?

How may be elements of the network be modeled in the simplest sense possible, so that good approximations to network analysis and performance may be readily obtained?

Finally, one global question that must be considered is that of reliability. How does the network maintain its viability in the event of link (or node) failure? In existing networks, as we shall see, this is sometimes done by providing alternate trunks (or links). This is particularly the case in the star or tree networks of Fig. 1-3. In the loop configuration, a duplex capability which is normally available anyway may be used to reverse the direction of traffic flow away from a failed link and into the CPU directly. In the mesh or distributed configuration of Fig. 1-1d, rerouting strategies may be used to avoid failed links. We shall not explore the question of reliability in detail in this book, except to point out that, in distributed topologies, the concept of two (or higher-)-connectivity is often invoked to ensure a rerouting capability in the event of link failure. Two-connectivity simply means that each node in the network is connected to at least two other nodes. The ARPA network to be discussed in the next chapter was designed on the basis of a two-connectivity reliability constraint. In centralized networks transmission paths are often duplicated to ensure transmission backup in the event of a link failure. The GE Information Services network described in the next chapter provides this duplicated capability. The reader is referred to an excellent tutorial paper for a quantitative discussion of reliability in data networks.*

In the next chapter we discuss in detail the operation of four existing computer-communication networks. The ARPA network already referred to provides interconnection between many large computer centers located throughout the continental United States plus connections to Hawaii and Europe via satellite links. It has a distributed (mesh-type) configuration, optimized in a least-cost sense with a specified minimum average time delay. The GE network, with a more centralized topological structure provides a large processing capability that may be accessed from anywhere in the United States, Canada, Europe, Australia, and Japan. Tymshare Inc.'s TYMNET is a distributed-type, terminal-oriented network that provides both a processing capability and a data transmission facility to users located in the United States and Europe. The SITA network is a worldwide airline reservation network, enabling airline agents' terminals located anywhere in the world to access their particular airline's computers. All four of these networks utilize packet- or message-switching. In addition to the differing topologies, we shall discuss the processes of message entry, message formatting, and routing and error control procedures adopted for all four networks, pointing out the different solutions possible to all of these design questions.

*R. S. Wilkov, "Analysis and Design of Reliable Computer Networks," *IEEE Trans. on Communications*, **COM-20**, no. 3, part II, June 1972, 660–78.

This should serve to put into more specific terms the design questions already raised in this chapter. The discussion also provides a focus for, and examples of the application of, the design techniques introduced in the chapters that follow.

Chapters 3 through 5 provide the basic introduction to design questions in computer communications by focusing on the simplest design problem— the appropriate choice of line capacity or transmission capability in bps required of the various links making up the network. In setting up and solving this design problem we become involved immediately in questions of concentrator modeling, message input statistics, and appropriate performance criteria. We discuss first some analytical approaches to capacity assignment that provide first-cut answers to the appropriate choice of capacities that minimizes network time delay. We then describe an algorithm specific to centralized network design that provides the appropriate link capacity assignments in the more realistic case when a selected number of capacities are available. In much of this discussion the centralized network design problem introduced in this chapter (Fig. 1-2) provides the example with which to develop the techniques introduced. A simple distributed network is also discussed, however, to provide an introduction to distributed network design.

The modeling introduced in Chap. 3 through 5 focuses on the buffering and queueing characteristics of the network concentrators. The design analysis carried out in these chapters relies on some simple results from queueing analysis. Since the principles of queueing theory are so vital to an understanding of the time delay performance to computer-communication networks, we take time out in Chap. 6 to introduce the elements of queueing theory. This serves to make this book as self-contained as possible. We discuss first the analysis of the M/M/1 queue, assuming Poisson message arrivals and exponentially-distributed message lengths, then go on to analyze the time delay characteristic of the M/G/1 queue, appropriate to messages that do not satisfy the exponential length distribution. We also include some material on priority queueing, since priority message transmission does play a role in many networks. Calculations based on the SITA network message characteristics are used to provide an example.

With this introduction to queueing theory, we then focus on the concentrator design problem in more detail in Chap. 7 and 8. Time response analysis, buffer size requirements to satisfy a specified blocking probability criterion, and the concept of statistical multiplexing are all discussed in these chapters. More realistic models than the M/M/1 and M/G/1 queues are introduced to cover packet or block transmission at a synchronous rate. These include geometrically-distributed message lengths and finite buffers storing data units (characters or bytes, for example) rather than the message storage of the M/M/1 queue.

In Chap. 9 and 10, we return to the overall or global network design area, focusing on the topological design of networks. In Chap. 9 we discuss algorithms developed to provide the least-cost connection of terminals or concentrators assuming one message destination point. In the former case this provides the best multidrop or multipoint connection of terminals to a concentrator. In the latter case this provides the least-cost connection of concentrators in a centralized network. In Chap. 10 we discuss first the problem of appropriate choice of concentrators and terminals to connect to them in a centralized network, and then the topological design of distributed networks. It is pointed out throughout both chapters that topological design of networks, although fundamental to least-cost design of networks, is so complex as to preclude truly optimal designs that incorporate all desired performance critieria. Network design must be carried out iteratively, determining, for example, the best location and connection of concentrators, then evaluating the best message routing paths, then determining the least-cost connection of terminals to each concentrator, then repeating the design again. In the concentrator and terminal connection problems heuristic algorithms are generally used because of the large-scale (complexity) of the networks involved. (For some of the subproblems, there are no optimum algorithms known.)

Chapter 11 continues the discussion of overall network design, comparing various routing strategies and analyzing some simple techniques for alleviating congestion in a network. The routing strategies discussed include both deterministic and random, centralized and local, fixed and adaptive techniques. Least time delay and shortest path algorithms for routing are included. The congestion or flow control techniques assessed include a simple model of an end-to-end control mechanism and a local control mechanism.

In Chap. 12 and 13, we return to the question of message access into the network. In Chap. 12 we discuss the principles of polling, using the IBM Passenger Airline Reservation System (PARS) as an example. In Chap. 13 we describe some of the random access techniques motivated by the Aloha system of the University of Hawaii. We provide some simple examples comparing polling with random access, discussing the trade-offs possible between time delay and network throughput.

In Chap. 14 we describe the basic problem of line control, the procedure used in any network for setting up the necessary connection between neighboring nodes, for establishing synchronism, for maintaining the integrity of messages transmitted, for maintaining error control, and for handling other foreseeable contingencies. Various protocols and codes to implement them are discussed, both of the character-oriented and bit-oriented (transparent) type. We describe, for example, the ISO-ANSI protocol and the corresponding ASCII code, the BSC (binary synchronous code), and the SDLC-HLDC category of protocols.

In the Appendix we include some descriptive material on current point-to-point data communication facilities for those readers with relatively little background in the area. This should make the terminology used throughout the book more readily understandable.

Examples
of Networks

2

In this chapter we provide a summary of the operating characteristics of four existing message- or packet-switched networks. All of these networks interconnect a multiplicity of large computer systems (so-called *Hosts*) and data terminals of various types, providing the transmission capability required to transmit data messages rapidly and reliably between source and destination anywhere in the network. We focus here, as in the rest of the book, on the backbone communications networks only. These consist, in all cases, of geographically-dispersed small computer-communications processors interconnected by communication links. The data terminals and Host computers connected to these processors are discussed only in passing.

The four networks chosen for discussion differ in their use and application. The ARPA network was primarily developed to interconnect large computer systems; the TYMNET and GE networks are commercial time-sharing networks; the SITA network is a worldwide airline reservations network and handles airline teletype messages of various kinds as well. They are similar, however, in their use of small computers as the basic message storage and switching elements of the network. These computers have been variously labeled *communications processor, programmable concentrator, message concentrator*, and the like. As will become apparent from the discussion of each network, they typically carry out a variety of tasks. They accept messages from data terminals or computer systems connected to them, recode message characters to a standardized message format for use throughout the network (if the input devices use other formats), and buffer the messages while awaiting transmission. This is the message combining, concentration, or multiplexing phase* already mentioned briefly in Chap. 1. Messages already in the network and enroute to their specified destinations are stored in the concentrators as well. The concentrators may block messages into smaller subunits (often called *packets*), append necessary address, control, and error-checking characters, and transmit the resultant block as a unit to the next concentrator enroute to a particular destination. This may be called the message distribution, routing, or switching function of the concentrator. Routing tables stored in the concentrator are used to determine the next concentrator enroute to the destination. The routing tables may be fixed and only updated at relatively infrequent intervals as in the SITA network; they may be reestablished on the basis of current information each time a user connects into the network, as in the case of the TYMNET; or they may be updated regularly and adaptively, once or twice a second, as in the ARPA network.

In addition to message combining and routing, the concentrators carry out error checking, transmit and receive acknowledgement messages as part of an error detection and retransmission procedure, and provide a flow control function to ease possible congestion which might develop in the network. The reader will find it useful to compare the different design solutions to these various data control problems developed by the designers of these different networks.

The four networks described in the sections following are representative of the different topologies used among the various data networks in existence throughout the world. Chapter 1 included a brief discussion of some typical topologies. The GE network is an example of a centralized topology, with all messages flowing into the center and back out again. The other three networks use a distributed topology of varying complexity. All four networks use a variety of transmission circuits, generally leased from the common carrier through whose territory they run. Included are satellite and submarine cable circuits for transcontinental transmission. These circuits are variously referred to as trunks, links, or lines. The concentrators to which they connect represent the nodes of the network.

As already noted these networks are all of the message-switched store-and-forward type. They contrast with line-switched networks in which dedicated circuits are established for any given source-destination pair. Multiplexers are commonly used in such networks, in contrast with the

---

*Three useful papers surveying the general area of concentration appear in the *Proc. IEEE*, **60**, no. 11, Nov. 1972. (This was a special issue devoted to computer-communications.) They are D. R. Doll, "Multiplexing and Concentration," pp. 1313–21; C. B. Newport and J. Ryzlak, "Communication Processors," pp. 1321–32, and D. L. Mills, "Communications Software," pp. 1333–41. Additional papers appear in a special issue of the *IEEE Trans. on Communications*, **COM-20**, June 1972, part II.

concentrators discussed here. As in the analogous public switched-voice telephone network, a data terminal or other data source desirous of entering the network calls in its destination. A complete path is set up, from end to end, and then, once the complete connection is established, messages may be multiplexed into the system.

A hierarchy of multiplexing procedures may be used. For example, the multiplexing system of the DATRAN line-switched network consists of time-division multiplexers (TDM) arranged in a three-level hierarchy.* The first-level multiplexer accepts data at a rate of 4.8 kbits/sec (kbps), 9.6 kbps, or 19.2 kbps and combines the various subscriber channels to form a high-speed output at either 56 kbps or 168 kbps. The second-level multiplexer accepts groups of 56 or 168 kbps inputs to form output at either 1.344 megabits/sec (Mbps) or 2.688 Mbps. These second-level outputs are in turn multiplexed to the third level of 21.504 Mbps. Two such data streams, capable of carrying 7854 4.8 kbps data channels, provide one 30 megahertz (MHz) radio channel over the microwave radio trunk system that constitutes the transmission system of the DATRAN network. Switching in the DATRAN network is carried out by means of computer-controlled time-space-time switch matrices.** Response time in this network is specified to be 3 sec or less, 99% of the time. This response time is defined as the interval between transmission of the destination address by the subscriber data set and the receipt by this set of a valid network response such as ring or busy. It is the time required to set up a call to the point of establishing a connection and to begin transmission. This time contrasts with the response time in message-switched networks, which varies from the interval between transmission of a message to receipt of an acknowledgement that the message has been received correctly at the destination, to the interval between transmission of a message and receipt of a reply.

As was pointed out in Chap. 1 we shall focus almost exclusively on message-switched networks throughout the remainder of this book. This brief discussion into line-switching technology was only introduced to better acquaint the reader with the distinctions between the two types of networks. It should be noted, however, that much of the topological design discussion of Chap. 9 and 10 is independent of the type of switching carried out. A design procedure that minimizes communication line costs, for example, would apply to *any* network including one carrying voice traffic only.

---

*F. T. Chen, H. D. Chadwick, and R. M. Penn, "The DATRAN Network: System Description;" and F. T. Chen et al., "Digital Multiplexing Hierarchy for an Integrated Data Transmission and Switching System;" both papers in the *Proc. IEEE National Telecommunications Conference*, New Orleans, Dec. 1975.

**T. Randall, J. Edwards, and P. Wallingford, "DATRAN's Time Division Data Switching System," *Proc. IEEE National Telecommunications Conference*, New Orleans, Dec. 1975.

GE INFORMATION SERVICES*

Overall Network

The GE Information Services MARK III® is the world's largest commercial data processing network. It provides both interactive and batch processing capability. Although the traffic carried in past years was primarily due to low-speed terminals accessing the network computers in an interactive mode, more recently the traffic mix has begun to change, with high-speed (400—600 lines/min.) remote job entry (RJE) data from synchronous terminals beginning to exceed the interactive traffic. The network provides local dial-up service in over 500 cities worldwide. Included is service in North America, service via satellite and undersea cable to Europe, as well as satellite service to Australia and Japan.

The network configuration follows a hierarchical star, as shown in Fig. 2-1: individual terminals are connected into 75 remote concentrators (RCs) located at 23 distribution points spread throughout the world.** The remote concentrators are in turn connected to central concentrators (CCs) located in Cleveland, Ohio; Rockville, Md.; London, England. The central concentrators then access the computer systems that are at the heart of the network.

Three types of minicomputer remote concentrators are currently in use. They consist of:

1. Honeywell H416s, with 48 ports connected to the public-switched telephone network, that handle 10–30 char./sec (110–300 bps) terminals

2. GE Diginet 1600 low-speed concentrators, with 96 ports each, accommodating 110–300 bps terminals as well as 1200 bps terminals

3. GE Diginet 1600 high-speed concentrators, with 16 synchronous full-duplex channels, 14 of which provide up to 9.6 kbps service, the other two going up to 50 kbps.

The low-speed concentrators are connected to the central concentrators by 9.6 or 14.4 kbps full-duplex lines. All lines are duplicated (i.e., alternate paths or circuits are used) to maintain reliability. The high-speed remote concentrators are connected via 14.4 or 19.2 kbps lines to the central concentrators, the lines again being duplicated for reliability. The Honeywell machine has 60 56-character buffers available for data storage, assigned using a modified buddy system. The Diginet 1600 is designed to accommodate a

---

*Based on private communications with Mr. Chris Brook, GE Information Services.

**These figures and those following in this section represent the characteristics of the network as of April 1976. As is true of most large networks the network is constantly in a state of improvement and development. A major upgrade was in fact underway at the time of this writing, to be completed during late 1976. Plans called for multicenter operation, the addition of poll and select terminal capability, an increase in the number of remote nodes in the network, and the insertion of software multiplexors between the remote and central concentrators. In addition, a major change in the protocol was planned to increase user throughput.

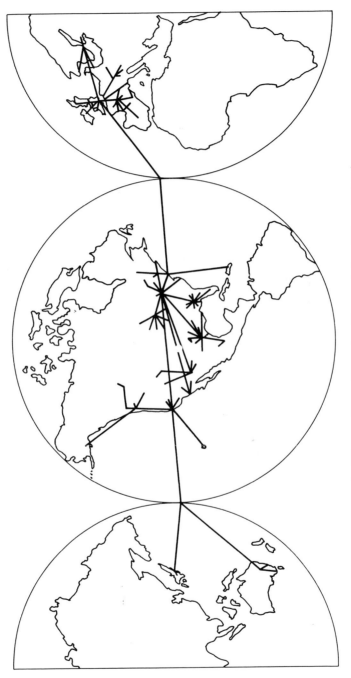

Fig. 2-1. GE network map. (Reproduced by permission of General Electric Co, Information Services Division.)

maximum of 70 users, one third of whom are assumed to be inputting data at any one time. Sixteen kwords of memory are available, with two 56-character buffers provided for each user. The high-speed concentrators used to process, concentrate, and store RJE messages have their memory systems divided into 168-character buffers, with six such buffers available per user.

A fourth remote concentrator currently being added to the network is a Honeywell 4000 series derivative. It is intended for use in cities with either low port usage or high measured error rates. Its line capability consists of 16 75—2400 bps asynchronous lines plus four 2.4—57.6 kbps synchronous lines. The mix of these can, however, be varied. Two of the four high-speed lines will provide the necessary connection to the network; the other two will be available as RJE lines for customers. (For this type of usage 168 incoming characters will be stored or handled at a time.)

The central concentrators for the network are Honeywell 4020 computers. They can each handle a maximum of seven remote concentrators. Each of these concentrators has 24-line capability; these lines include two full-duplex lines assigned to each of the seven remote concentrators, plus two lines connected to each of two switchers. The central concentrators serve two basic functions: they provide the necessary concentration of messages arriving from the remote concentrators connected, and they serve as preprocessors for the central computer systems to which they are connected. Messages arriving at a particular central concentrator from the remote concentrator into which they were originally inputted must be directed to the central concentrator handling the central system for which they are destined. This is done via the two switchers, Diginet 1600s (again duplicated for reliability) to which all central concentrators are connected. A more detailed breakdown of the network hierarchy, showing the connections from terminals to a remote concentrator, to the central concentrator to which they are connected, the connection to the switchers, and then to another central concentrator, if necessary, is sketched in Fig. 2-2. Also shown are the Host computer systems connected to the central concentrators.

There are 16 central concentrators currently available, 7 located in Cleveland, 5 in Rockville, 3 in London, and one used for development purposes. The network is currently switch-limited, the message-handling capacity of the switchers being 800 messages per second. The switchers can handle no more than 16 central concentrators each, and new switchers are being added. Central concentrators are connected to the switchers via 50 kbps full-duplex lines.

The computer systems in the network, access to which is made through the appropriate central concentrators, provide both interactive and batch processing capability. Those providing the interactive processing (time-shared tasks primarily) are called "foreground" systems. The batch processing computers are termed "background" systems. Each foreground machine (a Honeywell 6088) is connected to a particular central concentrator which serves as its processor. Foreground machines are also connected to the back-

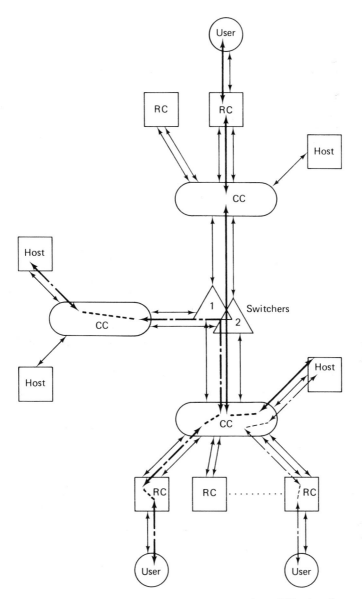

Fig. 2-2. Possible user-Host computer connections, GE network.

ground system, four foreground machines to one background one, for resource-sharing applications. The background systems may be accessed two ways: by way of the foreground systems or directly from a central concentrator. Direct access is made through a so-called "Brand X" interface for accessing a "foreign" Host. The Hosts in this case may be a Honeywell DN355 designed for remote batch operations or an IBM 370/158 driven by a PDP 11/40.

Message Format and Transmission

Users signing on for a session identify themselves with their user number and a password. The user number is eight characters long. The first five numbers represent the catalog number, and the last three the level in the catalog, the actual user number. The first character in the catalog number is the user's file system identifier and the next four are catalog identifiers within the file system.* The source central concentrator to which the user remote concentrator is connected determines from its own tables which central concentrator accesses the given file number; messages are then routed through the switchers to the appropriate destination central concentrator, as noted earlier. The source central concentrator (CC) determines which CC in the network that is connected to a processor with access to the user's file system (including itself) has the lowest number of users, and makes that the user's object CC. If the object CC is connected to two processors each of which has access to the specified file system, it will load balance between the two. Because access to the network is fairly random this provides a dynamic load-balancing scheme based on number of users. However, to protect against a processor with a fairly low number of users but with a high processor utilization, the selected processor has the ability to redirect users automatically (and invisibly, to the user) to another processor whose load factor is lower, even though it may have many more users.

The standardized ANSI message format and seven-bit ASCII code** are used for message transmission throughout the network. User input, from non-ASCII terminals, is converted at the remote concentrator to the stan-

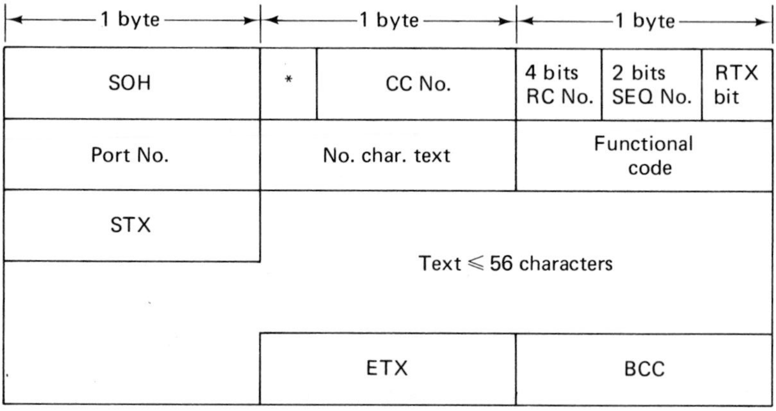

← 1 byte →		← 1 byte →	← 1 byte →		
SOH	*	CC No.	4 bits RC No.	2 bits SEQ No.	RTX bit
Port No.		No. char. text	Functional code		
STX	Text ≤ 56 characters				
	ETX		BCC		

*Direction bit: 1 = central to remote concentrator
                  0 = remote to central concentrator

Fig. 2-3. Message format, GE network, remote to central concentrator and reverse (excluding SYN characters).

*Files are kept on disks, separated from processors for reliability; they can be accessed by several processors. The foreground machines thus communicate with the central concentrator, files, and background machine to which they are connected.
**See Chap. 14 for a detailed discussion.

dardized format. User messages inbound from the remote concentrator to the central concentrator to which connected, as well as outbound messages in the reverse direction, are transmitted in block form. A block consists of two synchronization characters, denoted by the symbol SYN, followed by a 7-character header, up to 56 characters of text, an end-of-text character (ETX), and a block check character (BCC) used for error detection. The two synchronization characters are stripped off before entering the concentrator in either direction. The block format form excluding the SYN characters is sketched in Fig. 2-3. The central concentrators are 24-bit machines. Messages are thus formatted into 3-byte words, accounting for the format of Fig. 2-3. The SOH character is the standard ASCII character denoting start of header, and STX is the standard character denoting start of text. SOH and STX thus delimit between them the header portion of the message. As indicated in Fig. 2-3 the header contains both address and control characters. Six bits of the second character are used to denote the source central concentrator (CC); four bits of the third character are used to indicate which of the seven remote concentrators (RC) is transmitting (or receiving) the message; and the fourth character is used to indicate the port number on the RC to which the user data terminal is connected. Although the remote concentrators are connected via leased lines to the central concentrators and the central concentrators to the switchers, it has been found necessary in practice to include the CC number within the message block. (Several RC—CC links may share the same transmission facility, and under certain transmission conditions it is possible to have data appear at the wrong CC. Including the CC and RC number prevents messages from being misdirected.) A direction bit associated with the CC number indicates the direction of the block: inbound to the central concentrator, or outbound to the remote concentrator. The functional code character is used to describe buffer/data type: login, disconnect, break, user output, statistics, etc.

An error detection and acknowledgement scheme is used in this network, as in TYMNET, the ARPA network, SITA, (all to be described in later sections), and many other networks in existence, to correct for errors in transmission. The exclusive-or of all previous bits in the block is used to form the block check character (BCC). The receiving concentrator repeats the process. If no errors are detected, a positive acknowledgement (ACK message) is transmitted. This consists of the overhead plus address portion of the message block, as shown in Fig. 2-4. Should an error be detected the receiving con-

(SYN SYN) SOH, CC#, RC/SEQ#, Port #, STX, ETX, BCC

Fig. 2-4. Acknowledgement message block, GE network.

centrator does nothing. After a two second timeout waiting for receipt of the ACK message, the transmitting concentrator retransmits the entire message. The RTX bit in Fig. 2-3 denotes a retransmitted block; the sequence number is the number of the message being transmitted, for a particular user. All sequence numbering is on a user basis. Only one message, and so one retransmission, can be outstanding for a user on any link, but every user may have a message outstanding. The 0—3 sequence number is not used to limit forward transmission but to protect against duplicates due to a message being delayed through one switcher at the same time as it is retransmitted and acknowledged through the other; 0—1 sequencing formerly used could produce this condition. The RTX bit provides an extra level of sequence numbering protection under heavy queueing delays and retransmission without having to carry a 3-bit number in the user's control block.

A user message is read out of a buffer and transmitted whenever a 56-character buffer is full; in the interactive mode, whenever the carriage return key is pressed; in the file building mode, when 56 characters have been assembled.

Messages from source to destination central concentrators, and reverse, through the switchers are assembled into up to 168 characters of text and are transmitted in somewhat similar format, as shown in Fig. 2-5.* (The two synchronization characters have again been deleted.)** These blocks are acknowledged one at a time as well or retransmitted should an ACK message not be received. The "rubout" characters shown indicate that the message is being transmitted between central concentrators, as contrasted with system control messages moving between CC and switcher. As noted in the accompanying footnote the latter use the same initial six characters as in Fig. 2-3. Because of the rubouts the source CC number, RC/Seq. number, etc. are in the same position in both types of CC messages. The high-speed line direction bit in Fig. 2-5 is used for diagnostic purposes. A device can thus identify a line as being physically looped by the telephone company.

In transmission on any link in the network, first priority is given to ACK messages, second priority to retransmitted messages, and, finally, third priority to messages transmitted for the first time. There is a queue for each of these message categories at each remote concentrator. Each central concentrator has one such queue for each device to which connected including the two switchers. The three queues all feed the appropriate pair of output lines, whichever of the two lines first become available accessing the appropriate queue, in order of priority. Actually messages are not moved from queue to queue. Messages remain in the concentrator buffer until finally acknowledged. A copy of the message is read out onto the appropriate line when the line calls for it. Pointers or link listers corresponding to each of the messages move from queue to queue. The "transmit queue," for example, has a list of messages in buffers awaiting transmission. When a line interrupts to call for a

---

*The character count field shown is being enlarged to two bytes to accommodate the maximum of 168 characters of text indicated.

**Control messages, from central concentrator to switcher, use the RC—CC message format of Fig. 2-3.

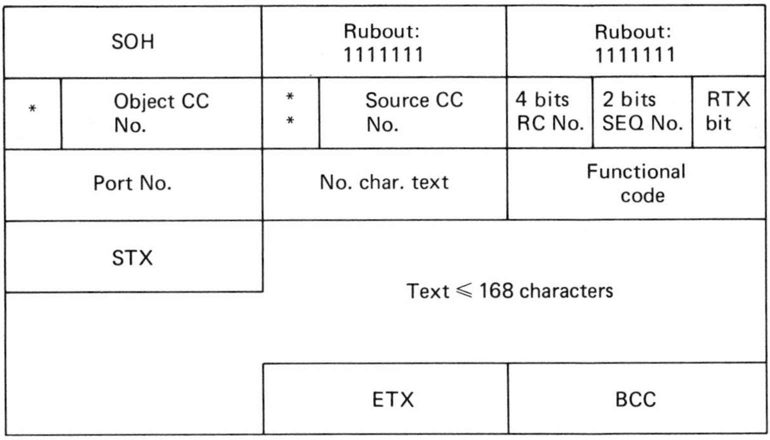

SOH		Rubout: 1111111		Rubout: 1111111		
*	Object CC No.	* *	Source CC No.	4 bits RC No.	2 bits SEQ No.	RTX bit
Port No.		No. char. text		Functional code		
STX		Text ≤ 168 characters				
		ETX		BCC		

* Direction bit: 1 = object to source direction
                    0 = source to object direction
** High-speed line direction bit

Fig. 2-5. Message format, GE network, transmission between central concentrators.

message, a copy of the message is immediately read over the line, and the pointer moves from the transmit queue to an "await-ACK queue" associated with that line, awaiting receipt of the acknowledgement message.

Message retransmission takes place in either of two cases:

1. An ACK message doesn't arrive within 2 sec. (This has been noted earlier.) In this case, the link lister for that message is appended to the retransmit queue.

2. If an ACK arrives for a message other than the first one in the appropriate await-ACK queue for that line, this is an indication that the message was lost or disfigured, or that the returning ACK was lost or disfigured. An ACK may be for the nth message in the await-ACK queue; in this case, 1 through $n - 1$ messages will be queued for retransmission.

Each remote concentrator has one await-ACK queue for each of the two physical lines connecting it to its central concentrator. The central concentrator, on the other hand, has one await-ACK queue for each *physical* line (remote concentrators plus the two switchers) connected to it, as well as for each *logical* link (central concentrator to central concentrator) it may establish. There are two logical links and hence two await-ACK queues for each other central concentrator for the transmission of regular messages, as well as one each for the two switchers, used for control messages between the concentrator and the switchers.

Each central concentrator has 48 kwords of 800 nanosec memory, split into buffers of three sizes: one for control messages; one for short text, up to 56 characters long; and one for central-central concentrator messages, up to 168 characters long.

Message transmission to and from a foreground system is also carried out using block format. Low-speed, asynchronous users have up to 168 characters at a time inputted and up to 504 characters (168 × 3) outputted. Synchronous user messages are handled in 1008-character (168 × 6) blocks, each way. High-speed users (e.g., a 300 card/min. card reader or a printer) are handled in up to 1008-character blocks, input and output. A 1028-character buffer in the central concentrator is used to serve each foreground system.

Network Performance Characteristics

Line utilization in this network is purposely kept low. This prevents queueing delay and eliminates a buffer management problem at the central concentrator (CC). In planning for network utilization, the assumption is made that one third of the active remote concentrator (RC) ports at any one time are idle (in a thinking mode), one third are inputting, and one third are outputting messages. In addition, as already noted, a user is allowed one message at a time only in the overall transmission path. Low-speed (110—300 bps) terminals are found to have an average input data rate of 5 char./sec. Outbound traffic averages 10 char./sec. An average user inputs 15 characters at a time. 1200 bps users average 10 char./sec inbound and 60 char./sec outbound. High-speed rates average 20 char./sec inbound and 200 char./sec outbound.

Round-trip response time in the continental United States is found to be about 400 msec. On international connections the response time is about 800 msec. The performance offered a user is given as 99.4% foreground system availability. The peak sustained network load is about 72 million char./hr.

As noted previously, load balancing for the system is done on a file system basis. Users are sent to the object central concentrator and foreground processor with access to the required file system with the smallest number of users. Users are thus directed anywhere in the network by the processors for load balancing. A completely automatic control system, involving the use of one of the central concentrators and a central system to which it is connected, has been developed to carry out statistical gathering and analysis, response measurement, automatic software distribution, network splitting for the development and testing of new software; to allow remote access to any node in the network; and to carry out many other necessary monitoring and control tasks for the network.* Using the statistical gathering and analysis procedure, for example, it is possible to evaluate the performance of each node and link in the network, to diagnose imminent hardware failure, to carry out network load-balancing and reconfiguration, to evaluate overall

---

*L. J. Mauceri, "Control of an Expanding Network—'An Operational Nightmare'," *Networks*, **4**, John Wiley & Sons, Inc., New York, 1974, 287–97.

network performance, and to determine the performance of the central systems.

TYMNET*

Overall Network

TYMNET is a computer-communications network developed in 1970 by Tymshare, Inc., of Cupertino, Ca. Although originally developed, like the GE network, for time-shared purposes, TYMNET has taken on a network function as well. In addition to providing connection to its own computer systems for interactive processing, remote job entry (RJE), and other user data processing requirements, TYMNET provides routing and connection facilities to the customer's own facilities as well. This service is provided under FCC Tariff 260 "Joint User" section. As an example, the U.S. National Library of Medicine uses TYMNET to provide access by remote terminals located anywhere in the United States to its own computer facilities distributed at several locations. As of September 1975, 40 user computers (roughly half the computer systems in the network) were connected into the network, to be accessed by the user terminals located elsewhere in the United States and in Europe. Such a service presumably provides higher efficiency at less cost than would be possible if the customer were to set up his own network using leased lines, for the network in this case is shared with the other TYMNET customers. The customer in this case also shares in the increased dependability and reliability made available through the network rerouting and error-detection capabilities.

The basic network itself is primarily a terminal-oriented network, enabling low-speed terminals anywhere in North America and Europe to access computers (whether belonging to the network or to the user in question) located geographically elsewhere. The terminals supported are those using ASCII code** with speeds of 10, 15, 30 char./sec. In addition some cities provide access to the network by IBM 2741 terminals or their compatible equivalents. Access in some cases is to EBCDIC-type 2741s, in other cases to those using correspondence code, and in still others to either type terminal. In all, 60 metropolitan areas are available, including four in Europe, that provide local calling access to the various terminals noted above.

Although as of early 1976 the network was primarily used for communication between low-speed asynchronous terminals and computers, it was beginning to handle more synchronous remote job entry terminal traffic at 2000 and 2400 bps. Later the capability of handling higher-speed 1200 bps asynchronous terminal traffic was added as well.

---

*Based primarily on private correspondence with Mr. LaRoy Tymes, Tymshare, Inc.
**See Chap. 14.

As in the GE system, concentration of terminal traffic is carried out by minicomputer concentrators called TYMSATS located throughout the United States and Europe. As of fall 1975, 75 such *remote* TYMSATS, each accommodating up to 32 terminals, were available in the network. In addition, 26 other TYMSATS were deployed as so-called *base* TYMSATS at the company's computer centers in Cupertino and Palo Alto, Ca.; Valley Forge, Pa., Houston, Tex., as well as in Paris, France. These base computers each support one or two of the network computer systems. (The base TYMSAT in Paris has seven remote TYMSATS homing in on it.) The network also contained 10 switchers, used for interconnecting up to eight synchronous lines, and 33 communication processors called TYMCOM-IIIs connecting to the user-Host computers. These latter processors thus serve to connect user computers to the network. The standard machine can handle up to 30 simultaneous users, with 30 ports that can be connected to one, two, or three Hosts.* Other options, such as 64 simultaneous users connected to up to four Hosts, are available as well.

The TYMSATS and TYMCOMS are all modified versions of Varian 620i, 620L, and 620L-100 minicomputers, with 12-kwords of memory. Interdata 7/32 minicomputers are being added as well, in a major network development effort to be briefly described later.

The over 150 minicomputers at network nodes are interconnected by 2400 bps, 4800bps, and 9600 bps lines. Transatlantic lines are cable with satellite backup. Satellites are avoided where possible because of the substantial delay introduced. There are over 260 links interconnecting the nodes of the network. The TYMCOMS connecting the user computers to the network home in on base TYMSATS in some cases and on remote TYMSATS in others. The network consists of 60,000 miles of leased circuits.

The network topology, in contrast to the hierarchical star of the GE network, is of a distributed type. A network map appears in Fig. 2-6. Note that in almost all cases network nodes have at least two links connecting them to the network so that alternate route capability is available.

Routing and Flow Control

Network routing is centrally determined by a supervisory program located in an Interdata supervisory computer. Multiple supervisors are available so that in the event of failure of the current supervisor another supervisor will be available to take over the supervisory tasks within a matter of min-

---

*J. R. Harcharik, "TYMNET, Present and Future," *IEEE Eascon Meeting*, Washington, D.C., Sept. 30, 1975.

utes.* A version of shortest path or least-cost routing** is used to determine the appropriate path (virtual circuit) from source to destination node over which to send messages for any particular user. The path is newly selected each time a user comes on the network, but, while the user maintains his current connection, the path chosen is unchanged. In this sense the route selection process is similar to that used in line- or circuit-switched networks (the modern telephone system is the most common example), in which a user is given a dedicated circuit from source to destination as long as he maintains his connection. The critical difference in the TYMNET system, however, is that messages are switched, in a store-and-forward fashion, from nodal computer to nodal computer, following the virtual circuit selected. Transmission on any link along the path is shared with a number of other users, again unlike the situation in circuit switching. The system typically supports up to 46 users on a 2400 bps line with very little degradation in response time.

The routing algorithm, as contained in the supervisory program, finds the path of current least cost, summed over the costs of each link on the path, from source TYMSAT to destination computer. Essentially arbitrary numbers are used in expressing the cost assignment. For example, the number 16 is assigned to a 2400 bps link, 12 to a 4800 bps link, 10 to a 9600 bps link, and 1 for certain internal high-speed connections. A penalty of 16 is added if a node at one end complains of "overloading".† The penalty is 32 if both nodes complain. A penalty of 16 is added to a satellite link for low-speed interactive users. (A 2400 bps land line provides a smaller time delay than a higher-speed satellite link.) An infinite cost is added if a link is nonfunctional, out of channels, or if a human operator has requested that the line not be used. In addition a node has a limited capacity for circuits passing through it (48—1024 circuits, depending on node type and amount of core). If this capacity is exceeded a penalty cost is added to all its links so that circuits can still be built *to* it as a destination node but not *through* it. The routing algorithm thus tends to reduce congestion in the network, spreading users out to make more efficient use of the facilities.

Once the appropriate circuit or route is determined nodal computers

---

*Until 1975 the supervisory program resided in two of the network Host computers in California, in one of the computers in Pennsylvania, and in one in Paris. Only one of these was active at any one time, however; another one could take over in 3 to 5 min.
**See Chap. 11.
†A line is said to be *overloaded* if the time to serve a channel exceeds half a second. This is to be contrasted with a *saturated* link in which the total data rate to be transmitted begins to approach link capacity. If one or two users, for example, are transmitting as much data as they can over a link, the link may saturate without being overloaded. An overload condition may result if enough circuits put enough traffic on a link. It may also result from a noisy link with a high error rate causing many retransmissions. The routing algorithm thus indirectly takes into account the number of users and the error rate on the link.

TYMNET

INTERNATIONAL DATA COMMUNICATIONS NETWORK

TYMSHARE

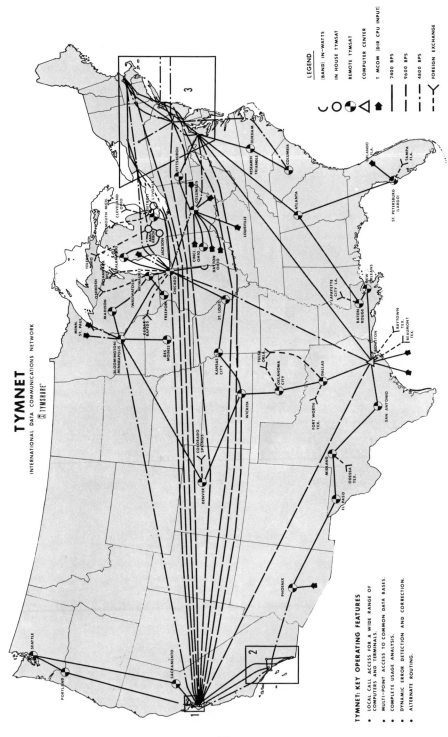

TYMNET: KEY OPERATING FEATURES

- LOCAL CALL ACCESS FOR A WIDE RANGE OF
  COMPUTERS AND TERMINALS.
- MULTI-POINT ACCESS TO COMMON DATA BASES.
- COMPLETE USAGE ANALYSIS.
- DYNAMIC ERROR DETECTION AND CORRECTION.
- ALTERNATE ROUTING.

LEGEND

(BAND) IN-WATTS
IN HOUSE TYMSAT
REMOTE TYMSAT
COMPUTER CENTER
T MCOM (DIR CPU INPUT)
2400 BPS
9600 BPS
4800 BPS
FOREIGN EXCHANGE

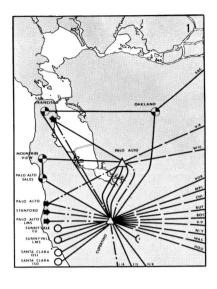

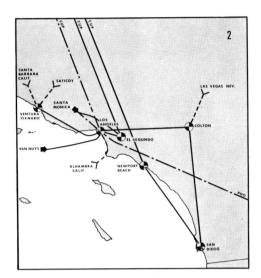

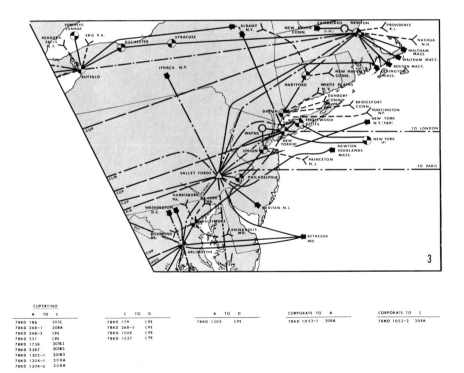

Fig. 2-6. (Reproduced by permission of Tymshare, Inc.)

along the path chosen are notified by the supervisor which sends control information to each TYMSAT along the route. Appropriate entries are made in each TYMSAT's routing or permuter tables, associating a particular channel number with one of the outgoing links from the TYMSAT in question. In the network redevelopment underway leading to the new TYMNET II, the supervisor will be able to choose alternate routes, in a manner transparent to the users, in case of line outages or intermediate node failures.

The channel number associated with an outgoing link at a node refers only to that link. A complete circuit, from source to destination node, thus consists of a series of channels or links. No one node knows anything about a circuit except for its own local portion of that circuit. The virtual circuit is thus defined solely by the routing or permuter table entries associated with its channels at the various nodes. The routing strategy serves to distribute the traffic more smoothly over the network and thus helps to avoid traffic pileups. In addition flow control is provided in the form of a computer-to-user direction shut-off feature that prevents traffic from building up. This is particularly necessary in buffering the output flow from computers in the system. For the computer output rate may run as high as 1000 char./sec, yet the terminal to which directed may only be able to print 10 char./sec. Intermediate node buffers are limited in size and so can't handle too large a data input. To prevent data from piling up on any one channel, a given sending node subtracts the number of characters sent out over the channel from a counter associated with the channel. When the counter reaches zero no more characters are sent over that channel. Twice a second the receiving node sends one bit back to the sending node, indicating whether it has less than or more than 32 characters in the receiving buffer for the channel. If it has less the sending node resets its counter to 32 and starts transmitting again.* (For high-speed channels that accommodate 120 char./sec, a count of 128 is used.)

Message Transmission

As already noted almost any low-speed (10—30 char./sec) terminal will be supported by the network. A user accesses the network by dialing a telephone number corresponding to the TYMSAT with which he is associated. This connects him into one of the TYMSAT ports. He then types a terminal identifier character. A software program at the incoming TYMSAT uses the character to identify the type of terminal, code used, and speed of character transmission.** The procedure is similar to that used in the GE network as

*L. Tymes, "TYMNET—A Terminal-Oriented Communications Network," *AFIPS Conference Proc.*, **38**, 1971, 211–16.

Some techniques for this purpose are described in J. F. Ossanna, "Identifying Terminals in Terminal-Oriented Systems," *IEEE Trans. on Communications*, **COM-20, June 1972, 565–68.

well as many other commercial data networks supporting any type of low-speed terminal. All characters following are then converted to standardized ASCII code, if necessary, for internal network transmission. As examples, a "D" is used as the identifying character for an ASCII 10 char./sec teletype; "carriage return" is used for the 13.5 char./sec EBCDIC IBM 2741; and an "E" is used for 30 char./sec thermal printers.

After the identifying character is typed in, the TYMSAT to which connected responds with the message "please log in". The user is then connected to the supervisor. The user types in his name and password. The supervisor checks the Master User Directory, validates the user name and password, sets up the virtual circuit or routing path, and then transfers control to the Host.

Any given TYMSAT handles traffic from its own ports as well as traffic coming through from the adjacent nodes to which it is connected. Messages from all these sources are stored (in ASCII code) in character buffers as they arrive. The character buffers as a group are allocated 2000—12000 bytes of concentrator memory, depending on the size of the node. This space is dynamically allocated as needed, with a maximum of 60 bytes for low-speed and 240 bytes for high-speed circuits. Each message—whether locally inputted from one of the local ports or passing through—has a virtual channel number associated with it, as noted in discussing routing in the previous paragraph.

Message transmission to adjacent nodes is accomplished by assembling a record or block of characters from those stored in the buffers, for each outgoing link. A block is assembled by searching through the character buffers, on a first-come-first-served basis, for those characters with virtual channel numbers associated with that particular link (i.e., those virtual channels associated with that link in the TYMSAT routing table). The search continues in round-robin fashion (returning to the first buffer queried for additional characters that might have been entered in the interim) until a maximum of 66 characters, including control and error detection characters (to be discussed below), have been assembled. If fewer than 66 characters are assembled, whatever is available is transmitted. If there are no data to be sent, control characters only are transmitted. Blocks are transmitted one after another with no gaps in between. Although channels are serviced in round-robin fashion, a channel whose turn was skipped because it had no data to send at the time its turn came up will have priority over the following channels if and when it suddenly has data to send.

The format of the block as finally assembled is shown in Fig. 2-7. A 16-bit header is first transmitted. This consists, in order as shown, of a 5-bit synchronization pattern, a 5-bit word count specifying the total number of 16-bit words in the block less 2, and three bits each for block number and acknowledgement. (These are discussed further below.) Each message associated with a particular user then follows. The user message, called a logical record, consists first of a 1-character virtual channel number, then of a 1-character logical

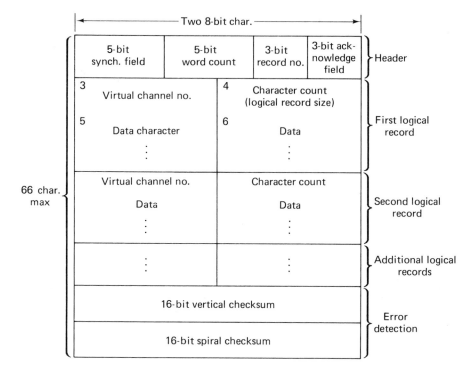

Fig. 2-7. TYMNET message format.

record count telling how many data characters are to follow, followed by the 8-bit data characters themselves. Additional logical records, for different users, follow. The final 32 bits or four characters of the block are used for error detection. They consist first of a 16-bit vertical checksum and then a 16-bit spiral checksum. The full 8 bits of each character are used in transmission. There is no parity bit, as in the ASCII-code characters to be discussed in Chap. 14.

The block as transmitted is dissembled at the next node at the end of the link, the message characters are stored in the appropriate buffers at that node, and the block assembly process is again repeated, as above.

Error correction is carried out by retransmission of the entire block if necessary; as soon as a block is received the number of that block is returned to the sending TYMSAT as part of the next outgoing block on the reverse path of the link in question. If a block is *not* acknowledged for any reason it is automatically retransmitted by the sending TYMSAT. If an error in the block is detected at the receiving TYMSAT the block is disregarded and not acknowledged. Retransmission then automatically takes place. In addition notification of the error is sent to the supervisor which keeps track of error counts on all links. The oldest unacknowledged record is retransmitted whenever there are four unacknowledged records (8 records on a satellite line to compensate for the delay). A line is considered to be out if 16 to 32 seconds pass with no valid records received. The checksum technique used for error detection (see Fig. 2-7) provides a very low error rate, theoretically of the order of 1 bit in 2^{32} or the order of 1 in 10^9 bits transmitted.

Note the differences between the message format in the TYMNET system and in the GE network. The messages from several TYMNET users may be combined in one block. In the GE case each user is allocated his own block. In the GE network separate acknowledgement messages are transmitted. Here acknowledgements are embedded within the message block, acknowledging correct receipt of a block received earlier in the reverse direction. The ARPA network described in a later section also embeds ACK messages within message blocks. The SITA network to be described next uses separate ACK messages. The GE network follows the ANSI protocol in transmitting two SYN characters followed by SOH, STX, and ETX characters. TYMNET uses quite a different protocol. Some of these points will be developed further in Chap. 14, in discussing line protocol and message transmission more generally.

Network Operating Characteristics

Topological reconfiguration of the TYMNET system is carried out on a regular basis. An attempt is made to locate network nodes in sales offices, computer centers, and other places where needed. Once nodes are installed various network configurations are simulated using recent accounting data and taking anticipated load into account. The configuration of lines finally installed is chosen to provide the best trade-off between cost, average response time, and reliability, with appropriate backup provided for line outages. The reliability figure for the TYMSATS has been 8 months mean time between failures. (The problems encountered have been primarily due to power failures.) Although line outages have been quite common, as is the case with all networks, the network has never been totally down since first brought up in November 1971.

The original network supervisor could handle up to 200 user logins/min., with 128 Host computers, and a total of 200 nodes. The maximum number of circuits set up, or users simultaneously accessing the network, was 2000. These numbers are being increased radically, as indicated in the next section, with a redevelopment effort underway. The actual network load in 1975 averaged 60 logins/min. on a 150-node network. The peak load on a normal business day runs to 800 users simultaneously accessing the network, with a 20 min. average connect time. Seventy-five percent of all logins are from 30 char./sec full-duplex ASCII terminals. Only 2% of the logins are from non-

ASCII devices. As an example, during October 1975 the total number of logins (sessions, or circuits built) was 495,000. The total number of connect minutes was 13,000,000. The number of characters transmitted was 3.65 × 10^9. This averages to 7300 char./login or 5 char./sec during a login and indicates the bursty nature of the interactive traffic carried.

Queueing delays on the network tend to be low, with lines rarely approaching saturation. The delay is primarily a function of line speed and block or record size. Record size normally averages 100 bits (recall from Fig. 2-7 that the maximum size is 66 characters or 528 bits) and the delay per node averages about 125 msec each way. The average circuit length is about $2\frac{1}{2}$ links, so that average network delay time, in each direction, is about 300 msec. (This of course excludes satellite links, with 300 msec added time delay in each direction on such a link.) When lines approach saturation (this occurs rarely) the block size goes to maximum, minimizing overhead, and the transmission time increases.

The average traffic utilization runs about 20% during peak periods. (On the average five 100-bit blocks are transmitted per second.) The reason for this low figure is that many of the nodes serve only a few low-speed users at a time. Although, as noted earlier, a 2400 bps line can handle 46 users, most of the lines do not have that much traffic. When a 2400 bps line begins to saturate because of intercomputer transfers or remote job entry (RJE) terminals coming on line, it is upgraded to 4800 or 9600 bps.

New Developments

As already noted earlier the network is undergoing a large change to a TYMNET-II configuration. Interdata 7/32 multiple minicomputers, 64—512 kbytes, 32-bit word size machines are being installed as network supervisors, wholly dedicated to the supervisory task. The supervisor will handle global tasks only, with all local tasks turned over to nodal minicomputers. The supervisor will continue to carry out the circuit building or routing task for users as they log in; it will provide rerouting in case of line outages and node failures, as already noted; it will handle accounting for the entire network; it will provide more effective security for Host computers accessing each other's files; it will provide for optimal network interconnections; and it will decide if several are available to which of several Hosts to connect a user. (Note that the supervisory tasks are, other than that of routing, similar to those carried out by the GE central control facility.) All supervisory communication to nodes will be enciphered using the IBM Lucifer cipher scheme, for added security.

Using the new supervisory system the number of logins/sec handled by a supervisor will rise from the current limit of 3/sec to 50/sec. Multiple supervisors will be used. No design limit is indicated on the size of the network to be handled, in nodes, or on the number of circuits simultaneously in operation.

The nodal computers will take on additional tasks as well. They will handle, for example, buffer layout, channel, and port assignments. The nodes will consist almost exclusively of Interdata 7/32 minicomputers. These will have 96 low-speed (up to 300 baud) ports; 32 1200 bps ports; and 8 synchronous (2000—9600 bps) dial-up ports to support RJE users. All switchers will be eliminated and, in some cities, several smaller nodes will be replaced by one large node. (Installation of these minicomputers actually began in mid-1976.) The maximum block or record size will be increased to 1000 bits to provide increased efficiency on high volume traffic. This longer record size will be offset by increased use of 9600 bps lines instead of 2400. As the network grows in the number of nodes, the connectivity will also increase, so that the average circuit length of $2\frac{1}{2}$ links will remain about the same. The internode line discipline in TYMNET II will be a direct extension of the TYMNET I discipline described above. In addition to the change to a longer record, an improved polynomial checksum for error detection will be incorporated, and there will be an expanded record header with provision for a larger number of outstanding, unacknowledged records. A 3-bit field will specify one of seven different record sizes. An escape convention will be used to allow more than 256 channels per link. Links may have several parallel lines available to them. All circuits then use all lines on the link. The transmission capability of one circuit may temporarily equal the combined capacity of all lines forming the links. When traffic is light, a record may be sent on all lines simultaneously. A record may be sent on one line and acknowledged on another. The bit rate, error rate, and transmission delay will all be used in optimizing the trade-off between capacity available and response time.

THE SITA NETWORK*

SITA (Société Internationale de Télécommunications Aeronautiques) is a cooperative company of international air carriers organized to provide to its members a worldwide data communications capability via a message-

*The material contained in this section has been taken from the paper by G. J. Chretien, W. M. König, and J. H. Rech, "The SITA Network, Summary Description," *Computer-Communication Networks Conference*, University of Sussex, Brighton, U. K., Sept. 1973. Network charts are updated regularly by SITA. Additional information, some of which will be presented in Chap 6, appears in an earlier paper by G. J. Brandt and G. J. Chretien, "Methods to Control and Operate a Message-Switching Network," *Proc. Symposium on Computer-Communications Networks and Teletraffic*, Polytechnic Press, New York, 1972, pp. 263–76. D. W. Davies and D. L. A. Barber, *Communication Networks for Computers*, John Wiley & Sons, Inc., London, 1973, also discuss the SITA network in detail.

switching network. More than 160 carriers belong to SITA. The backbone of the network consisted in April 1975 of nine computer centers, or high-level centers, comprising the so-called high-level network and interconnected by voice-grade, medium-speed (4800 bps) circuits. The nine centers with associated satellite processors to be discussed later, make up the medium-speed network shown in Fig. 2-8. Two kinds of traffic are carried by the SITA network: conversational (inquiry/response) traffic labeled "Type A" and telegraphic traffic labeled "Type B." The former comprises inquiry messages and responses flowing between agent sets (CRT terminals) located in airline offices and their associated reservation computers located geographically distant. The Type B traffic consists of telegraphic messages destined to and generated by airline teleprinters and computers, as well as local Telex networks. Type B telegraphic traffic, in addition to using the high-level network of Fig. 2-8, flows over a complex low-speed network, interconnected with the medium-speed network. We shall focus on the medium-speed network of Fig. 2-8 only in this section. Details of the low-speed operation and a map of the

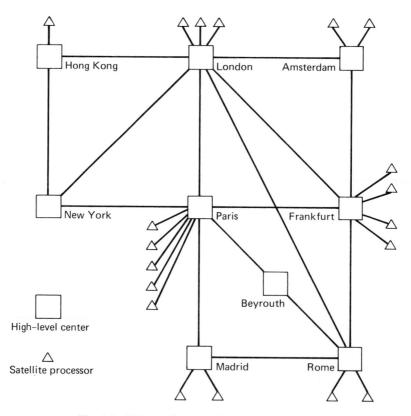

Fig. 2-8. SITA medium-speed network, April 1975.

complete SITA network as of September 1973 appear in the paper referenced.*

Type A messages receive priority over Type B messages in traversing the
high-level network. The Type A messages are generally short, consisting on
the average of 30 characters inbound from the agent set to the reservations
computer and 120 characters in the reverse direction. The ISO (International
Standards Organization) 7-bit character code or the IBM BCD code are
used for Type A message transmission. (The ASCII code used in the GE
network, and discussed in detail in Chap. 14, is the U.S. version of the ISO
code.) Type B messages are generated using the 5-digit CCITT code no. 2
that is standard for 50 bps Telex machines. They are then padded up to 7-bit
characters (plus parity bit) for transmission over the high-level network.
These messages average 200 characters in length. The response time required
for the Type A messages is 3 sec, while that for Type B messages is of the
order of several minutes.

Connected to the high-level computer centers are minicomputer satellite processors or concentrators which together with the centers comprise
the medium-speed network of Fig. 2-8. Agent sets are connected to the
satellite processors, and reservation computers to the high-level centers. A
Type A message thus enters the network at the center to which its satellite
processor is connected and is routed via a fixed path to the exit center to
which the reservation computer is connected. The high-level centers are
connected to both the reservation computers and satellite processors via
medium-speed (2.4 or 4.8 kbps) lines. In addition to these connections teleprinters and local Telex networks may access both the high-level centers and
the satellite processors through low-speed (50 or 75 bps) lines.

Messages traversing the high-level network are transmitted in block
form with an appropriate header for each. A block consists of at most 240
characters, and no more than 16 blocks/message can be transmitted. Blocks
are sent continuously between any two centers in the network. A sequence
number within the block header is used to ensure that blocks are received in
the same order in which transmitted. If a block received is in the proper
sequence and a block check indicates no error detected, it is acknowledged
as correctly received. An acknowledgement block is then transmitted in the
reverse direction. If the block received is not accepted as valid, a negative
acknowledgement is sent back. A timeout at the sending center is used to
check for acknowledgements. If an acknowledgement is not received after a
specified time interval, all blocks following the first unacknowledged blocks
are repeated. In addition to this link control procedure for maintaining correct flow over links between adjacent centers, special end-to-end control
messages are used to acknowledge the correct reassembly of multiblock mes-

*Chretien, König, and Rech, "SITA Network."

sages at the destination or exit high-level center. Each block header contains for this purpose a sequence number per entry/exit pair. The block header must contain, in addition, the sequence number for point-to-point link control noted above, the entry address, the exit address, and a priority indication distinguishing between message types. A block check character based on longitudinal (column) and transversal (row) parity checking is appended at the end of each block. Link control blocks such as the ACK and negative ACK blocks receive the highest priority for transmission, just as in the GE network discussed previously.

The routing of blocks between any two centers in the network is fixed according to predetermined priorities. For each route there is one outgoing link. A high-level center enroute selects the highest priority route available and hence the corresponding outgoing link for each block ready to leave the center. Routing tables are updated three times a year. Note from Fig. 2-8 that there are at least two outgoing links from each center. This provides the alternate route capability needed to establish a priority structure, or, in general, to reroute should one of the links fail.

Three types of high-level computer systems are in use in the SITA network. These consist of a Phillips DS-714 Mark II 32-bit word machine and Univac 418-II and 418-III 18-bit word machines. Processors are duplicated for reliability. The Phillips systems utilize two types of communication multiplexers: one that can handle up to 125 asynchronous (low-speed) lines of 45—100 bps each; a second that can accommodate up to 30 synchronous or asynchronous lines of 200—9600 bps capacity. The Paris center for example in 1973 had three multiplexers of the first type, accommodating 300 low-speed lines, and one of the second, used for 12 lines. The Univac centers are equipped with communication line controllers that can control up to 32 low-speed asynchronous lines or up to 16 synchronous lines. The Rome center in 1973 was equipped with two line controllers to handle two medium-speed lines, 50 low-speed lines, plus two remote multiplexer lines.

Two types of machines are used as satellite processors in the network: the Raytheon 706 16-bit word computer with 32 kwords of memory, and the Thomas Houston (GE) 24-bit word computer with 32 kwords of memory. The Raytheon machine can control 8 full-duplex synchronous lines and 72 full-duplex asynchronous (low-speed) lines. The Thomas Houston system can control 64 synchronous or asynchronous full-duplex lines.

Agent sets connected to a satellite processor are polled cyclically by the processor asking them to transmit any waiting inquiry messages. On receipt of a polling message (the topic of polling will be considered in detail in Chap. 12), the agent set addressed will transmit its inquiry message, if one is waiting, to the processor. If none is waiting it so indicates. In either case the next set in order is interrogated and so on down the line. (Polling is quite common in inquiry-response systems of various kinds and is used as an access technique for groups of terminals sharing a communication line. The terminals are thus effectively connected in series.) Messages are assembled into blocks at the processor and then transmitted, block by block, to the high-level center to which the processor is connected. A full-duplex synchronous link control procedure similar to that described above for handling point-to-point transmission between neighboring high-level centers is used to control the exchange of data between the satellite processor and its center. Messages are reassembled on drum at this entry center. They are then routed through the high-level network, following the procedure described earlier, to the exit center to which the appropriate reservations computer is connected. Type A response messages generated by the reservations computer are returned in block form through the network, as described earlier, to the entry high-level center. They are then forwarded, block by block, to the satellite processor. Appropriate line control is utilized as noted above to ensure the correct block and message (if multiblock) arrival at the processor. Multiblock messages are reassembled at the processor before being sent out on the agent set line. An example of a typical Type A message path, from agent set to reservation computer and return, is shown in Fig. 2-9.

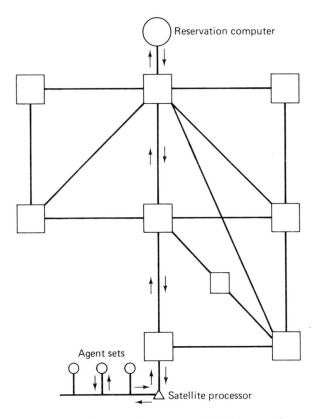

Fig. 2-9. Typical Type A message path, SITA network.

Blocks correctly received at a processor are stored in fixed length buffers in the main memory. These buffers are assigned, using a chaining technique, from the available pool and are returned to the pool as soon as available. After each buffer is assigned the processor checks to see if memory is still available. In the case of saturation, teleprinters are first informed to stop transmitting; the poll rate on the agent set lines is then reduced if necessary; finally, if necessary, traffic from the high-level center to which the processor is connected is shut off.

Some operating statistics and performance figures for the SITA network as of 1973 are of interest.*

The average response time for Type A messages ranges from 1.4 sec to 3 sec, depending on the number of links traversed over the route. This is the time between transmission of the agent query and the instant the first character of the response appears on the CRT screen. It clearly agrees with the 3 sec response time figure quoted earlier. A typical response time distribution shows a median value of 2 sec and a maximum delay of 4.7 sec.** The mean transit time, or time taken for a block to traverse the high-level network, is 0.7 sec.†

Most of the traffic handled by the SITA network was Type B in 1973, but a rapid increase in the Type A volume was expected in the next few years.‡ The average number of messages leaving the high-level network during peak periods in 1973 was about 7/sec. The high-level center in Paris, as an example, switched 1.2 messages/sec from the low-level network to the high-level network and reverse during peak periods. (If messages switched from low-level to low-level were also to be considered, the Paris figure increased to four messages received per sec.) The line loads ranged from 30% to 40% of capacity during peak periods. As a check, assume the average message traverses two links in going from entrance to exit center. There are then an average of 14 messages/sec traversing the network. If Type B messages of 200 characters constitute 75% of the load, while the remaining 25% are evenly divided between 30-character inquiry and 120-character response messages, the average message length works out to be 170 characters. In 1973 the high-level network had 11 links interconnecting the eight centers in operation at that time. Assuming, for simplicity, that the line load was equally-distributed, we then find $\frac{14}{11} = 1.3$ messages/sec or 220 characters/sec traversing each link, on the average. For 4800 bps or 600 char./sec lines, this corresponds to a line load or relative traffic intensity of 0.37. The calculation of traffic intensity or relative line throughput will be explored in detail in the remainder of this book.

*Ibid.
**Ibid., Fig. 16.
†Details of a typical calculation of delay times for the SITA network appear in Chap. 6. See also Brandt and Chretien, "Message-Switching Network."
‡Chretien, König, and Rech, "SITA Network."

Network availability is of considerable interest in assessing the operation of a network. Downtimes of the high-level centers in the SITA average about two hours per month, including scheduled stops for service reasons. The probability that any pair of high-level centers is completely isolated, with no route available between them, is found to be negligible.* The corresponding downtimes are in the order of minutes per month. Satellite processor downtime, including both unscheduled stops (system failures) and scheduled stops (e.g., for preventive maintenance and for configuration changes), comes to about 2% per month.

ARPA NETWORK

The ARPA network has probably generated more interest and excitement in the field of computer networking than any other network in the world. It has spawned a tremendous amount of research in such diverse areas as: computer-to-computer protocol, interconnection of dissimilar networks, line protocol, communication processor hardware and software design, network topological design, network reliability, adaptive routing and flow control, packet-switching concepts, and so on. Some of these topics in computer-communications will be discussed in detail in later chapters. The development of the ARPA network has led, directly or indirectly, to the development of a whole host of large-scale computer-communication networks worldwide, both commercial as well as government-owned in many cases.

The network was originally conceived by the Advanced Research Projects Agency (ARPA) of the U.S. Department of Defense as an experiment in computer resource sharing: a network that would interconnect dissimilar computers throughout the United States, allowing users and programs at one computer center to access and interactively use facilities at other centers geographically remote from one another. The network began operation in 1969 with four nodes (computer center sites) interconnected; by June 1975 more than 100 large computers of all types were connected into the system. The growth rate in that period of six years was phenomenal. Although a major portion of the research activity during the development of the network was devoted to the difficult problems of establishing and maintaining communication between dissimilar computers (these involve aspects of "handshaking" and computer-to-computer protocol), we shall focus in this section on design questions relating to the communications subnet only.

Emphasis in the ARPA network has been on the segmentation of messages. It was decided at the beginning of the ARPA network design to use the store-and-forward rather than the line-switched technology. In addition, emphasis was placed on the segmentation of messages from a computer sys-

*Ibid.

tem (*Host*) at a source node into blocks called *packets*. This was done to decrease possible delays. (Long messages, if stored at intermediate nodes along a path for error checking, could result in excessive time delay. The first packets of a message can be forwarded ahead of the later ones, however, reducing the time delay. Too short a packet size on the other hand results in suboptimum buffer utilization.) Individual packets are then stored and forwarded at intermediate nodes as they move across the network to the computer system at the destination node. As a result of this emphasis on packets the ARPA network has been labeled a *packet-switched* network. Other networks discussed in this chapter use the words "blocks" or "records" to denote their basic transmission unit. We shall not attempt to distinguish between the terms "message-switched" and "packet-switched" in this book; in fact we sometimes use them interchangeably, since data most often will be assumed transmitted in block form.

The communication functions of the ARPA network are similar to those previously discussed in describing other networks. These involve message storage, coding into standardized network format, routing and flow control, and error control, among others. The communications function is again carried out by nodal minicomputer communication processors called, in the ARPA network, *Interface Message Processors*, IMPs for short. (These are modified versions of the Honeywell DDP-516 machine.) In 1972 provision was made to have terminals connect directly to the network without going through a large computer system or Host computer. For this purpose modified IMPs called *Terminal Interface Message Processors*, TIPs, were introduced into the network as nodal concentrators as well. (These are based on the Honeywell H-316 computer.) The IMPs and TIPs comprising the communication subnet are interconnected with wideband communications lines or links primarily of 50 kbps capacity. The geographical map of the network in February 1976 appears in Fig. 2-10. It consists of 56 nodes interconnected by 74 links. Two of the links are 7.2 kbps satellite links (one to Hawaii, the other to Europe). There were 23 TIPs and 33 IMPs in the network at that time. A logical map of the network in February 1976, showing the communication links with more clarity and indicating the various computer systems connected in, is shown in Fig. 2-11. From one to four Hosts are connected to each IMP. Each node (except for two in the continental U.S., plus the Hawaiian and European links) is connected to from two to four other nodes to provide alternate path capability. (IMPs actually have the capability of being connected to five lines.)

Note that the distributed topological form of the ARPA network with its alternate path capability is similar to that of TYMNET discussed previously. The major difference is in line capacity. The ARPA network uses 50 kbps lines while the TYMNET lines are primarily voice-grade.

In the summer of 1975 the ARPA network was turned over to the De-

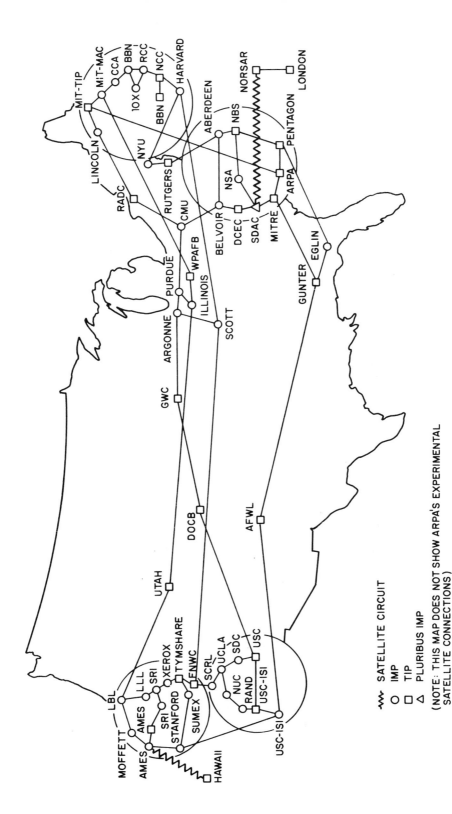

Fig. 2-10. ARPA network, geographic map, Feb. 1976.

SATELLITE CIRCUIT
○ IMP
□ TIP
△ PLURIBUS IMP

(NOTE: THIS MAP DOES NOT SHOW ARPA'S EXPERIMENTAL
SATELLITE CONNECTIONS)

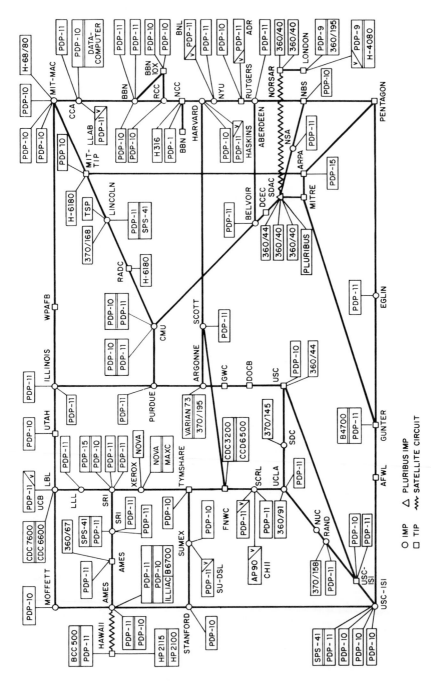

Fig. 2-11. ARPA network, logical map, Feb. 1976.

○ IMP   △ PLURIBUS IMP
□ TIP   〜〜 SATELLITE CIRCUIT

(PLEASE NOTE THAT WHILE THIS MAP SHOWS THE HOST POPULATION OF THE NETWORK ACCORDING TO THE BEST
INFORMATION OBTAINABLE, NO CLAIM CAN BE MADE FOR ITS ACCURACY)

fense Communications Agency of the U.S. Department of Defense. This concluded the experimental phase of the network with the network now taking on more of an operational character. Because of its experimental character in the period from 1969–1975 and the great deal of research carried out during its evolution into all areas of computer-communications, the ARPA network has been extensively documented in the literature. We shall reference some of the papers describing various aspects of the network design and operation in this section. Other references appear in later chapters of this book. These papers in turn contain much more detailed references for the interested reader. An overall discussion of the network with a summary of experiences gained during the ARPA experimental period appears in a paper by D.C. Walden.* Much of the material following is based on a paper by J.M. McQuillan, W.R. Crowther, et al., "Improvements in the Design and Performance of the ARPA Network."

As noted above, messages from a Host computer are segmented into packets before being transmitted to the desired destination node. To limit possible congestion in the network and to ease the requirements on nodal buffers for storing packets, messages from Host computers are limited to 8063 bits. A message from a Host computer transmitted to its IMP for processing and forwarding through the communications subnetwork is segmented at the IMP into at most 8 packets with a maximum of 1008 bits each. In practice the vast majority of messages transmitted are one packet long. Control and destination characters are added at the source IMP before the packet is released to the network. A typical data packet is shown sketched in Fig. 2-12.** Standardized 8-bit synchronization patterns are used to delimit the beginning and end of each packet. Two DLE STX characters (8 bits each) are used to indicate the start and end of packet framing. All of these are generated by hardware. Two levels of overhead are shown (not including the higher-level Host-to-Host protocol bits). Level-0 is used to control packet transmission between adjacent nodal processors. As in the case of the networks previously discussed in this chapter error detection with positive acknowledgement is utilized in the ARPA network. A 24-bit checksum is generated by the sending interface hardware and checked by the receiving interface hardware to detect line errors. The program also puts a 16-bit software checksum on the packet in memory before it is sent, and checks it after it is stored in the receiver's memory to detect processor, memory, and software errors. This checksum is passed along through the entire network path.

---

*D. C. Walden, "Experiences in Building, Operating, and Using the ARPA Network," *Second USA-Japan Computer Conference*, Tokyo, Aug. 1975.

L. Kleinrock, W. E. Naylor, and H. Opderbeck, "A Study of Line Overhead in the ARPANET," *Communications of the ACM*, **19, no. 1, Jan. 1976, 3–13, Fig. 1. This format was the one used until 1975. Changes in packet format are noted briefly at the end of this section in discussing new and proposed ARPA network implementations.

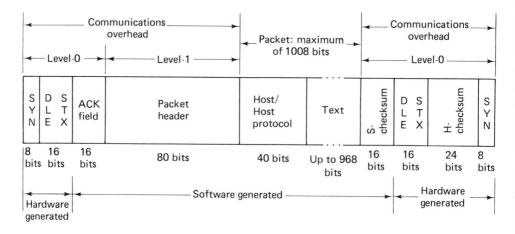

Fig. 2-12. Data packet format, ARPA network. (Courtesy of L. Kleinrock et al., "A Study of Line Overhead in the ARPANET," *Communications of the ACM*, Jan. 1976, Fig. 1.)

If no line error is detected at the receiving node, an acknowledgement message is embedded in (or piggybacked onto) an outgoing packet in the reverse direction. This is shown as the 16-bit ACK field in Fig. 2-12.* The level-1 overhead shown as an 80-bit packet header is used for transmission control between source and destination IMPs. It contains, among other data, source and destination addresses, sequence control, and buffer allocation bits (to be discussed further later).

Packets are individually routed through the network to the destination node. Once a complete message is received at the destination IMP and in turn passed on to the appropriate Host computer, a 118-bit *ready for next message* (RFNM) packet is returned to the source node. Acknowledgements are thus used to certify the correct delivery of individual packets from node to node, while RFNMs indicate the delivery of a completed message to the destination Host.

*Source-to-Destination Flow Control***

Although the vast majority of messages in the ARPA network have been found to be single-packet messages, provision must be made to handle multipacket messages at the destination node. Since the number of packet buffers

*In the original ARPA network design, separate acknowledgement packets were used. See F. G. Heart, R. E. Kahn, S. M. Ornstein, W. R. Crowther, and D. C. Walden, "The Interface Message Processor for the ARPA Computer Network" *AFIPS Conference Proc.*, Spring Joint Computer Conference, 36, June 1970, 551–67.

**J. M. McQuillan, W. R. Crowther, B. P. Cosell, D. C. Walden, and F. G. Heart, "Improvements in the Design and Performance of the ARPA Network," *AFIPS Conference Proc.*, Fall Joint Computer Conference, 41, Dec. 1972, 741–54.

at each node is limited it is possible, if precautions are not taken, to have a phenomenon called *reassembly lockup* occur. A typical example occurs when all reassembly storage buffers at a given node are filled with partially reassembled messages, while neighboring IMPs are filled with packets destined for the node in question. The partially reassembled messages cannot be released to their respective Hosts until completely assembled, but the packets necessary to complete reassembly are barred from arriving because of lack of buffer space. Deadlock ensues. Buffer allocation is used in the ARPANET to prevent lockup from occurring.* A source IMP with a multipacket message to transmit first sends a request for the allocation of up to eight buffers of reassembly space to the destination IMP. The latter replies with an "allocate" message. When this is received at the source IMP, message transmission may begin. To reduce the request/allocate overhead and to allow as much transmission of multipacket messages as possible in the case of a steady flow of traffic, the destination IMP automatically allocates new assembly buffers after delivering the reassembled multipacket message to its Host. An "allocate" message to this effect is then sent to the source IMP piggybacked on the RFNM. If the source responds within 125 msec the message can be transmitted right away. Otherwise the source "returns" the allocation with a special "give back" message. When the Host in question wants to transmit a multipacket message its IMP must again initiate the allocation procedure. In the case of single-packet messages, the message and request for allocation are combined. If the destination IMP can accept the message it does so and returns an RFNM to the source. If buffer storage is not available at the destination the message is dropped. The destination IMP sends back an "allocate" message when storage becomes available. The source then retransmits the message.

The flow control procedure described above is an example of an end-to-end flow control procedure. The GE network also maintains end-to-end control. The TYMNET system uses a local shut-off mechanism at each individual node to control possible congestion in the network. In Chap. 11 we discuss some analytical models of both local and end-to-end control techniques to limit congestion in a network. Although they are not directly applicable to the specific control mechanisms described here, they do provide insight into the congestion control problem and help in carrying out designs for such mechanisms.

Routing in the ARPA Network

The ARPA network has pioneered the use of locally-determined adaptive routing. Unlike TYMNET in which a complete source-destination path is specified by the central supervisor on a least-cost basis or the SITA system

*Ibid.

in which fixed path routing is used, each node in the ARPA network makes its own decision as to which node to next forward a given packet destined for a specific IMP. Each node maintains a routing table which associates each destination node in the network with the particular one of the node's outgoing lines estimated to provide the shortest time path to the desired destination. (Further discussion of the algorithm and related approaches to routing appear in Chap. 11.) Basically, the estimates as to the appropriate outgoing link to check for a particular destination are obtained by periodically exchanging least-time estimates for each destination with the adjacent nodes. A given node then adds its own estimate as to the length of time a packet would take to get to each of the neighboring nodes (based on the queue on each of its outgoing lines), and chooses, for each destination, the outgoing line (or nearest neighbor) that minimizes the sum. The routing table is then updated using this new estimate. In practice, routing messages of 1160 bits are exchanged at least every 625 msec. (If the lines are lightly loaded, the nodes exchange routing more often.) Details of the ARPA routing algorithm as well as a description of other algorithms and references to the literature appear in a report by J.M. McQuillan.* With the local adaptive routing approach used in the ARPA network, packets from the same message may be independently routed along different paths, arriving out of sequence. This again demonstrates the need for the source-to-destination or end-to-end flow control mechanism described earlier.

Source-to-Destination Sequence Control**

In addition to the flow control procedure the ARPA network has incorporated a source-to-destination message sequence control that allows several messages between a given source IMP—destination IMP pair to be in the transmission path simultaneously. This serves to increase the throughput rate. In addition priority classes are available, and priority messages so designated by a Host can move ahead of nonpriority messages. This sequence control is set up by associating with each source IMP—destination IMP pair a single logical "pipe". For this purpose each IMP maintains an 8-bit sequence number for every other IMP in the network. This number (accommodating 256 different messages) has been chosen large enough to avoid problems with identically numbered messages; e.g., a prior message will have long since been received at the destination. Each Host at a given IMP has a separate set of sequence numbers for its communication with each other Host in the

*J. M. McQuillan, "Adaptive Routing Algorithms for Distributed Computer Networks," Bolt, Beranek, and Newman Report no. 2831, May 1974 (Harvard Ph.D. thesis); available from National Technical Information Service, AD781467.
  **McQuillan et al., "Improvements of the ARPA Network."

network, at each priority level. A small subset or window, at present capable of accommodating eight separate numbers, represents the numbers currently valid in each sequence. This allows up to eight messages to be in transit at any one time between each of the Hosts in the network. The size of this window is chosen to allow high throughput given the network response time. This control results in an ordering of the eight messages and allows detection of duplicate messages.

The source control procedure is a level-1 or source-destination control procedure, as noted earlier, and the eight bits allocated to this appear in the packet header of Fig. 2-12. Error control, on the other hand, is carried out on both a node-to-node basis and an end-to-end basis. Error control for the ARPA network, as noted earlier, involves the use of 40 checksum bits (Fig. 2-12) to detect errors. Theoretically, this should reduce the undetected bit error rate to 2^{-40} or approximately 10^{-12} below the raw error rate of a physical line. For a line transmitting 30,000 bps continuously, this represents one undetected bit error on the average in many, many years!

Node-to-Node Acknowledgement*

The acknowledgement procedure adopted for the ARPA network in 1972 (prior to that time separate ACK packets were used) is similar to one described earlier in the literature.** Each physical line is visualized as divided into eight "logical channels" in each direction. Each packet is assigned to one of the eight outgoing channels, carrying the channel number and an odd/even bit for that channel, used to detect duplicate packet transmissions. The packet also carries eight ACK bits, one for each channel in the reverse direction. The receiving IMP carries out error detection, comparing the appropriate first checksum calculation with the checksum bits of the packet. If they agree the packet is accepted as valid. The odd/even bit of the packet, as received at the next node to which directed, is then compared to the odd/even bit associated with the appropriate receive channel. If there is a match this indicates the packet is a duplicate, and it is discarded. If the bits do not match the packet is accepted and the odd/even bit is complemented. An ACK is piggybacked onto an outgoing packet in the reverse direction. For this purpose the received odd/even bit is copied into the ACK bit (of eight available) associated with that channel. When the original sending IMP receives a packet it checks the odd/even ACK bit in each channel with the transmit odd/even bits. For *each* match found the corresponding packet is discarded, its channel is marked as unused, and the transmit odd/even bit is complemented. This ACK pro-

*Ibid.
K. Bartlett, R. Scantlebury, and P. Wilkinson, "A Note on Reliable Full-Duplex Transmission Over Half-Duplex Links," *Communications of the ACM*, **12, no. 5, May 1969, 260–61.

cedure has been found to provide from 10—20% improvement in line utilization over the previous scheme involving separate ACK messages.

A transmission ordering scheme is used to avoid too long a time for transmission. The order of transmission consists of:

1. previously transmitted and unacknowledged packets (if unacknowledged for 125 msec)

2. priority packets not yet transmitted

3. regular packets not yet transmitted.

Overall Network Design Considerations

The original ARPA network design goal was to provide a least-cost network with a packet time delay of less than 0.2 sec from source-to-destination IMP. Since the number and location of nodes and their associated communication concentrators (IMPs or TIPs) are given for the network, the least-cost topological design for a specified traffic throughput must be based on an appropriate choice of lines (links) interconnecting the nodes, and the transmission capacity of these lines. The topology chosen depends on the routing strategy adopted for the packets as well. Since this is not really known in advance and in fact depends on the network topology, iterative design procedures are required to ultimately determine the optimum network design. Some of the network design techniques developed during the research phase of the ARPA network development are described in Chap. 10 and 11, and the references contained therein.

In addition to a least-cost design that satisfied a 0.2 sec time delay criterion, various constraints had to be met as well.* These included a measure of reliability, specified in practice by requiring a network design with at least two-connectivity (i.e., each node must be connected to the network by at least two links), the ability to accommodate variations in traffic flow without significant degradation in performance, and the ability to grow in an orderly, low-cost manner as new nodes and links were added.

The original network in 1969 consisted of a 4-node configuration on the West Coast. Some months later, in mid-1970, there were 10 nodes in the network; by early 1971 the network had 15 nodes, by mid-1971 there were 26 nodes; by late 1972 there were 34 nodes; and in early 1973 there were 40 nodes. In 1975 as already noted, there were 56 nodes. The network thus grew extremely rapidly. Through much of this time additions only to the existing network were made with links being added only as required while maintaining the low-cost, time delay, and reliability criteria mentioned above. It

---

*H. Frank, I. T. Frisch, and W. Chou, "Topological Considerations in the Design of the ARPA Computer Network," *AFIPS Conference Proc.*, **36**, June 1970, 581–87.

wasn't until the network reached the 26-node size that fundamental changes were made in the network structure.* A redesign at this time resulted in a reduction in cost with a corresponding increase in throughput and improvement in reliability. As the network has grown the designs produced have resulted in a reduction of link cost/node/year from $44,000 at 15 nodes to $26,000 at 40 nodes. The design throughput level has been reduced from 10.7 kbps/node to 7.3 kbps/node. The line cost per thousand packets transmitted has remained relatively constant at $0.07.**

IMP Program Structure†

We have in previous sections outlined the various steps involved in transmitting messages through the network. These are carried out by the nodal communication processors, IMPs, in the network.

Most of these tasks involved in the handling of packets are stored as programs in core at each IMP. These program functions include the segmenting of Host messages into packets; the processes of receiving, routing, and transmitting store-and-forward packets; the retransmission of unacknowledged packets; the reassembly of packets into messages for transmission to the appropriate associated Host; and the generation of RFNMs and other control messages. In addition, the IMP carries out various miscellaneous tasks, such as that of gathering statistics, performing on-line testing, and monitoring network status.

A schematic diagram indicating the various steps involved in the IMP's handling of packets and maintaining their flow appears in Fig. 2-13.†† The packet processing and other routines to carry out the various functions noted above are shown within the dashed lines. Queueing and buffering points are indicated as well.

The code for these various program functions is stored in 24 516-word pages of core. The code is centered in each page, surrounded for the most part by buffers. (There is an integral number of buffers between the last word of code on one page and the first word of code on the next page to reduce breakage.) There are buffers in the IMP set aside for three specific functions:

1. *Line buffering.* One buffer is allocated for output packets on each line connected; two buffers are provided for input on each line. This latter feature permits all input traffic to be examined by the program, so that ACKs can always be processed.

---

*H. Frank and W. Chou, "Network Properties of the ARPA Computer Network," *Networks*, **4**, John Wiley & Sons, Inc., New York, 1974, 213–39.

**Ibid., Table 1, p. 218.

†McQuillan et al., "Improvements of the ARPA Network," pp. 745–48.

††Ibid., Fig. 5, p. 747.

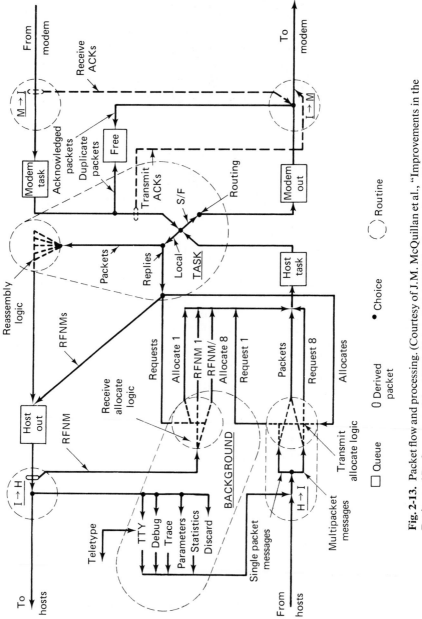

Fig. 2-13. Packet flow and processing. (Courtesy of J.M. McQuillan et al., "Improvements in the Design and Performance of the ARPA Network," *AFIPS Conference Proc.,* **41,** 1972, 747, Fig. 5.

2. *Store-and-forward pool.* Each line is limited to eight or fewer buffers from a set maximum in the pool.

3. *Reassembly storage.*

A description of some of the packet processing routines stored in the IMP program, as shown in Fig. 2-13, follows:*

1. *Host-to-IMP.* This routine appends a message number to each message. The message is then passed through the transmit allocation logic which requests a reassembly allocation from the destination IMP. Once the allocation is received, the message is packetized, and the packets are passed to the Task routine via the Host–Task queue.

2. *Task.* This routine directs packets to their proper destination. Three categories of packets are involved:

   a. Packets going to a local Host are passed through the reassembly logic. When message reassembly is complete, the message is passed to the IMP-to-Host routine via the Host Out queue, as shown in Fig. 2-13.
   b. Control messages for the local IMP are passed to the transmit or receive allocate logic.
   c. Packets for other destinations are placed on the appropriate modem output queue as specified by the routing table.

3. *Imp-to-Modem.* This routine transmits packets from the modem output queue to the associated modem and outgoing line. It also transmits piggy-backed ACKs for packets correctly received by the Modem-to-Imp routine and accepted by the Task routine.

4. *Modem-to-Imp.* This routine handles inputs from modems. It also forwards packets that have been correctly received to the Task routine via the Modem Task queue. It processes incoming piggybacked ACKs and frees buffers holding correctly acknowledged packets.

5. *Imp-to-Host.* This program delivers reassembled messages to the local Hosts. It notifies the background routine that an RFNM should be sent to the source Host.

6. *Background.* These programs carry out miscellaneous tasks. They interact with the IMP's console teletype, they send out incomplete transmission messages, they send and return allocations, and they send RFNMs. (Messages from the last three Tasks are put directly on the Task queue.) In addition, there are debugging, statistics, and trace programs, as well as several routines used to generate control messages.

*Ibid.

7. *Timeout*. This routine carries out periodic functions. It checks tables, queues, and program states to see if the entries and routines remain in a particular state for too long. It sends routing information to each one of the IMP's neighbors every 625 msec as noted earlier.

Measured Network Characteristics

The measured traffic on the ARPA network increased exponentially from 10^5 packets/day in 1971 to 4.5×10^6 packets/day in 1973 and then appeared to level off in growth beyond that point.* In a series of measurements carried out during a one-week period in August 1973, single packet messages were found to predominate;** 97—98% of the messages were a single packet in length, and the average message size was 1.12 packets.

The mean message length in the same set of tests was found to be 243 bits, while the mean packet length was 218 bits. Transmission efficiency is thus rather low since the overhead per packet is 168 bits. Buffer storage in the IMPs is even less efficient, since buffers are designed to accommodate 1008-bit data packets. Adding 176 bits of overhead required per packet, as stored in the IMP, gives an effective average efficiency of 18.4%. Based on these measurements calculations indicate that the efficiency could be doubled to 36.6% by reducing the buffer size to one-quarter of its 1008-bit size.†

The average round-trip message delay (measured from the time the message enters the network until an RFNM is received, acknowledging delivery of the complete message at the destination) was found to be 93 msec, substantially below the 0.2 sec design figure quoted earlier. The reason for this is apparently due to the short length of most messages, the relatively low traffic intensity, as well as the very short path messages were found to traverse on the average. In particular 22% of the traffic measured was found to be *intranodal*, i.e., traffic between Hosts at the same site.†† In addition 16% of the traffic was found to travel one hop only, i.e., between neighboring nodes. The mean path length for these measured statistics can be calculated to be 3.3 hops, or number of links traversed. If one assumes traffic flowing along shortest paths only, one gets a value of 3.2 hops, indicating that most of the traffic *was* essentially following a shortest path route.§ (This may very well be due to the relatively low utilization of the network. With a lightly-loaded network, all least-time routing algorithms tend to favor the shortest path

---

*L. Kleinrock and W. E. Naylor, "On Measured Behavior of the ARPA Network," *AFIPS Conference Proc.*, National Computer Conference, **43**, May 1974, 767–80. See Fig. 2.

**Ibid.

†Ibid.

††Walden, "Building the ARPA Network," speculates on the various reasons for this.

§Kleinrock and Naylor, "Behavior of the ARPA Network."

route. See Chap. 11.) In addition, it was found that 44% of all traffic was directed to a most favored destination, while 90% of the traffic was directed to the nine most favored sites of the roughly 40 available at the time of the experiment.

As noted above, the measured utilization of the network was rather low. (As mentioned in previous sections, commercial networks tend to operate the same way to reduce transmission delay and to cut down on the costs involved in buffer management at intermediate nodes.) Specifically in the seven days of tests mentioned above, the total network traffic was 6.3×10^9 bits or 25×10^6 messages. There was thus an average network arrival rate of 47 messages/sec. (The peak rate measured was 110 messages/sec.)* Including overhead this corresponds to a utilization (in percent of transmission capacity) of 7% on the average. Excluding overhead this comes to 0.8% utilization. The maximum utilization of the network overall during the 7-day period measured was found to be 13.4%, with overhead included. This corresponded to 600 kbps of *internal* network flow. (A message requiring three hops to be delivered to its destination must be counted three times in determining the internal flow. In addition, control messages generated by data messages such as RFNMs for example should be included as well. See Chap. 3, 4, and 6 for discussions and typical calculations involving these points.) The busiest line of any hour was found, on the other hand, to have a 48% utilization with overhead included and 22.5% without.

Other measurements made indicate that 49% of all packets transmitted are communication subnet control messages.** Of these 89% are RFNMs for single-packet messages. The request allocation message discussed earlier, used to request eight buffers at a destination node for a multipacket message, only accounts for 1% of the control messages, as does the return allocation message. This of course reflects the fact that only 2—3% of messages transmitted are multipacket messages. In addition to these and the other control messages mentioned earlier, there is background traffic flowing in the network, consisting primarily of the 1160-bit routing messages sent every 624 msec.†

New and Proposed ARPA Network Implementations

As was the case with the other networks discussed in this chapter, changes in the ARPA network structure, message- and packet-handling techniques, and minicomputer architecture have been taking place regularly. Some of these changes have already been noted earlier. Others will be men-

*Ibid.
**Kleinrock, Naylor, and Opderbeck, "Line Overhead in ARPANET."
†Ibid.

tioned briefly here. Some of these changes are due to the introduction of two new IMPs, the so-called Pluribus IMP and the Satellite IMP. Others, such as format changes, are due to the growth of the network.

The Satellite IMP, a modified version of the IMP discussed earlier, was developed specifically with the expectation that satellite links would play an increasingly larger role in ARPA network operations. The Satellite IMP uses some of the packet broadcast ideas (pioneered by the ALOHA system at the University of Hawaii, and discussed in some detail in Chap. 13) that enable several network nodes to statistically share a communications channel to a satellite. Because of the long round-trip propagation delay (0.27 sec), as many as 32 packets can be sent out before the acknowledgement for the first returns. Buffer space must thus be provided for these packets. As will be discussed in Chap. 13, two or more nodes attempting to transmit simultaneously over the same channel will result in packet destruction. To prevent this from happening again packets must be retransmitted randomly. The Satellite IMP uses a software algorithm to carry this out. Other features of this IMP are discussed in the reference.* Two such IMPs were in use on the network in 1976.

The Pluribus IMP was developed specifically for packet-switching applications, using the experience of the Honeywell 516 and 316 communication processors as a guide.** The Pluribus concentrators have a minicomputer-multiprocessor architecture and are highly modular. They are based on the Lockhead SUE computer which connects multiple processors, multiple memories and input-output (I/O), on a single bus. In the Pluribus configuration multiple buses are used to expand the capability of the system. A configuration incorporating 14 processors would be expected to have 10 times the traffic-handling capability of the 316 IMP for example. The Pluribus IMP design was undertaken with the idea of developing flexibility in configuration, to provide cost savings for small systems yet have the ability to grow easily and modularly to accommodate added traffic and larger numbers of interfaces, and, finally, to provide improvement in reliability. As of early 1976 one Pluribus IMP had been installed in the ARPA network.

In addition to new developments in minicomputer architecture a modified packet format was introduced in 1976 to accommodate the increased size of the network. For packets concerned with the actual transmission of data, the basic packet structure is organized around 16-bit words in addition

---

*S. Butterfield, R. Rettberg, and D. Walden, "The Satellite IMP for the ARPA Network," Computer Nets Supplement, *Proc. Seventh Hawaii International Conference on System Sciences*, Jan. 1974.

S. M. Ornstein and D. C. Walden, "The Evolution of a High Performance Modular Packet-Switch," *Proc. IEEE International Conference on Communications*, San Francisco, June 1975, pp. 6–17 to 6–21; S. M. Ornstein et al., "Pluribus—A Reliable Multiprocessor," *AFIPS Conference Proc.*, National Computer Conference, **44, 1975, 551–59.

to the data portion and error detection characters. A 16-bit field, called the NETH field, is provided for modem control. The TYPH field is used to designate one of four packet types: data, network control, switch control such as routing, or special. It also has a priority message bit, a tracer bit, and flag bits for other control purposes. The CHKH field provides the software checksum noted earlier; there is a 16-bit source IMP field, a 16-bit message number field SEQH containing eight bits for message number and eight bits for receive message block number, a packet number field which also includes a multipacket message designation bit and other flags, a destination IMP field, and the message ID field MIDH. Other packet types use somewhat different formats.

Finally, a new set of message processing procedures is being implemented on the ARPA network. Tables kept at each IMP are structured for a network of up to 64 IMPs, four Hosts per IMP, line capacities of 50 kbps, and round-trip delays of $\frac{1}{2}$ sec. With the network now approaching the 64-node size, with new types of IMPs being introduced, and satellite circuits being utilized, it is clear that the constraints noted above have to be reexamined. Three major changes have been either introduced or planned. These include the use of dynamic message blocks, a restructuring of message tables, and a set of changes to the IMP—Host protocol.* In the dynamic block concept message tables are structured in the form of small blocks of storage. These blocks are kept only as long as a conversation between two Hosts is active. This replaces permanent tables indexed by IMP, Host, etc., which become prohibitive with a large enough network.

*J. M. McQuillan, "The Evolution of Message Processing Techniques in the ARPA Network," *Infotech International State of the Art Report*, "Network Systems and Software," 1975, 541–78.

Capacity Assignment
in Networks

3

With an introduction into overall questions of network design provided by Chap. 1, and the detailed discussion of some existing networks provided by Chap. 2, we are now ready to begin a quantitative discussion of some of the problems raised. In this chapter and the two following, we focus on the question of link capacity assignment: What capacity throughput (in bits per second (bps)) should be made available on each link of the network to provide a specified grade of service (or network performance)? In most of this material we shall assume the network structure specified, although we shall discuss briefly the effect of changing network topology. We also assume the network traffic statistics known; i.e., average message lengths and rate of occurrence, as well as average number of messages flowing between any two points in the network. The subject of capacity assignment is chosen first because of its obvious importance in network design and because it provides a simple introduction to other elements of network design to be discussed later in this book. The more complex questions of choice of topology, of connections between concentrators, and of routing of messages arise naturally in the context of the discussion of capacity assignment. An introduction to the concentration (statistical multiplexing) process and the modeling of concentrators by queues arise naturally out of this discussion as well.

We shall, by example, outline several approaches to capacity assignment, utilizing different performance criteria. Much of this is based on the pioneering work of L. Kleinrock.* In the first (and simplest) case, due specifically to Kleinrock, we assume cost linearly proportional to capacity. Holding the overall network cost fixed is then equivalent to keeping the total capacity fixed. We then ask for the best allocation of capacity, link by link, in the sense of minimizing average message time delay. Details of this design approach appear in this chapter. This gives rise to a so-called square-root capacity assignment strategy, with the capacity in any link proportional to the *square root* of the traffic flowing through that link. In the next chapter we compare this approach, again by example, with two other assignment strategies: an equal assignment strategy, in which the *same* capacity is assigned to each link, and a proportional assignment strategy in which the capacity is proportional to the traffic flowing in any link.

Although the assumption of a linear cost-capacity relationship is not truly valid in real life (costs depend nonlinearly on a host of parameters: capacity, type of leased line or service, length of line, etc., etc.), it does provide a reasonable first approximation to the choice of capacity. It answers the question of where to start in capacity assignment—roughly what capacities will be needed to keep the average message time delay to within the desired range? It also enables us to assess, in a rather simple way, the effect of changing network structures as well as the choice of message strategy.

In the next chapter we extend this rather simple analysis to other classes of performance criteria. One criterion in particular that has been suggested is that of choosing link capacities to minimize the largest time delay expected anywhere in the network. This has the effect, as we shall see, of equalizing the link time delays. Equivalently, it has the effect of providing the same service to both light and heavy network users.

In Chap. 5 we approach the more realistic case of nonlinear cost-capacity relationships, and outline a least-cost algorithm for assigning capacity to links, with the maximum time delay specified. This particular algorithm is valid for centralized computer-communication networks only, i.e., the tree-type structure discussed in Chap. 1, Fig. 1-3b. In working out an example we are able to compare two configurations, the tree of Fig. 1-3b and the star of Fig. 1-3a.

To begin our quantitative discussion of capacity allocation, we take the simplest case possible. We start with the example introduced in the first chapter and diagrammed there in Fig. 1-2—there are seven cities, each with a specified number of data terminals (teletypewriters (TTYs)), to be connected to a central computer (CPU) in Washington, D.C. Consider first the star network configuration of Fig. 1-3a, repeated in more detail in Fig. 3-1. Recall that each

---

*L. Kleinrock, *Communication Nets*; *Stochastic Message Flow and Delay*, McGraw-Hill, New York, 1964. Reprinted, Dover Publications, 1972.

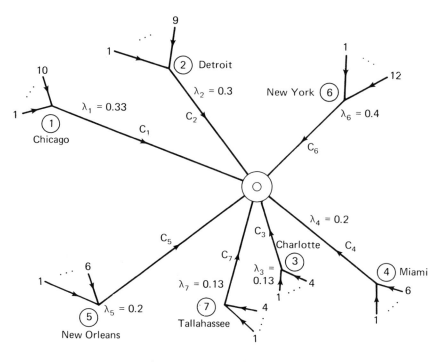

$\lambda_i = i^{th}$ link message rate (messages/sec)
$C_i = i^{th}$ link capacity (bps)

Fig. 3-1. Example of Fig. 1-2, star configuration (active terminals for each city indicated).

terminal (labeled in Fig. 3-1) was assumed to produce a message, on the average, once every 30 sec. Each message was assumed to have an average message length of 120 bits. The object is to determine the trunk capacity, in bps, to allocate to each of the seven links in the network of Fig. 3-1. The capacity of the ith link is indicated as C_i, $i = 1, \ldots, 7$.

To determine this we first focus on the concentrator at a typical node, which serves to combine incoming messages and route them over the appropriate outgoing link, after some necessary processing and buffering. The simplest model is to assume all input ports scanned essentially instantaneously with any messages available at the ports dumped first-come-first-served into an appropriate buffer. This is shown schematically in Fig. 3-2a. Details of the scanning and/or interrupt operations are thus suppressed in this simple approach. Other techniques for entering messages into a concentrator, including polling and random access or contention, are discussed in detail in later chapters. The type of concentration studied here is often referred to as statistical or asynchronous multiplexing. In a more general network than the

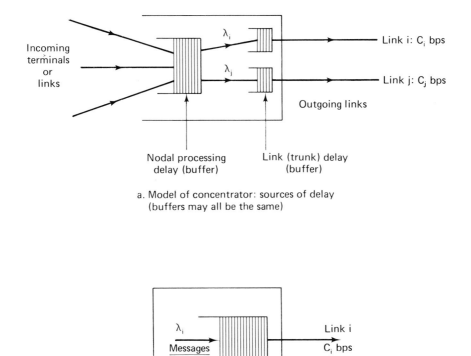

a. Model of concentrator: sources of delay
(buffers may all be the same)

b. Simplest model: one input, one output, infinite
buffer, appropriate to Fig. 3-1

Fig. 3-2. Message time delays in concentrator: simplified models.

star network under consideration here, the input ports correspond to both terminals and trunks (links) feeding messages into this particular concentrator model. After the necessary processing (indicated by a delay element or buffer in Fig. 3-2a), messages destined for link i are routed one at a time onto the appropriate outgoing line. The time delay incurred in waiting for the line to be available is modeled as an additional buffer in Fig. 3-2a. (In practice there may only be one buffer.) For a general network there may be any number of outgoing links. In the star of Fig. 3-1 each concentrator has one outgoing link only.

Since our interest is in link capacity allocations, we ignore details of the concentration and buffering operations. We ignore message overhead, storage in block form, etc. (These are considered, to some extent, in later chapters.) A great simplification ensues by assuming the nodal processing delay to be negligible compared to the delay incurred waiting for the outgoing link to be made available. The time delay model then reduces to the one shown in Fig. 3-2b. The average message rate λ_i destined for link i is the sum of all incoming messages routed over that link. As an example, in the star network of Fig. 3-1, the terminals each have the same average message rate, $\frac{1}{30}$ messages/sec; λ_i for the ith link is then the number of terminals connected in, times $\frac{1}{30}$. For example, $\lambda_1 = \frac{10}{30} = 0.33$ messages/sec, on the average, corresponding to 10 terminals associated with the Chicago concentrator.

Queueing theory may now be applied to the simple model of Fig. 3-2b. Details will be given in Chap. 6. Assuming a Poisson message arrival rate with λ_i messages/sec arriving, on the average, exponentially-distributed message lengths with $1/\mu_i$ bits per message on the average (the bit length thus does not have to be discrete in this simple model), and an infinitely-large buffer capacity, it turns out that the average time delay in seconds incurred by messages is given by

$$T_i = \frac{1}{\mu_i C_i - \lambda_i} \tag{3-1}$$

Here C_i in bps is the link capacity noted earlier. This delay includes the time taken to transmit an average message, $1/\mu_i C_i$ sec, plus the message buffering delay.

Finite buffers will be considered in later chapters, as well as more realistic models for message and traffic statistics. The assumption of an infinite buffer immediately precludes the possibility of message blocking—messages turned away due to full buffers. We shall see later, however, that buffers large enough to keep the blocking probability to less than 10^{-2} or 10^{-3}, for example, may be assumed essentially infinite so far as *average* time delay is concerned.

Equation (3-1) exhibits the characteristic time delay buildup of queues— as λ_i, the average rate of traffic flow, approaches $\mu_i C_i$, the time delay increases without limit. This is often indicated by defining a traffic intensity parameter

$$\rho_i \equiv \frac{\lambda_i}{\mu_i C_i} < 1 \tag{3-2}$$

In terms of this parameter

$$T_i = \frac{1}{\mu_i C_i (1 - \rho_i)} \tag{3-3}$$

For $\rho_i \ll 1$, $T_i = 1/\mu_i C_i$, just the time required to transmit an average message. For $\rho_i \rightarrow 1$, T_i becomes very large. As an example, if $\lambda_i = 0.33$ messages/sec, and $1/\mu_i = 120$ bits/message, as in node ① of Fig. 3-1, then $C_i = 100$ bps produces an average time delay per message transmitted on the outgoing link of 2 sec. Of this, $1/\mu_i C_i = 1.2$ sec is the time required to transmit 120 bits over a 100 bps line, and 0.8 sec is the average buffering delay. The traffic intensity parameter is $\rho_i = 0.4$. Time delays on the New York—Washington link in Fig. 3-1 would be 2.3 sec with the same capacity, while delays on the Tallahassee—Washington link would be 1.43 sec. Increasing the capacity to 900 bps on the Chicago—Washington link reduces the delay to 0.14 sec, of which $1/\mu_i C_i = 0.13$ sec is the message transmission time.

With this simple equation for time delay, we can begin to handle the question of allocating link capacity in a network such as that of Fig. 3-1. In this chapter we assume that the object is to minimize the time delay averaged over the entire network with total capacity assumed fixed. (In Chap. 5, as already noted, we consider other criteria and obtain different results for this network.) Specifically, let γ be the total incoming message rate for the network. In this example a check with Fig. 3-1 shows $\gamma = 1.7$ messages/sec. The average message delay for the network is then defined to be

$$\bar{T} = \frac{1}{\gamma} \sum_i \lambda_i T_i \qquad (3\text{-}4)$$

where we sum over all the network links. $\bar{T}$ thus represents the *weighted* time delay, with T_i given by Eq. (3-1). In the network of Fig. 3-1, i ranges from 1 to 7. This expression for time delay, first used by Kleinrock* in his studies of capacity assignment, will be shown in Chap. 6 to arise quite naturally from some simple arguments in queueing theory. Assuming the total capacity $C = \sum_i C_i$ is held fixed we would like to choose each C_i to minimize $\bar{T}$. This is conveniently carried out by using Lagrange multipliers: it may be shown that the constrained minimum is found by minimizing $\bar{T} + \alpha C$.** The Lagrange multiplier α is chosen to ensure $\sum_i C_i = C$, the fixed quantity.

Actually carrying out the minimization by differentiating $\bar{T} + \alpha C$ with respect to C_i, one finds the optimal solution given by

$$C_i\big|_{\text{opt}} = \frac{\lambda_i}{\mu_i} + \frac{C(1-\rho)\sqrt{\lambda_i/\mu_i}}{\sum_j \sqrt{\lambda_j/\mu_j}} \qquad (3\text{-}5)$$

Here the constant ρC is the representation for $\sum_i (\lambda_i/\mu_i)$ with ρ a parameter playing the role of equivalent traffic intensity parameter for the entire network. With this choice of capacity, link by link, one may substitute into Eq. (3-1) to find the corresponding link time delay T_i. From Eq. (3-4) one then gets the following expression for minimum average message delay:

$$\bar{T}_{\text{min}} = \frac{(\sum_i \sqrt{\lambda_i/\mu_i})^2}{\gamma C(1-\rho)} \qquad (3\text{-}6)$$

Note that the parameter ρ defined above does in fact play the role of a *network* traffic intensity parameter. This assignment of capacity is called the *square-root assignment rule*† since C_i has a term proportional to $\sqrt{\lambda_i}$. Note that the

---

*Ibid.

**Equivalently, one may minimize $\bar{T} + \alpha(C - \sum_i C_i)$.

†Kleinrock, *Communication Nets.*

minimum average time delay $\bar{T}_{\min}$ varies inversely with the capacity C, or, effectively, the cost in this case, since C has been assumed linearly proportional to cost. This inverse relation is an example of the type of trade-off we shall encounter throughout this book. One can always reduce time delays due to queueing in a given network by increasing the line capacities. The price paid is, of course, increased cost. For a specified cost, then, Eq. (3-6) establishes the minimum average time delay possible under the assumption made. In Chap. 5 using more realistic relations between capacity and cost, we shall in fact come up with a typical trade-off curve, such as those that might be used in practice for design purposes, that provides the cost required for varying choices of time delay.

The form of the optimum capacity expression of Eq. (3-5) is also of interest. Note that the capacity term has two parts. The first, (λ_i/μ_i), represents the absolute minimum capacity assignment that must be allocated to link i to enable the traffic over that link to be transmitted. For with λ_i the average number of messages/sec to be handled, and $1/\mu_i$ their average length in bits, (λ_i/μ_i) represents the average *offered load* on link i in bps. This obviously must be less than the transmission capability C_i in bps. This is of course exactly the motivation for defining the traffic parameter ρ_i of Eq. (3-2). Note from Eq. (3-3) as well that with the model of message arrival and length statistics used here (to be justified in detail in Chap. 6), the link time delay increases beyond bound as λ_i/μ_i approaches the capacity C_i. Interestingly then the optimum capacity relation of Eq. (3-5) first assigns the absolute minimum capacity to each link and then allocates the remaining capacity to each link following a square-root assignment strategy. As already noted we shall compare this assignment with several others in the next chapter.

How does the square-root assignment strategy now apply to the network of Fig. 3-1? Here $\mu_i = \mu = \frac{1}{120}$ for all links. From this and summing λ_i over all the links, we find

$$\rho C = \sum_{i=1}^{7} \frac{\lambda_i}{\mu_i} = 204 \text{ bps}$$

If we don't want inordinate time delay we must pick ρ substantially below one (see Eq. 3-6). Specifically then, let $C = 4500$ bps as the total capacity allocation for the network. (In practice, as already noted, one would try different choices of C, each corresponding to a different cost, find $\bar{T}_{\min}$ for each, and plot a time delay cost curve. One could then determine from this the appropriate C for a specified $\bar{T}_{\min}$. A curve like this will be obtained under more realistic conditions in Chap. 5.) For these numbers we find, from Eq. (3-6), that $\bar{T}_{\min} = 0.19$ sec for the network of Fig. 3-1. The actual link capacity assignments in bps obtained from Eq. (3-5) and the corresponding link time delays are shown tabulated in Table 3-1. Also included are the choice of capacities and the corresponding link time delays that one might use if one were constrained to choose C_i from either 450 or 900 bps lines. This is obvi-

TABLE 3-1

STAR NETWORK

| Link | Optimum Case | | Discrete Case | | |
	$C_i|_{opt}$ (bps)	T_i (sec)	C_i (bps)	T_i (sec)	Cost ($/mo)
1	767	0.165	900	0.140	1000
2	726	0.174	900	0.139	650
3	471	0.264	450	0.284	450
4	588	0.212	450	0.282	1288
5	588	0.212	450	0.282	2090
6	845	0.150	900	0.141	388
7	471	0.264	450	0.284	948
	$\bar{T}_{min} = 0.19$ sec		$\bar{T}|_{discrete} = 0.192$ sec		
			Total cost = $6,814 mo		

ously a much more realistic choice, since one never has a continuum of line capacities from which to choose. The square-root assignment strategy thus provides a starting point on which to base realistic choices of capacity.

Note that because of the rather large initial choice of C the capacity choices are not critical. The restriction to *two* discrete capacities thus provides an average time delay for the network that differs inconsequentially from the minimum possible. With C given as 2250 bps, Eq. (3-3) indicates the minimum time delay would have increased from 0.19 sec to 0.38 sec.

To focus attention on network communication cost (to be considered in more detail in Chap. 5) we have indicated in Table 3-1 a typical cost breakdown, link by link, obtained by assuming the 450 bps line rental charges are $1.4/mo/mile, while the 900 bps line costs $1.7/mo/mile.* The monthly costs shown in Table 3-1 were obtained by using the mileages shown in Fig. 1-2. We emphasize this point because for the next example we take the tree network of Fig. 1-3b. Although the delays are found to be substantially greater than those for the star network just considered, the *cost* is much less as well, because of the elimination of some long distance, low-capacity links. In Chap. 5 we shall return to this question showing that the tree network time delay-cost curve is superior to that of the star network for this example.

Consider now the same problem of connecting seven cities to a CPU in Washington, but with the tree structure of Fig. 1-3b used instead of the star previously analyzed. This structure is reproduced, with somewhat more detail shown, in Fig. 3-3. Note here that the four long distance lines connecting Chicago, New Orleans, Tallahassee, and Miami directly to Washington have been eliminated, resulting, as we shall see, in substantial savings in cost.

*These are quite arbitrary figures, chosen for illustrative purposes only. Examples of typical line costs appear in various problems throughout the book and in the Appendix.

Queueing delays are correspondingly greater, however, since messages must now go through intermediate concentrating points, being stored and forwarded as they progress through the network. The delays may be reduced by increasing the network capacity. We shall show in Chap. 5 that although this results in correspondingly higher costs the delay-cost locus is still much better than that for the star network of Fig. 3-1.

To analyze this network and determine the appropriate link capacity allocation, we must take into account in calculating queueing delays not only messages from terminal ports at each nodal concentrator, but messages forwarded from previous links as well. Assuming statistical multiplexing, message arrival rates can again be summed to determine the overall message arrival rate (as shown schematically in Fig. 3-2b), but the message statistics on successive links are now related to one another. Time delays are therefore related as well. (Heavy traffic through link 1 in Fig. 3-3 ensures heavy traffic in link 2, with correspondingly large queueing delays at nodes ① and ②.) The analysis in this case becomes quite difficult for most networks.* Experience has shown, however, that in most cases one can ignore this dependence of successive delays on one another. This is particularly true in light traffic situations and in those where external messages enter in large enough numbers to wash out the dependence of internal messages arriving from other nodes in the network. We therefore invoke the so-called *independence assumption,*** essentially *ignoring* queueing dependencies. (One can always argue that we are only interested in approximate results anyway, since one never really knows the network statistics. The Poisson and exponential models for the message statistics, as well as the averages used for terminal message rates and message lengths, are of course only coarse approximations to the truth.)

Under this assumption, messages are assumed independently generated at each node, with lengths independently chosen from an exponential distribution. We then simply add previous link message rates to those entering a concentrator from external ports, treating them as if they were independently generated by equivalent terminals. In the case of Fig. 3-3, for example, the queueing delay for messages required to traverse link 2 is due to messages externally generated, with rate 0.3 messages/sec at node ② (Detroit: the summed effect of the 9 TTYs assumed located there and accessing the network), plus messages at the rate of 0.33/sec coming from Chicago. Under the independence assumption the messages generated at Chicago are assumed to have their lengths at Detroit selected independently of the lengths at Chicago. The total message rate through link 2, to be used in evaluating the time delay

---

*Analyses of certain special cases are considered by I. Rubin in two papers: I. Rubin, "Communication Networks: Message Path-Delays," *IEEE Trans. Information Theory*, **IT-20**, Nov. 1974, 738–45; and "Message Path-Delays in Packet-Switching Communication Networks," *IEEE Trans. on Communications*, **COM-23**, no. 2, Feb. 1975, 186–92.

**Kleinrock, *Communication Nets*.

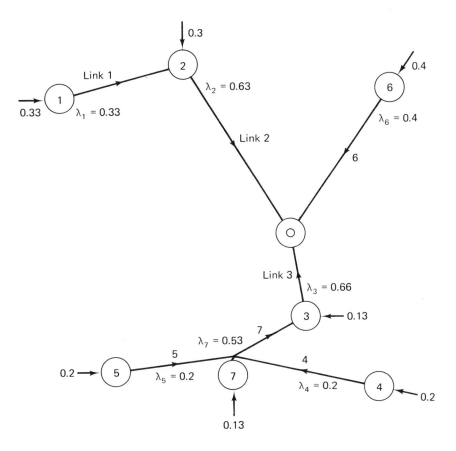

$\lambda_i = i^{th}$ link message rate, messages/sec

Fig. 3-3. Example of Fig. 1-2, tree configuration.

of messages queueing up for transmission over that link, is thus 0.63 message/sec, as shown in Fig. 3-3. The other λ_i's shown may be found similarly. The sum of the λ_i's is no longer equal to the sum of external message rates, as was the case for the star network of Fig. 3-1. (As a matter of fact, $\sum_i \lambda_i/\gamma$, summed over all the links, and with γ the total external message arrival rate, is just the average number of links traversed by a typical message.) But the equations used previously still apply, providing we accept the independence assumption. Thus, using the λ_i's shown in Fig. 3-3, one may again calculate optimum link capacity assignments for the tree network of that figure, using Eq. (3-5) as previously. The results of the calculations are shown in Table 3-2, again for a total capacity $C = 4500$ bps, and again compared with discrete capacity assignments of 450 or 900 bps. (The choice of an optimum discrete assignment is considered in Chap. 5.) The links have been labeled to correspond to the node at the input to the link.

TABLE 3-2

TREE NETWORK

Link	Optimum Case	Discrete Case	
	$C_i|_{opt}$ (bps)	C_i (bps)	T_i (sec)
1	575	450	0.29
2	819	900	0.146
3	842	900	0.146
4	441	450	0.28
5	441	450	0.28
6	638	450	0.298
7	743	900	0.143
	$\bar{T}|_{min} = 0.333$ sec	$\bar{T}|_{discrete} = 0.39$ sec	
		Total cost $= \$3,500/mo$	

Note as already mentioned, that this network results in a larger average time delay than the star previously considered. This cost is correspondingly less because of the elimination of the four long distance links, however. We can reduce the time delay if desired by increasing the capacity assignments appropriately. Since the incremental cost of using larger capacity lines is smaller as the line size increases, considerable delay-cost improvement may be obtained. This point is considered in detail in Chap. 5.

PROBLEMS

3.1 The average time delay due to buffering in a message-switched, store-and-forward network is given by

$$\bar{T} = \frac{1}{\gamma} \sum_i \lambda_i T_i, \qquad T_i = \frac{1}{\mu_i C_i - \lambda_i}$$

(1) The total network capacity $C = \sum_i C_i$, in bps is to be held fixed. Use the Lagrange multiplier technique to find the link capacity assignment that minimizes $\bar{T}$ above. Show this is given by

$$C_i = \frac{\lambda_i}{\mu_i} + C(1 - p) \frac{\sqrt{\lambda_i/\mu_i}}{\sum_j \sqrt{\lambda_j/\mu_j}}$$

Here $pC \equiv \sum_i \lambda_i/\mu_i$.

(2) Show the minimum average time delay is given by

$$\bar{T}_{min} = \frac{\left(\sum_i \sqrt{\lambda_i/\mu_i} \right)^2}{\gamma C(1 - p)}$$

3.2 In Fig. P3.2, programmable concentrators in each of the five boroughs of
New York City are to be connected to a large computer in lower
Manhattan. Teletype terminals are in turn connected to the concentrators. Each terminal transmits at a rate of 100 bps. Messages are, on the
average, 1000 bits long. A typical terminal transmits a message on the
average of once a minute. The number of terminals in each borough is
as follows:

Bronx	10
Brooklyn	15
Manhattan	20
Queens	10
Richmond	5

(1) Determine the minimum average time delay for the network if
the total capacity available is $C = 2000$ bps. Repeat for $C = 5000$ bps. (Assume one-way delay, into the CPU, only.)

(2) Find the optimum capacity allocation for each of the five links to
the large computer for the two total capacities of (1).

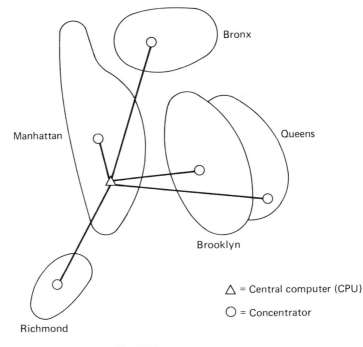

Fig. P3.2

(3) 300, 600, 900, and 1200 bps lines only are available. Adjust the link values found in (2) to the closest of these available capacities, with the total capacity kept close to 2000 and 5000 bps respectively, and compare the average time delays in these cases with the minimum possible.

3.3   Refer to Problem 3.2. Two other capacity assignments are to be investigated for the case of $C = 2000$ bps:

(1) The total capacity C is assigned equally to all five links.

(2) Proportional assignment is used, with $C_i = \lambda_i C/\lambda$,

$$\lambda = \sum_{i=1}^{5} \lambda_i$$

For each scheme find the average time delay per link and the average overall time delay for the network, and compare with the corresponding result of Problem 3.2(1).

3.4   Refer to the 7-city centralized network example of this chapter. Determine the optimum capacity assignment for minimum time delay, assuming a star connection, and verify the entries in Table 3-1. Use the line rental charges given to check the monthly communications cost obtained for the discrete capacity case.

3.5   Use the current tariff structure available from ATT, Western Union, or from any of the specialized data carriers in the United States to obtain a more realistic and up-to-date cost picture of the 7-city star network of Problem 3.4. Use a realistic set of discrete capacity assignments as in Problem 3-2(3). Include as many other costs as necessary to make the cost estimate as realistic and all-inclusive as possible.

3.6   Repeat Problem 3.4 for the tree structure of Fig. 3-3. Check the entries in Table 3-2.

3.7   As in Problem 3.5, calculate an up-to-date set of costs required to implement the tree network of Fig. 3-3, using the discrete capacity assignments of Problem 3-2(3). For this purpose consult the tariffs published by ATT, Western Union, or any specialized data carrier.

Capacity Assignment

in

Distributed Networks

In the previous chapter we discussed capacity assignment for a very simple network—terminals at seven cities feeding in to a central processor located at one central point. More generally, we have data messages flowing between various points in a network. This gives rise to the mesh-type network of Fig. 1-1d. The ARPA network, TYMNET, and the SITA network, discussed in Chap. 2, are existing examples of this type of network.

Capacity assignment strategies in these types of network are *identical* to those discussed in conjunction with the simple configuration of the previous chapter, *provided* one is again willing to invoke the independence assumption discussed there. To be specific consider the hypothetical network shown in Fig. 4-1. This has been taken from the book by L. Kleinrock previously referenced.* With the traffic, its statistical characteristics, and routes taken by messages given between all pairs of five cities shown, we shall, repeating the approach of the last chapter, indicate how one optimally assigns capacity to each of the seven links in the network. We shall then compare this square-root capacity assignment for minimizing average time delay with two other assignment strategies, proportional and equal assignment.

The capacity assignments depend on the routing strategies adopted. We shall investigate the effect of routing briefly by changing the routing strategy somewhat and noting the effect on capacity assignment. Routing algorithms will be considered in detail in Chap. 11.

*Kleinrock, *Communication Nets*, p. 23.

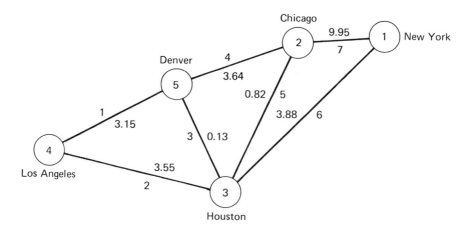

Fig. 4-1. Network example, λ_i's (messages/sec) shown, either direction (shortest distance routing).

This particular example will be discussed in this chapter because it has appeared in follow-up work in the literature in discussions relating to different types of performance criteria used in assigning capacity. These include, in contrast to the minimum time delay criterion, minimum mean-square time delay and minimum of the maximum time delay. We shall summarize these papers extending Kleinrock's work to other cost functions and compare, for the same network, the effect of using different cost functions.

In determining the capacity allocations for this network one must know the traffic flowing between cities as well as the route assigned to messages entering the network at one city and destined for another. As an example, the traffic matrix of Table 4-1, indicating the average rate of message flow (messages/sec) between all city-pairs, is assumed given.*

Note that the traffic flowing has been assumed symmetrical (N.Y. to L.A. traffic = L.A. to N.Y. traffic) for simplicity. Asymmetrical traffic flows could easily be handled in the same manner. The *total* average message traffic emanating from any one city is of course given by summing along the appropriate horizontal row. The average number of messages/sec arriving at a particular city is found by summing the appropriate column. The sum of all the entries in the table provides the total network traffic input.

All seven links in the network of Fig. 4-1 are assumed to be full-duplex so that the capacity in either direction is the same. In addition, because of the symmetrical nature of the traffic flow shown in Table 4-1, it is apparent that

*Ibid., p. 22. This specific example is used, as noted earlier, because extensions of it have appeared in the literature. Although the entries shown are in messages/sec, they can easily be converted to bps (bits/sec) by multiplying by average message length in bits. For example, if messages were all on the average 1000 bits long, all entries would be multiplied by 1000. The case of unequal message lengths is considered in a later paragraph.

TABLE 4-1

TRAFFIC MATRIX, NETWORK, FIG. 4-1*

Source City	Destination: New York 1	Chicago 2	Houston 3	Los Angeles 4	Denver 5
1. New York		9.34	0.935	2.94	0.610
2. Chicago	9.34		0.820	2.40	0.628
3. Houston	0.935	0.820		0.608	0.131
4. Los Angeles	2.94	2.40	0.608		0.753
5. Denver	0.610	0.628	0.131	0.753	

*From L. Kleinrock, *Communication Nets*, p. 22

average traffic characteristics in either direction of traffic flow along a particular link will be the same, as will queueing delays at the nodes at either end of a particular link. This enables us to focus attention on the traffic in any one direction only, reducing the problem from that of calculating queueing delays over 14 one-way links to only 7. We shall thus focus on one-way message flow over seven links only. The *total* network flow is obviously double this.

To determine the capacity assignment for each of the seven links we invoke as noted earlier the independence assumption: traffic queueing up for transmission over any link is statistically independent of traffic appearing anywhere else in the network. We must also determine the average message rate flowing over each of the links. For this purpose assume the routing of messages takes the *shortest geographical route*:

1. Los Angeles—Chicago traffic routed through Denver

2. Los Angeles—New York traffic through Houston

3. Denver—New York traffic through Chicago.

Specifically, letting γ_{jk} messages/sec represent the appropriate entry in the matrix of Table 4-1 showing messages entering city j and destined for city k, we have as the average one-way message rate in each of the seven links of Fig. 4-1:

$$\lambda_1 = \gamma_{45} + \gamma_{42} \qquad = 3.15 \text{ messages/sec, one-way}$$
$$\lambda_2 = \gamma_{43} + \gamma_{41} \qquad = 3.55 \text{ messages/sec, one-way}$$
$$\lambda_3 = \gamma_{53} \qquad\qquad = 0.13 \text{ messages/sec, one-way}$$
$$\lambda_4 = \gamma_{52} + \gamma_{42} + \gamma_{51} = 3.64 \text{ messages/sec, one-way}$$
$$\lambda_5 = \gamma_{23} \qquad\qquad = 0.82 \text{ messages/sec, one-way}$$
$$\lambda_6 = \gamma_{31} + \gamma_{41} \qquad = 3.88 \text{ messages/sec, one-way}$$
$$\lambda_7 = \gamma_{21} + \gamma_{51} \qquad = 9.95 \text{ messages/sec, one-way}$$

The total average message traffic through each of the links is of course twice the one-way figures, as noted earlier. The total one-way link traffic is

$$\lambda = \sum_{i=1}^{7} \lambda_i = 25.12 \text{ messages/sec}$$

on the average. The total number of messages/sec entering the entire network on the average is

$$\gamma = \sum_{jk} \gamma_{jk}$$

where we sum over all the entries in the matrix of Table 4-1. This is just 38.3 messages/sec on the average. The one-way traffic is thus $\gamma' = \gamma/2 = 19.15$ messages/sec. The average number of links traversed by a typical message is $(25.12/19.15) = 1.3$.

The link capacity assignments in bps (bits/sec) depend not only on the link traffic (the *demand* or offered load, in messages/sec), but on the message lengths as well. Recall from Eq. (3-1) in the previous chapter, that the average time delay on the ith link due to message transmission and buffering, while waiting for transmission to begin, is given by

$$T_i = \frac{1}{\mu_i C_i - \lambda_i}$$

(This assumes Poisson message arrivals, exponentially-distributed message lengths, and an infinite buffer for the queue, as noted earlier.) What shall we use for $1/\mu_i$, the average message length in bits, if the messages flowing come from various sources and nodes? We shall essentially ignore the issue here by simply assuming all messages in the network have the same average length $1/\mu$. This enables us to get reasonable numbers quickly. In more complex situations different types of messages may be flowing over a given link. (Recall the network examples of Chap. 2 in which different types of messages of varying lengths may be flowing in the same direction over any link. These could be different message categories; control or data messages; ACK messages if not embedded in a message block; varying message lengths inbound to and outbound from a computer, if not blocked into fixed-length packets, etc.) Some sort of average thus has to be taken. One simple possibility is to weight message lengths in link i by the relative number of messages of the particular length flowing through the link. Thus, we define

$$\frac{1}{\mu_i} \equiv \sum_{\text{link } i} \frac{\gamma_{jk}/\mu_{jk}}{\sum_{\text{link } i} \gamma_{jk}}$$

$$= \sum_{\text{link } i} \frac{\gamma_{jk}/\mu_{jk}}{\lambda_i} \tag{4-1}$$

The summation shown over link i refers to those messages from source j to destination k that are routed through link i. As an example, consider link 7, Chicago—N.Y., in Fig. 4-1. This carries Denver—N.Y. and Chicago—N.Y.

traffic. Say the Chicago—N.Y. messages are 200 bits long, on the average, while the Denver—N.Y. messages are 500 bits long. Using the traffic data from Table 4-1 we have

$$\frac{1}{\mu_7} = \frac{0.61(500) + 9.34(200)}{9.95} = 218 \text{ bits}$$

on the average. (More generally, we would have to account for different message lengths in the two different directions. For duplex lines one would choose capacities to account for the heavier direction of traffic.)

With both the link traffic demand λ_i and the average message length $1/\mu_i$ defined in a typical case, we are now in a position to determine the effect of link capacity allocation on the message time delay. The *optimum* capacity assignment, in the sense of minimizing the average time delay throughout the network, is the same as that found previously in Chap. 3. (A little thought will indicate that with message statistics assumed independent from link to link, the analysis of Chap. 3 holds true here as well.) We thus have, as in that chapter, the optimum capacity assignment for link i given by the same Eq. (3-5)

$$C_i\big|_{\text{opt}} = \frac{\lambda_i}{\mu_i} + \frac{C(1-\rho)\sqrt{\lambda_i/\mu_i}}{\sum_j \sqrt{\lambda_j/\mu_j}}$$

Recall that $C = \sum_i C_i$ is the overall capacity of the network that we keep fixed, while $\rho C \equiv \sum_i (\lambda_i/\mu_i)$. The average time delay for messages in the network is again given by Eq. (3-4),

$$\bar{T} = \frac{1}{\gamma} \sum_i \lambda_i T_i$$

while the *minimum* time delay, found using the capacity assignment of Eq. (3-5), is given by Eq. (3-6),

$$\bar{T}_{\min} = \frac{(\sum_i \sqrt{\lambda_i/\mu_i})^2}{\gamma C(1-\rho)}$$

To apply these equations to the network of Fig. 4-1 assume first that all messages have the same average length $1/\mu$. Assume further that the overall network message capacity in messages/sec is fixed at $\mu C = 192$ messages/sec. For the network under question we then have a traffic intensity factor

$$\rho = \frac{\lambda}{\mu C} = \frac{25.12}{192} = 0.13$$

The network is then rather lightly loaded. (Recall again that we are considering traffic in any *one* direction only.)

Equations (3-1), (3-5), and (3-6) can now be used to determine the capacity allocations for the network of Fig. 4-1 to minimize message time delay. The resultant capacity allocation and time delays, by link, are indicated in Table 4-2. Also shown are capacities and time delays obtained using two other capacity assignments:

1. An equal assignment strategy in which the total capacity C is simply divided equally among all the links, independent of traffic on the link. (In this case, then, $\mu C_i = \mu C/7 = 192/7 = 27.4$ messages/sec capacity allotted to each link.)

2. A proportional assignment strategy* in which C_i is proportional to the traffic demand λ_i; i.e., we let

$$C_i\big|_{\text{prop}} = \frac{C\lambda_i}{\lambda} \qquad (4\text{-}2)$$

The corresponding time delays for these two alternative ways of assigning capacity are found by using Eqs. (3-1) and (3-4).

TABLE 4-2

CAPACITY ASSIGNMENTS, NETWORK OF FIG. 4-1 (FULL-DUPLEX)

Link	Demand, λ_i one-way, messages/sec	Capacity Allocation μC_i (one-way, messages/sec)				
		square root	T_i (msec)	equal assign-ment	T_i (msec)	propor-tional
1	3.15	28	40.4	27.4	41.3	24
2	3.55	30	37.8	27.4	41.9	27.5
3	0.13	5	206	27.4	36.6	1
4	3.64	30	38	27.4	42.1	28
5	0.82	13.5	78.8	27.4	37.6	6.3
6	3.88	31.5	36.2	27.4	42.5	30
7	9.95	54	22.6	27.4	57.3	76.5
		$\bar{T}_{\min} = 42$ msec		$\bar{T}_{\text{equal}} = 57.6$ msec		$\bar{T}_{\text{prop}} = 54.8$ msec

Several factors bear notice. First note that in order to minimize the overall time delay the light traffic links receive less capacity than do the heavy traffic links. (Compare links 3 and 5 with 7, as an example.) The time delays incurred on the light traffic links are thus much higher than those incurred on the heavy traffic areas. Link 3, for example, has an average time delay of 206 msec with the square-root assignment strategy, while link 7 has a time delay of 22.6 msec. The light user is thus penalized in favor of the heavy user. We shall discuss shortly an alternate time delay criterion in which this penalty does not occur, *all* links involving, on the average, the same time delay.

Second, note that the proportional capacity assignment scheme exaggerates the distinction between light and heavy links even more. The disparity

*Ibid.

between capacity assignments is even greater than in the square-root assignment case, while the average time delay incurred is increased somewhat. Third, note that the equal assignment strategy, while increasing the overall average time delay per message, does reduce the difference in time delays on light and heavy traffic links. Thus, comparing square-root and equal assignment results, the light traffic link 3 has had its average time delay reduced six times, from 206 msec to 36.6 msec. The corresponding increase in time delay on the heavy traffic link 7 is proportionally less, going from 22.6 msec to 57.3 msec. As noted above we shall discuss shortly a capacity assignment technique that eliminates time delay penalties incurred by light users altogether, with link time delays equalized throughout the network.

What is now the effect on capacity assignments and corresponding time delay of changes in the routing strategy? Although routing will be discussed in detail in Chap. 11 it does pay to consider one example at this point. For this purpose we make just one change in the shortest distance strategy used in all the calculations above. Assume that Los Angeles—New York traffic is now routed by way of Denver and Chicago, rather than Houston, as in Fig. 4-1.

It is left for the reader to check the following one-way traffic flows obtained for this alternate route network:

$$\lambda_1 = 6.1 \quad \text{messages/sec}$$
$$\lambda_2 = 0.61$$
$$\lambda_3 = 0.13 \quad \text{(no change)}$$
$$\lambda_4 = 6.58$$
$$\lambda_5 = 0.82 \quad \text{(no change)}$$
$$\lambda_6 = 0.93$$
$$\lambda_7 = 12.89$$

These flows are indicated in the network diagram of Fig. 4-2.

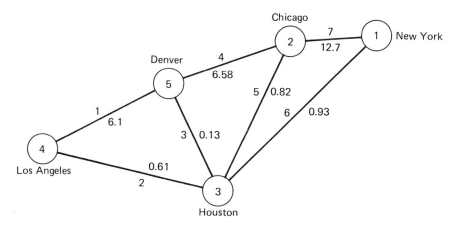

Fig. 4-2. Alternate routing, λ_i's (messages/sec) shown, either direction.

The total message flow for the network is now $\lambda = \sum_i \lambda_i = 28.1$ messages/sec (one-way), while the average number of links traversed by a typical message is $\bar{n} = \lambda/\gamma = 1.47$. The increased flow of traffic (from 25.12 to 28.1 messages/sec) and larger number of links traversed is of course due to changing from the shortest distance routing strategy. The overall minimum time delay, with square-root capacity assignment, doesn't change very much in this case, however. A calculation shows that $\bar{T}_{\min} = 43.1$ msec (compared to 42 msec in the previous case), while the time delay with proportional capacity assignment is 63.2 msec (compared to 54.8 msec previously).

Although we have chosen to discuss link capacity assignment for networks in the context of simple and relatively artificial examples, the techniques outlined have been utilized in design studies for the ARPA network.* The approach used has been extended as well to include nonlinear capacity-cost relations, nodal processing delays, and the minimization of time delays other than the average time delay discussed thus far. In the remainder of this chapter we consider a relatively simple yet useful extension of Kleinrock's work which equalizes the disparity between light and heavy users of a network, as noted earlier.** The reader is referred to the literature for other extensions that include nodal processing delay and nonlinear cost functions that appear in this case.† In the next chapter we consider algorithms for taking into account the *nonlinear* capacity-cost relations typical of real networks, but specialized to the case of centralized computer-communication networks only.

The work on capacity assignment discussed thus far can be generalized with very little additional effort in the following two ways:††

1. A fixed cost $D = \sum_{i=1}^{N} d_i C_i$ is to be constrained. The summation is again over the N links of the network, but associated with each choice of link capacity C_i is a cost $d_i C_i$ linearly proportional to it. (If $d_i = 1$ we have the case previously discussed.)

2. Choose C_i to minimize

$$T^{(k)} = \left[\sum_{i=1}^{N} \frac{\lambda_i}{\gamma} (T_i)^k \right]^{1/k} \tag{4-3}$$

For $k = 1$ we have the average time delay criterion already considered, for $k = 2$ we have a mean-squared delay to be minimized, and for $k \to \infty$, we

---

*L. Kleinrock, "Models for Computer Networks," *Proc. IEEE International Conference on Communications*, June 1969, pp. 21.9 to 21.16.

B. Meister, H. R. Mueller, and H. R. Rudin, Jr., "New Optimization Criteria for Message-Switching Networks," *IEEE Trans. on Communications Technology*, **COM-19, no. 3, June 1971, 256–60.

†B. Meister, H. R. Mueller, and H. R. Rudin, Jr., "On the Optimization of Message-Switching Networks," *IEEE Trans. on Communications*, **COM-20**, no. 1, Feb. 1972, 8–14.

††Meister, Mueller, and Rudin, Jr., "Optimization Criteria."

have the so-called Chebyshev or min-max criterion. It is this last criterion that turns out to be *user*-oriented. For with $k \longrightarrow \infty$ a little thought indicates that the largest time delay on any of the links dominates. It is then this time delay that is minimized, subject to the constraint on cost. This gives rise to the appelation min-max criterion. The time delay on each link turns out in this case (using this criterion) to be equal. Light users are thus not penalized as they are in the $k = 1$ case, hence the suggestion that this is a user-oriented approach to design.

The minimization of $T^{(k)}$ of Eq. (4-3) subject to a fixed cost constraint is readily carried out using the Lagrange multiplier technique of Chap. 3. The resultant optimum capacity assignment for arbitrary k turns out to be

$$C_i^{(k)} = \frac{\lambda_i}{\mu_i} + \left[\frac{k\lambda_i}{\gamma d_i \mu_i^k L^{(k)}} \right]^{1/(k+1)} \tag{4-4}$$

where

$$L^{(k)} \equiv \left\{ \frac{\sum_i \left[\frac{k\lambda_i d_i^k}{\gamma \mu_i^k} \right]^{1/(k+1)}}{D_a} \right\}^{(k+1)} \tag{4-5}$$

Note that for $k = 1$ we have the square-root capacity assignment result found earlier.

The parameter

$$D_a \equiv D - D^*, \quad \text{with} \quad D^* \equiv \sum_i d_i \frac{\lambda_i}{\mu_i}$$

Now D^* is the *minimum* possible network cost. For the smallest capacity (in bps) that can possibly be assigned on link i is as already noted λ_i/μ_i (the demand on that link), and $d_i\lambda_i/\mu_i$ is the corresponding cost. D_a is then the freely-assignable portion of the total cost D.

As a check let $d_i = 1$. This is just the case considered in Chap. 3 and up to this point in this chapter. Then

$$D^* = \sum_i (\lambda_i/\mu_i) \equiv \rho C \quad \text{and} \quad D_a = C(1 - \rho)$$

using the parameters introduced earlier. Also from Eq. (4-5)

$$[\gamma L^{(1)}]^{1/2} = \sum_i \frac{\sqrt{(\lambda_i/\mu_i)}}{C(1 - \rho)}$$

and from Eq. (4-4)

$$C_i^{(1)} = \frac{\lambda_i}{\mu_i} + \frac{\sqrt{(\lambda_i/\mu_i)}\, C(1 - \rho)}{\sum_j \sqrt{(\lambda_j/\mu_j)}}$$

checking Eq. (3-5).

With $k \longrightarrow \infty$, Eq. (4-4) results in

$$C_i^{(\infty)} = \frac{\lambda_i}{\mu_i} + \frac{1}{\mu_i} \frac{D_a}{\sum_j (d_j/\mu_j)} \tag{4-6}$$

Note that with equal average message lengths ($\mu_i = \mu$) on all links, this is essentially a constant plus proportional assignment strategy. It is intermediate between the equal assignment and proportional assignment cases. The corresponding time delay *on each link* turns out to be

$$T_i^{(\infty)} = \frac{1}{D_a} \sum_j \frac{d_j}{\mu_j} \tag{4-7}$$

while the min-max time delay incurred by each message, on the average, is just

$$T^{(\infty)} = \bar{n} T_i^{(\infty)} = \frac{\bar{n}}{D_a} \sum_j \frac{d_j}{\mu_j} \tag{4-8}$$

with $\bar{n} = \lambda/\gamma$ the average number of links traversed by a message.

We can apply these results to the network of Fig. 4-1 to compare with the capacity assignment strategies previously discussed. Specifically, we again let $\mu_i = \mu$ and take $\mu C = 192$ messages/sec. Let $d_i = 1$. Then $D_a = C(1 - p)$ as already noted and

$$\mu C_i^{(\infty)} = \lambda_i + \frac{\mu C(1 - p)}{N} \tag{4-9}$$

with N the total number of links (7 in this case). We again take $p = 0.13$. Then for this example,

$$\mu C_i^{(\infty)} = \lambda_i + 23.8 \text{ messages/sec}$$

$$T_i^{(\infty)} = \frac{N}{\mu C(1 - p)} = \frac{1}{23.8} = 42 \text{ msec}$$

and

$$T^{(\infty)} = 1.3(42) = 54.6 \text{ msec}$$

The capacity assignments and corresponding time delays, by link, are listed in Table 4-3.

TABLE 4-3

CAPACITY ASSIGNMENTS, NETWORK OF FIG. 4-1
(includes min-max assignment)

Link	λ_i (messages/sec, one-way)	$\mu C_i^{(1)}$ (messages/sec)	$T_i^{(1)}$ (msec)	$\mu C_i^{(\infty)}$ (messages/sec)	$T_i^{(\infty)}$ (msec)	μC_i T_i (equal assignment)	
1	3.15	28	40.4	27	42	27.4	41.3
2	3.55	30	37.8	27.4	42	27.4	41.9
3	0.13	5	206	24	42	27.4	36.6
4	3.64	30	38	27.5	42	27.4	42.1
5	0.82	13.5	78.8	24.6	42	27.4	37.6
6	3.88	31.5	36.2	27.7	42	27.4	42.5
7	9.95	54	22.6	33.8	42	27.4	57.3
		$\bar{T}_{\min} = 42$ msec		$T^{(\infty)} = 54.6$ msec		$\bar{T}_{\text{equal}} =$ 57.6 msec	

Note that except for the light traffic links (3 and 5) and the heavy traffic link 7, the min-max capacity assignments are almost the same as those for the equal assignment case. This is because we have picked a relatively low traffic intensity in this example ($\rho = 0.13$). Note from Eq. (4-9) that for $\rho \ll 1$, $\mu C_i^{(\infty)} = \mu C/N$, just the equal assignment case. (For $\rho \ll 1$, $\lambda_i \ll \mu C_i$, and the first term is negligible.) For $\rho \rightarrow 1$, $\mu C_i^{(\infty)} = \lambda_i$, essentially the proportional assignment strategy noted earlier. The min-max approach does make a difference on the light and heavy traffic links, however. Note from Table 4-3 that the equal assignment approach favors the light user too much (providing a relatively low time delay), while penalizing the heavy user. The min-max capacity assignments equalize these two extremes.

The effect on the various users of changing the criterion is shown graphically in Fig. 4-3, taken from the references.* The curves are sketched for the case $\rho = 0.25$ and $\mu C = 100.5$ messages/sec as the total capacity to be allocated ($\lambda = 25.12$ messages/sec). It demonstrates the *large* improvement in the time delay characteristic possible for the lightest load (link 3), at the cost of a relatively small increase in average time delay. The heaviest load (link 7) incurs a penalty but this time delay characteristic is still always below the average delay curve.

The stress in this chapter as in Chap. 3 has been on minimizing link time delays, or averages of them. The min-max criterion, for example, minimizes

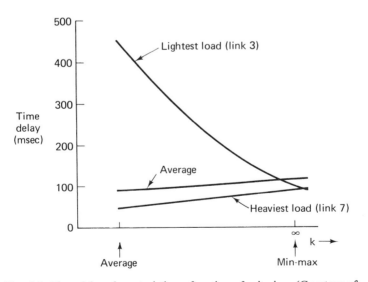

Fig. 4-3. Time delay characteristic as function of criterion. (Courtesy of B. Meister et al., *IEEE Trans. Communications Technology*, **COM-19**, no. 3, June 1971.)

*Ibid.

the time delay on any link. In the next chapter in discussing capacity allocations where capacity is nonlinearly related to cost, we focus on minimizing the
maximum message time delay *from source to destination.*

PROBLEMS

4.1 A map of a proposed data network connecting five European cities
appears in Fig. P4.1. A concentrator is used in each of the cities to
statistically multiplex messages from terminals located within the
vicinity of each. The terminals output messages on the average of 1
message/min. each. The average message length is 1000 bits. The traffic
matrix for this network, indicating the average number of messages/min.
between any two cities, is as follows:

γ_{ij} (MESSAGES/MIN)

$j \rightarrow$	1	2	3	4	5
$i \downarrow$ 1		40	10	20	30
2	40		30	20	10
3	10	30		20	10
4	20	20	20		10
5	30	10	10	10	

Full-duplex lines connect the cities as shown in the map.

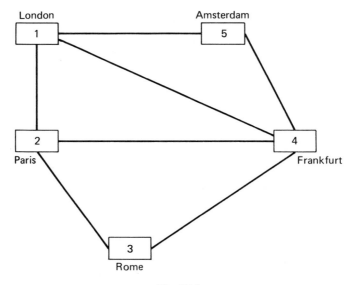

Fig. P4.1

(1) Find the capacity of each line if the minimum average time delay for the network is to be 5 sec with total capacity C fixed. (*Note*: Recall that

$$\rho C \equiv \sum_i \frac{\lambda_i}{\mu_i})$$

Use shortest-path (least number of links) routing, with London—Rome traffic routed via Paris, and Paris—Amsterdam traffic routed via Frankfort.

(2) Using the same total capacity as in (1) above, find the minimum time delay for the network if the routing strategy now routes messages from London—Rome via Frankfort, and Paris—Amsterdam traffic via London. Compare with (1).

(3) All line capacities in the network are chosen to be 1200 bps. Find the total capacity, effective ρ, and average time delay, and compare with (1) above.

4.2 Verify the capacity allocations and corresponding average time delays of Table 4-2 under the three different capacity assignment strategies indicated.

4.3 Consider the routing strategy for the network of Fig. 4-1 that routes Los Angeles—New York traffic by way of Denver and Chicago. Verify the one-way traffic flows shown in Fig. 4-2. Show that the minimum average time delay for this network with the flows shown is 44 msec. This ignores propagation delay. Indicate how you might take this into account and calculate the time delay including propagation effects. Consider two possible propagation delay estimates: 10 msec/1000 miles, and 40 msec/1000 miles.

4.4 Refer to the generalized capacity assignment analysis of this chapter. Specifically, with a fixed cost linearly proportional to the sum of the capacities on each link, and time delay defined as in Eq. (4-3), show the optimum capacity on each link is given by Eq. (4-4).

4.5 Min-max criterion: Let $k \longrightarrow \infty$ in Eq. (4-4). Show that the capacity assignment on each link is given by Eq. (4-6) while the link time delays are all *equal* and given by Eq. (4-7).

4.6 Apply the min-max results of Eqs. (4-6) to Eq. (4-9) to the network of Fig. 4-1. Find the capacity assignments and corresponding time delays, by link, comparing with the minimum average delay results. These should agree with the entries of Table 4-3. Check the equal assignment results shown in that table as well.

4.7 Refer to the 5-city European network of Problem 4.1. Determine the capacity assignment, by link, using a min-max criterion, for the same total capacity as in part (1) of that problem. Compare the resultant average time delays, both per link and overall average, with the minimum time delay result. Compare with the equal assignment result of part (3) of Problem 4.1.

Centralized Networks:

Time Delay—

Cost Trade-offs

5

||||||||||||||||||||||||||||||||||||||||||||||||||||||||||||||||||||||||||||||||||||||||||||||||||||||||||||||||||||||||||||||||||||||||||||||||||||||||||||||||||||||||||||||||||||||||||||||||

In the capacity assignment discussion of the last two chapters we have emphasized a technique in which average message time delay is minimized with total capacity held fixed. A variation of this, leading to essentially the same results, assumes cost linearly proportional to capacity and assigns capacity to minimize the average time delay with the overall cost held fixed.

This is an appropriate design approach in many situations. It provides insight into the network operation. It enables trunk capacities to be relatively quickly chosen for complex networks, it allows comparison between other assignment techniques chosen from a fixed number of capacities, equal or proportional assignment, among others, and is readily extended to take network routing into account, as was done in the last chapter.

This approach is at the same time unrealistic in many design situations in which cost truly plays the overriding role and in which capacity-cost relations are far from linear. Examples would include those in which *incremental* cost is proportional to the capacity, the relative cost thus decreasing with capacity, or in which the cost of a particular link is based upon a complex array of many variables: capacity, use for which intended, time of day, type of traffic, whether or not part of a larger package arrangement, location of trunks involved, etc., etc. (In the United States, for example, leased line tariffs differ from state to state, and intrastate tariffs differ from interstate tariffs.)*

*See, for example, M. Gerla, "New Line Tariffs and their Impact on Network Design," *AFIPS Conference Proc.*, National Computer Conference, **43**, 1974, 577–82.

These more complex situations can be handled by computer search routines in which a minimum cost or class of minimum cost networks is chosen after a series of iterative trials. These approaches rely on the use of algorithms that are efficient and effective, coming up with solutions that are optimum or close to optimum in a reasonable number of trials. We shall have more to say about the subject of network algorithms in subsequent chapters in connection with overall network design. There the more complex problem of the appropriate choice of network configuration is considered. Here, as an introduction to algorithm formulation, we consider the simple problem of assigning capacities to a given network. By iterating the approach suggested here, changing one portion of the network structure at a time, a comparison between network configurations becomes possible.

The price we pay for using an algorithmic rather than an analytical formulation is to lose some insight into the network design process. It does enable us to handle more realistic problems, however, as noted above.

In this chapter we concentrate on centralized (i.e., tree-type) networks only for which algorithms are particularly simple to understand and apply. In addition to solving the problem of capacity assignment in a more realistic sense in such a network, as well as allowing comparisons to be made between different configurations, the formulation here serves as a good introduction to network algorithms discussed later.

The approach we use is based on that of Frank et al.,* in which capacity is assigned to links in the network to *minimize* the *maximum time* delay from anywhere in the network to the CPU. An equivalent criterion assigns capacity to minimize the overall cost, with the maximum time delay anywhere in the network specified not to exceed some fixed quantity. Actually, in the example of the seven cities to be connected to Washington, D.C., first introduced in Chap. 1 (see Fig. 1-2), and then analyzed in Chap. 3 (Fig. 3-1, 3-3), we shall come up with a time delay-communication cost curve, showing the trade-offs possible between these two parameters. Different configurations can be compared as well on the basis of such a curve, and we shall in fact show that the star network of Fig. 3-1 is far poorer, on the basis of the criterion used here, than the tree-type structure of Fig. 3-3.**

A similar approach to the design of centralized networks has been adopted by D. Doll.† In fact, the example of the seven cities used here, as well as the choice of numbers used, has been taken from his work. He has con-

---

*H. Frank, I. T. Frisch, R. Van Slyke, and W. S. Chou, "Optimal Design of Centralized Computer Networks," *Networks*, **1**, no. 1, John Wiley & Sons, New York, 1971, 43–58.

**It can be shown that the tree structure chosen here is the minimum distance spanning tree for this example. See Chap. 9 for a discussion of minimum spanning tree algorithms.

†D. R. Doll, "Efficient Allocation of Resources in Centralized Computer-Communication Network Design," University of Michigan, Systems Engineering Laboratory, Nov. 1969.

centrated primarily on multiplexed, line-switched networks, however, rather than the message-switched type of network with concentration under discussion here.

The technique to be discussed here as an example of an efficient algorithm or search procedure for assigning capacity is readily discussed in terms of an example.*

Consider the tree-type network of Fig. 5-1, in which nodes may only communicate by first going through the CPU at the center. For each link we have available its delay-cost characteristics, provided as an array of pairs of

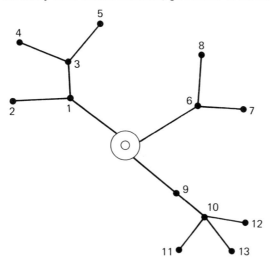

Fig. 5-1. Tree-type network.

numbers. These arrays are determined by the capacity assignment and the traffic carried. (Actual calculations will be carried out later for the 7-city example.) As an example, link (2,1) (the link from node 2 directed to node 1) might have the following delay-cost array, with delay and cost both measured in arbitrary units.

	1	2	3	4	5	6	7
(2, 1) Delay	110	101	83	66	52	40	30
Cost	10	13	17	22	27	34	42

There are thus seven choices of capacity possible, each at a specified cost and providing a given delay.

*Frank et al., "Optimal Design." The algorithm used, which systematically searches out the best time delay-cost choices in a step-by-step fashion, is essentially a dynamic programming procedure.

With an array like this given for each link in the network, the object is to choose the pair of values for each link that provides the smallest value of maximum time delay in the network at least cost. Actually what we end up with is a set of assignments that provides an optimum delay-cost characteristic.

A little thought will indicate that the maximum time delay *must* emanate from one of the outermost or "pendant" nodes—those with only one link connected to them. (These are nodes 11, 12, 13, 7, 8, 2, 4, 5.) The basic procedure is to calculate the time delay to the CPU from each of these for different cost (capacity) choices. This becomes a difficult combinatorial problem, particularly if there are many nodes in the network, each with several capacity choices. The algorithm discussed here is a technique for systematically and efficiently solving this combinatorial problem.

It consists essentially of two parts: the links between pendant nodes connected to a common node (11, 12, 13, or 7, 8, or 4, 5 in Fig. 5-1) are first converted to an equivalent link with its own cost-delay lists (or array), by a so-called *parallel merge*. In this merge, to be described by example below, various cost assignments are made and the lowest cost assignment for each delay only retained. The resultant configuration for the network after carrying out the parallel merge on these sets of pendant nodes is shown in Fig. 5-2a.

The second part of the algorithm consists of a serial merge, adding time delays of all outlying links that are now in series. (These consist of the links connected at nodes 3, 6, and 10 in Fig. 5-2a.) Again the lowest cost assignment for each delay only is retained. Working inward through the network, calculating time delays and corresponding costs, this process of parallel and serial merge is then repeated until the final reduced network of Fig. 5-2b is obtained. The equivalent link with the largest time delay, of the three shown, obviously determines the network time delay, and one would choose for the remaining two links the lowest cost assignments possible.

As an example of the parallel merge technique consider the three links (11, 10), (13, 10), and (12, 10) of Fig. 5-1. Say their delay-cost lists, as indexed by increasing cost, are as shown below:*

		1	2	3	4	5	6	7
(11, 10)	Delay	120	111	92	66	54	40	31
	Cost	13	17	23	29	36	45	58
(12, 10)	Delay	150	139	118	87	75	70	67
	Cost	6	9	14	21	30	40	56
(13, 10)	Delay	94	86	80	61	55	48	32
	Cost	8	12	18	26	34	43	57

Ibid.

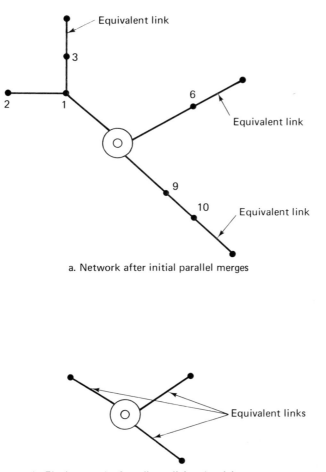

a. Network after initial parallel merges

b. Final network after all parallel and serial merges

Fig. 5-2. Two steps in the reduction process.

It is apparent that there are $7^3 = 343$ possible choices of delay-cost combinations from which to choose here. However, note that if the index 1 delay-cost combination (150, 6) is chosen for link (12, 10), it is senseless to use any but the index 1 combinations for the other two links (11, 10) and (13, 10). For with this choice for link (12, 10) the 150-unit delay dominates the time delay to node 10. Choosing any but the index 1 assignments for the other two links can only result in increased cost but no decrease in the time delay to that node.

A possible delay-cost combination for the three parallel links thus consists of using the capacity assignment corresponding to index 1 for each. Can the delay to node 10 be decreased, however? This is obviously possible only by decreasing the (12, 10) link delay to 139 units, or by indexing that link assignment 2. The entire procedure may be systematized by setting up a so-called *testing block*: each link is assigned a column. Links are first set to index 1, corresponding to the lowest cost, highest delay choice of capacity. For the example under discussion here the testing block appears as follows:

Link	(11, 10)	(12, 10)	(13, 10)	
Delay	120	(150)	94	Delay = 150
Cost	13	6	8	Cost = 27
Index	1	1	1	

The total cost of this choice of capacities is obviously the sum of the link costs or 27, while the maximum delay is 150, shown circled. Both these numbers are now stored as entries in the delay-cost lists for an equivalent link.

Now let link (12, 10) have its capacity increased to the value corresponding to index 2. This decreases the time delay to 139 units, as already noted. We set up a testing block to find another possible entry for the equivalent link:

Link	(11, 10)	(12, 10)	(13, 10)	
Delay	120	(139)	94	Delay = 139
Cost	13	9	8	Cost = 30
Index	1	2	1	

Again note that the maximum delay still appears in the (12, 10) link column. It therefore doesn't pay to increase the capacities of the other two links. (These will only result in increased costs but no corresponding decrease in the time delay to node 10.) The delay and total cost pair (139, 30) provide another entry in the delay-cost lists for the equivalent links.

To reduce the delay further we can only assign more capacity to link (12, 10) indexing it to 3:

Link	(11, 10)	(12, 10)	(13, 10)	
Delay	(120)	118	94	Delay = 120
Cost	13	14	8	Cost = 35
Index	1	3	1	

But now note that the dominant delay of the three links is that provided by link (11, 10). Increasing the capacity of the other two links can only result in increased cost, but no attendant reduction in time delay. The 120 units of delay and 35 units of cost shown above thus provide another pair for the equivalent link.

This procedure is now repeated, reducing the maximum delay in the testing block (the circled delay) by increasing the index by 1 unit in that column. A few typical entries in the testing block, with corresponding entries for the equivalent link table shown, follow:

Link	(11, 10)	(12, 10)	(13, 10)	
Delay	111	(118)	94	Delay = 118
Cost	17	14	8	Cost = 39
Index	2	3	1	
Delay	(111)	87	94	Delay = 111
Cost	17	21	8	Cost = 46
Index	2	4	1	
Delay	92	87	(94)	Delay = 94
Cost	23	21	8	Cost = 52
Index	3	4	1	

The process is repeated until any largest (circled) entry appears at its maximum index (7 in this case). This terminates the process, since the delay cannot be reduced anymore. (Increasing the indices of the other links only increases the cost, with no decrease in time delay.) The search procedure in this case requires at most $1 + 6(3) = 19$ steps to come up with an ordered set of delay-cost lists for the equivalent merged link. (This corresponds to the initial step plus at most 6 more for each of the three links until one of them reaches its maximum index of 7.) This contrasts with the 343 possible different capacity assignments noted earlier that might have to be checked, one by one, without the use of this merge technique, or some systematic procedure like it.

In this particular example it turns out that 13 iterations are required for the procedure to terminate. The first six pairs in the resultant ordered delay-cost array of the equivalent merged link are given by:

Delay	150	139	120	118	87	94	...
Cost	27	30	35	39	46	52	...

This same procedure can now be repeated for the other sets of pendant nodes in Fig. 5-1, and then later on, after serial links are merged.

Rather than carry this example any further, however, we return specifically to the 7-city example of Chap. 1 and 3. The object here is to actually determine the delay-cost arrays or lists for each link for some discrete set of capacities that may be used, and then determine the best capacity assignments for both a tree-type and star network. Specifically consider first the tree-type structure of Fig. 3-3, repeated here as Fig. 5-3. The link message rates, λ_i, $i = 1, 2, \ldots, 7$, are indicated, repeated from Fig. 3-3.

A discrete set of trunk capacity choices is assumed available at each link,

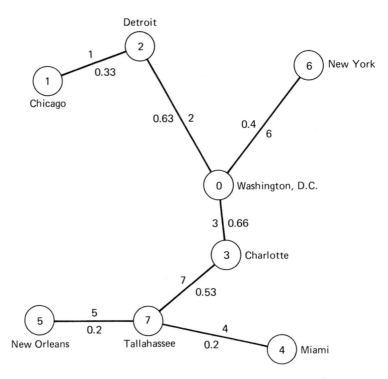

Fig. 5-3. Centralized computer network, link message rates shown.

the object then being to choose the appropriate capacity for each link to minimize the maximum time delay anywhere in the network, for fixed cost, or, equivalently, to find the minimum cost network for a specified maximum time delay. Note how this criterion differs from the one chosen for the same network in Chap. 3. Four such capacity choices (all that are needed to carry out the desired optimization for this example) and the corresponding cost in dollars/mo/mile appear in the following table:*

TABLE 5-1

Capacity C (bps)	$/mo/mile
450	1.4
900	1.7
1350	1.875
1800	2.0

*Doll, "Allocation of Resources in Network Design." Note again, as mentioned in earlier chapters, that we ignore here the cost of the programmable concentrators, assumed the same at each node.

As was the case in Chap. 1 and 3 we assume all messages to be Poisson-distributed, with lengths exponentially-distributed and of average length $1/\mu = 120$ bits. Then, as in previous chapters, we have the average link message delay for messages transmitted over the ith link given by

$$T_i = \frac{1}{\mu C_i - \lambda_i} \text{ sec} \qquad (5\text{-}1)$$

For $1/\mu = 120$ and λ_i as indicated in Fig. 5-3, one can calculate the time delay for each of the four capacities in the previous table. Knowing the length of each of the seven links in Fig. 5-3 we can determine as well the cost in dollars/mo for each of the four capacities. Carrying out these calculations we get the following delay-cost arrays for the seven links:

TABLE 5-2

DELAY-COST ARRAYS, NETWORK OF FIG. 5-3

Link	Capacity $\longrightarrow$ Index $\longrightarrow$	450 1	900 2	1350 3	1800 4
1 (235 mi)	Delay (sec) Cost ($/mo)	0.292 329	0.139 399	0.092 440	0.068 470
2 (383 mi)	Delay (sec) Cost ($/mo)	0.320 537	0.146 652	0.094 720	0.070 766
3 (321 mi)	Delay (sec) Cost ($/mo)	0.325 450	0.146 546	0.095 602	0.070 642
4 (381 mi)	Delay (sec) Cost ($/mo)	0.282 534	0.137 644	0.091 715	0.068 762
5 (347 mi)	Delay (sec) Cost ($/mo)	0.282 485	0.137 590	0.091 650	0.068 694
6 (228 mi)	Delay (sec) Cost ($/mo)	0.298 319	0.141 388	0.092 427	0.069 456
7 (378 mi)	Delay (sec) Cost ($/mo)	0.310 529	0.143 642	0.093 709	0.069 756

The optimum assignment of capacities in the network of Fig. 5-3 is almost trivially carried out because of the simplicity of the network. Note that the only parallel merge needed (until the final reduced configuration) combines links 4 and 5. In this case this parallel merge can be done by inspection since the delays for each index number are the same for each link. For each index we simply add the two costs and use the delay corresponding to the index number. The resultant equivalent merged link, indicated as 4' in Fig. 5-4a, has the following delay-cost lists:

Link 4′	Index	1	2	3	4
	Delay (sec)	0.282	0.137	0.091	0.068
	Cost ($/mo)	1019	1234	1365	1456

We now use a *serial merge*, combining links 4′ and 7, incident at node 7, to give an equivalent link 7′. This is shown in Fig. 5-4b. Links 7′ and 3 can then be combined in a serial merge, as can links 1 and 2, to give the final reduced form of the network, as shown in Fig. 5-4c. The serial merge algorithm should be one that systematically compares all capacity assignment of the two links in series, eliminating the poorer assignments (those that provide larger delays at higher costs), and arranging or indexing the resultant lists in order of

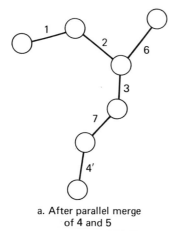

a. After parallel merge
of 4 and 5

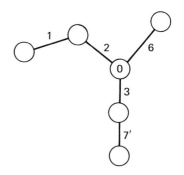

b. After serial merge of
4′ and 7

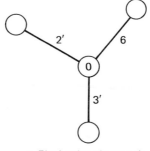

c. Final reduced network

Fig. 5-4. Step-by-step reduction of network of Fig. 5-3.

increasing costs. Again the object is to come up with *efficient* algorithms, computational procedures that produce the desired output in a reasonable number of iterations. One such procedure that is particularly simple to implement* (more efficient algorithms have been found) consists of comparing the different capacity choices of one of the two links to be combined, one at a time, with the first capacity assignment (index 1) of the other link in series. The two delays and costs are *added* for each of the choices. This is repeated for each index number, in increasing order, of the second link. Poor choices, as noted earlier, are discarded.

As an example, consider the serial merge of links 4′ and 7 in Fig. 5-4a. The delay-cost lists for the two links are repeated below to make it easier to follow the procedure:

Link	1	2	3	4
4′	0.282	0.137	0.091	0.068
	1019	1234	1365	1456
7	0.310	0.143	0.073	0.069
	529	642	709	756

Note that there are 16 different possibilities here. After systematically checking each one of them (keeping link 4′ at a given index and then scanning through each index of 7, adding the two costs and delays), we retain the five delay-cost pairs shown below. These correspond to an equivalent merged link denoted by 7′ in Fig. 5-4.

Link 7′	Index	1	2	3	4	5
indices corresponding to 4′ and 7		11	12	22	33	44
	Delay	0.59	0.43	0.28	0.16	0.13
	Cost	1550	1660	1880	2070	2210

Of the 16 original possibilities some were discarded as poor choices, some because they provided insignificant delay-cost variation. As an example, the choice 21 (index 2 for 4′, 1 for 7) gives Delay = 0.45, Cost = 1760, clearly worse than choice 12 shown as index 2 above for link 7. Similarly, choice 31 gives Delay = 0.40, Cost = 1890, poorer than 22, shown as index 3 above.

Repeating this serial merge two more times to get the final reduced network of Fig. 5-4c, and retaining only six significant entries in the lists for equiv-

*Frank, et al., "Optimal Design."

alent links 2′ and 3′ as shown, we are finally left with the following three arrays:

Link	Index	1	2	3	4	5	6
3′	Delay (sec)	0.92	0.74	0.58	0.43	0.28	0.21
	Cost ($/mo)	2000	2100	2210	2430	2570	2850
2′	Delay (sec)	0.61	0.46	0.39	0.29	0.19	0.14
	Cost ($/mo)	870	940	1010	1050	1160	1240
6	Delay (sec)	0.30	0.14	0.09	0.07		
	Cost ($/mo)	320	390	430	460		

A final parallel merge will now produce the desired minimum delay-cost characteristic for the original network. Actually carrying out the parallel merge by the testing block approach noted earlier we get the following table of delay-cost pairs, each corresponding to the link indices below:

TABLE 5-3

DELAY-COST CHARACTERISTIC, NETWORK OF FIG. 5-3

Link					
3′	2′	6			
Index			Delay (sec)		Cost ($/mo)
1	1	1	0.92		3190
2	1	1	.74		3290
3	1	1	.61	A	3400
3	2	1	.58		3470
4	2	1	.46		3690
4	3	1	.43		3760
5	3	1	.39		3900
5	4	1	.30	B	3940
5	4	2	.29		4110
5	5	2	.28		4220
6	5	2	.21	C	4400

There are thus 11 iterations required before the procedure terminates, compared to $4 \times 6^2 = 144$ possible combinations. Note that the capacity assignment of link 6 plays a role only in the last three iterations. The maximum time delay for the first indices, corresponding to relatively low capacity assignments throughout the network, is due principally to the cascading of three time delays corresponding to equivalent link 3′.

The delay-cost characteristic of Table 5-3 is plotted as Fig. 5-5. This provides the locus of optimum capacity assignments in the sense of smallest time delay anywhere in the network for a specified cost *or*, equivalently, the least cost for a specified maximum time delay. Any other of the $7^4 = 2401$ possible capacity assignments not lying on the locus would provide costs and time delays lying *above* the characteristic shown.

Each point shown in Fig. 5-5 corresponds to a different set of capacity assignments for the network of Fig. 5-3. As an example, three typical points (A, B, C) are indicated. The three sets of capacity assignments corresponding to these as well as the maximum time delay in the network and corresponding monthly costs are shown in Fig. 5-6. Capacities of each link, in bps, are printed alongside each link. Note the dramatic improvement in delay possible with relatively little increase in cost. The capacity choices for B, with half the

Fig. 5-5. Optimum delay-cost characteristic, network, Fig. 5-3.

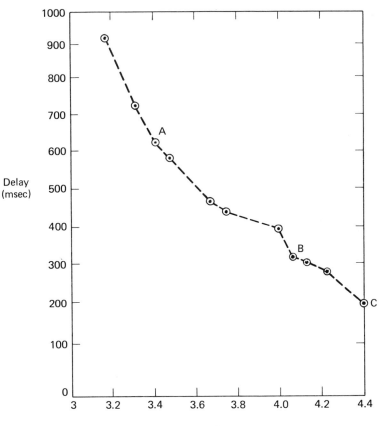

Cost ($1000/mo)

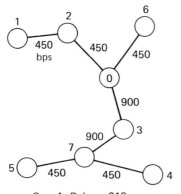

a. Case A, Delay = 610 msec
Cost = $3400/mo

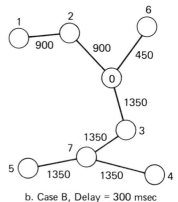

b. Case B, Delay = 300 msec
Cost = $4040/mo

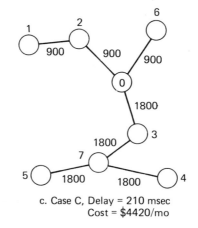

c. Case C, Delay = 210 msec
Cost = $4420/mo

Fig. 5-6. Examples of optimum capacity assignments.

delay of case A, cost less than 20 % more in line charges/mo. This is of course due to the capacity-cost characteristic per link, originally specified in Table 5-1.

It is possible, by changing one connection at a time and repeating the delay-cost analysis, to iterate the structure of the network as well, searching for improved network topologies. Algorithms for this purpose are discussed in Chap. 10. D.Doll has shown that the minimum distance spanning-tree network of Fig. 5-3, the one for which the optimum capacity assignments have just been found, is the optimum one for a line-switched network using multiplexers.*

*Doll, "Allocation of Resources in Network Design."

One may readily show that a star configuration for this 7-city problem, as sketched in Fig. 3-1, is far poorer in the sense of maximum time delay for a fixed cost, than the tree network of Fig. 5-3 or 5-6. These capacity allocations for the star are indicated in Fig. 5-7. Note that the delay-cost numbers shown fall far above the locus plotted in Fig. 5-5. The star network is of course much more costly because of the need to run lines directly from each city to the CPU. It is much more efficient to combine the traffic of cities in the same general region, using only one trunk to carry the traffic. This is of

Fig. 5-7. Capacity assignments, star configuration.

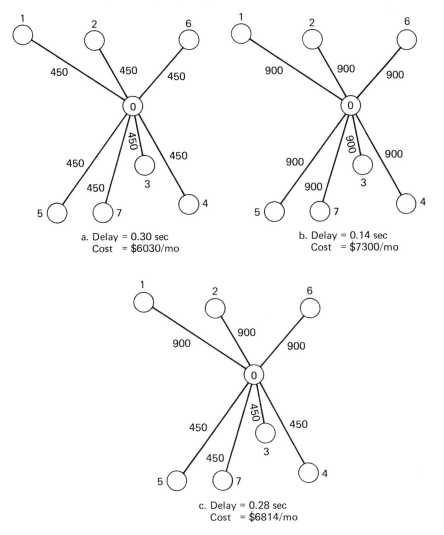

a. Delay = 0.30 sec
   Cost = $6030/mo

b. Delay = 0.14 sec
   Cost = $7300/mo

c. Delay = 0.28 sec
   Cost = $6814/mo

course the reason for the delay-cost improvement provided by the tree network of Fig. 5-3.

Note that the capacity assignment of Fig. 5-7c is the same as that selected much earlier in Table 3-1 of Chap. 3. The *average* time delay through the network was then shown to be 0.19 sec. The maximum time delay is of course larger and is in this case 0.28 sec. This is apparent as well by noting the link time delays shown in Table 3-1. For a star network of this type the maximum delay corresponds to the most heavily-loaded link.

It should be stressed, however, that we have considered communication line costs only in the 7-city example of this chapter. Concentrator and/or multiplexer costs as well as modem costs have been ignored. In some design situations these could very well turn the balance the other way. Examples of the cost calculation for some simple network configurations, incorporating modems, concentrator or multiplexer, and other fixed costs, are considered in the Appendix. Single capacity assignments are assumed in all cases to simplify the calculations, however. Time delay thus does not enter the picture. A more detailed discussion of the extent of concentrator cost on network design appears in Chap. 10. But there, too, single capacity assignments only are considered. The discussion there is also developed for star-type configurations only. As noted in passing in Chap. 1, and as will be emphasized again in Chap. 9 and 10, a complete network design involving choice of topology, type of connection of terminals to concentrators, choice of line capacities, and routing paths, among others, is so complex that it can generally only be done iteratively. In this chapter and the ones preceding we have focused on capacity assignment only to develop a flavor for network design and algorithms used in carrying out the design. The capacity assignment problem is the simplest design problem to consider providing topology is assumed beforehand, and device costs are neglected. In Chap. 9 and 10 we return to the network design question focusing on the more complex problems of multipoint connection, concentrator location and connection, and distributed network design. Capacity assignments will be assumed given, however, as already noted.

PROBLEMS

5.1 A large retail chain with stores in Chicago, St. Louis, Cleveland, Detroit, Baltimore, Philadelphia, New York, and Boston is planning a data network connecting concentrators in each of these cities to a central processor at its headquarters in Buffalo. The capacity assignments for the two proposed topologies shown in Fig. P5.1 are to be investigated.

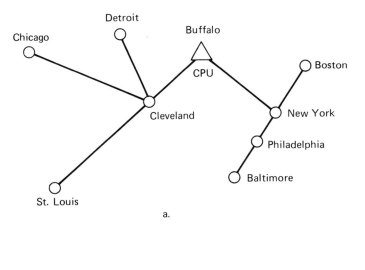

a.

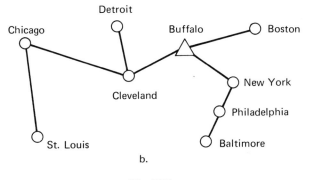

b.

Fig. P5.1

The rates for the various channel capacities available consist of a fixed monthly charge plus a charge dependent on distance. These rates are as follows:

Capacity (kbps)	Mileage ($/mi/mo)	Fixed ($/mo)
2.4	0.50	145
4.8	.65	210
9.6	1.00	285

Establish the time delay-cost curve for each of the two networks that provides the smallest maximum delay in the network for fixed cost.

Messages are expected to be on the average 1000 bits long. The average rates of messages originating at each city are expected to be: St. Louis—0.6 message/sec; Chicago—1.4 messages/sec; Detroit—0.8 message/sec; Cleveland—0.8 message/sec; Baltimore—0.6 message/sec; Philadelphia—1 message/sec; New York—2 messages/sec; Boston—1 message/sec.

5.2 Repeat Problem 5.1 using an alternate set of rates as specified in the table below. These provide for a higher monthly mileage leasing charge but a smaller monthly fixed charge:

Capacity (kbps)	Mileage ($/mi/mo)	Fixed ($/mo)
2.4	0.90	80
4.8	1.30	120
9.6	1.55	150

5.3 Repeat Problem 5.1 using some other topological connections and compare with the results of Problem 5.1. Can you develop some algorithms that both vary the concentrator connections and the capacity assignments in some systematic way that iteratively generates improved network designs?

Elements of
Queueing Theory

6

||||||||||||||||||||||||||||||||||||||||||||||||||||||||||||||||||||||||||||||||||||||||||||||||||||||||||||||||||||||||||||||||||||||||||||||||||||

Queueing theory plays a key role in the quantitative understanding of computer-communication networks. It is apparent from our discussion of these networks thus far that queues develop at each concentration point (node) in the network as messages arrive and wait for service. In fact, as has been stressed over and over again, one of the primary factors in the time delay messages encounter in traversing a network is just the queueing delay due to waiting for service.

The actual queueing delay encountered depends on the statistics of the messages arriving and the so-called service discipline—the way in which messages are handled at each concentrator. The overall network itself can be visualized as an interactive network of queues. The concentration and buffering aspects of network design, as well as routing, flow control, and other overall network operating characteristics, depend critically on an understanding of queueing theory for their quantitative characterization. We have already used one simple equation from queueing theory, the average time delay $T = 1/(\mu C - \lambda)$ of a message queued in an infinite buffer, to carry out the capacity assignment calculations of previous chapters.

Because of the intimate connection of queueing theory to the analysis and design of computer-communication networks, we shall take time out in this chapter to provide a simple introduction to some of the basic aspects of queueing theory. Later chapters will take up additional topics in the context of applications where needed. The reader is referred to the ever-growing literature on queueing theory for additional information and more thorough

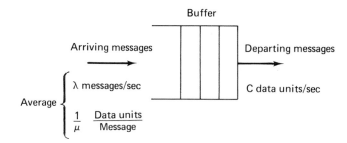

Fig. 6-1. Model of buffering process at a concentrator.

presentations where desired. A good first book in the subject is *Queues*, by D. R. Cox and W. L. Smith, Chapman and Hall, London, 1961. The two-volume series, *Queueing Systems*, by L. Kleinrock, Wiley-Interscience, 1975-76, is particularly up-to-date and comprehensive.

To approach queueing as simply as possible consider the simplest model of the queueing process at a concentrator node, as shown in Fig. 6-1. This is of course the same model used in earlier chapters in determining time delay at a node in message store-and-forward systems. We intend now as the first task in approaching queueing theory to derive the expression $T = 1/(\mu C - \lambda)$ used in previous chapters, and to indicate the underlying assumptions involved.

Messages are shown arriving at the input to the buffer. (These can be coming from a group of message sources directly connected to the concentrator or coming in on a line from another concentrator.) These messages are shown as having length $1/\mu$ data units (bits, bytes, characters, etc.). Messages in the buffer are serviced by the outgoing trunk, capable of transmitting C data units/sec. (Transmission takes place of course only if there are messages waiting in the buffer.)

Say a message arrives and n messages are waiting ahead of it in the buffer. The time taken to serve this message to completion, or the total delay time, is

$$T = \text{service time} + \text{waiting time}$$

$$= \frac{1}{\mu C} + \frac{n}{\mu C} \text{ sec} \tag{6-1}$$

Here for simplicity all messages are assumed to have the same length $1/\mu$ and to be served first come-first served. The delay time thus depends, in addition to the message length and the trunk capacity C, on the state n of the buffer. It is this state that we must in general determine statistically. The average of T in Eq. (6-1) over all states will then lead to a desired expression for *average* time delay.

This state depends on several things:

1. Statistics of the incoming messages, the so-called arrival process. This includes message length, or the service-time distribution.

2. Service discipline—

    a. first-come-first-served or, possibly, some form of priority structure

    b. size of buffer (finite or whether assumed infinite)

    c. number of outgoing trunks or the number of servers

    d. whether the queue is truly independent of other queues, or connected in some sort of network.

In the next section we choose the simplest example, that of an infinite buffer handling Poisson arrivals with exponentially-distributed message lengths. It is this model that gives rise to the expression for average time delay used in previous chapters.

M/M/1 QUEUES:
POISSON ARRIVALS,
EXPONENTIAL SERVICE TIMES

We have already noted several times in this book that we assume Poisson arrivals as the model for the message arrival process. It is the most common description of the arrival process in queueing theory and has been used in almost all applications of that theory. Telephone traffic, for example, is often modeled as a Poisson process. The limited measurements taken to date of message statistics in computer-communication networks substantiate this model as well.

The defining assumptions for a Poisson process are as follows: Consider a small time interval Δt, with $\Delta t \rightarrow 0$.

1. The probability of one arrival in Δt sec is then $\lambda \Delta t \ll 1$, *independent* of arrivals in adjacent (past or future) time slots. The assumption then is that the chance of an arrival is proportional to the time interval; λ, the proportionality constant, is thus assumed to be a fixed known constant in this case.

2. The probability of *no* arrivals in Δt is $1 - \lambda \Delta t$. The process then effectively rules out more than one arrival in Δt as $\Delta t \rightarrow 0$.

It may then be shown, through quite elementary methods, that the statistics of arrivals in a much larger interval, say T, obey the Poisson distribution.* Specifically, the probability of K arrivals in T sec is then

$$P(K) = P(K \text{ arrivals in } T \text{ sec}) = \frac{(\lambda T)^K e^{-\lambda T}}{K!} \tag{6-2}$$
$$K = 0, 1, 2, \ldots$$

The *average* number of arrivals in T sec is then

$$E(K) = \sum_{K=0}^{\infty} KP(K) = \lambda T \tag{6-3}$$

(The E( ) notation is the standard one representing expectation or mean value.) So the Poisson parameter λ introduced as a proportionality factor in defining the Poisson process turns out to be the *average* message arrival rate as well.

It may then also be shown** that the time τ between arrivals is a continuously-distributed exponential random variable:

$$f(\tau) = \lambda e^{-\lambda \tau} \tag{6-4}$$

Here $f(\tau)$ is the probability density function of τ and is sketched in Fig. 6-2. The *average* time between arrivals is just

$$E(\tau) = \int_0^\infty \tau f(\tau) \, d\tau = \frac{1}{\lambda} \tag{6-5}$$

as might be expected.

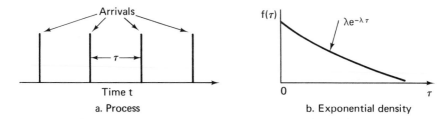

a. Process   b. Exponential density

Fig. 6-2. Poisson arrivals and exponential time between arrivals.

Now consider the message lengths. The service time, or time to complete the message transmission, is of course intimately related to the message lengths. (The emphasis in this application is somewhat different than in other applications of queueing theory. In those cases one refers most commonly to *customer* arrivals, and the service time is related to the *server* characteristic. Customers are served in a statistically-varying manner because of the server characteristics. Here the server is essentially a fixed capacity outgoing line

*D. R. Cox and W. L. Smith, *Queues*, Chapman & Hall, London, 1961.
**Ibid.

which continually outputs C data units/sec if messages are available to be transmitted. Statistical variations then arise because the messages—the customers—are themselves varying in length.) We again invoke the simplest queueing theory assumption; messages are now assumed to be exponentially-distributed in length, with average length $1/\mu$. (In the queueing theory terminology the service distribution is exponential.)

Specifically, if messages are r units long, the probability density function of r is

$$f(r) = \mu e^{-\mu r} \qquad (6\text{-}6)$$

and

$$E(r) = \frac{1}{\mu} \text{ data units/message}$$

Shorter messages $(r < 1/\mu)$ are then more likely than longer messages $(r > 1/\mu)$. Note that this is clearly a physically implausible distribution since data messages are discrete in length (multiples of the data unit used), whereas r in Eq. (6-6) is continuous. In chapters following we shall in fact introduce a discrete message length model that is physically more valid and fits the experimental data in many situations. The exponential message length assumption does provide quick results very simply, however. It allows extension to more complex network models quite readily since it is the simplest service time model available and the literature is replete with applications of its use. In actual practice the exponential message length assumption has been found to lead to relatively good design results and analysis of existing data networks. We shall discuss the applicability of this assumption in later chapters.

If an outgoing trunk of capacity C data units/sec is now used, it is clear that messages r data units long take r/C sec to be transmitted or serviced. We can then write as the *service-time distribution*

$$f(t) = \mu C e^{-\mu C t} \qquad (6\text{-}7)$$

Here $E(t) = 1/\mu C$ is the average time to transmit a message. We shall henceforth focus on μC rather than μ in describing message service time. (In the queueing literature the symbol $1/\mu$ alone is often used to represent the average service time. We shall in fact do the same occasionally to simplify the notation. In that case the units of $1/\mu$ are seconds, rather than data units, and the capacity C of the outgoing trunk is understood to be included.)

Note that the service time distribution is identical with that of the message interarrival distribution of Eq. (6-4) and Fig. 6-2. A little thought will then indicate that there are Poisson-type assumptions behind the exponential service time distribution as well. Specifically, consider a message already in service. It is then readily shown that with the exponential service time model, the probability of a message *completion* in a Δt sec interval is $\mu C \Delta t$, while the probability of no completion is just $(1 - \mu C \Delta t)$. Completions from one Δt sec interval ($\Delta t \rightarrow 0$) to the next are statistically independent. The number of message departures (service completions) in T sec obeys the same Poisson distribution as that of Eq. (6-2) with μC replacing λ.

Now consider the queueing model of Fig. 6-3: Poisson arrivals enter an infinite buffer with an exponential service time distribution. Messages are handled first-come-first-served. This queueing model is called an M/M/1 queue and is the simplest one available in queueing theory. (The notation used is due to D. G. Kendall and has now become standardized in the queueing literature. The Kendall notation in its most general form is given as A/B/C, with "A" a symbol denoting the arrival distribution, "B" the service discipline and "C" the number of servers used. The symbol "M" denotes Poisson or the equivalent exponential distributions. An M/G/1 queue would have Poisson arrivals, a *general* service distribution, and one server. The "D" denotes fixed (constant) service time, so a queue with this characteristic and Poisson arrivals would be written M/D/1.*)

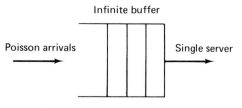

Infinite buffer

Poisson arrivals   Single server

Exponential service-time distribution

Fig. 6-3. M/M/1 queue.

We would like to find the probability $p_n(t)$ for the M/M/1 queue that n messages are present in the buffer at time t. This provides a state description of the buffer from which various statistical parameters (e.g., average buffer occupancy, probability of exceeding a given level of occupancy, and so on) may be found. For $t \rightarrow \infty$ we shall find steady-state conditions setting in and will develop the steady-state description of the buffer.

Because of the Poisson assumptions involved, a simple way of analyzing the buffer is to focus on two successive times intervals t and $t + \Delta t$ ($\Delta t \rightarrow 0$). These are shown in Fig. 6-4. Say that the buffer happens to be in state n at time $t + \Delta t$ as shown. With the Poisson assumptions for message arrival and completion, it is apparent that the buffer could only have occupied one of the three states shown in Fig. 6-4, ($n + 1, n, n - 1$) at time t, Δt sec prior. For in the Δt sec time interval no more than one message could have arrived, and no more than one could have had its transmission completed (service completion). $p_n(t + \Delta t)$ can then be readily found in terms of the probability of

*See T. L. Saaty, *Elements of Queueing Theory*, McGraw-Hill, New York, 1961, as well as other books on queueing for details and analysis of many types of queues.

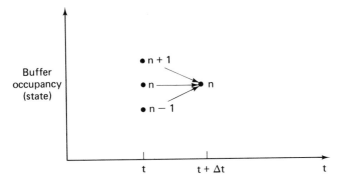

Fig. 6-4. Analysis of M/M/1 queue.

occupying each of the three states at time t, and the probabilities of arrivals and departures (the so-called transition probabilities). Specifically, we have

$$p_n(t + \Delta t) = p_n(t)[(1 - \mu C \Delta t)(1 - \lambda \Delta t) + \mu C \Delta t \, \lambda \Delta t]$$
$$+ p_{n+1}(t) \, [\mu C \Delta t \, (1 - \lambda \Delta t)] \qquad \text{(6-8)}$$
$$+ p_{n-1}(t) \, [\lambda \Delta t \, (1 - \mu C \Delta t)] \qquad n \geq 1$$

The terms in brackets multiplying $p_n(t)$ represent the probabilities of no arrivals and no departures, or one arrival and one departure—just the quantities needed to maintain the buffer at its same state. Similarly, the term in brackets multiplying $p_{n+1}(t)$ represents the probability of one departure (service completion) and no arrival, so that $n + 1$ drops to n. Finally, the last term in brackets represents the probability of one arrival and no departure.

Equation (6-8) can be used to solve for $p_n(t)$ by letting $\Delta t \rightarrow 0$. Assuming the various probabilities of state are continuous, one can represent $p_n(t + \Delta t)$ by the first two terms in its Taylor series:

$$p_n(t + \Delta t) \doteq p_n(t) + \frac{dp_n(t)}{dt} \Delta t \qquad \text{(6-9)}$$

Substituting Eq. (6-9) into Eq. (6-8), cancelling terms, and letting $\Delta t \rightarrow 0$ (second-order terms involving $(\Delta t)^2$ then vanish), one obtains a differential-difference equation governing $p_n(t)$. We shall focus on stationary statistical behavior only. Thus we assume the state probabilities are independent of time. (This implies the buffer system of Fig. 6-3 has been in operation for a long period of time with transient effects negligible.) This also implies $dp_n(t)/dt = 0$. From Eq. (6-8) and Eq. (6-9), the equation of state governing the stationary queueing process is then readily shown to be given by

$$(\lambda + \mu C)p_n = \mu C p_{n+1} + \lambda p_{n-1} \qquad n \geq 1 \qquad \text{(6-10)}$$

Equation (6-10) may be diagrammed in the form of Fig. 6-5 which represents the two ways in which state n may be reached from $(n - 1)$ and $(n + 1)$

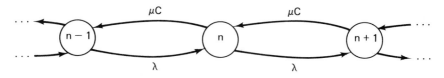

Fig. 6-5. State representation of steady-state queue.

respectively. The solution of this difference equation with appropriate boundary conditions incorporated provides the desired expression for p_n, the probability that n messages occupy the buffer. One condition of course is that as $n \rightarrow \infty$, p_n must approach zero. For $\sum_{n=0}^{\infty} p_n = 1$. Higher states must thus have decreasingly smaller probabilities of occupancy.

Another condition relates p_1 and p_0. An equation similar to Eq. (6-8) may be written for these two states. It is then left to the reader to show that in the steady-state

$$\lambda p_0 = \mu C p_1 \tag{6-11}$$

The interpretation here of course is that an arrival while the queue is in state 0 (empty) moves the queue to state 1, while a departure from state 1 moves the queue to state 0.

One simple method of solution starts with Eq. (6-11) and then uses Eq. (6-10) recursively. Thus, from Eq. (6-11)

$$p_1 = \frac{\lambda}{\mu C} p_0 = \rho p_0 \tag{6-12}$$

with $\rho \equiv \lambda / \mu C$ often called the traffic intensity. This is of course the parameter already introduced in previous chapters. From Eq. (6-10) with $n = 1$, we find

$$p_2 = (\rho + 1)p_1 - \rho p_0 = \rho^2 p_0 \tag{6-13}$$

using Eq. (6-12). Repeating, the general expression for p_n is readily shown to be given by

$$p_n = \rho^n p_0 \tag{6-14}$$

It is apparent that we must have $\rho = \lambda / \mu C < 1$ from the comment above that the state probabilities must decrease with n. This agrees with our intuitive notion that the average number of arrivals per unit time, λ, must be less than the system capacity μC. Otherwise the buffer begins to build up indefinitely. (Recall we are dealing with an infinite buffer here. In the finite buffer case to be discussed later too many arrivals simply means arrivals are blocked and do not enter the buffer if it is full.)

Since

$$\sum_{n=0}^{\infty} p_n = 1 = p_0 \sum_{n=0}^{\infty} \rho^n = \frac{p_0}{1 - \rho} \tag{6-15}$$

we also find
$$p_0 = (1 - \rho) \tag{6-16}$$
and
$$p_n = (1 - \rho)\rho^n \tag{6-14a}$$

This again indicates that we must have $\rho < 1$. It also indicates that as ρ increases, the higher states become relatively more probable.

Note the physical interpretation of ρ provided by Eq. (6-16): $\rho = (1 - p_0)$ is the probability that the buffer is not empty.

An alternate method of solving Eq. (6-10) consists of *assuming* a solution for p_n. Since Eq. (6-10) is a linear homogeneous difference equation an exponential-type (actually geometric) solution is indicated. Thus one *assumes* a solution of the form
$$p_n = K\rho^n$$

with K and ρ constants to be determined. Substituting into Eq. (6-10) the equation becomes an algebraic one. It is left to the reader to show that the resultant equation is only satisfied for $\rho = \lambda/\mu C$.

Equation (6-14a), representing the probability of occupancy of the various states of the M/M/1 queue, may be used to find all statistical quantities of interest for the queue. Specifically, the *average* queue size is given by
$$E(n) = \sum_{n=0}^{\infty} np_n = \frac{\rho}{1 - \rho} \tag{6-17}$$

The average queue occupancy thus increases beyond bound as $\rho \to 1$. This is the same phenomenon first noted in the discission of the average time delay equation in earlier chapters. $E(n)$ is sketched in Fig. 6-6. For $\rho < 0.5$ the

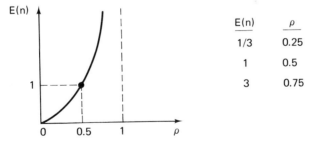

E(n)	ρ
1/3	0.25
1	0.5
3	0.75

Fig. 6-6. Average queue occupancy, M/M/1 queue.

average number of messages in the queue is less than 1. For $\rho > 0.5$ the number increases rapidly. Thus for $\rho = 0.75$, $E(n) = 3$; for $\rho = 0.8$, $E(n) = 4$; for $\rho = 0.9$, $E(n) = 9$; and so on.

In Eq. (6-1) we indicated that time delay is related to queue occupancy. We can thus use Eq. (6-17) for the average queue occupancy to find the average time delay $E(T)$. Specifically,

$$E(T) = \frac{1}{\mu C} + \frac{E(n)}{\mu C} = \frac{1}{\mu C(1 - \rho)} = \frac{1}{\mu C - \lambda} \qquad (6\text{-}18)$$

from Eq. (6-17). Note that this is the identical expression used in earlier chapters in discussing the choice of capacity to minimize average time delay in a network. We have thus shown how one derives this very basic equation. The basic assumptions made previously were that each queue in the network could be modeled as an M/M/1 queue, and that each queue was statistically independent of all the others. This latter assumption is particularly subject to challenge, since it implies message lengths are *independently* chosen from an exponential distribution at *each* concentration or nodal point. This is clearly not valid in practice. Yet as pointed out earlier, studies of real networks indicate the results of analysis using this assumption do agree fairly well with practice.

An alternate and more general derivation of Eq. (6-18) comes from *Little's formula** which will be used in other applications later in this book. This theorem simply says that under some broad conditions the average occupancy of a buffered system must equal the average delay time for the system multiplied by the average arrival rate. The system in question can be a network of queues and the M/M/1 hypothesis doesn't have to be invoked so that the theorem is quite broad in its applicability. As applied here for one queue we have

$$E(T) \cdot \lambda = E(n) \qquad (6\text{-}19)$$

Substituting Eq. (6-17) in for $E(n)$ we get Eq. (6-18) directly.

The application of Little's theorem to a large network is of interest and leads directly to the average time delay Eq. (3-4) of Chap. 3. Consider such a network made up of many nodes connected by links. Let the outgoing buffer associated with the ith link have an average arrival rate λ_i, average number of messages either waiting or in service $E(n_i)$, and an average delay time $E(T_i)$. Then $E(T_i) \cdot \lambda_i = E(n_i)$, from Little's theorem. Now visualize the entire network enclosed in the proverbial "black box" and focus attention on arrivals into this box. Say γ messages per unit time enter the network, on the average; there is an average delay time $E(T)$ for the entire network, and $E(n)$ is the average number of messages stored inside. The black box itself behaves as a queue for which, by Little's theorem, we have $E(T) \cdot \gamma = E(n)$. From average statistics we have

$$E(n) = \sum_{i=1}^{m} E(n_i) = \sum_{i=1}^{m} \lambda_i E(T_i)$$

summing over all the buffers in the network and applying Little's theorem to

*D. C. Little, "A Proof of the Queueing Formula: $L = \lambda W$," *Operations Research*, **9**, 1961, 383–87.

each one in turn. It is apparent that this then gives us

$$E(T) = \frac{1}{\gamma} \sum_{i=1}^{m} \lambda_i E(T_i) \qquad (6\text{-}19a)$$

just Eq. (3-4) used previously in determining network capacity assignments.

It is often of interest to know the probability that the queue exceeds a specified number. We shall use this calculation in later chapters in determining the buffer size needed for a prescribed probability of buffer overflow. From Eq. (6-14a) the probability that the number of messages waiting in an M/M/1 queue exceeds some number N is given by

$$P(n > N) = \sum_{n=N+1}^{\infty} p_n = (1 - \rho) \sum_{n=N+1}^{\infty} \rho^n = \rho^{N+1} \qquad (6\text{-}20)$$

after using the geometric sum formula.

As an example, the following table indicates $P(n > N)$ for $\rho = 0.6$ and various N:

N	$P(n > N)$
1	0.36
3	0.13
9	6.1×10^{-3}
19	3.7×10^{-5}

The probability decreases exponentially with N as shown by Eq. (6-20). Recall that the *average* occupancy for $\rho = 0.6$ is $E(n) = 0.6/(1 - 0.6) = 1.5$. It is apparent from the table above that the chance of exceeding 10 times the average buffer occupancy is less than 10^{-3}. A buffer capable of holding 15 messages would then appear effectively like an infinite buffer for this value of ρ.

As a check consider a *finite* buffer now with Poisson arrivals and exponential message lengths. The derivation of Eq. (6-14) for the steady-state probability of state occupancy didn't really involve the infinite buffer assumption. The solution for p_n is thus still appropriate in the finite buffer case. The only difference now is that the probabilities of the finite set of states must sum to 1. Thus, we have

$$\sum_{n=0}^{N} p_n = 1 = p_0 \sum_{n=0}^{N} \rho^n = p_0 \left[\frac{1 - \rho^{N+1}}{1 - \rho} \right] \qquad (6\text{-}21)$$

again using the geometric sum formula.

We thus have in this case

$$p_0 = \frac{1 - \rho}{1 - \rho^{N+1}} \qquad (6\text{-}22)$$

and

$$p_n = \frac{(1 - \rho) \rho^n}{1 - \rho^{N+1}} \tag{6-23}$$

For $\rho^N \ll 1$ it is apparent that this result reduces to the infinite buffer result of Eq. (6-14a). The probability that the buffer is *filled* and that messages are turned away (blocked) is simply the probability that there are N messages in the buffer or

$$p_N = \frac{(1 - \rho)\rho^N}{1 - \rho^{N+1}} \tag{6-24}$$

This expression for blocking probability may be substantiated in an instructive fashion that focuses on average message throughput. In this approach the average net rate of message arrivals, or message throughput, is equated to the average message departure rate. Statistical equilibrium is of course presumed to prevail. This approach will be used again in a later chapter in calculating the blocking probability of a finite queue using a more realistic model of data unit arrivals. The principle of statistical equilibrium may also be invoked to derive Eq. (6-10) for the M/M/1 state equation directly. Generalizations of these ideas are used in studying the equilibrium properties of queueing networks. We shall in fact use this approach in analyzing congestion control procedures in Chap. 11.

To derive the blocking probability Eq. (6-24), consider the finite M/M/1 queue of Fig. 6-7. (As noted above this is also readily generalized to more general queueing structures.) λ messages/sec on the average are assumed to arrive at the input to the queue capable of holding, at most, N messages only. If the blocking probability is P_B, the *net* arrival rate *into* the queue must be $\lambda(1 - P_B)$. For equilibrium to exist this must equal the average message departure rate and is just the system throughput. Now the probability of a message departure in an interval Δt is just $\mu \, \Delta t$ *if* there is a message waiting in the queue.* The probability that a message is waiting is just the prob-

Fig. 6-7. Blocking probability and average throughput, M/M/1 queue.

ability $(1 - p_0)$ that the queue is nonempty. The average departure *rate* is thus $(1 - p_0)\mu$, and we have

$$\lambda(1 - P_B) = (1 - p_0)\mu \tag{6-25}$$

---

*For simplicity's sake, as noted earlier, we are letting the previous parameter μC be labeled μ. The capacity C is thus subsumed in μ.

This is indicated in Fig. 6-7.

In particular for the finite M/M/1 queue, p_0 is readily found from Eq. (6-23). Substituting this into Eq. (6-25), noting that $\rho = \lambda/\mu$, and solving for P_B, we find exactly Eq. (6-24) arising. As a check, for an infinite queue we must have, from Eq. (6-25), $\rho = (1 - p_0)$, if $P_B = 0$ which agrees with Eq. (6-16). The traffic intensity parameter ρ is thus just the average throughput for an infinite queue as well. We shall also invoke this approach in Chap. 8.

QUEUES WITH DEPENDENCE ON STATE OF SYSTEM

The M/M/1 queue results given in the previous section may be generalized readily in a few cases of specific interest. One such case involves the multiserver situation in which additional servers or transmission channels are added as the state occupancy increases. Another case has the message arrival rate decreasing with queue occupancy to keep the average occupancy down. Both of these are special cases of a queue in which arrivals and departures, although based on Poisson-type assumptions, depend on the state of the system.

We shall discuss these cases briefly here.* All of these Poisson-type processes are examples of generalized birth-death processes** in which the probability of an arrival (birth) in an interval Δt is proportional to Δt, $\Delta t \rightarrow 0$, while the corresponding probability of a departure (death) is proportional to Δt as well. The generalization consists of relating the proportionality constants to the state of the system.

Thus let the arrival coefficients be called λ_n and the departure coefficient be μ_n to denote their dependence on the state n. (The capacity C is now subsumed in the μ_n coefficient, as noted earlier. The results obtained are thus applicable to queueing situations other than those involving data messages.) Assume these coefficients are independent of time and that statistical equilibrium has set in as well. It is then apparent by comparison with Eq. (6-10) for the M/M/1 case in which the coefficients are state independent that the difference equation relating p_n to p_{n-1} and p_{n+1} is now given by

$$(\lambda_n + \mu_n)p_n = \mu_{n+1}p_{n+1} + \lambda_{n-1}p_{n-1} \qquad n \geq 1 \qquad (6\text{-}26)$$

This equation may again be solved recursively, as was Eq. (6-10), by first writing an equivalent equation relating p_1 to p_0 and then continuing for higher

---

*Cox and Smith, *Queues*, pp. 43–48.

**D. R. Cox and H. D. Miller, *The Theory of Stochastic Processes*, Methuen & Co., London, 1965.

state probabilities. It is left for the reader to show that the resultant expression for p_n is given by

$$p_n = \frac{\lambda_0 \lambda_1 \lambda_2 \lambda_3 \ldots \lambda_{n-1}}{\mu_1 \mu_2 \ldots \mu_n} p_0 \qquad (6\text{-}27)$$

The probability p_0 that the queue is empty is in turn found by summing all the states and setting the sum equal to 1.

As a specific case say $\mu_n = n\mu$. This is the case of a queue with multiple servers; as a new message (or "customer," in the queueing jargon) arrives, an additional server is pressed into service. There can be a limit on the number of servers available* but we shall leave that case for the reader to develop. If we assume no limit on the number of servers we have

$$p_n = \left(\frac{\lambda}{\mu}\right)^n \frac{p_0}{n!} = \frac{\rho^n}{n!} p_0 \qquad (6\text{-}28)$$

with $\rho \equiv \lambda/\mu$ again.

Then with

$$\sum_{n=0}^{\infty} p_n = 1 = p_0 \sum_{n=0}^{\infty} \frac{\rho^n}{n!} = p_0 e^\rho \qquad (6\text{-}29)$$

we have

$$p_0 = e^{-\rho} \qquad (6\text{-}30)$$

and

$$p_n = \frac{\rho^n e^{-\rho}}{n!} \qquad (6\text{-}28a)$$

The probability of higher state occupancy is relatively less here for the same ρ than in the M/M/1 case since the additional servers brought in clear the system out more rapidly. We compare this queue discipline (multiple servers) with the M/M/1 case in the following table:

Parameter		Multiple Server Case		M/M/1 Queue
1. Probability queue is empty p_0	$=$	$e^{-\rho}$	$>$	$1 - \rho$
2. Probability queue is nonempty (server is busy) $1 - p_0$	$=$	$1 - e^{-\rho}$	$<$	ρ
3. Average queue occupancy $E(n)$	$=$	ρ	$<$	$\rho/(1 - \rho)$

*Cox and Smith, *Queues*, p. 45.

Note that the average queue occupancy rises only linearly with ρ in this case and does not show the rapid increase with ρ as $\rho \rightarrow 1$ in the M/M/1 case (Fig. 6-6). In fact, here $\rho > 1$ is allowed since more servers are simply brought in to accommodate the increased demand as λ increases.

Another example that leads to the identical result as the many-server case is the so-called queue with discouragement.* Here the model used is $\mu_n = \mu$, $\lambda_n = \lambda/(n+1)$. Thus as the queue size increases, the arrival rate drops accordingly. The server discipline remains the same, however. (The number of trunks does not increase.) It is left to the reader to show that the equation for p_n is exactly that of Eq. (6-28) from which Eq. (6-28a) again follows. The previous table thus applies here as well with the multiple server case replaced by the queue with discouragement.

M/G/1 QUEUES:
GENERAL SERVICE TIME DISTRIBUTION

We now extend the queue analysis to one involving a general service time distribution. In the data transmission context this implies messages with nonexponentially-distributed lengths. We shall show that the average buffer occupancy and hence, by Little's formula, the average time delay expression may be found for this case quite generally. The resultant expression is called the *Pollaczek-Khinchine formula*. It enables us to handle models of message length statistics that represent true data more accurately. It also enables us to see how different choices of statistics affect the average time delay determined on the basis of exponentially-distributed (M/M/1) message lengths. One example is that of fixed length messages, a fairly common model for inquiry-response data networks or packet-switched networks, in which most messages traversing the network are of a fixed length. The approach used here will be extended in later chapters to include discrete message length statistics.

To handle the general message length (or service time) case we approach the problem quite differently than in the previous section. We shall handle general service time first, independent of the arrival distribution, then focus on the M/G/1 case, with Poisson arrivals. The approach here is to focus on the times (randomly-distributed) at which service on a message is completed. (Transmission of the message in question is then concluded and the message leaves the concentrator in question.)

Thus, assume a sequence of messages arrives at a buffer, each with randomly-varying length (or service time). The server works on one message at a time (i.e., the transmission trunk handles one message at a time) until completion. Then service begins on the next message, first-come-first-served. Let n_j be the queue length *after the departure* of the jth message (j is the

*Ibid., p. 44.

running time index). We can write a simple equation relating n_j to the queue length n_{j-1} after the departure of the $(j-1)$ message. Specifically, we have

$$n_j = (n_{j-1} - 1) + v_j \qquad n_{j-1} \geq 1$$
$$= v_j \qquad\qquad\qquad n_{j-1} = 0 \tag{6-31}$$

Here v_j is the number of messages arriving during the service time of the jth message (or jth customer). This is itself of course a random variable. The times involved are diagrammed in Fig. 6-8. Equation (6-31) simply states the obvious fact that the queue length decreases by 1 after departure of a message (*if* there was a message in the queue) and increases by the number of arrivals.

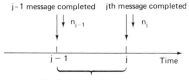

Fig. 6-8. General service time distribution.

The equation may be written in an alternate and instructive fashion as

$$n_j = (n_{j-1} - 1)^\dagger + v_j \tag{6-31a}*$$

The $(\ )^\dagger$ notation used is defined as follows:

$$a^\dagger = a \qquad \text{if } a \geq 0$$
$$a^\dagger = 0 \qquad \text{otherwise} \tag{6-32}$$

The quantities on the right-hand side of Eq. (6-31a) are independent random variables. The state variable n_j is thus the sum of two independent random variables. Its probability distribution is therefore the convolution of the two respective probability distributions. This suggests the use of transforms, for in this case transforms multiply. The appropriate transforms here are the so-called moment-generating functions defined for a random variable n as follows:

$$G_n(z) \equiv E(z^n) = \sum_{k=0}^{\infty} P(n = k)z^k \tag{6-33}$$

Here $P(n = k)$ is the probability that n equals k. We shall use p_k to represent this expression in the interest of notational economy. As is usually the case with transforms, once one finds $G_n(z)$ one can always determine p_k (at least conceptually) by expanding $G_n(z)$ in an infinite series in z. The use of the transform approach simplifies the problem considerably since we immediately

*An alternate representation in terms of step functions appears as Eq. (7-2) of Chap. 7, as well as in Problem 6.9.

have from Eq. (6-31a)

$$G_{n_j}(z) = G_a(z)G_{v_j}(z) \tag{6-34}$$

with each function the generating function of the corresponding variable in Eq. (6-31a),* and defined as in Eq. (6-32). If we now assume the system has been operating a long time with statistical equilibrium or stationarity having set in, we can drop the j subscripts. We thus have, in the steady-state case,

$$G_n(z) = G_a(z)G_v(z) \tag{6-35}$$

The statistics of v (the number of messages arriving during the service time interval) are assumed known so that $G_v(z)$ can be found from these. Details of this procedure will be demonstrated shortly. We now show how to calculate $G_a(z)$ from the statistics of n. The resulting relation between $G_a(z)$ and $G_n(z)$ will then enable us to develop an explicit equation relating $G_n(z)$ to $G_v(z)$. For given message arrival statistics then, one can in principle find the desired probabilities $P(n = k)$ of state occupancy.

Specifically, we have from the defining Eq. (6-33) for moment-generating functions

$$G_a(z) = P[(n - 1)^{\dagger} = 0] + P[(n - 1)^{\dagger} = 1]z + \dots \tag{6-36}$$

But from Eq. (6-31), (6-31a), and (6-32), $(n - 1)^{\dagger} = 0$ corresponds to $n = 0$ *or* 1, $(n - 1)^{\dagger} = 1$ corresponds to $n = 2$, and so on. The probabilities for $(n - 1)^{\dagger}$ can thus be written as equivalent probabilities in n. Equation (6-36) thus becomes

$$G_a(z) = p_0 + p_1 + p_2 z + p_3 z^2 + \dots \tag{6-36a}$$

with $p_k \equiv P[n = k]$, as noted earlier.

Comparing Eq. (6-36a) with Eq. (6-33), it is apparent that we can also write

$$G_a(z) = p_0 + \frac{G_n(z) - p_0}{z} \tag{6-36b}$$

Substituting Eq. (6-36b) into Eq. (6-35) and solving for the desired (unknown) $G_n(z)$, we have

$$G_n(z) = \frac{p_0(z - 1)G_v(z)}{[z - G_v(z)]} \tag{6-37}$$

The moment-generating function $G_n(z)$ of the number of messages buffered at the completion of a message transmission is thus written, as desired, in terms of the generating function of the number of arrivals during the time of message transmission. All desired properties of the buffer state—average buffer occupancy, probability that the buffer contents exceed a specified value, etc., can then at least in principle be found from $G_n(z)$.

---

*Say $w = x + y$, with x and y discrete independent random variables. Then

$$G_w(z) = E(z^w) = E(z^{x+y}) = E(z^x)E(z^y)$$

by virtue of the independence assumed.

Note however that p_0 in Eq. (6-37), the probability that the buffer is empty, is still unknown. We shall show quite simply however that p_0 depends on the average number of arrivals $E(v)$ during a message transmission interval:

$$p_0 = 1 - E(v) \qquad (6\text{-}38)$$

This is an extension of the M/M/1 result of the previous section that $\rho = 1 - p_0$ and, as we shall see shortly, includes that result as a special case. This says that the average number of arrivals during message transmission must be less than 1. Equation (6-37) as modified thus becomes

$$G_n(z) = \frac{[1 - E(v)](z - 1)G_v(z)}{[z - G_v(z)]} \qquad (6\text{-}37\text{a})$$

To demonstrate Eq. (6-38) we note that Eq. (6-37) as it stands is indeterminate at $z = 1$. For, from the definition of the moment-generating function in Eq. (6-33), $G_n(1) = 1$. Also $G_v(1) = 1$, as well. This is a general property of moment-generating functions. Substituting $G_v(1) = 1$ into Eq. (6-37) we find $G_n(1)$ is indeterminate. It is in actually evaluating $G_n(1)$ in Eq. (6-37) and setting it equal to 1 that we find Eq. (6-38) must be satisfied.

A Taylor series expansion of $G_v(z)$ about the point $z = 1$ provides the means of bypassing the indeterminacy in Eq. (6-37). Specifically, we have

$$G_v(z) = G_v(1) + \frac{dG_v(z)}{dz}\Big|_{z=1}(z - 1) + \frac{d^2G_v(z)}{dz^2}\Big|_{z=1}\frac{(z - 1)^2}{2!} + \ldots \qquad (6\text{-}39)$$

Now from the definition, Eq. (6-33), of the moment-generating function we have

$$\frac{dG_v(z)}{dz}\Big|_{z=1} = \frac{d}{dz}E[z^v]\Big|_{z=1} = E[vz^{v-1}]\Big|_{z=1} = E(v) \qquad (6\text{-}40)$$

Similarly, it is left for the reader to show that

$$\frac{d^2G_v(z)}{dz^2}\Big|_{z=1} = E(v^2) - E(v) \qquad (6\text{-}41)$$

Successive derivatives of the moment-generating function thus produce the various average values or moments of the random variable in question. It is for this reason that the moment-generating function, defined in Eq. (6-33), gets its name. Using Eq. (6-40) and (6-41) and the fact that $G_v(1) = 1$, the Taylor series expansion of Eq. (6-39) is simply given as

$$G_v(z) = 1 + E(v)(z - 1) + [E(v^2) - E(v)]\frac{(z - 1)^2}{2!} + \ldots \qquad (6\text{-}39\text{a})$$

Hence

$$z - G_v(z) = (z - 1)[1 - E(v) + \ldots] \qquad (6\text{-}42)$$

Here higher-order terms in $(z - 1)$ have been subsummed in the dot notation. Substituting Eq. (6-42) into the denominator of Eq. (6-37), cancelling the

$(z - 1)$ term in the numerator and denominator, setting $z = 1$ and $G_n(1) = 1$, Eq. (6-38) results.

Equation (6-37a) is deceptively simple. For except in certain cases, the evaluation of the statistics of message arrivals during the (random) service time of a message, as required to find $G_v(z)$, can be quite tricky. One case of great interest for which results can be found quite readily is the one involving Poisson arrivals, or just the case of the M/G/1 queue. We shall derive the statistics for this case shortly. Before considering the M/G/1 case, however, it is of interest first to consider a special and important subclass: that of fixed length messages arriving at a Poisson rate. As already noted earlier this is often taken as a model for inquiry-response systems in which messages all tend to be of the same fixed length. Equation (6-37a) is also easily applied in this case, so we can get some idea of its significance.

Let the messages be of length τ_0. Since the messages are all of the same length, the number arriving in τ_0 sec (the service time) depends strictly on the arrival process and is easily found. If the process is Poisson, for example, we have as the statistics of v,

$$p_k = P[v = k] = e^{-\lambda \tau_0} \frac{(\lambda \tau_0)^k}{k!} \qquad (6\text{-}43)$$

Also

$$E(v) = \lambda \tau_0 < 1 \qquad (6\text{-}44)$$

is required, so this limits the arrival rate of messages in this process. (This is of course equivalent to $\rho = \lambda/\mu < 1$ in the M/M/1 case. Here τ_0 is exactly equivalent to $1/\mu$, the average message length in the exponentially-distributed case. These limits on $E(v)$ and ρ are necessary to ensure statistical equilibrium, as noted earlier.)

The moment-generating function $G_v(z)$ is now readily found to be given by

$$G_v(z) = \sum_{k=0}^{\infty} p_k z^k = \sum_{k=0}^{\infty} e^{-\lambda \tau_0} \frac{(\lambda \tau_0 z)^k}{k!} = e^{\lambda \tau_0 (z-1)} \qquad (6\text{-}45)$$

upon recalling that $e^x = 1 + x + x^2/2! + \ldots$. As a check,

$$\left. \frac{dG_v(z)}{dz} \right|_{z=1} = \lambda \tau_0 = E(v)$$

Higher moments of the Poisson process may be found similarly. Using Eq. (6-44) and Eq. (6-45) in Eq. (6-37a), the moment-generating function of the buffer state, for *this special case*, is found in closed form. By appropriate differentiation desired moments may be found. By expanding $G_n(z)$ in an infinite series in z (not an obvious task even in this special case), the various probabilities of buffer occupancy may be found as well.

We now apply Eq. (6-37a) to the more general case of the M/G/1 queue; i.e., one with Poisson arrivals and arbitrary service (message length) distribution. To do this we must first find the probabilities $P(v = k)$ of message arrivals during a random service time. Say a message (or customer service time) has a known distribution of lengths, in time, given by $f_\tau(\tau)$. (The discrete message length case can be handled by writing $f_\tau(\tau)$ as an appropriate sum of weighted impulse functions.) Let $P(v = k \mid \tau)$ be the probability of k arrivals in τ sec. Then it is apparent that $P(v = k)$ is given by

$$P(v = k) = \int_0^\infty P(v = k \mid \tau) f_\tau(\tau)\, d\tau \tag{6-46}$$

Specifically, say the arrivals constitute a Poisson process. Then

$$P(v = k \mid \tau) = \frac{(\lambda \tau)^k e^{-\lambda k}}{k!} \tag{6-47}$$

The moment-generating function $G_v(z)$ in this M/G/1 case is given by

$$G_v(z) = \sum_{k=0}^\infty P(v = k) z^k = \sum_{k=0}^\infty \left[\int_0^\infty \frac{(\lambda \tau)^k e^{-\lambda \tau}}{k!} f_\tau(\tau)\, d\tau \right] z^k \tag{6-48}$$

using Eq. (6-46) and (6-47).

Interchanging the order of integration and summation in Eq. (6-48) and recognizing that the infinite series resulting is again the series for the exponential, we have

$$G_v(z) = \int_0^\infty e^{-\lambda(1-z)\tau} f_\tau(\tau)\, d\tau = F_\tau[\lambda(1 - z)] \tag{6-48a}$$

with $F_\tau(s)$ defined to be the Laplace transform of $f_\tau(\tau)$:

$$F_\tau(s) = \int_0^\infty e^{-s\tau} f_\tau(\tau)\, d\tau \tag{6-49}$$

So if the message length distribution is known, $G_v(z)$ is readily found in terms of its Laplace transform. For example, if the messages are all of fixed length τ_0, $f_\tau(\tau) = \delta(\tau - \tau_0)$. Substituting into Eq. (6-48a), Eq. (6-45) results. If $f_\tau(\tau) = \mu e^{-\mu \tau}$ (the exponential distribution discussed in the M/M/1 case in the previous section), $F_\tau(s) = \mu/(s + \mu)$, and

$$F_\tau[\lambda(1 - z)] = \frac{\mu}{\lambda(1 - z) + \mu} = \frac{1}{\rho(1 - z) + 1}$$

Other examples are left to the reader to work out.

From Eq. (6-48a) we also have

$$E(v) = \frac{dG_v(z)}{dz}\bigg|_{z=1} = -\lambda \frac{dF_\tau(s)}{ds}\bigg|_{s=0} \tag{6-50}$$

But,

$$\frac{-dF_\tau(s)}{ds}\bigg|_{s=0} = \int_0^n \tau f_\tau(\tau)\, dz = E(\tau) \tag{6-51}$$

using Eq. (6-49). (The Laplace transform of a continuous random variable, the so-called characteristic function, plays the same role as the moment-generating function of a discrete random variable. By appropriate differentiation one can obtain the various average values or moments.) If we call the average value of the message length $1/\mu$, as in previous sections, we have

$$E(v) = \lambda E(\tau) = \frac{\lambda}{\mu} \equiv \rho < 1 \qquad (6\text{-}52)$$

an exact extension of the previous M/M/1 result. (As noted earlier, the capacity C of the outgoing trunk is here subsumed in μ. The units of μ here are time, say seconds, while in previous sections they were in data units, bits, bytes, etc.)

Finally then for the M/G/1 case,

$$G_n(z) = \frac{(1 - \rho)(z - 1)F_\tau[\lambda(1 - z)]}{z - F_\tau[\lambda(1 - z)]} \qquad (6\text{-}53)$$

As an example and as a check, say the service time is exponential. We have already noted that $F_\tau[\ ]$ in this case is given by $1/[\rho(1 - z) + 1]$. Substituting into Eq. (6-53) and simplifying, we have

$$G_n(z) = \frac{1 - \rho}{1 - \rho z} \qquad (6\text{-}54)$$

Since $\rho < 1$ and $|z| \leq 1$ for the moment-generating functions to converge, we can expand $(1 - \rho z)^{-1}$ in an infinite series in z. Equation (6-54) then becomes

$$G_n(z) = (1 - \rho) \sum_{k=0}^{\infty} (\rho z)^k = \sum_{k=0}^{\infty} \underbrace{(1 - \rho)\rho^k}_{p_k} z^k \qquad (6\text{-}54a)$$

The coefficient of z^k is then

$$p_k = P(n = k) = (1 - \rho)\rho^k \qquad (6\text{-}55)$$

exactly as found previously for the M/M/1 case! Other message length distributions may be handled similarly, although not as simply. (Even the fixed message length case, using Eq. (6-45) in Eq. (6-37a), involves a lot of algebra in the expansion into a series in z.)

We noted earlier in this section that very useful formulas for the average number $E(n)$ of messages in the buffer and the average time delay may be derived for the M/G/1 queue. This can be done by using Eq. (6-37a) or (6-53). Thus differentiating Eq. (6-37a) once with respect to z and setting $z = 1$, it can be shown after some algebraic manipulation that

$$E(n) = \left.\frac{dG_n(z)}{dz}\right|_{z=1} = \frac{1}{1 - E(v)}\left[\frac{E(v)}{2} - E^2(v) + \frac{E(v^2)}{2}\right]$$
$$= \frac{1}{2(1 - \rho)}[\sigma_v^2 + \rho(1 - \rho)] \qquad (6\text{-}56)^*$$

*A much simpler derivation uses the buffer dynamics Eq. (6-31) directly. Squaring left- and right-hand sides of Eq. (6-31) and taking statistical averages, at equilibrium, Eq. (6-56) results. The details are carried out in the next chapter in the context of another queueing model for the concentration process.

Here $\rho \equiv E(v)$ [see Eq. (6-52)] and $\sigma_v^2 = E(v^2) - E^2(v)$ is the variance of the number of messages arriving during a random service interval.

For the M/G/1 queue we can further simplify Eq. (6-56) into a more specific form. Thus we have, from the definition of the moment-generating function,

$$\sigma_v^2 = G_v''(1) + \rho - \rho^2 \tag{6-57}$$

with G'' standing for the second derivative with respect to z. (The reader is asked to check Eq. (6-57) for himself.) But from Eq. (6-48a) for the M/G/1 queue, we have

$$G_v''(1) = \lambda^2 \left.\frac{d^2 F_\tau(s)}{ds^2}\right|_{s=0} = \lambda^2 E(\tau^2) = \lambda^2 \left[\sigma^2 + \left(\frac{1}{\mu}\right)^2\right] \tag{6-58}$$

Here σ^2 is the variance of the message-length distribution, $E(\tau^2)$ is its second moment, and use has been made of Eq. (6-49) in recognizing that the second derivative of $F_\tau(s)$ at $s = 0$ is just $E(\tau^2)$. Substituting Eq. (6-57) and (6-58) into Eq. (6-56), and recalling that $\rho = \lambda/\mu$, we get after some rewriting of terms,

$$E(n) = \left(\frac{1}{1-\rho}\right)\left[\rho - \frac{1}{2}\rho^2(1 - \mu^2\sigma^2)\right] \tag{6-59}$$

The average buffer size is thus related directly to the traffic intensity factor ρ, the average message length $1/\mu$, and the variance of the message lengths.

As an example, say the message lengths are exponentially-distributed. Then $\sigma^2 = 1/\mu^2$, and $E(n) = \rho/(1 - \rho)$, the M/M/1 result found in the previous section. Now let the messages be of *fixed* length $\tau_0 = 1/\mu$. Then $\sigma^2 = 0$, and

$$E(n) = \left(1 - \frac{1}{2}\rho\right)\left(\frac{\rho}{1-\rho}\right)$$

The average buffer occupancy is thus *reduced* over the M/M/1 case.

The average time delay of messages arriving at the buffer is now found again utilizing Little's formula. Recalling that $\rho = \lambda/\mu$, we have for the M/G/1 queue

$$E(T) = \frac{1}{\lambda}E(n) = \frac{1}{2\mu(1-\rho)}[2 - \rho(1 - \mu^2\sigma^2)] \tag{6-60}$$

For exponential message lengths with $\sigma^2\mu^2 = 1$ we again have $E(T) = 1/\mu(1 - \rho)$. For fixed-length messages we find the time delay reduced and given by $E(T) = (1 - \rho/2)/\mu(1 - \rho)$. Other cases may be found similarly.

The average time delay expression for the M/G/1 queue is thus very similar to the one found earlier for the M/M/1 queue. It differs in the second term inside the bracket of Eq. (6-60), depending only on how different $\mu^2\sigma^2$ is from 1. For message length distributions with $\sigma^2 < 1/\mu^2$, the average time delay is reduced compared to the exponential message length case. For message length distributions with $\sigma^2 > 1/\mu^2$, the average time delay is lengthened. This is intuitively obvious since a distribution with increased variance has a higher probability of longer messages, and hence the delay time is increased.

The Pollaczek-Khinchine formula of Eq. (6-60) focuses on average time delay in an M/G/1 queue. An equivalent formula in much more compact form can be written for the average time spent in the queue waiting to be served. This time is simply the delay time less time required for service (transmission). The formula for waiting time will be found useful in the next section in discussing priority queues. Specifically, let $E(W)$ be the average waiting time. The average delay time $E(T)$ is then just $E(W)$ plus the average service time (message transmission time) $1/\mu$.

$$E(T) = E(W) + \frac{1}{\mu} \qquad (6\text{-}61)$$

Substituting Eq. (6-61) into (6-60), solving for $E(W)$ and simplifying we find

$$E(W) = \frac{\lambda}{2} \frac{E(\tau^2)}{1 - \rho} \qquad (6\text{-}62)$$

The average waiting time $E(W)$ thus depends on the second moment $E(\tau^2)$ of the message-length distribution. Interestingly, a very similar expression will be found to hold true for the case of nonpreemptive priority queueing, to be discussed in the next section.

PRIORITY QUEUEING: MULTI-USER QUEUES

Messages of various priorities are very common in computer-communication systems. Short acknowledgement messages are often given priority over normal messages, users may have classes of urgent messages as contrasted to normal message traffic, two or more categories of message may traverse the network (e.g., in the SITA network teletype messages are handled at a lower priority than conversational messages), or some users may transmit shorter messages on the average than other users with priority given to these to expedite delivery overall.

It is thus of interest to extend the average time delay analysis to the case of an M/G/1 queue with multiple classes of users, each of different priority. To carry out this analysis most simply we focus on average waiting time rather than delay time. As shown by Eq. (6-61) we can always convert to delay time by adding the average message transmission time. We use the approach of A. Cobham.* We assume *nonpreemptive* priority, in which a message may move ahead of lower priority messages on the queue, but cannot preempt service of a lower priority message undergoing service (transmission).

The queueing system under study is assumed to have priorities labeled $p = 1, 2, 3. . . , r$ in order of *descending* priority. Consider a message of prior-

---

*Saaty, *Elements of Queueing Theory*, p. 232. For the original work refer to A. Cobham, *Journal of ORSA*, **2**, 1954, 70–76; **3**, 1955, 547.

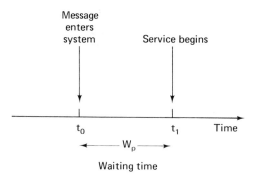

Fig. 6-9. Waiting time in a queueing system.

ity p. It arrives at time t_0 and enters service (begins transmission) at time t_1, W_p units of time later. (See Fig. 6-9.) We would like to develop a general relation for $E(W_p)$, the average waiting time of messages of priority class p. To do this we focus on the various components of W_p: there is a time T_0 required to complete the current service, there are times T_k to service m_k messages of priority $k = 1, 2 \ldots, p$ already waiting when the message under consideration arrives, and times T'_k, $k = 1, 2 \ldots, p - 1$, to service messages of higher priority that may arrive during the waiting interval and be put ahead of this message. Averaging over all of these we thus have

$$E(W_p) = E(T_0) + \sum_{k=1}^{p} E(T_k) + \sum_{k=1}^{p-1} E(T'_k) \qquad (6\text{-}63)$$

To evaluate $E(T_k)$, say there are on the average $E(m_k)$ messages of priority k waiting. If each of these requires, on the average, $1/\mu_k$ time units for service, we must have

$$E(T_k) = \frac{E(m_k)}{\mu_k} \qquad (6\text{-}64)$$

But $E(m_k)$ is just the difference between $E(n_k)$, the average number of messages waiting and in service, and the average number in service. The latter is just $\rho_k = \lambda_k/\mu_k$, assuming λ_k arrivals per unit time, on the average, of category-k messages.* From Little's theorem

$$E(n_k) = \lambda_k \bar{T} = \lambda_k \left[E(W_k) + \frac{1}{\mu_k} \right]$$

$$= E(m_k) + \rho_k$$

with $\bar{T}$ the average delay time of the average number of messages waiting. Hence,

$$E(m_k) = \lambda_k E(W_k) \qquad (6\text{-}65)$$

*The probability that a category-k message is present, when ready to be served, is ρ_k; the probability that a message of this type is missing is $1 - \rho_k$.

and
$$E(T_k) = \rho_k E(W_k) \tag{6-66}$$

Consider now the term $E(T'_k)$ in Eq. (6-63). Recall that this is the average time required to service the messages of priority k higher than p that arrive during the average waiting time $E(W_p)$. By an argument similar to that used in finding $E(T_k)$ we have
$$E(T'_k) = \rho_k E(W_p) \tag{6-67}$$

Putting all of this together we have
$$E(W_p) = E(T_0) + \sum_{k=1}^{p} \rho_k E(W_k) + E(W_p) \sum_{k=1}^{p-1} \rho_k \tag{6-68}$$

This may be solved recursively, first for $E(W_1)$, then for $E(W_2)$, and so on. It is left to the reader to show that the average waiting time for messages of priority p is then found to be given by
$$E(W_p) = \frac{E(T_0)}{(1 - \sigma_{p-1})(1 - \sigma_p)} \tag{6-69}$$

with
$$\sigma_p = \sum_{k=1}^{p} \rho_k$$

Now what is the time $E(T_0)$ required, on the average, to complete an existing service? Consider a single priority M/G/1 queue first. Comparing Eq. (6-69) and (6-62) we must have $E(T_0) = \lambda E(\tau^2)/2$ for that case. As a check, assume the message lengths are exponentially-distributed. Then it is readily shown that $E(T_0) = \rho/\mu$. This is just the probability ρ that a message is available to be served (the queue is nonempty) times the average message length $1/\mu$. More generally, for multiple priority message classes, we have
$$E(T_0) = \frac{\lambda}{2} E(\tau^2) = \frac{1}{2} \sum_{k=1}^{r} \lambda_k E(\tau_k^2)$$
$$\lambda = \sum_{k=1}^{r} \lambda_k \tag{6-70}$$

This is just the weighted sum over all priority classes of the average time required to complete service.

As an example, say there are two priority classes, $p = 1$ and 2. Assume also, for simplicity, that messages are exponentially-distributed, with average lengths $1/\mu_1$, and $1/\mu_2$, respectively. Then it is readily found from Eq. (6-69) and (6-70), with $\sigma_k^2 = 1/\mu_k^2$, and $E(\tau_k^2) = 2/\mu_k^2$, that
$$E(W_1) = \frac{(\rho_1/\mu_1) + (\rho_2/\mu_2)}{(1 - \rho_1)} \tag{6-71}$$

and
$$E(W_2) = \frac{(\rho_1/\mu_1) + (\rho_2/\mu_2)}{(1 - \rho_1)(1 - \rho_1 - \rho_2)} \tag{6-72}$$

The average waiting time of the lower prority messages ($p = 2$) is of course longer than that of the higher priority ($p = 1$) messages. The higher priority messages see effectively an M/M/1 queue (moving ahead of lower priority messages on the queue), *except* for the time required to service a message. This can be due to *either* class of messages. To find the average delay time for each, one must add the appropriate average service time to the waiting time.

It is of interest to compare these results for priority classes of messages with time delays encountered by the same messages in the no priority case. When there is no priority structure and messages are simply served first come-first served, the general M/G/1 formulation holds, and the average waiting time for any message is given by Eq. (6-62). The average delay time for a particular message class is then again given by adding the appropriate service (transmission) time parameter. As an example, again consider two classes, 1 and 2, of exponentially-distributed message lengths. The average waiting time for both types of message is

$$E(W) = \frac{(\rho_1/\mu_1) + (\rho_2/\mu_2)}{(1 - \rho)} \qquad (6\text{-}73)$$

with $\rho = \rho_1 + \rho_2$. Note by comparing this with Eq. (6-71) and (6-72) that the effect of introducing priorities is, as was to be expected, to *reduce* the time delay of the higher priority messages at the expense of the lower priority ones.

Consider some specific examples. Say that $\rho = 0.5$, with $\rho_1 = \rho_2 = 0.25$. First take the case in which both message classes have the same average message length $1/\mu = 1$ sec. Then $\lambda_1 = \lambda_2 = 0.25$ messages/sec arriving, on the average. If there is no priority structure, the two classes are obviously indistinguishable, the average waiting time is $E(W) = 1$ sec, and the average delay time is then 2 sec. Now introduce priority. Class 1 messages then wait, on the average, $0.5/0.75 = \frac{2}{3}$ sec, and their average delay time is $1\frac{2}{3}$ sec. Class 2 messages wait, on the average, $0.5/(0.75)(0.5) = 1\frac{1}{3}$ sec, and their average delay time is $2\frac{1}{3}$ sec.

Now consider a case in which the higher priority messages are relatively short acknowledgement messages and the lower priority messages are longer data packets. Let $1/\mu_1 = 0.1$ sec and $1/\mu_2 = 1$ sec. Since each message generates an acknowledgement we must have $\lambda_1 = \lambda_2$. Say this average message arrival rate is 0.5 messages/sec. Then $\rho_1 = 0.05$, $\rho_2 = 0.5$, and $\rho = 0.55$ sec. The average waiting time for acknowledgement messages is 0.53 sec (due mostly to waiting while a data message completes its service), and for data messages this is $0.53/0.45 = 1.18$ sec. If there were no priority structure, both the acknowledgement and the data messages would have to wait on the average $0.505/0.45 = 1.12$ sec. Note the large reduction in waiting time (and hence delay time) for the acknowledgement messages due to the priority scheme. The corresponding increase in delay for the data messages is relatively small. This is the reason why short messages are often given priority over long ones.

They are helped a great deal by the priority scheme, while the corresponding increase in delay of the long messages is relatively small.

An even better approach is to embed the acknowledgement message in outgoing data messages in the reverse direction. TYMNET and the ARPA network, discussed in Chap. 2, use this method as do many other networks. There are two basic reasons for using this approach where possible. First, the traffic in the network is reduced. (There are fewer pure acknowledgement messages traversing the network. These are now only needed when there is no data to send.) Second, the system is more efficient since the overhead required for ACK messages is no longer needed. The ACK portion of a data message is thus shorter than a separate ACK message. Consider the example above. Say the acknowledgement message is embedded in the data message and can now be reduced to one half of its previous length. The average data message length is thus increased to 1.05 sec. The effective traffic at the queue is now $\rho = (0.5)(1.05)$, the waiting time is $E(W) = 1.16$ sec, and the average delay time is 2.21 sec.

The above examples have been for the case of exponentially-distributed message lengths. We now conclude this section with a sample calculation of time delay in a priority queue for which messages are not exponentially-distributed. We thus use the general M/G/1 priority results of Eq. (6-69) and (6-70). This example is taken from published calculations on the SITA network,[*] described briefly in this book in Chap. 2. The SITA network has three types of messages traversing the system: conversational or Type A messages with mean length 400 bits, telegraph or Type B messages with mean length 1600 bits, and 40-bit link control messages used to control both Type A and Type B messages. The link control messages are given priority 1, the Type A messages priority 2, and the Type B messages priority 3. Assuming a 2400 bps transmission speed, the message length (service time) statistics are found to have the following characteristics:[**]

Message Type (by priority)	Mean Length $1/\mu_p$ (sec)	$E(\tau_p^2)$
1	1/60	$(1/\mu_1)^2$
2	1/6	$1.7(1/\mu_2)^2$
3	2/3	$1.4(1/\mu_3)^2$

Note that neither Type A nor Type B messages is exponentially-distributed. (For that case $E(\tau^2) = 2/\mu^2$.)

---

[*]G. J. Brandt and G. J. Chretien, "Methods to Control and Operate a Message-Switching Network," *Proc. Symposium on Computer-Communications Networks and Teletraffic*, Polytechnic Press, New York, 1972, pp. 263–76.

[**]Ibid., p. 272.

We can now apply Eq. (6-69) and (6-70) directly to calculate the waiting time and hence the average delay time for the three messages. Of primary interest is the delay time of the Type A messages (conversational and reservation-type traffic). Take the case of

$$\rho = \sum_{i=1}^{3} \rho_i = 0.7 \quad \text{and} \quad \lambda_2 = 4\lambda_3$$

(Type A messages arrive four times as often as Type B, on the average.) Letting $\lambda_1 = \lambda_2 + \lambda_3$, we have

$$E(T_0) = \frac{1}{2} \sum_{k=1}^{3} \lambda_k E(\tau_k^2) = 0.2 \text{ sec}$$

Then $E(W_2) = 0.33$ sec, and $E(T_2) = 0.5$ sec. With no priority in the system the average waiting time would be $E(T_0)/(1 - \rho) = \frac{2}{3}$ sec and the average delay time 0.83 sec. So nonpreemptive priority improves the delay time characteristic of the Type A messages considerably. It is found for this case that preemptive priority improves the characteristic even more.* (Preemptive priority, with application to this example, is considered in Problem 6.16.) These results are critical in assessing the operation of a complex network such as SITA, since the network response time (i.e., time for a message to be delivered from the sender, possibly an agent's data set, to a processing CPU and back again to the sender) is one of the critical parameters determining performance. This response time is the sum of the queueing delays, propagation delay, and computer processing time, just as pointed out in previous chapters. The system using nonpreemptive priority has an average response time, to Type A messages, worldwide, of less than 4 sec. It is apparent from the above discussion that without priority this parameter would be increased considerably.

PROBLEMS

6.1 (1) Derive the equation of state of an M/M/1 queue given by

$$(\lambda + \mu C)p_n = \mu C p_{n+1} + \lambda p_{n-1} \qquad n \geq 1$$

(2) Show that the solution for an infinite buffer is given by

$$p_n = (1 - \rho)\rho^n \qquad \rho \equiv \frac{\lambda}{\mu C}$$

(3) Show the average buffer occupancy is given by

$$E(n) = \sum_n n p_n = \frac{\rho}{1 - \rho}$$

*Ibid., p. 273.

6.2   Find the average buffer occupancy, in messages, at the outgoing link of a concentrator for the following cases (assume the infinite buffer, M/M/1 model is valid):

(1) 10 terminals, each generating on the average of one message every 4 sec, are statistically multiplexed at the concentrator. The messages are 40 bits long, on the average. The capacity of the outgoing link is $C = 1000$ bps. How does this result compare to *one* data source generating a 40-bit message every 0.4 sec, on the average?

(2) Same as (1) above, but 50 such terminals are now multiplexed. Compare this result with the 10 terminal case, each generating a message every 0.8 sec, on the average.

(3) 50 terminals as in (2) are multiplexed, but C is reduced to 600 bps.

(4) Same as (1) above, but the messages are now 200 bits long, on the average.

6.3   A concentrator buffer is modeled as an infinite M/M/1 queue.

(1) Find the average time delay (transmission time plus queueing delay) for each of the four cases of Problem 6.2.

(2) Compare the average time delay in each of the following situations:

(a) outgoing line capacity is 100 bps, $\rho = 0.1, 0.5, 0.8$

(b) capacity is 1000 bps, $\rho = 0.1, 0.5, 0.8$

(c) capacity is 10,000 bps, $\rho = 0.1, 0.5, 0.8$

The average message length is 100 bits in each of the cases.

6.4   The 10 terminals of Problem 6.2(1) each transmit at 250 bps. What capacity would be needed if they were time-multiplexed? Repeat for 50 terminals.

6.5   A concentrator buffer holds a maximum of N messages. Modeling it as an M/M/1 queue with finite buffer, find the probability that messages are blocked in each of the following cases. Compare results.

(1) $N = 2,$ $\rho = 0.1$

(2) $N = 4,$ $\rho = 0.1$

(3) $N = 4,$ $\rho = 0.8$

What is the probability the buffer is empty in each of these cases?

6.6   Consider a queue with state-dependent Poisson arrival rate λ_n and departure rate μ_n. Show that the equation governing the state probabilities after statistical equilibrium has set in is given by

$$(\lambda_n + \mu_n)p_n = \mu_{n+1}p_{n+1} + \lambda_{n-1}p_{n-1} \qquad n \geq 1$$

Show the solution to this equation is given by

$$p_n = \frac{\lambda_0 \lambda_1 \lambda_2 \dots \lambda_{n-1}}{\mu_1 \mu_2 \dots \mu_n} p_0$$

6.7 The "queue with discouragement" is one in which the arrival rates decrease with increasing queue size. Specifically, let $\lambda_n = \lambda/(n+1)$ and $\mu_n = \mu$. Show that the probability of state of the queue is given by

$$p_n = \frac{\rho^n e^{-\rho}}{n!} \qquad \rho \equiv \frac{\lambda}{\mu}$$

6.8 Extend the analysis of the queue with multiple servers discussed in this chapter to the case of a limit on the number of servers available. Thus,

$$\mu_n = n\mu \qquad n \le M$$
$$= M\mu \qquad n \ge M$$

Also $$\lambda_n = \lambda$$

Find the probability of state p_n and compare with that of Eq. (6-28a) with no limit on the number of servers.

6.9 Consider the infinite buffer with general service time distribution.

(1) Show that Eq. (6-31), relating the queue length n_j after the departure of the jth message to n_{j-1}, may be written

$$n_j = n_{j-1} - U(n_{j-1}) + v_j \qquad (6.9\text{–}1)$$

with $U(x)$ the unit step function defined by

$$U(x) = 1 \qquad x > 0$$
$$= 0 \qquad x \le 0$$

(2) Let $j \to \infty$ and assume equilibrium has set in. Show that from Eq. (6.9-1) above that

$$E(v) = E[U(n)] = P(n > 0) \equiv \rho$$

with the variables replaced by their equilibrium values.

(3) Square both sides of Eq. (6.9-1), simplify, take expectations of both sides, and let $j \to \infty$ again. Solve for the average number of messages either waiting or being transmitted and show it is given by

$$E(n) = \frac{E(v)}{2} + \frac{\sigma_v^2}{2(1 - E(v))} \qquad (6.9\text{–}2)$$

Here $E(v) < 1$ is the average number of arrivals in a service interval and $\sigma_v^2 = E(v^2) - E^2(v)$ is the variance of the arrivals in a service interval. This is exactly Eq. (6-56) derived much more simply, extending the M/M/1 queue result to the much more general case. [Hint: $nU(n) = n$, $U^2(n) = U(n)$. Why?

Also,

$$E(n_{j-1}v_j) = E(n_{j-1})E(v_j)$$

if messages arrive independently in adjacent service intervals.]

6.10 *Drill on moment-generating functions.*

Consider a discrete random variable x with probabilities $p_k \equiv P(x = k)$, $k = 0, 1, 2, \ldots$. Then

$$G_x(z) \equiv E(z^x) = \sum_{k=0}^{\infty} p_k z^k$$

(1) Show
$$G_x(1) = 1$$

$$\frac{dG_x(z)}{dz}\bigg|_{z=1} = E(x)$$

$$\frac{d^2G_x(z)}{dz^2}\bigg|_{z=1} = E(x^2) - E(x)$$

(2) Find $G_x(z)$ and $E(x)$ and σ_x^2 directly from $G_x(z)$ for the following examples:

(a) *Bernoulli distribution.* Let $x = 1$ with probability p, $x = 0$ with probability $q = 1 - p$.

$$(G_x(z) = q + pz, \quad E(x) = p, \quad E(x^2) = p, \quad \text{and} \quad \sigma_x^2 = pq)$$

(b) *Binomial distribution.*

$$p_k = \binom{m}{k} p^k q^{m-k} \qquad q = 1 - p$$

$$(G_x(z) = (pz + q)^m, \quad E(x) = mp, \quad \sigma_x^2 = mpq)$$

(Hint: Let $x = \sum_{i=1}^{m} x_i$, the x_i's independent Bernoulli variables.)

(c) *Poisson distribution.*

$$p_k = \mu^k \frac{e^{-\mu}}{k!} \qquad k = 0, 1, 2, \ldots$$

$$(G_x(z) = e^{-\mu}e^{\mu z}, \quad E(x) = \mu = \sigma_x^2, \quad \text{from} \quad G_x(z))$$

(d) *Geometric distribution.*

$$p_k = pq^{k-1} \qquad q = 1 - p$$

$$\left(G_x(z) = \frac{pz}{1 - qz}, \quad E(x) = \frac{1}{p}, \quad \sigma_x^2 = \frac{q}{p^2}\right)$$

6.11 Starting with Eq. (6-53), derive Eq. (6-59) for the average number of messages waiting in an $M/G/1$ queue. From this find the *Pollaczek-Khinchine* formula, Eq. (6-60), for the average time delay in an $M/G/1$ queue.

6.12 Service-time distributions in queueing studies are often modeled by the gamma distribution*

$$\frac{\beta(\beta x)^{k-1}e^{-\beta x}}{\Gamma(k)} \qquad x > 0, \quad k > 0$$

(1) Sketch this distribution for $k = \frac{1}{2}, 1, 2, 4$.

(2) Show $E(x) = k/\beta$ and $\sigma^2 = k/\beta^2$

(3) Specialize the Pollaczek-Khinchine formula to messages whose lengths obey a gamma distribution. Compare the ratio of average delay time to average service (transmission) time for $k = \frac{1}{2}, 1, 2, \infty$. What types of messages do the cases $k = 1$ and ∞ represent?

6.13 Assume there are r classes of messages, each arriving randomly at a Poisson rate at a queue. Service is first-come-first-served, with no priority. Use the approach used in the analysis of priority queueing in this chapter to find the average waiting time in the queue and show Eq. (6-62) results. Use that result to derive the Pollaczek-Khinchine formula of Eq. (6-60).

6.14 Derive Eq. (6-69), the average waiting time equation for an M/G/1 queue with priority classes.

6.15 Refer to the discussion at the end of this chapter on the priority structure of messages in the SITA network.** Calculate and plot the average time delay for Type A (conversational) and Type B (telegraph) messages as a function of the total traffic intensity ρ, and compare. Assume $\lambda_2 = 4\lambda_3$.

6.16 The equation for the average time delay of priority 2 messages in an M/G/1 queue with *preemptive priority* may be shown to be given by†

$$E(T_2) = \frac{1}{2}\frac{\sum\limits_{i=1}^{2}\lambda_i E(\tau_i^2)}{(1 - \rho_1)(1 - \rho_1 - \rho_2)} + \frac{1/\mu_2}{1 - \rho_1}$$

Use this equation to calculate the average time delay of Type A messages in the SITA network under a preemptive priority discipline for the case of $\lambda_2 = 4\lambda_3$ and compare with the nonpreemptive calculation of Problem 6.15.††

---

*W. Feller, *An Introduction to Probability Theory and Its Applications*, vol. **II**, John Wiley & Sons, Inc., New York, 2nd ed., 1971, pp. 47, 48.

**G. J. Brandt and G. J. Chretien, "Methods to Control and Operate a Message-Switching Network," *Proc. Symposium on Computer-Communications Networks and Teletraffic*, Polytechnic Press, New York, 1972, pp. 271–74.

†Saaty, *Elements of Queueing Theory*.

††See Brandt and Chretien, "Message-Switching Network," Fig. 3, p. 273, for additional curves.

Concentration and Buffering in Store–and–Forward Networks

7

In Chap. 3 through 5 we concentrated on overall network design—the allocation of trunk capacity to links of a network and its relation to message time delay, time delay-capacity-cost trade-offs, the effect of network structure and message routing strategy on time delay and cost, and so on. We shall return to some of these global questions in later chapters, discussing in more detail, for example, routing in networks, flow control and topological optimization. In this chapter and the one following we focus more specifically on the design of concentrators using asynchronous or statistical multiplexing for entering messages into the network. In Chap. 12 and 13 we shall discuss two other techniques, polling and random access, for entering messages into a network. The design questions to be considered in this part of the book, focusing on buffering considerations at a concentrator, include the following:

1. What size buffers should be used to keep the message blocking probability to within specified design limits?

2. How is this related to message statistics and to outgoing trunk capacity?

3. What are the time delays expected for varying traffic and message statistics?

4. What is the effect of dynamic buffering and message block storage?

Some of these questions can be answered rather quickly to a first approximation by assuming Poisson statistics and exponential message lengths and using the M/M/1 queue analysis discussed in the previous chapter. We have already used the simple time delay result $T = 1/(\mu C - \lambda)$ in discussing network capacity allocations. In this chapter and the one following we shall try to be more realistic, however, using more appropriate models for message statistics. We shall in fact compare these possibly more realistic models with the much simpler M/M/1 approach.

Some of the basic problems involved in allowing messages to enter a network, in allocating buffer storage, in assembling them, either singly or in combined fashion, in block form, and then reading them out over a specified trunk, have been noted in Chap. 2 in discussing examples of representative systems. More detailed discussions of the various types of concentration methods, of typical processor configurations, and of the software problems involved, may be found in the current literature.* In this chapter and Chap. 8 we focus on more quantitative aspects in an attempt to come up with specific design information.

Note from the above summary of the concentration process that there are essentially three parts to the process:

1. entry of messages

2. message assembly

3. message readout.

Entry may be carried out by a scanning process (either sequentially or with priority) in which the various ports are continually scanned following a predetermined strategy to see if messages are waiting to enter the system, or an interrupt procedure may be used in which an incoming message notifies the processor that it desires entry. For the purposes of this chapter we assume that entry into the nodal processor is so rapid as to be almost instantaneous so that we shall effectively ignore the type of strategy used. (The various strategies differ of course in their hardware and software requirements.) We shall focus here, as already noted, on the buffering problems related to message assembly and message readout.

A simplified model of the processor now might look as shown in Fig. 7-1. The outgoing block assembly box represents the process of forming message packets and adding control and header information. It could very

---

*See, e.g., the following three papers in the special issue on Computer-Communications, *Proc. IEEE*, **60**, no. 11, Nov. 1972, as well as references included therein:

D. R. Doll, "Multiplexing and Concentration," pp. 1313–21;

C. B. Newport and J. Ryzlak, "Communication Processors," pp. 1321–32;

D. L. Mills, "Communication Software," pp. 1333–41.

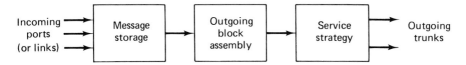

Fig. 7-1. Simplified model, processor.

well be combined with the message storage box. The service strategy box includes the process of scanning the buffer for messages destined for a particular output link as well as the strategy of assigning one or more trunks needed to handle messages over that link.

Some of the particular design questions that have been considered in the literature and which we would like to discuss in these two chapters include, as already noted in part, buffer sizes needed, the effect of a varying number of output trunks, dynamic buffering, message storage by block and optimum block size, the effect of message overhead, etc. Software considerations play a key role in the entire process of message concentration. The complexity of the software needed and the resultant program storage requirements are critical in any real design. These problems are difficult to handle quantitatively, however. Instead we shall focus here on the much simpler queueing-type questions relating to the probability of buffer overflow, the average message time delay due to buffering (determined from the average buffer occupancy), and the number of customers (traffic) that may be accommodated for specified values of buffer overflow probability and time delay.

In developing design parameters for the concentrator or communications processor we shall start with the simplest model and work our way up, adding complexity as needed. Thus the first model we shall assume, essentially a simplification of Fig. 7-1, consists of an infinite length buffer, with discrete length messages arriving according to some specified statistical distribution, and with an output trunk *synchronously* removing message units at a rate of 1 message unit/Δ sec.* (The unit here can be bit, byte, character, or group of characters, of fixed duration.) The line capacity C is then just $C = 1/\Delta$ units/ sec. A diagram of this simple model is shown in Fig. 7-2a. The analysis of this simple queueing model is readily extended to the multiple user model of Fig. 7-2b, with inputs assumed statistically multiplexed.

We shall be able to come up with expressions in both cases for the average buffer occupancy or average message time delay as a function of the input traffic as well as buffer sizes needed to attain a specified blocking probability. These differ from the previous M/M/1 or M/G/1 queueing

---

*W. W. Chu and A. G. Konheim, "On the Analysis and Modeling of a Class of Computer-Communication Systems," *IEEE Trans. on Communications*, **COM-20**, no. 3, June 1972, part II, special issue on computer-communications, 645–60.

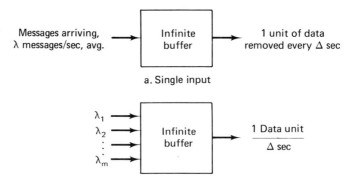

Fig. 7-2. Processor queueing model for analysis.

results: first, in the more realistic assumption of *discrete* rather than continuous message statistics; second, in the emphasis on storage of data units rather than messages as in the M/M/1 case. Buffer design focuses on data unit (bit, byte, or character) storage. We shall show how one determines the probability of exceeding a specified level of buffer occupancy. For this probability small ($\ll 1$) it is very nearly the same as the probability of buffer overflow (or message blocking) in the finite buffer case, so that design curves can be obtained relating buffer size to the expected number of message arrivals and average message length, for a specified probability.

We shall check these results in the next chapter by reviewing some work appearing in the literature that takes finite buffer size into account. We shall then go on to discuss dynamic buffering and the storage of messages from multiple inputs in block format. In all of this we try where possible to compare the results obtained with those obtained assuming exponential message lengths, the M/M/1 queue assumption.

To begin our analysis of the single input model of Fig. 7-2, we resort to the strategem used in the previous chapter in discussing M/G/1 queues, as well as the analysis there of time delay in priority queues. We focus on significant time intervals encountered in the queueing process. In the case of the M/G/1 queue these times were the message completion times and were, of necessity, themselves random variables (see Fig. 6-8). In this case we assume a synchronous output line (trunk) outputting precisely one data unit (bit, byte, or character, for example) every Δ sec.* The time interval is then always Δ sec. The statistics of operation of the processor models of Fig. 7-2 will be written in terms of the states of the buffer at the end of each time interval Δ sec long. Except for the emphasis here on time intervals required to transmit one data unit, the approach used is essentially the same as that of the

*Ibid.

M/G/1 queue in the previous chapter, and the equations developed will be identical: the ones here focusing on the number of data units residing in the buffer, the ones in Chap. 6 on messages. Consider therefore the timing diagram shown in Fig. 7-3. In any one time interval Δ sec long, one unit of data is removed from the buffer *if* the buffer had at least one unit stored at the beginning of that interval. Any unit of data entering the buffer during that time interval must wait to at least the next time interval to be served. Let L_j be the number of data units residing in the buffer at the end of the jth time

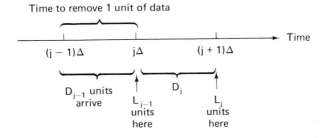

Fig. 7-3. Timing diagram.

interval just prior to the beginning of the $(j + 1)$ interval as shown in Fig. 7-3. Let D_j units be the number of data units arriving during the jth interval. (It is apparent that the average of D_j must be less than 1 to prevent the buffer from building up indefinitely.) Then the relation between the number of units buffered at the end of the jth time interval and those buffered at the end of the $(j - 1)$ interval must be given by

$$
\begin{aligned}
L_j &= (L_{j-1} - 1) + D_j, \quad \text{if} \quad L_{j-1} \geq 1 \\
&= D_j \qquad\qquad\quad \text{if} \quad L_{j-1} = 0
\end{aligned}
\tag{7-1}
$$

Using this simple relation one can obtain the essential statistics of operation of the processor models of Fig. 7-2. As noted above, this equation is exactly of the form of Eq. (6-31) of Chap. 6, showing the variation of message queue lengths with time in the M/G/1 queue.

Equation (7-1) can be rewritten in various equivalent forms from which equilibrium statistics can be found. For example, the form of Eq. (6-31a) gives rise to an expression suitable for analysis with moment-generating functions, from which the equilibrium probabilities of state of the buffer can be derived. This was carried out in detail in Chap. 6 in discussing the M/G/1 queue. We review the application of that approach to the case here, involving synchronous transmission and data unit storage, later in this chapter. We focus instead at this point on another form of Eq. (7-1) from which average buffer lengths and average time delay are more readily found. The application to the M/G/1 queue appears in Problem 6.9.

Specifically, a little thought will indicate that Eq. (7-1) may be written in the following equivalent form,* with $U(x)$ the unit step function:

$$L_j = L_{j-1} - U(L_{j-1}) + D_j \tag{7-2}$$

Here $U(x) = 1$, $x > 0$; $U(x) = 0$, $x \leq 0$. If the system has been under operation for some time, statistically stationary conditions prevail. The average buffer occupancy must thus be independent of time and $E(L_j) = E(L_{j-1}) = E(L)$, with $E(\ )$ the symbol commonly used to represent statistical average. Then from Eq. (7-2), $E[U(L_{j-1})] = E(D_j) = \mu_D$, with μ_D the average number of data units entering the buffer in Δ sec.

To find $E(L)$, the average number of units of data in the buffer as a function of μ_D, the average number entering in Δ sec, we use a simple trick.** Square both sides of Eq. (7-2), note that $xU(x) = x$, if $x \geq 0$ (as must be true for L_{j-1}) and $U^2(x) = U(x)$. Taking the average of both sides with the system assumed to be statistically stationary and then collecting terms, we find

$$E(L) = \frac{\mu_D}{2} + \frac{\sigma_D^2}{2(1 - \mu_D)} \tag{7-3}$$

with $\mu_D = E(D)$, as already noted, and $\sigma_D^2 = E(D^2) - E^2(D)$, the variance of the units of data arriving in Δ sec. This is identical with Eq. (6-56) of Chap. 6, with all parameters there referring to *message* arrivals in a *random* service interval. Here the parameters refer to *data unit* arrivals in a *fixed* service interval Δ.

Equation (7-3) is the basic relation from which we can study the processor models of Fig. 7-2. Note incidentally that $\mu_D < 1$. Otherwise $E(L)$ would blow up. This is exactly the point made above. μ_D thus plays the role of the traffic intensity parameter ρ introduced in Chap. 6. (See Eq. (6-56), for example.) We shall in fact use ρ for μ_D later in this chapter after introducing some specific models for message statistics. The fact that μ_D is the same as the traffic intensity parameter is readily demonstrated by considering the basic definition of that parameter: it is the ratio of average traffic rate into the system (the load or demand on the system) to the system transmission capacity. Let the average rate of arrival of data units be α. The capacity of the system is just $C = 1/\Delta$ data units/sec. Then $\rho = \alpha\Delta$ = the average number of data units arriving in Δ sec, or just $\mu_D = E(D)$.

To go any further with the development in this chapter, in particular to obtain design curves and tables for statistical concentrators, we must know something of the characteristics of the input data. This is necessary, for example, to calculate the appropriate parameters in Eq. (7-3). Studies have been made of typical computer-communication systems for this purpose. For

---

*J. D. Spragins, "Loop Transmission Systems—Mean Value Analysis," *IEEE Trans. on Communications*, **COM-20**, no. 3, part II, June 1972, 592–602.
**Ibid.

example, a study of long holding-time systems (i.e., those in which connections are maintained for from 15—30 min., typical of business and scientific applications requiring extensive computations) has shown that messages may be modeled as a Poisson process with the length of messages geometrically-distributed.* The studies also show that the traffic in the outbound direction, from computer to user, is an order of magnitude greater than in the inbound, user-computer direction. (This point has been noted by operators of many typical systems.)** Furthermore during the call interval the user is active only 5% of the time, the computer 30% of the time. This demonstrates the desirability of statistically multiplexing a group of terminals at the concentrator, as is the case in our discussion of the processor.

For short holding-time systems, those with holding times of seconds to 1—2 minutes, and typical of inquiry-response systems (airline reservation, on-line banking, credit bureau, production control, etc.), character interarrival times were found in a related study to be given by the sum of two gamma distributions (not quite the exponential characteristics of Poisson distributions), while the number of data segments per call was again geometrically-distributed.† The user send-time was only 15% of the holding time, again showing the desirability of statistical multiplexing.

To apply Eq. (7-3) we shall assume input messages to be Poisson-distributed with the message *length* given by the geometric distribution. This agrees with the measured results for long holding-time systems quoted above. Thus, say M messages are received in the Δ sec interval. M can be 0, 1, 2, ..., k, ... For a Poisson distribution having an average of λ messages/sec, or $\lambda\Delta$ messages in Δ sec, the probability of receiving k messages in Δ sec is

$$P[M = k] = \frac{(\lambda\Delta)^k e^{-\lambda\Delta}}{k!} \qquad k = 0, 1, 2, \ldots \qquad (7\text{-}4)$$

Let X_j be the length, in data units (bits, bytes, characters, etc.) of the jth message. By geometric distribution we mean the probability of one unit of length is some number $p \leq 1$, the probability of two units is pq, with $q = 1 - p$, the probability of three units is pq^2, and so on. The probability that

---

*E. Fuchs and P. E. Jackson, "Estimates of Distributions of Random Variables for Certain Computer-Communications Traffic Models," *Communications of the ACM*, **13**, no. 12, Dec. 1970, 752–57.

See, for example, the discussion of the TYMNET and GE networks in M. Schwartz et al., "Terminal-Oriented Computer-Communication Networks," *Proc. IEEE*, **60, no. 11, Nov. 1972, 1411, 1415.

†A. L. Dudick et al., "Data Traffic Measurements for Inquiry-Response Computer-Communication Systems," Info Process 71, *Proc. IFIP*, Ljubljana, Yugoslavia, Aug. 1971, North-Holland Publishing Co., pp. 634–41. Both this reference and the one noted above by E. Fuchs and P. E. Jackson have been reprinted in the book, *Advances in Computer-Communications*, W. W. Chu, ed., Artech House, Inc., Dedham, Mass., 1974, 2–15.

the message is r units in length is

$$P[X_j = r] = pq^{r-1} \qquad r = 1, 2, \ldots \qquad q = 1 - p \qquad (7\text{-}5)$$

This distribution is diagrammed in Fig. 7-4 for the special case of $p = q = \frac{1}{2}$. Note that the probabilities decrease in geometric proportion, hence the name geometric distribution. (Note also that this is essentially an *exponential* decrease. We shall, in fact, find this *discrete* exponential well-approximated by the *continuous* exponential of M/M/1 theory for $p \ll 1$, in which case the messages have relatively high probabilities of being much more than one unit in length. For long messages the discreteness of the message length is less noticeable, and a continuous approximation would be expected to be quite valid.)

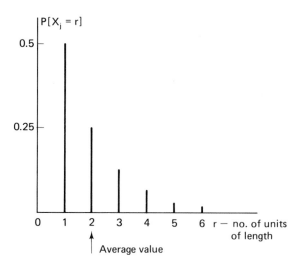

Fig. 7-4. Geometric distribution ($p = 0.5$).

As a check, we know that all the probabilities must sum to 1. Using the well-known sum of geometric series we have

$$\sum_{r=1}^{\infty} pq^{r-1} = \frac{p}{1 - q} = 1$$

In addition, the average value of the message is given by

$$E(X_j) = \sum_{r=1}^{\infty} rP[X_j = r] = \sum_{r=1}^{\infty} rpq^{r-1} = \frac{1}{p} \qquad (7\text{-}6)$$

The average length is just $1/p$ units. $1/p$ thus plays the same role here as $1/\mu$ in the exponential distribution. For $p = 0.5$, the average message length is two units. This is indicated in Fig. 7-4. One also finds that the variance of the geometric distribution is given by

$$\sigma_x^2 = \frac{q}{p^2} \tag{7-7}$$

To find the arrival statistics of the data units entering the buffer, we must combine the Poisson-distribution of messages with the geometric distribution of lengths for each message. We write the number of units of data received in an interval Δ sec long as

$$D = X_1 + X_2 + X_3 + \cdots + X_M \tag{7-8}$$

A little thought will indicate that if each message is assumed to have the same average length $1/p$, the overall average of the units of data received in Δ sec is

$$E(D) = \mu_D = E(M)E(X) = \frac{\lambda\Delta}{p} \tag{7-9}$$

This is just the expression we use in evaluating the expected buffer occupancy $E(L)$, given by Eq. (7-3). Some calculation, using Eq. (7-8), also provides the variance of D, appearing in Eq. (7-3):*

$$\sigma_D^2 = E(M)\sigma_x^2 + \sigma_M^2 E^2(X) \tag{7-10}$$

For Poisson message arrivals, $E(M) = \sigma_M^2 = \lambda\Delta$. Hence, for this case,

$$\sigma_D^2 = \lambda\Delta E(X^2)$$

$$= \frac{\lambda\Delta}{p^2}(1 + q) = \frac{\mu_D}{p}(1 + q) \tag{7-10a}$$

using Eq. (7-6) and (7-7).

Using Eq. (7-10a) in (7-3) provides an expression for the average data unit buffer occupancy that is reminiscent of the result obtained for average message occupancy in M/G/1 queues. Here we have

$$E(L) = \frac{\mu_D}{2} + \frac{\lambda\Delta}{2} \frac{E(X^2)}{1 - \mu_D} \tag{7-11}$$

The M/G/1 result obtained by rewriting Eq. (6-59), with $E(\tau^2) = \sigma^2 + 1/\mu^2$, is readily found to be

$$E(n) = \rho + \frac{\lambda^2}{2} \frac{E(\tau^2)}{(1 - \rho)} \tag{7-12}$$

Here $E(\tau^2)$ is the second moment of the message length distribution. As a check, the average time delay in the M/G/1 case is just

$$E(T) = \frac{E(n)}{\lambda} = \frac{1}{\mu} + \frac{\lambda}{2} \frac{E(\tau^2)}{(1 - \rho)}$$

The second term is just the waiting time expression of Eq. (6-62) in Chap. 6. Note the similarity in the two results. In particular note again the similarity

---

*This is done by forming the expression for the variance of D and then, conditioning on M, averaging first with respect to the random variable X. Then, averaging over M, Eq. (7-10) is obtained. Details are left to the reader. (See Problem 7.2.)

of μ_D and p. But recall again that $E(L)$ represents the average number of *data units* stored, while $E(n)$ is the average number of *messages* stored.

As a check, assume messages are all one unit long. This is then the case of fixed length packets. It is then left for the reader to show that both Eq. (7-11) and (7-12) provide the same expressions. For example

$$E(n) = \left(\frac{p}{1-p}\right)\left[1 - \frac{p}{2}\right] \tag{7-13}$$

and

$$E(L) = \left(\frac{\mu_D}{1-\mu_D}\right)\left[1 - \frac{\mu_D}{2}\right] \tag{7-14}$$

$\mu_D = \lambda\Delta$ in this case. This is as to be expected since with fixed length messages, the average number of messages stored must be the same as the average number of data units stored. The dimensions of Eq. (7-13) and (7-14) are however different—the first being given in messages, the second in data units. Note again, from the form of Eq. (7-14) in comparison with Eq. (7-13), that the parameter μ_D plays the role of a traffic intensity parameter. That this is generally true for all values of average message length $1/p$ is readily appreciated from the expression for μ_D given by Eq. (7-9). For, as stated earlier, the capacity of the trunk in the case of Fig. 7-2 is just $C = 1/\Delta$ units of data/sec. The quantity λ/p represents the average rate of arrival of data units. (λ is the average rate of arrival of messages, and each message has an average length of $E(X) = 1/p$ data units.) The ratio of the average rate of arrival of data units to the output trunk capacity, in data units/sec, is just the traffic intensity ρ and is of course also $\mu_D = \lambda\Delta/p$. As a check, note that $1/p$, the average message length, is equivalent to $1/\mu$ in the exponentially-distributed length case. ($\lambda\Delta/p$) here is thus equivalent to the parameter ($\lambda/\mu C$) introduced in earlier chapters as a measure of traffic intensity. We thus have

$$\rho \equiv \mu_D = \frac{\lambda\Delta}{p} < 1 \tag{7-15}$$

We now use Eq. (7-3), (7-9), (7-10a), and (7-15) to carry out some calculations of average buffering occupancy and message time delay (to be discussed shortly) for various traffic intensities and message lengths obeying a geometric distribution. The results are tabulated in Table 7-1. They are there compared with the time delays calculated using an M/M/1 model as an approximation. Consider the average buffer occupancy $E(L)$ first, as shown in the table.

Note from the table that for a given traffic intensity ρ, the average buffer occupancy $E(L)$ goes up more than proportionately as the average message length increases. For example, for $\rho = 0.6$, 1.05 units of data wait in the buffer, on the average, if the messages are of unity length. (This could be 1 bit, 1 byte, or 1 character, for example.) If the messages are now doubled to two units of length on the average, but with ρ still held fixed at 0.6, $E(L) = 2.55$,

TABLE 7-1

AVERAGE BUFFER OCCUPANCY AND MESSAGE TIME DELAY

$1/p$ (message length in units of data)	p	Buffer occupancy, $E(L)$ (units of data)	Time delay $E(T)/\Delta$	$E(T)/\Delta$ (M/M/1 approx)
$1\ (\sigma_D^2 = p)$	0.1	0.105	1.05	1.1
	0.2	0.225	1.125	1.25
	0.4	0.534	1.33	1.67
	0.6	1.05	1.75	2.5
	0.8	2.4	3	5
	0.9	5	5.6	10
$2\ (\sigma_D^2 = 3p)$	0.1	0.217	2.17	2.2
	0.2	0.475	2.375	2.5
	0.4	1.2	3	3.3
	0.6	2.55	4.25	5
	0.8	6.4	8	10
	0.9	14	15.4	20
$4\ (\sigma_D^2 = 7p)$	0.1	0.439	4.39	4.4
	0.2	0.975	4.88	5
	0.4	2.53	6.32	6.6
	0.6	5.55	9.25	10
	0.8	14.4	18	20
	0.9	32	35	40

more than twice 1.05. Doubling the average message length again to 4, $E(L) = 5.55$, again more than twice 2.55. This is readily explained by referring to Eq. (7-10a) for the variance of the data units arriving in Δ sec. According to this equation the variance or *spread* of the number of units of data arriving increases as the average message length $1/p$ *increases*. For a fixed traffic intensity p (say $p = 0.2$, for example), the message arrival rate λ must decrease as $1/p$ increases to keep the average number of data units $\mu_D = p$ fixed. But the increase in spread means a correspondingly greater probability that larger numbers of data units will arrive, and hence the average buffer occupancy must increase. This is borne out by Eq. (7-3) showing $E(L)$ increasing with σ_D^2.

Now consider the two columns of average time delay shown in Table 7-1. The last column has been calculated simply by using the M/M/1 equation

$$E(T) = \frac{1}{\mu C - \lambda} = \frac{1}{\mu C(1 - p)} = \frac{\Delta}{\mu(1 - p)}$$

using $C = 1/\Delta$, as noted previously. This assumes messages are exponentially-distributed in length rather than geometrically-distributed, as has been the case here, and takes $1/\mu = 1/p$, i.e., the same average length as with the geometric model. The other column represents the average time delay calculated using the geometric distribution. It has already been pointed out that for long messages, the discrete (geometric) and continuous (exponential) models should approach one another, and this is borne out by the case $1/p = 4$. The exponential (M/M/1) assumption tends to provide conservative estimates of time delay.

The time delay calculation for the geometric model is carried out by again invoking Little's formula. Recall from the previous chapter that this is a queueing theory formula stating generally that average time delay times customer arrival rate must equal the average number of customers waiting on a queue. For our application we have the average arrival rate of units of data given by μ_D/Δ. Hence we get

$$E(T) \cdot \frac{\mu_D}{\Delta} = E(L) \tag{7-14}$$

Then

$$\frac{E(T)}{\Delta} = \frac{E(L)}{\mu_D}$$

$$= \frac{1}{2} + \frac{\sigma_D^2}{2\mu_D(1 - \mu_D)} \tag{7-15}$$

$$= \frac{1}{2} + \frac{\sigma_D^2}{2p(1 - p)}$$

from Eq. (7-3). For the case of Poisson message arrivals with geometric message lengths we have, using Eq. (7-9) and (7-10a),

$$\frac{E(T)}{\Delta} = \frac{1}{p(1 - p)}\left(1 - \frac{pp}{2}\right) \tag{7-16}$$

Eq. (7-16) was used in calculating the entries in Table 7-1. Note that for $p \to 0$ $((1/p) \gg 1)$, the case of long message lengths, on the average,

$$\frac{E(T)}{\Delta} \longrightarrow \frac{1}{p(1 - p)} \qquad \frac{1}{p} \gg 1 \tag{7-17}$$

just the M/M/1 result, if we let $1/p = 1/\mu$. Eq. (7-16) also indicates that, for the shorter message lengths, the time delay is less than that calculated assuming an M/M/1 model.

As an application of this material, say data traffic of intensity $p = 0.6$ is buffered prior to being released over a trunk of capacity $C = 2400$ bps or 300 characters/sec, assuming 8-bit characters as the unit of data. Then $\Delta = \frac{1}{300} = 3.3$ msec is the time for transmission of 1 character of data. (On the average, 0.6 character arrives in this time arrival.) If the messages arriving are all 1 character in length $(1/p = 1)$, the average buffer occupancy will be 1.05 characters, and the average message time delay, due to buffering *and* to transmission time, will be $E(T) = 1.75\,\Delta = 5.8$ msec. The M/M/1 approximation would have given 2.5 Δ or 8.3 msec. If the messages arriving average two characters in length $(1/p = 2)$, $E(L) = 2.55$ characters is the average buffer occupancy, and the average time delay is $E(T) = 4.25\,\Delta = 14$ msec. The corresponding M/M/1 result is 16.5 msec. Finally, if $1/p = 4$ characters, $E(L) = 5.55$ characters, and $E(T) = 9.25 \, \Delta = 31$ msec. The M/M/1 result is 33 msec.

Now consider the extension of the results just found to the very important case of the concentration or combining of several terminals. This is the example shown in Fig. 7-2b. If we assume statistical multiplexing of several inputs on a first come-first served basis, as was mentioned in the beginning of this chapter, then it is apparent that we are simply adding up the message arrivals on a statistical basis. If the ith input port of m ports connected provides D_i units of data in Δ sec, the total number of units of data arriving is

$$D = \sum_{i=1}^{m} D_i \tag{7-18}$$

Equations (7-3) and (7-15) for average buffer occupancy and message time delay are still applicable with

$$\rho = \mu_D = \sum_{i=1}^{m} \mu_{Di}, \qquad \sigma_D^2 = \sum_{i=1}^{m} \sigma_{Di}^2 \tag{7-19}$$

with μ_{Di} and σ_{Di}^2 the statistical parameters of the ith terminal.

In particular, if the messages at all inputs have the same geometric length distribution so that $p_i = p$ for each terminal while the message arrival rates are λ_i, $i = 1, 2, \ldots, m$, as in Fig. 7-2b, we have

$$\mu_D = \frac{\lambda \Delta}{p}$$

as before, with

$$\lambda = \sum_{i=1}^{m} \lambda_i \tag{7-20}$$

The previous results are thus still appropriate, with an equivalent message rate defined given by the sum of the individual message rates. When we talk of a traffic intensity $\rho = \mu_D$ we thus talk of the *overall* intensity. For $\rho = 0.6$ and 10 terminals inputting the concentrator of Fig. 7-2b, the 10 terminals *together* should not produce more than 0.6 units of data in the Δ sec interval. We shall return to these considerations with some specific design calculations after first discussing probabilities of buffer occupancy.

Note that thus far we have only discussed the *average* occupancy of a buffer as a function of input message statistics. This is extremely useful information since it provides us quickly with some knowledge of the number of data characters typically stored in a buffer and, perhaps more important, is related by Little's formula to the average time delay expected to be incurred by messages entering an outgoing link buffer. It doesn't provide us with specific design information as to buffer size needed for a particular system. For this purpose we must talk more precisely of the buffer size needed for a specified probability of buffer overflow.

In this chapter we have focused on infinite buffers (Fig. 7-2) to simplify the analysis. Strictly speaking, for such buffers one never gets buffer overflow. However, if for such a buffer we find the probability of N characters or more stored to be a rare event (say a probability of 10^{-3} or less), then it stands to reason that limiting the buffer size to N characters shouldn't affect the results very much. This is precisely the procedure followed: Assume an infinite buffer, as in Fig. 7-2. Calculate for this model of the buffer and specified input message statistics the probability that the buffer occupancy is greater than some number N for various values of N. For this probability small ($<10^{-3}$, for example), it should be very nearly the same as the probability of buffer overflow for a finite buffer with a maximum capacity of N. In the next chapter we substantiate this approach by summarizing some work in finite buffers reported on in the literature.

The calculation of the probability that the number of characters L (or any other units of data) in the buffer exceeds a specified number N depends of course on the determination of the probabilities of state of the buffer. It turns out that the analysis here is identical to that carried out in Chap. 6 on the M/G/1 buffer, with the crucial difference being that there we were calculating the probability of having n *messages* in a buffer, while here we are evaluating the probability that L *data units* reside in the buffer.

Specifically, the approach used here to determine the probabilities of state of a buffer with data units synchronously removed, 1 per Δ sec, starts with the basic Eq. (7-1) governing the flow of data units into and out of the buffer. But note that this is identical with Eq. (6-31) of Chap. 6 describing the message contents of an M/G/1 queue. That equation led to Eq. (6-37a) relating the moment-generating function $G_n(z)$ of the number of messages residing at equilibrium in the M/G/1 buffer to the moment-generating function $G_v(z)$ of the message arrivals. It is thus apparent that a similar equation must hold here with data units replacing messages. In particular, we must have as the moment-generating function of the data units stored in the buffer,

$$G_L(z) = \frac{(1 - \mu_D)(z - 1)G_D(z)}{z - G_D(z)} \qquad (7\text{-}21)$$

with $G_D(z)$ the moment-generating function of the data unit arrival process D. This is the basic equation from which the desired state probabilities may be found. For recall again the definition of the moment-generating function

$$G_L(z) = \sum_{j=0}^{\infty} p_j z^j \qquad (7\text{-}22)$$

with p_j the probability that there are $L = j$ data units in the buffer. With $G_D(z)$ given, we find $G_L(z)$. Expanding this in a power series in z and picking off the appropriate coefficients of z^k, $k = 1, 2, \ldots$, we can find the desired probabilities of buffer occupancy, p_1, p_2, p_3, etc. The probability that the number of characters L in the buffer exceeds some number N is then given by

$$P(L > N) = p_{N+1} + p_{N+2} + \cdots$$

$$= \sum_{k=N+1}^{\infty} p_k \qquad (7\text{-}23)$$

Chu and Konheim have used this technique to analyze the synchronous system of Fig. 7-2.*

As an example, say the input messages are Poisson-distributed and all are of single character length. (This corresponds to $1/p = 1$ in the discussion earlier.) The probability that k data units (characters) arrive in Δ sec is then just the probability that k messages arrive. But from Eq. (7-4) we have, with $D = M$,

$$P(D = k) = \frac{(\lambda\Delta)^k e^{-\lambda\Delta}}{k!} \qquad k = 0, 1, 2, \ldots \qquad (7\text{-}24)$$

The moment-generating function in this case is given by

$$G_D(z) = \sum_{k=0}^{\infty} P(D = k)z^k$$

$$= \sum_{k=0}^{\infty} \frac{(\lambda\Delta z)^k e^{-\lambda\Delta}}{k!} \qquad (7\text{-}25)$$

$$= e^{-\lambda\Delta} e^{\lambda\Delta z}$$

recognizing that $\sum_{k=0}^{\infty} (\lambda\Delta z)^k/k!$ is just the series for $e^{\lambda\Delta}$. Substituting Eq. (7-25) into (7-21), one finds $G_L(z)$ for this case.

The more general case of Poisson message arrivals and geometric message lengths is handled by recalling from Eq. (7-8) that the number of characters D arriving is the sum of a random number M (Poisson-distributed) of messages, each with random length X. One can again use generating functions to find $G_D(z)$ in terms of $G_X(z)$. (The form of Eq. (7-8) suggests the use of generating functions.) Specifically, we find

$$G_D(z) = e^{-\lambda\Delta} e^{\lambda\Delta\,G_X(z)} \qquad (7\text{-}26)$$

as the general form for $G_D(z)$ if the message arrivals are Poisson-distributed with *any* length distribution. (If the messages are all of unit length, $G_X(z) = z$, and we get the result of Eq. (7-25).) For the geometric length distribution we have

$$G_X(z) = \sum_{k=1}^{\infty} P(X = k)z^k = \sum_{k=1}^{\infty} (pq^{k-1})z^k = \frac{pz}{1 - qz} \qquad (7\text{-}27)$$

Eq. (7-27) inserted into Eq. (7-26), and in turn into Eq. (7-21), enables $G_L(z)$ to be found for this case.

*Chu and Konheim, "Analysis and Modeling of Computer-Communication Systems."

As a check, we may differentiate $G_L(z)$ to find the moments of the buffer occupancy. Specifically, one finds from Eq. (7-21)

$$E(L) = \frac{dG_L(z)}{dz}\Big|_{z=1} = \frac{\mu_D}{2} + \frac{\sigma_D^2}{2(1 - \mu_D)} \tag{7-28}$$

as already found previously and much more simply in Eq. (7-3). By differentiating Eq. (7-21) once more, one may find the variance of L if desired. (See Eq. (6-41) and (6-57) in Chap. 6, for example.)

Typical results of a calculation of the probability that the number of characters L (or any other units of data) in the buffer exceeds a specified number N, taken from the work of Chu and Konheim* appear as Fig. 7-5.

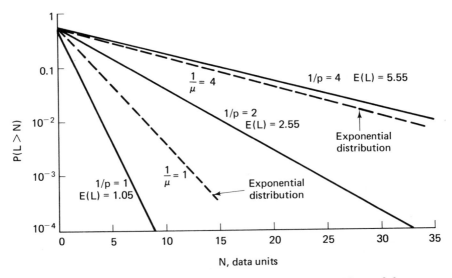

Fig. 7-5. Probability that buffer occupancy is greater than N, $p = 0.6$, geometrically-distributed message lengths.

The curves shown are plotted for a traffic intensity $\rho = 0.6$, assuming messages to be Poisson-distributed, with geometrically-distributed lengths of varying average length. Note that in all cases the *average* value $E(L)$ of buffer occupancy is far less than the value of N for which the probability of buffer occupancy is greater than 10^{-3}. The average value of occupancy, although useful in determining average message time delay, is not helpful in determining the buffer size needed to maintain a certain specified probability of buffer overflow. As an example, if messages are all of 1 unit length ($(1/p) = 1$), a six or seven unit buffer (six or seven characters, if that is the unit of length used) will

*Ibid., plus some unpublished work.

provide a probability of buffer overflow of 10^{-3}. The average number of data units in the buffer is, however, little more than 1. If the message lengths are now doubled to two units, on the average, 24 units of buffer are needed to have a probability of buffer overflow of 10^{-3}. If the messages are four units in length, on the average, the buffer size needed is about 55, for an overflow probability of 10^{-3}. Roughly speaking, the buffer size needed is about 10 times the average buffer occupancy. This assumes $p = 0.6$. For lighter traffic the buffer sizes needed are of course less.

Also plotted in Fig. 7-5 is a set of curves for the probability of buffer occupancy assuming exponentially-distributed message lengths.* Note that for an average message length of four units, the exponential- and geometric-distribution curves essentially coincide. This is in agreement with the previous comments in connection with average message time delays, that for relatively long messages the exponential assumption may be expected to be valid.

We now consider some simple numerical examples of the material just discussed.

1. Say a message concentrator allows 46 data terminals to access it. Assume each terminal transmits on the average of one message every 5 sec. Each message as assembled is four characters long, on the average. (This then includes overhead characters.) The outgoing trunk has a capacity of 60 char./sec (480 bps, if 8-bit characters are used). The effective rate of incoming messages is $\frac{46}{5} = 9.2$ messages/sec, on the average; the average number of char./sec in and out of the buffer is 9.2(4) = 36.8 char./sec; and the traffic intensity is $p = 36.8/60 \doteq 0.6$. The average message time delay at the buffer is, from Table 7-1, 9.25/60 = 0.15 sec. The buffer size needed to keep the probability of buffer overflow to 10^{-3} turns out to be 55 characters. (This is beyond the range of Fig. 7-5.) Note that this is a little more than 1 char./terminal.

2. 90 terminals transmitting 1 message/sec each, with average message length of two characters including overhead, are combined at a concentrator. The capacity of the output line is 300 char./sec (2400 bps for 8-bit characters).

---

*These were calculated from Eq. (6-20), Chap. 6, with the added loose assumption that the number of data units was simply the number of messages times the average message length $1/\mu$. Hence

$$P(L > N) \doteq p^{N\mu+1} \qquad p = \frac{\lambda}{\mu C}$$

in the M/M/1 case. A more comprehensive discussion of the equivalence between data unit statistics in the synchronous buffer case and message statistics in the M/M/1 case appears in M. Rich and M. Schwartz, "Buffer Sharing in Computer-Communication Nodes," *Proc. IEEE International Conference on Communications*, San Francisco, June 1975, pp. 33–17 to 33–21. Since the M/M/1 model is always simpler to analyze it is useful to know under what conditions it serves as a valid first-order approximation to the analysis of more complex buffers.

Then $\rho = 0.6$ again. (Conversely, to keep $\rho = 0.6$, a line of 300 char./sec capacity is needed.) The average message time delay at the buffer is $4.25/300 = 14$ msec, and the buffer size needed for a probability of buffer overflow of 10^{-3} is, from Fig. 7-5, 24 characters. Here about one character of storage for every four terminals is needed, as contrasted with the previous example, because of the 2 to 1 reduction in average message length.

PROBLEMS

7.1   Consider the geometric distribution described by Eq. (7-5). Show by averaging appropriately over the probability space that the average value and variance of a geometrically-distributed random variable are given by Eq. (7-6) and (7-7), respectively. (Compare with Problem 6.10, part (2d).)

7.2   Derive Eq. (7-10) for the variance of the data units received in an interval Δ sec long if message arrivals are Poisson and message lengths are geometric.

7.3 N terminals are connected to a concentrator. The concentrator output transmission line rate is one data unit per Δ sec. Each terminal is synchronized to this output rate and feeds in either one data unit with probability p every Δ sec, or none with probability $1 - p$. Show the average queue length of the concentrator buffer, in data units, is

$$E(L) = \frac{\mu_D}{1 - \mu_D}\left[1 - \frac{\mu_D}{2}\left(1 + \frac{1}{N}\right)\right], \qquad \mu_D = Np$$

(*Hint:* The input to the buffer is the sum of N Bernoulli random variables.)

7.4   For the model of Problem 7.3, calculate the average queue length (buffer occupancy) and average time delay in sec if the output line operates at 1000 char./sec, 10 terminals are connected, and each terminal inputs 10 char./sec, on the average.

    Repeat the problem if 50 terminals are now connected, all parameters remaining the same, and then again with 50 terminals if $p = 0.015$. Compare the three cases.

7.5   60 terminals are connected to a concentrator. Half of them transmit, on the average, 1 message/15 sec; the other half transmit 1 message/30 sec, on the average. The message lengths are geometrically-distributed, with the average 10 characters long. Find the average queueing delay if the output line capacity is 60 char./sec. Compare with the time delay obtained by using the M/M/1 result.

7.6 Repeat Problem 7.5 and compare if the message lengths are all five characters long, on the average, while the message rates are all doubled.

7.7 Repeat Problem 7.5 if all terminals transmit at a rate of 1 message/10 sec, on the average. Messages are now eight characters long, on the average. Again compare with the M/M/1 approximation.

7.8 30 terminals are connected to a concentrator. Each generates fixed-length 1200-bit messages ("packets") on the average of once a minute. Find the output line capacity, in bps, required if the traffic intensity is to be $\rho = 0.6$. Find the buffer size in packets required if the probability of overflow is to be 10^{-4}. What is the average queueing delay in this case? Compare both buffer size and time delay with the values found assuming an M/M/1 queue.

Concentration:

Finite Buffers,

Dynamic Buffering,

Block Storage

In Chap. 7 we focused on the buffering problem in concentrators for store-and-forward networks, using models for message statistics that appear to agree with those measured in practice, and determining for these the average message time delays expected due to buffering, as well as the buffer size needed to accommodate the messages. We also showed that for long message lengths the exponential message length model used in earlier chapters gave results in fairly close agreement with geometric length statistics.

The buffer was assumed infinite in size in carrying out the analysis in the previous chapter, however. How valid is this assumption in practice? Is this a valid assumption in developing design curves? In this chapter we draw on work reported in the literature that handles the more realistic finite buffer case. We shall see, as was noted in the last chapter, that the infinite buffer approach appears to be quite accurate if the probability that the buffer occupancy exceeds a specified value is less than 10^{-3}. In this range this probability is essentially the same as the probability of buffer overflow for finite buffers, often used as a design criterion in computer systems.

Continuing the attempt to make the models more realistic, we then summarize work reported in the literature that treats the dynamic buffering of incoming messages and assumes them stored in block form rather than the storage by character assumed up to now. Out of this comes, as an interesting byproduct, an expression for optimum block size, showing the proper split between message units and overhead units in a block.

FINITE BUFFER SIZE

Various papers have appeared indicating the effect of finite buffer size and providing design curves relating the probability of buffer overflow (or message blocking) to message statistics and buffer size.* The papers by Chu that are referenced use the Poisson message arrival model with geometric lengths introduced in the previous chapter, so we shall summarize his approach and reproduce some of his results here. This enables us to directly compare the finite buffer results with the infinite buffer ones summarized in the previous chapter.

The paper by Rudin parallels the work of Chu, but uses binomial message arrival statistics instead. (All messages are assumed to be one character in length.) This corresponds specifically to the case of a multiplicity of terminals connected to a concentrator, using statistical multiplexing, each one of which has a specified probability of being active at any given time interval. As the number of terminals becomes larger, the overall arrival statistics (or statistics of active terminals) becomes Poisson, so that one would expect Rudin's results to approach Chu's. Such is in fact the case. Rudin also handles the nonstationary situation in which the number of terminals connected changes instantaneously. This could correspond to the onset of a busy period, for example.

The approaches of both Chu and Rudin consist of actually writing down explicit expressions for the probabilities of buffer occupancy, with a maximum buffer size N, and solving the resultant equations recursively by computer. Specifically, let Δ again be the service time introduced in Chap. 7 during which at most one character is released by the buffer. Assume the system has been in operation for a long enough time for equilibrium to have set in. A random number of characters k may arrive every Δ sec interval, and a random number n characters are present in the buffer. This is shown in Fig. 8-1. Let Π_k be the

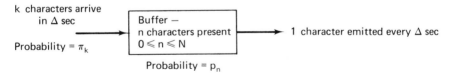

Fig. 8-1. Finite buffer model.

*W. W. Chu, "A Study of Asynchronous TDM for Time-Sharing Computer Systems," *AFIPS Conference Proc.*, Fall Joint Computer Conference, **35**, 1969, 669–78.

W. W. Chu, "Buffer Behavior for Batch Poisson Arrivals and Single Constant Output," *IEEE Trans. on Communication Technology*, **COM-18**, no. 5, Oct. 1970, 613–18.

H. Rudin, Jr., "Performance of Simple Multiplexer-Concentrators for Data Communications," *IEEE Trans. on Communication Technology*, **COM-19**, no. 2, April 1971, 178–87.

probability of k characters arriving in Δ sec and p_n be the probability that n characters (the buffer state) are present in the buffer. Although the actual number of characters k arriving will vary from interval to interval as will the number n in the buffer, their *probabilities* of occurrence will be fixed numbers at equilibrium.

A little thought will indicate that we then get the following set of equilibrium equations relating the various probabilities:

$$p_0 = \Pi_0 \, p_1 + \Pi_0 \, p_0$$
$$p_1 = \Pi_0 \, p_2 + \Pi_1 \, p_1 + \Pi_1 \, p_0$$
$$p_2 = \Pi_0 \, p_3 + \Pi_1 \, p_2 + \Pi_2 \, p_1 + \Pi_2 \, p_0$$

$$\vdots$$

$$p_n = \Pi_0 \, p_{n+1} + \sum_{i=1}^{n} \Pi_{n-i+1} \, p_i + \Pi_n \, p_0$$

$$\vdots$$

$$p_N = p_N \sum_{i=1}^{\infty} \Pi_i + p_{N-1} \sum_{i=2}^{\infty} \Pi_i \ldots + p_2 \sum_{i=N-1}^{\infty} \Pi_i + (p_1 + p_0) \sum_{i=N}^{\infty} \Pi_i$$
$$= p_N(1 - \Pi_0) + p_{N-1}(1 - \Pi_0 - \Pi_1) + \ldots$$

$$p_{i>N} = 0 \qquad \sum_{i=0}^{N} p_i = 1 \tag{8-1}$$

These equations simply relate the probability of having a particular buffer state (number of characters) present at the end of a Δ sec interval to the possible states that could have existed at the end of the previous interval, given no more than 1 character removed in Δ sec.

Thus, for example, the first equation of the set says that an empty buffer (with probability p_0) could have risen if the buffer were previously empty and no character arrived in the Δ sec interval (the probability of this is $\Pi_0 \, p_0$), *or* if there had been one character present (this character was then removed in the Δ sec interval) and none arrived. (The probability of this is $\Pi_0 \, p_1$.) Since these are mutually exclusive events one simply adds the probability of the two events. The second equation equates the probability p_1 of one character being present in the buffer to the probabilities of the three events that might have contributed to this state:

1. Two characters were present during the previous interval, one was emitted, none arrived.

2. One was present and left, one arrived.

3. The buffer was empty (hence none left) and one arrived.

The final equation of the set, involving the maximum buffer occupancy N, differs from the others since any number of characters greater than the minimum required to reach state N could have arrived. The excess number are simply blocked or turned away.

The model of the buffer operation assumes that messages arriving cannot be emitted over the output link during the interval in which they arrive. Even if the buffer is empty on arrival they must wait until the next Δ sec time interval before processing begins.

With the input message statistics given, the Π's are known explicitly and the p_n's can be found by solving the system of Eq. (8-1). This Chu has done for Poisson message arrival statistics with geometrically-distributed lengths. For design purposes we would actually like to find the probability of buffer overflow and relate this both to the buffer capacity N, in characters or other units of data, and to the traffic intensity. The probability of buffer overflow P_{of} can be related to p_0, the probability that the buffer is empty, which is in turn found from the solution of Eq. (8-1) by a throughput argument similar to those discussed in Chap. 6. (Refer to Fig. 8-2.) Let λ/p characters/sec

Fig. 8-2. Calculation of buffer overflow probability.

attempt to enter the buffer, on the average. (Recall from Chap. 7 that λ is the Poisson arrival parameter, and $1/p$ the average length of a message, in characters or other data units.) Let α char./sec represent the average number leaving the buffer; α must differ from the number attempting to enter by exactly those blocked due to the buffer overflow. The fraction of those blocked is just $P_{of}(\lambda/p)$. Hence by equating the net number entering on the average in Δ sec to those leaving, we get

$$\alpha\Delta = (1 - P_{of})\frac{\lambda\Delta}{p} \qquad (8\text{-}2)$$

An argument similar to that used in Chap. 6 relates α to p_0, the probability the buffer is empty. For, by definition, the average number of characters leaving in Δ sec is $\alpha\Delta$. Characters can only leave when the buffer has at least one character stored or is *not* empty. The probability of this event is $1 - p_0$, and one character only can leave in Δ sec. The average number leaving in Δ sec is thus $1 \cdot (1 - p_0)$. We thus get

$$\alpha\Delta = 1 - p_0 \qquad (8\text{-}3)$$

With the input message statistics specified and N, the buffer capacity, given, the solution of the set of Eq. (8-1) determines p_0. From Eq. (8-3) we find α, and from Eq. (8-2), P_{of}.* Table 8-1 following, taken from Chu's work, shows the buffer capacity N needed for two values of buffer overflow probability. Also indicated are numbers obtained assuming an infinite buffer, as in the last chapter, and finding N such that $P(L > N) = 10^{-3}$, as well as numbers obtained assuming exponential message statistics. Note that the infinite buffer results agree closely with the finite buffer solutions.

TABLE 8-1

BUFFER CAPACITY AND OVERFLOW PROBABILITY

Avg. Message Length $\frac{1}{p}$ (characters)	P_{of}	$p = 0.6$ Buffer Capacity N (characters)		
		Finite Buffer	Infinite Buffer	Exponential
1	10^{-3}	5	6	12
1	10^{-7}	16		30
2	10^{-3}	22	24	24
2	10^{-8}	63		69
4	10^{-3}	50	55	47
4	10^{-8}	153		144
10	10^{-3}	150	150	118
10	10^{-8}	410		393

The exponential approximation numbers in Table 8-1 were obtained in a manner similar to the calculations of the exponential distribution curves of Fig. 7-5. For the finite M/M/1 buffer it is readily found that the probability of message blocking and the overflow probability calculated from the message throughput equation equivalent to Eq. (8-2) (see the discussion in Chap 6) are the same. In particular they both turn out to be the probability that the buffer is full. For an M/M/1 buffer accommodating M messages this is just

$$P_{of} = P_B = p_M = \frac{(1 - \rho)\rho^M}{1 - \rho^{M+1}} \tag{8-4}$$

Assuming as an approximation that the number of characters stored in an M/M/1 buffer is just the number of messages stored times the average message length $1/\mu$, we have as the data unit or character capacity of an M/M/1 buffer

$$N \doteq \frac{M}{\mu} \tag{8-5}$$

*Note that the overflow probability calculated here relates to the overflow of *data units*. It is thus not the same as *message blocking probability* which refers to the probability that an *entire message* will be blocked. In the case of fixed length messages or a buffer whose state is defined in terms of messages (the M/M/1 queue, for example), rather than data units, the two quantities become the same.

Combining Eq. (8-5) with (8-4) we get an equation relating overflow probability to buffer capacity and average message length. This simple expression was used to obtain the exponential entries in Table 8-1.*

In Fig. 8-3 we have sketched some typical curves relating the buffer size N needed as a function of message legnth $1/p$ ($1/\mu$ in the exponential approximation case) for overflow probability $P_{of} = 10^{-6}$. These curves are taken from the work referenced by Chu. Also shown for comparison are the equivalent curves found using Eq. (8-4) and (8-5), assuming an exponential message length distribution. Note that Eq. (8-5) predicts a buffer size directly proportional to the message length $1/\mu$. (As noted in the preceding footnote, the actual relation is found empirically to depend on the traffic intensity p as well.)

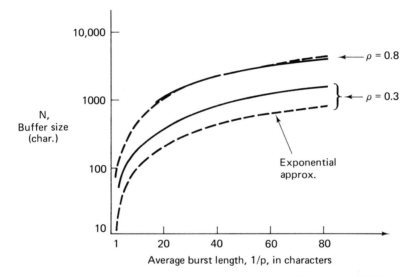

Fig. 8-3. Buffer size vs. message length, $P_{of} = 10^{-6}$. (Courtesy of W.W. Chu, "Buffer Behavior for Batch Poisson Arrivals and Single Constant Output," *IEEE Trans. on Communication Technology*, **COM-18**, no. 5, Oct. 1970, 613-18.)

*A more detailed study of the relation between message blocking probability determined using an M/M/1 analysis and the overflow probability for data characters found through Chu's approach, as outlined in this section, indicates that the two provide comparable results if one assumes a more complex relation between N and M than that of Eq. (8-5). More specifically, one finds

$$N \doteq \frac{M}{\mu} f(p) \qquad (8\text{-}6)$$

with $f(p)$ an empirical function found to depend on the traffic intensity p only. Further discussion and a typical plot of $f(p)$ appear in the paper by M. Rich and M. Schwartz, "Buffer Sharing in Computer-Communications Network Nodes," *Proc. IEEE International Conference on Communications* June 1975, San Francisco, pp. 33–17 to 33–21.

These results and others like them can be used for some simple design calculations. For example, the form of Fig. 8-3 plotting N vs. $1/p$ for relatively large message lengths or bursts indicates that it is appropriate for modeling the outbound or computer-user direction in a centralized computer network. Fig. 8-4 indicates the distinction between inbound and outbound directions

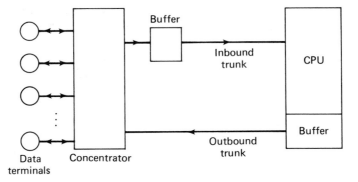

Fig. 8-4. Model of rudimentary network. (Courtesy of W.W. Chu, "Buffer Behavior for Batch Poisson Arrivals.")

and the two separate buffers to be designed. As an example, say the central processor (CPU) ultimately connects with 46 data terminals. Assume that each terminal transmits, at a Poisson rate, an average of one message every 2.84 sec, or $\lambda = 0.35$ message/sec. The CPU replies at the same rate so that the number of Poisson-distributed messages leaving the computer is $46\lambda = 16.1$ messages/ sec. Assume the CPU messages to each terminal are geometrically-distributed in length, with a mean length $1/p = 20$ characters to each terminal. Say 20% is added for overhead, so that the average message or burst length is 24 characters. If a 480 char./sec trunk is used leaving the CPU, the effective traffic intensity is

$$\rho = \frac{16.1(24)}{480} \doteq 0.8$$

What size buffer is now needed at the CPU to accommodate messages outbound over this trunk? For an overflow probability of 10^{-3}, Chu's analysis shows N is somewhat more than 500 characters. If $P_{of} = 10^{-8}$ is desired, $N = 1650$ characters. The average time delay incurred by messages waiting to be transmitted over the outgoing trunk is, from Chap. 7,

$$\frac{E(T)}{\Delta} = \frac{1}{2(1 - \rho)}\left[\frac{2 - p\rho}{p}\right] \tag{8-7}$$

For the numbers used here this is about 120 character times or $\frac{120}{480} = 0.25$ sec. (Since the overflow probability is small, one can neglect its effect in calculating average time delay and assume essentially an infinite buffer.)

What if the trunk capacity is now increased to 960 char./sec? Then $p = 0.4$, and for $P_{of} = 10^{-3}$, $N \doteq 200$ characters of buffer storage are needed. For $P_{of} = 10^{-8}$, $N \doteq 600$ characters are needed. The average time delay now becomes 40 character times or $\frac{40}{960} = 0.042$ sec. Note particularly the great improvement in time delay effected by doubling the line capacity. This is of course due to a very high p to begin with. Since $E(T)$ is proportional to $1/(1-p)$, the time delay is very sensitive to changes in p at p near 1. These results are summarized in Table 8-2.

TABLE 8-2

EFFECT OF CAPACITY CHANGE, $P_{of} = 10^{-8}$

C (char./sec)	p	N (char.)	$E(T)$ (sec)
480	0.8	1650	0.25
960	0.4	600	0.042

For the inbound or user-computer direction (Fig. 8-4), shorter message lengths are more common. (This is particularly true for inquiry-response systems.) As a special case, assume inbound messages are one data unit long (one character, say). This corresponds of course to $1/p = 1$. A set of curves for this case, relating the buffer overflow probability P_{of} to the buffer size N, in data units (say characters), is shown sketched in Fig. 8-5. These are again

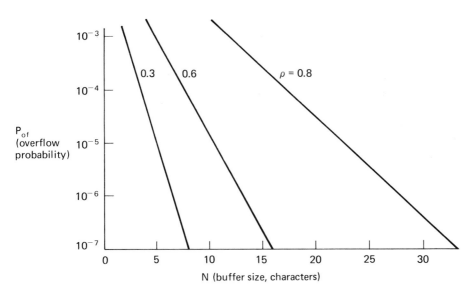

Fig. 8-5. Buffer design curves, average message length = one character. (Courtesy of Chu, "Buffer Behavior for Batch Poisson Arrivals.")

taken from the work of Chu. They are of course very similar to the infinite buffer curves of Chap. 7. The buffer in this case would be at the concentrator, as shown in Fig. 8-4. Examples similar to the one worked out above can be carried out to determine the buffer sizes needed at the concentrator for a specified traffic (number of data terminals combined), link capacity, and over-flow probability specified. Examples of this type were worked out in the previous chapter. Others are left for the reader as problems at the end of this chapter. Note of course that the concentrator buffer size required is generally considerably smaller than that of the CPU buffer (compare Fig. 8-3 and 8-5) because of the difference in message length that is generally expected.

In practice the lines between terminal and CPU (or concentrator and CPU) would be either full-duplex or identical half-duplex lines. The choice of line capacity, and trade-off between buffer size and capacity in an inquiry-response system would thus be dictated by the outbound or computer-user direction, since this is carrying much larger messages, on the average. For example, if the outbound message lengths are 20 characters on the average, as assumed in calculating the entries of Table 8-2, while inbound message lengths are only a few characters long, the effective ρ's inbound are consider-ably below those outbound. There would thus be no need to use a set of curves such as those of Fig. 8-5. A minimal buffer size, presumably enough to handle one data unit, would be all that would be required on the inbound side. As the message size inbound increases, the effective traffic intensity increases correspondingly, and larger buffer sizes become warranted.

DYNAMIC BUFFERING AND BLOCK STORAGE

Note that in the discussion of concentration and buffering thus far, we have steadily moved to more realistic models. We began, in the introductory chapters on capacity assignment, by assuming infinite buffers and exponen-tially-distributed (i.e., continuously-varying) message lengths. In the last chapter we took the more realistic case of messages with discrete lengths, in particular choosing the geometric distribution as the model for message lengths. (For long message lengths, as we have been pointing out, the need for modeling of message lengths in terms of discrete units becomes less critical, and the continuously-varying message length assumption is often quite valid.) In this chapter we added the condition of finite buffer size in obtaining design curves relating buffer size to buffer overflow probability and message statistics. We showed that for low probabilities ($\leq 10^{-3}$), results obtained assuming infinite buffers were still valid.

In the remaining portion of this chapter we focus more closely on storage in the buffer. Messages are generally stored as blocks, with overhead charac-ters assigned to link more than one block corresponding to one message together. Questions to be asked here are the overall word size needed to accommodate the expected traffic for a specified overflow probability (similar to the buffer size needed, as shown in Fig. 8-3 and 8-5) as well as the optimum choice of block size in which to distribute messages.

That an optimum size should exist is apparent after some thought: if the block size is made too small, overhead characters account for too much of the block allocation resulting in buffer inefficiency. If the block size is too large, messages may occupy only a portion of a block (or overflow into a portion of the last block for long messages). This is also wasteful of buffer storage.

In addition it would be of interest to compare different types of dynamic buffering strategies developed for both time-shared computer systems and communication processors. We shall describe only one simple strategy, however, referring the reader to the references for further discussion.

Several papers have appeared discussing quantitatively the question of dynamic buffering and block storage. We list these below.* For the purposes of this discussion, however, we focus primarily on the work of G.D. Schultz.

Consider a computer accessed by M lines or ports. (See Fig. 8-6.) Although we are considering the concentration problem here, with the computer generally a minicomputer functioning as a communications processor,

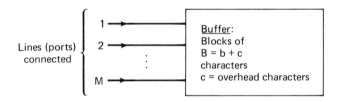

Fig. 8-6. M ports connected to computer.

the discussion could apply equally well to terminals accessing a CPU in a time-sharing mode, or to a multiplicity of concentrators in turn communicating with a CPU. When a request for service is made on any line (the lines may be rapidly scanned or an interrupt procedure may be used, as noted in Chap. 7), a block of B characters from the buffer is assigned instantaneously. When

*G. D. Schultz, "A Stochastic Model for Message Assembly Buffering with a Comparison of Block Assignment Strategies," *J. of the ACM*, **19**, no. 3, July 1972, 483.

D. P. Gaver, Jr. and P. A. W. Lewis, "Probability Models for Buffer Storage Allocation Problems," *J. of the ACM*, **18**, no. 2, April 1971, 186–98.

J. H. Chang, "An Analysis of Buffering Techniques in Teleprocessing Systems," *IEEE Trans. on Communications*, **COM-20**, no. 3, part II, June 1972, 619–29.

R. D. Pedersen and J. C. Shah, "Multiserver Queue Storage Requirements with Unpacked Messages," *IEEE Trans. on Communications*, **COM-20**, part I, June 1972, 462–65.

the block is filled up another block is in turn assigned instantaneously, the process continuing until the message on that particular line has been completely deposited in the buffer. This is the simplest form of dynamic buffering. In other versions a fixed number of blocks may be reserved for each incoming line and additional blocks assigned as needed; an additional buffer block may be assigned to a line on the arrival of a message in anticipation of message overflow beyond one block, etc.

Each block assigned has B characters, b of which are set aside for message characters, c for the necessary overhead (including chaining characters for linking blocks of the same message assigned in different parts of the buffer). The number of blocks assigned times B is thus the buffer storage N required in units of characters. The approach here is to again assume an unlimited buffer pool and then to find the number of blocks S typically required by the M ports connected such that the probability of exceeding S is some small specified number. According to our previous discussion this should be close to the overflow probability for a finite buffer with S blocks. In calculating this probability we assume tacitly that on the completion of a message the entire message is immediately removed from the buffer and the blocks occupied returned to the pool. This thus differs from the previous concentrator and buffer calculations in which we assumed no more than one character to be removed every Δ sec. The assumption here is that the outgoing line capacity is large enough to make buffering delays negligible.* We focus here on the buffer design problem only.

In calculating the number of blocks of buffer storage needed, the approach, following Schultz, differs from those outlined previously in focusing on the number of incoming lines that are *active*. Thus, each of the M lines connected is assumed alternately active and inactive (or idle). During the active period the message is assumed exponentially-distributed with an average message transmission time of $1/\gamma$ sec. For a terminal transmitting synchronously at a rate of r char./sec, this corresponds to an average message length in characters, of $1/\mu = r/\gamma$. The idle interval, the period between the end and start of an active period (see Fig. 8-7), is also assumed to be exponentially-distributed in length, with average length $1/\lambda$ sec. The message model adopted is thus similar to that used earlier, with continuous message lengths assumed, however. The active-idle approach is needed to keep the messages on individual lines separated. This is due to the buffer block format used, in which individual messages rather than messages combined from the various input lines are loaded into blocks.

Some typical numbers are of interest. Say a data terminal transmits, on the average, 3 char./sec, at a rate of $r = 10$ char./sec. In any time interval it is

---

*Recall from Chap. 2 that some networks are designed on this basis to reduce the buffer management problem.

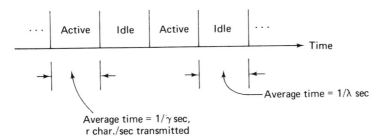

Fig. 8-7. Input line alternately active and idle.

thus active, on the average, 0.3 of the time and idle 0.7 of the time. The user send-time is thus 30% of the holding time (the time the line is connected). If the average message is 10 characters in length ($1/\mu = 10$), $1/\gamma = 1$ sec. A little thought then indicates that the average idle period is $1/\lambda = 2.33$ sec. With these assumptions and the approach indicated one can proceed to find the number of blocks needed for a specified number of the input lines active. First, how many blocks does a typical message on any one of the incoming lines need? Since each block contains b message characters, any message of length b characters or less requires one block. A message with length between b and $2b$ characters requires two blocks, etc. This is shown in Fig. 8-8, in which the exponential message length distribution in *time* is sketched. A message of length b characters requires b/r sec to be transmitted.

Let f_1 be the probability that one block is needed when a terminal at one of the ports requests service. This is just the probability that the message length in sec is less than b/r, or the length in characters is less than b. This is indicated as the area under the curve from 0 to b/r in Fig. 8-8. This is just

$$f_1 = \int_0^{b/r} \gamma e^{-\gamma\tau} \, d\tau = 1 - e^{-\gamma b/r} = 1 - e^{-\mu b} \tag{8-8}$$

with $\mu = \gamma/r$ introduced, to convert from message length in sec to length in characters. To simplify the notation let $q = e^{-\mu b}$, $p = 1 - q$. Then we also have

$$f_1 = 1 - q = p = 1 - e^{-\mu b} \tag{8-8a}$$

The probability that *two blocks* are needed is just

$$f_2 = \int_{b/r}^{2b/r} \gamma e^{-\gamma\tau} \, d\tau = q(1 - q) = qp \tag{8-9}$$

Continuing, the probability that j blocks are needed is just

$$f_j = q^{j-1}p \qquad j = 1, 2, \ldots \tag{8-10}$$
$$q \equiv e^{-\mu b} \qquad p = 1 - q$$

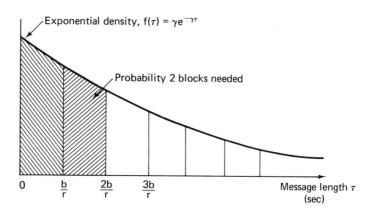

Fig. 8-8. Calculation of blocks needed.

The number of blocks needed thus follows the geometric distribution! The *average* number of blocks needed is then $1/p = 1/(1 - e^{-\mu b})$.

Equation (8-10) represents the probability distribution of blocks needed for a typical active line. The probability that a line is active can be shown to be given simply by the fraction of the time the line is active.

$$Q = \frac{1/\gamma}{1/\gamma + 1/\lambda} = \frac{\lambda}{\gamma + \lambda} \tag{8-11}$$

(Refer to Fig. 8-7.) For the example used earlier, with $1/\gamma = 1$ sec, $1/\lambda = 2.33$ sec, $Q = 0.3$, just the fraction of the time the line is active. The average number of blocks needed by a given line is just Q/p. For the M lines connected to the concentrator, then, the *average* number of *blocks* of buffer storage needed is

$$E(S) = \frac{MQ}{p} \tag{8-12}$$

with Q and p defined in terms of the traffic on any one line by Eq. (8-11) and (8-8a), respectively. As an example, if $Q = 0.3$, $1/\mu = 20$, and $b = 2$, an average of three blocks per line will be utilized.

The average number of characters needed in the buffer is then just

$$E(N) = (b + c)E(S) = \frac{MQ(b + c)}{1 - e^{-\mu b}} \tag{8-13}$$

with b the message characters per block and c the overhead characters. Using the same example as above, if $c = 2$ overhead characters are used, an average of 16 characters per incoming line will be needed at the buffer. It is apparent from this equation that there is an optimum block size b, in terms of minimizing the number of characters needed. This agrees with the intuitive argument noted earlier. Differentiating Eq. (8-13) with respect to b and setting the derivative equal to 0, one finds the optimum value of b given by the solution of the equation

$$\mu c + \mu b + 1 = e^{\mu b} = 1 + \mu b + \frac{(\mu b)^2}{2} + \ldots$$

If we now assume $\mu c \ll 1$ to simplify the equation (this then implies the number of overhead characters c is small compared to the average message length $1/\mu$), we get

$$\mu b \doteq \sqrt{2\mu c} \quad \text{or} \quad b \doteq \sqrt{2c\left(\frac{1}{\mu}\right)} \tag{8-14}$$

as the optimum choice of message block size to minimize the average buffer size.

As an example, say $1/\mu = 20$ characters is the average message length. Let $c = 2$ characters be the overhead required. Then $b \doteq 9$ characters is the appropriate message block size. The actual block size is $B = b + c = 11$ characters. If the average message length is 10 characters and three overhead characters are needed, then the appropriate value of $b \doteq 8$ characters, and a total of 11 characters are still needed for each block.

We already know from Chap. 7 that the average number of characters residing in the buffer is a very poor measure of the buffer size needed for a specified probability of overflow. The buffer size required should correspond to a value whose probability of being exceeded is some specified small value. The method of doing this is fairly straightforward. It involves finding the probability that say i blocks are needed, summing the probabilities that $i, i + 1, i + 2, \ldots$ blocks are needed, and calculating the resultant probability that the number of blocks $S > i$ for various values of i. We shall not carry out this calculation but refer the reader to the paper by Schultz* for details. We only indicate the approach here.

If h_i is defined to be the probability that the buffer occupancy in number of blocks is i, we must have

$$h_i = P[S = i] = \sum_{n=0}^{M} P[A = n]P[X_1 + X_2 + \ldots + X_n = i \,|\, A = n] \tag{8-15}$$

Here A is the number of lines of the M total that are active and X_l is the number of blocks required by the lth active line. Equation (8-15) is basically a tabulation of the various ways in which the active lines may combine to produce a requirement of i blocks in the buffer. $P[A = n]$ represents the probability that n of the M lines are active, and n may range in general from 0 to M. For each possibility the sum of the blocks needed ($X_1 + X_2 + \ldots + X_n$) must exactly equal i.

*Schultz, "Stochastic Model for Message Assembly Buffering."

The probability that n of M lines are active is just the binomial distribution, with the probability Q (Eq. 8-11) that any one line is active as the basic parameter:

$$P[A = n] = \binom{M}{n} Q^n (1 - Q)^{M-n} \qquad n = 0, 1, 2, \ldots M \qquad (8\text{-}16)$$

The probability $P[X_1 + X_2 + \ldots + X_n = i \,|\, A = n]$ that n active lines require i blocks can be found in terms of the probability f_j (Eq. 8-10) that a given line requires j blocks. The results of a typical calculation for $M = 1$ and $M = 2$ lines are tabulated in Table 8-3.

TABLE 8-3

BUFFER STORAGE REQUIREMENTS

$Q = 0.3 \quad P[S > i] = 10^{-3} \quad 1/\mu = 20 \text{ char.} \quad c = 3 \text{ overhead char.}$

b (Message char./block)	No. of blocks needed		N: no. of char. needed	
	1 line	2 lines	1 line	2 lines
1	114	140	456	560
2	57	70	285	350
4		35		245
10	12	14	156	182
20		7		161
40		4		172

In all cases the number of blocks needed for the specified probability of 10^{-3} of not exceeding that number is far greater than the average number. This is true as well for the number of characters. For example, if each buffer block contains two message characters and three overhead characters, Eq. (8-13) indicates an average of 16 characters of buffer storage will be utilized when one line is connected in and the average message length is 20 characters. Table 8-3 shows the number of characters needed to be 285.

Schultz has carried out the calculations for the case of very long message bursts and large numbers of terminals connected in. (This is then more appropriate to a time-shared CPU environment than to the communications processor under discussion here.) His curves are reproduced here as Fig. 8-9. They assume an average message length of 600 characters and have each terminal active 50% of the time. The number of overhead characters in each block is 4, and the probability of exceeding the buffer pool size shown is 10^{-2}. Note that the curves all have a minimum point at the dotted line indicated by $b_{\text{opt}} = 69$. This is the point calculated using Eq. (8-14) that minimizes the average pool size $E(N)$. It thus appears to provide an optimum value as well (albeit quite broad) for buffer design predicted on statistical considerations.

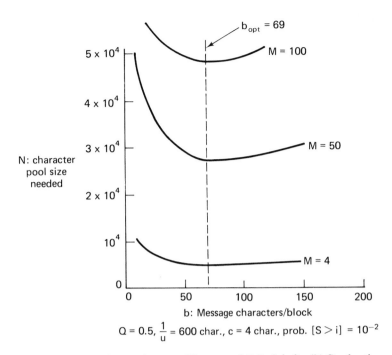

Fig. 8-9. Buffer size requirement. (Courtesy of G.D. Schultz, "A Stochastic Model for Message Assembly Buffering with a Comparison of Block Assignment Strategies," *J. of the ACM*, **19**, no. 3, July 1972, 483.)

PROBLEMS

8.1 30 data terminals are connected via a concentrator to a central processing system. The data terminals each generate geometrically-distributed messages which are, on the average, 10 characters long. Messages are generated, on the average, once every six sec. Each inbound message receives a reply from the CPU which is, on the average, 40 characters long. A full-duplex line is used so that the inbound and outbound line capacities are the same. Assuming 0.2 sec computer processing time, choose a line capacity such that the total average response time is no more than one sec. (*Note*: The response time is normally measured from the time a message is read in by a terminal to the time a reply is received. In this case neglect the time required to transmit messages from the individual terminals to the concentrator, as well as the replies back from the concentrator. These times can be quite sizeable, but are normally limited by the terminal speed and thus not attributable to the network.) Determine the buffer size needed at both the concentrator and the outbound trunk of the CPU if the probability of overflow is to be 10^{-6}. (See Fig. 8-4.) Make any reasonable assumptions required.

8.2 It is felt that the buffer size required at the CPU in Problem 8.1 is too large. To reduce the buffer size, a larger line capacity C is to be chosen. C can be no more than 20% larger than the previous capacity. Find the effect on time delay and buffers required at both the concentrator and CPU.

8.3 Refer to Problem 8.1 again. The system designer feels that the prime consideration is to reduce the buffer requirement at the central processor. For this purpose it is decided to keep the traffic intensity on the outbound link to no more than 0.5. There are two options possible: to either increase the line speed appropriately or to decrease the message throughput by limiting the number of messages per unit time allowed per user. Investigate both of these possibilities for blocking probabilities of 10^{-6} and 10^{-3}. Compare the buffer requirements with those of Problem 8.1. Find the corresponding response times. Make any necessary assumptions in solving the problem.

Centralized

Network Design:

Multipoint Connections

We have noted several times in this book the basic questions of network design: given a multiplicity of terminals and other data sources spread over a geographic area, with some measure of traffic expected between the various sources, how does one decide on the number of concentrators needed, where should they be placed, how should they be interconnected? At a lower level yet the same questions arise—which terminals shall be connected to a particular concentrator (this is often called the terminal clustering problem), and how shall the terminals associated with a particular concentrator be connected (this is the terminal layout problem)?

A definitive answer to all these questions and others involving network topology and design is still far from being available. The complexity of the problem is of course enormous. The network design questions are generally attacked one at a time and then iteratively. Heuristic approaches have been widely adopted in recent years and with some measure of success in those networks to which applied.

In this first introductory chapter on network design we focus again on the simplest type of network—a centralized system with all messages flowing inward to some central processing facility. Recall that our first examples on network capacity assignment in the early chapters of this book also stressed the centralized network. As a matter of fact in our early discussions of capacity assignment and routing we did a rudimentary type of network design as well. We showed for example that the communication line costs for a tree-type structure were inherently less costly than a star-type configuration for the same centralized system application. (As noted elsewhere in this book and as carried out in the Appendix, equipment cost must also be included to determine the complete cost trade-offs.)

The centralized network model described in this chapter applies to two extremely important problems: the terminal layout problem noted above, in which terminals are to be connected in so-called multidrop fashion or multipoint to a specified concentrator; and the centralized network problem in which concentrators themselves are connected to a central processing facility. Combinations are of course possible as well, with both terminals and concentrators connected in a tree fashion to a central facility. An example of such a network is shown in Fig. 9-1.

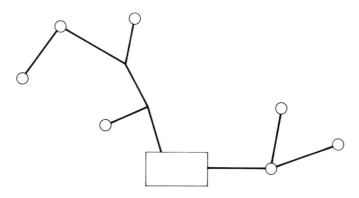

Fig. 9-1. Multipoint (tree) network.

Thus the two problems—terminal connection and concentrator connection—are really the same, although they may sometimes differ in the network hierarchy. In all cases one looks for a minimum cost connection or set of linkages in the network subject to certain constraints. This is exactly the approach we have taken in the capacity assignment problem discussed earlier in this book. An obvious constraint desired here is again the usual one discussed earlier: that time delay shall not exceed a specified value. Another one might be a reliability constraint. This could be interpreted several ways. One way would insist that alternate path (or two-connectivity) routing be available at all times. Another interpretation of reliability that arises, particularly in multipoint connection networks, is that no more than a specified number of terminals or concentrators be disconnected if any link in the network fails.

The time delay constraint is a difficult one to invoke directly in the context of minimum cost network design. Instead we shall focus in the examples given below on a flow constraint: the flow in any particular link shall not exceed a specified maximum value. This of course implies a maximum link time delay on each link in the network.

In describing techniques developed for multipoint or centralized network design we shall first describe an algorithm due to Chandy and Russell* using a branch-and-bound technique that provides the minimum cost solution to this constrained network design problem. We shall then focus on heuristic algorithms that generally provide suboptimum solutions that are quite close to the optimum but at a considerable saving in computation time. (For very large networks with many nodes to be connected in multipoint fashion, the optimum algorithm may require a considerable number of iterations for convergence.) The discussion of the heuristic algorithms draws heavily on the paper by Kershenbaum and Chou** who have shown that many such algorithms developed in the past years may be considered special cases of one unified algorithm.

Without the constraints the minimum cost network reduces precisely to the *minimum spanning tree* of the network of nodes (terminals or concentrators) to be connected together. Since the minimum spanning tree appears in the Chandy-Russell algorithm and since it provides a lower bound on the cost of the minimum cost network, it pays to digress a little at this point to discuss this concept. The minimum spanning tree is by definition the spanning tree, a connected network containing all the nodes and no circuits or closed paths, the sum of whose link costs is a minimum.† Many constructions or algorithms exist to find the minimum spanning tree of a network. We shall outline one such algorithm here. It is based essentially on an algorithm by Kruskal.†† The heuristic algorithms considered later in this chapter lead to the minimum spanning tree as well if there are no constraints in the problem.

In finding the minimum cost network, with the unconstrained minimum spanning tree as one example, the cost considered is that of setting up a link between any pair of nodes in the network. For each pair of nodes that may be connected, the link cost is assumed known. The Kruskal algorithm simply connects the least-cost links, one at a time starting with the lowest cost link, until all nodes have been connected into the network. A precise formulation of this algorithm, one of several possibilities, may be phrased as follows:§

*K. M. Chandy and R. A. Russell, "The Design of Multipoint Linkages in a Teleprocessing Tree Network," *IEEE Trans. on Computers*, **C-21**, no. 10, Oct. 1972, 1062–66.

A. Kershenbaum and W. Chou, "A Unified Algorithm for Designing Multidrop Teleprocessing Networks," *IEEE Trans. on Communications*, **COM-22, no. 11, Nov. 1974, 1762–72.

†T. C. Hu, *Integer Programming and Network Flows*, Addison-Wesley, Reading, Mass., 1969, pp. 122–23; H. Frank and I. T. Frisch, *Communication, Transmission, and Transportation Networks*, Addison-Wesley, Reading, Mass., 1971, pp. 206–10.

††J. G. Kruskal, "On the Shortest Spanning Subtree of a Graph and the Traveling Salesman Problem," *Proc. Amer. Math Society*, **7**, 1956, 48–50.

§Frank and Frisch, *Communication, Transmission, and Transportation Networks*, p. 209.

Carry out the following step until no longer possible. Among the links not yet selected choose the least-cost link, checking to make sure it does not form a circuit (closed path) with the links already selected.

An example appears in the next section.

OPTIMUM SOLUTION

As noted earlier we follow the work of Chandy and Russell. They have compared their optimum algorithm to heuristics suggested by various authors and have found the heuristics are generally within 10% and often 5% of the optimum solution in those examples for which they have carried out tests. Kershenbaum and Chou have also found that the heuristic solutions came within 5% of the best solution. Note, however, that although this 5% difference may be quite tolerable in many cases, it could still mean considerable losses in some large networks. (This corresponds to $50,000/year for every $1 million/year of network costs. On this basis it may sometimes pay to carry out the more costly computations required to find the optimum network design.)

We shall describe the Chandy-Russell algorithm, as they do, in terms of a simple example. We shall compare the solution obtained with that obtained by several heuristic algorithms and then repeat with another example motivated by the Kershenbaum-Chou work. This will then enable us to demonstrate their unified algorithm.

Consider the simple network problem of Fig. 9-2.* Four terminals (or concentrators) numbered 2, 3, 4, 5 are to be connected to the central facility at 1. The traffic or average number of data units per unit time generated at each of the four nodes is assumed known,** as is the cost of establishing a link between any node pair, including the central facility. We shall focus here on minimizing the total cost subject to a constraint on the traffic flow in each link. The additional reliability constraint for this application is discussed in the paper by Chandy and Russell.

Specifically, let the traffic generated per unit time at each of the four source nodes be

$$a_2 = 2, \quad a_3 = 3, \quad a_4 = 2, \quad a_5 = 1$$

In addition the cost of establishing a link between any pair of nodes (including

---

*Chandy and Russell, "Design of Multipoint Linkages."

**Note that this corresponds to the traffic matrix discussed in earlier chapters. Here because all messages are destined for the center, the matrix formulation is not needed. At the ith node this corresponds to λ_i/μ_i, in terms of previous notation. All messages are assumed to have the same average length so that we could equally well talk of λ_i messages/time generated at the ith node.

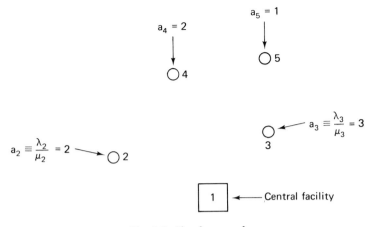

Fig. 9-2. Simple example.

the central node 1), is assumed given by the following symmetrical cost matrix:

node →		1	2	3	4	5
node	1	–	3	3	5	10
↓	2	3	–	6	4	8
$C =$	3	3	6	–	3	5
	4	5	4	3	–	7
	5	10	8	5	7	–

The units used here are arbitrary but typically might be in hundreds of dollars/month. The symbol c_{ij} will be used to denote the i-j entry in the matrix, representing the cost of establishing link i-j between nodes i and j. In an actual problem the cost would of course be determined by the applicable tariffs and would depend on line capacity, type of connection and line leased, distance between the nodes, etc. The assumption here is that one type of line only can be used with capacity specified. The case of choosing from a set of capacities, with corresponding variations in cost, as described in earlier chapters, compounds the design problem and makes it more difficult to solve.

Assume also that the maximum flow allowed on any link is 5 units. This could be the capacity of the lines themselves (in arbitrary units of data units/time) or a maximum flow determined from time delay considerations, as noted earlier.

It is left to the reader to show that the minimum spanning tree for this network, or the *unconstrained* minimum cost network, is the one shown in Fig. 9-3. Note that the flow in the link connecting node 3 to the center is 6

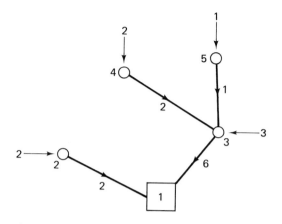

Fig. 9-3. Minimum spanning tree connections, link flows shown. (Unconstrained least-cost solution.)

units, exceeding the maximum allowable. This solution is therefore infeasible. It does provide a lower bound on the minimum cost feasible solution, however. The cost for this network is

$$c_{21} + c_{31} + c_{43} + c_{53} = 14 \text{ units}$$

as obtained from the C matrix.

To find the optimum *feasible* solution one would normally have to test all possible link connections. For even a moderate size network one can appreciate that the computation required can get out of hand. The branch-and-bound technique, as adapted by Chandy and Russell to this problem, provides one way of searching in a systematic fashion so as to ease the computational requirements. Even with this technique the number of iterations to be carried out may become too large to justify its use. Heuristic techniques to be described later must then be utilized.

The approach in the Chandy-Russell algorithm is to partition the complete set of possible connections (or feasible solutions) into smaller and smaller subsets, always testing to see if a lower bound based on a minimum spanning tree connection for that subset is reached. When the lower bound is reached, the algorithm terminates.

The algorithm is based on the observation proved in the Chandy-Russell paper* that those links in the unconstrained solution connected directly to the center (e.g., 2-1 and 3-1 in Fig. 9-3) remain connected to the center in the constrained solution.

In this example initialize by partitioning the complete set of possible connections into two subsets A and B. Let A contain the two links, 2-1 and

*Ibid., Appendix.

3-1; let B have one or both of them lacking. Then clearly the constrained solution must be contained in A, with a lower bound cost of 14 units. The object is now to partition A further, update the lower bound, and check feasible solutions. If one satisfies the bound, the algorithm terminates.

Let A be divided into two subsets AA and AB. To determine subset AA, let one of the tree links in A (one not already connected nor not allowed by constraint considerations) be connected. Subset AB then excludes this link. As an example, establish or connect link 4-3. The two subsets are then defined as follows:

AA—established links 2-1, 3-1, 4-3; links not allowed—none

AB—established links 2-1, 3-1; links not allowed—4-3.

(AA and AB are sketched in Fig. 9-4.)

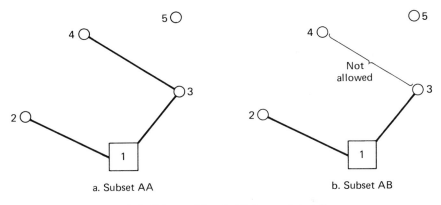

a. Subset AA   b. Subset AB

Fig. 9-4. Subsets AA and AB shown pictorially.

Now find lower bounds (using the minimum spanning tree approach) on cost for AA and AB. Call these bounds L_{AA} and L_{AB}, respectively. The smaller of the two is labeled L. If a feasible solution in that subset has the cost L, the algorithm terminates. If not, subdivide that set further into two sets and proceed, repeating the procedure again.

The algorithm must thus have a way of finding the lower bound on the cost at any iteration. A minimum spanning tree approach can be used here, as noted above. Specifically, consider subset AA. The cost of connecting the established links 2-1, 3-1, and 4-3 is a fixed cost U_{AA}. These can thus be eliminated from consideration, and the minimum spanning tree involving the remaining links found. Call the cost of this tree Z_{AA}. Then clearly the desired lower bound is

$$L_{AA} = U_{AA} + Z_{AA}$$

In this example with 2-1, 3-1, and 4-3 established, $U_{AA} = 9$. The minimum spanning tree to be found is also trivial. For the only remaining node to be connected is node 5. Clearly links 5-3 and 5-4 are not allowed since they lead to infeasible solutions. (The flow through 3-1 would then again be $6 > 5$, the maximum allowable. Chandy and Russell point out that the algorithm may often be speeded up by noting that some links are not allowed in the subsets.) The only possibilities are links 5-2 and 5-1. Since $c_{52} = 8$ and $c_{51} = 10$ from the cost matrix, connection 5-2 is favored. The desired lower bound is thus $L_{AA} = 17$.

Now consider subset AB. For this subset

$$U_{AB} = c_{21} + c_{31} = 6$$

This is again the cost of the established links. To find the minimum spanning tree involving the remaining links, set the c_{ij} entries for the established links in the original C matrix equal to 0. (This effectively eliminates them from consideration.) Set the entries c_{43} and c_{34} for the link not allowed equal to ∞. Call the resultant cost matrix D_{AB}. The unconstrained minimum spanning tree for this matrix is now to be found. Its cost Z_{AB} when added to U_{AB} gives the desired lower bound L_{AB} on the cost of subset AB.

In this example we have as the D_{AB} cost matrix,

node →	1	2	3	4	5
node 1	–	0	0	5	10
↓ 2	0	–	6	4	8
$D_{AB} =$ 3	0	6	–	∞	5
4	5	4	∞	–	7
5	10	8	5	7	–

The minimum spanning tree for this matrix (see Fig. 9-4b also) is readily shown to be the one sketched in Fig. 9-5. It consists of the established links

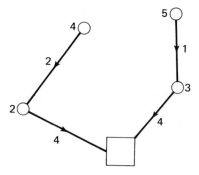

Fig. 9-5. Minimum spanning tree, subset AB, link flows shown. (Optimum constrained solution.)

plus the lowest cost connections of nodes 4 to 2 and 5 to 3. The additional cost of making these connections is

$$Z_{AB} = 4 + 5 = 9$$

Thus

$$L_{AB} = U_{AB} + Z_{AB} = 15$$

Since $L_{AB} = 15$ is less than $L_{AA} = 17$, L_{AB} is chosen as the new (updated) lower bound L. The feasible solutions in AB are now tested against this lower bound. Clearly, however, the unconstrained minimum spanning tree of Fig. 9-5 is feasible as well, since all flows are less than the maximum allowable. Fig. 9-5 thus represents the *optimum* feasible solution in this example, and the algorithm terminates.

A general description of the Chandy-Russell algorithm may be summarized as follows:

Let the subsets in the current (ith) partition be written $s_1^{(i)}, s_2^{(i)}, \ldots, s_k^{(i)}$, with k subsets in all. Let the corresponding lower bounds on the costs be $L_1^{(i)}, L_2^{(i)}, \ldots L_k^{(i)}$. This can then be written generally as the indexed pairs

$$(s_1^{(i)}, L_1^{(i)}; s_2^{(i)}, L_2^{(i)}; \ldots, s_k^{(i)}, L_k^{(i)})L^{(i)}$$

Here $L^{(i)}$ represents the lowest of the lower bounds. Say this is subset j so that $L_j^{(i)} = L^{(i)}$. Test subset $s_j^{(i)}$ for its feasible solutions. If a feasible solution exists that has cost $L_j^{(i)}$, it is obviously the optimum solution as well. The algorithm then terminates.

If no feasible solution has cost $L_j^{(i)}$, relabel set j as set k. Then partition set $s_k^{(i)}$ into sets $s_k^{(i+1)}$ and $s_{k+1}^{(i+1)}$. (The relabeling allows a systematic and straightforward labeling notation to be used as new sets are added.) The partitioning consists of connecting a previously free link in $s_k^{(i)}$ to form subset $s_k^{(i+1)}$ while not allowing this connection in $s_{k+1}^{(i+1)}$. Again lower bounds $L_k^{(i+1)}$ and $L_{k+1}^{(i+1)}$ are computed and the procedure repeats. Note that the lower bound increases or remains the same on successive partitions; i.e., $L^{(i+1)} \geq L^{(i)}$.

HEURISTIC ALGORITHMS

As has already been noted several times in passing, the algorithm for finding the optimum constrained multipoint network may sometimes require very large computer running times, particularly for large networks. It is thus appropriate to consider heuristic algorithms that provide suboptimum solutions in general, with considerable reduction in computational effort. There is thus a trade-off involved in improving the network performance versus the computational effort involved in doing so.

Many algorithms have appeared in the literature that are appropriate for handling multipoint connection problems of the type we are considering.

We shall consider three of these. As already noted Kershenbaum and Chou have presented an algorithm that unifies these various approaches, allowing some comparison of the algorithms to be made.

The three algorithms to be discussed here are the Esau-Williams algorithm, the Prim algorithm,* and the Kruskal algorithm described previously. All three produce a minimum spanning tree solution when constraints are removed. In that case they then differ in their running time (complexity of computation) requirements. In the constrained multipoint design problem with which we are concerned in this chapter, they produce somewhat different designs as well. Experience has shown that the Esau-Williams algorithm generally provides network designs that are closer to optimum,** although the unified algorithm of Kershenbaum-Chou can be modified to provide even better solutions.

The Esau-Williams algorithm essentially searches out the nodes that are furthest from the center (in a cost sense) and connects them to neighboring nodes that provide the greatest cost benefit. Prim's algorithm does the reverse: initially it selects the node closest to the center (again in a cost sense), then connects in those nodes that are closest to those already in the network. Kruskal's algorithm simply connects the least-cost links, one at a time. For application to the multipoint problem, constraints have to be checked as a possible connection is made.

We now demonstrate each of these algorithms using the previous example (Fig. 9-2) as a test problem.

Esau-Williams Algorithm

Step 0. Initialize by calculating all trade-off parameters†

$$t_{ij} = c_{ij} - c_{i1} \qquad \text{all } i, j$$

with c_{ij} the appropriate entry from the cost matrix C. This parameter thus measures the difference in cost between connecting node i to node j, and node i directly to the center.

---

*L. R. Esau and K. C. Williams, "A Method for Approximating the Optimal Network," *IBM System Journal*, **5**, no. 3, 1966, 142–47; R. C. Prim, "Shortest Connection Networks and Some Generalizations," *Bell System Technical Journal*, **36**, Nov. 1957, 1389–1401.

**Kershenbaum and Chou, "Designing Multidrop Teleprocessing Networks"; Chandy and Russell, "Design of Multipoint Linkages."

†We use the notation and formulation of Kershenbaum and Chou here. In the original Esau-Williams paper all nodes are first connected to the center. A trade-off function is then calculated for each pair of nodes representing the saving gained by removing the central connection and creating a link connection. The algorithm then *maximizes* the savings. In the notation used here the trade-off function is the negative of the Esau-Williams function, and one chooses to *minimize* it.

A few examples from the problem of Fig. 9-2 are

$$t_{24} = c_{24} - c_{21} = 4 - 3 = 1$$
$$t_{42} = c_{42} - c_{41} = 4 - 5 = -1$$
$$t_{53} = c_{53} - c_{51} = 5 - 10 = -5$$
$$t_{35} = c_{35} - c_{31} = 5 - 3 = 2$$

Thus node 2 is closer to the center than to node 4, while node 4 is closer to 2 than to the center.

In addition we have

$$t_{21} = t_{31} = t_{41} = t_{51} = 0$$

All parameters > 0 may be disregarded since it obviously pays to connect the node in question directly to the center rather than to the other node selected.

Step 1. Select the minimum t_{ij} and consider connecting i to j.
In this example $t_{53} = -5$ is the minimum. Hence we consider connecting 5 to 3.

Step 2. Check to see if the constraints are satisfied. If yes, go to Step 3. If not, set $t_{ij} = \infty$, go back to Step 1 and select again.

In this example the flow through link 5-3 if connected would be $a_5 = 1$, which is less than the maximum 5. Thus the constraint is satisfied.

Step 3. Add link i-j; label node i with the label of node $j(i \leftarrow j)$ to show i is connected to j; reevaluate the constraints and update the trade-off functions. Then go back to Step 1.

For example, with link 5-3 connected in the example of Fig. 9-2, $5 \leftarrow 3$, flow a_3 is now $a_3' = a_5 + a_3 = 4$, and node 5 can no longer be connected to the center. Trade-off functions t_{53} and t_{35} can thus be expunged from the list.

Continuing with this example, the next link connection to be considered (Step 1) is $t_{43} = -2$. If 4 is connected to 3, however (Step 2), the new flow through 3 is $a_4 + a_3' = 6 > 5$. This is thus not allowed, $t_{43} \leftarrow \infty$, and we return to Step 1. This time min $t_{ij} = t_{42} = -1$. The constraints in this case are satisfied ($a_2' = a_2 + a_4 = 4 < 5$), and the connection can be made. Repeating again, we finally obtain the complete network connection of Fig. 9-6. Details are left to the reader. The numbers in parentheses indicate the order in which the various connections were made. Note that this network is exactly the optimum network of Fig. 9-5!

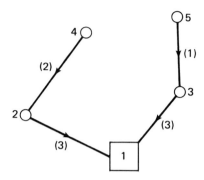

Fig. 9-6. Steps in Esau-Williams algorithm; numbers represent order in which connections are made.

Prim's Algorithm

Again we use the Kershenbaum-Chou notation for consistency and apply the algorithm to the same simple network already considered (Fig. 9-2).

> *Step 0.*   Here to initialize each node is assigned a weighting factor w_i, with $w_1 = 0$; $w_i = -\infty$, $i \neq 1$. The trade-off function t_{ij} is then defined as

$$t_{ij} \longleftarrow c_{ij} - w_i$$

Initially then, all $t_{ij} = \infty$, except t_{1j}, representing the cost of connecting each node to the center. The only node initially connected in the network is thus the central node 1.

> *Step 1.*   Find the minimum t_{ij}. The algorithm thus searches out the minimum cost of connecting a node to one already connected in the network.

In the example of Fig. 9-2, initially all $t_{ij} = \infty$ except $t_{12} = c_{12} = 3$, $t_{13} = 3$, $t_{14} = 5$, $t_{15} = 10$. Then either 2 or 3 may be connected to 1. Say t_{12} is chosen.

> *Step 2.*   Check to see if the constraints are violated. If not, go to Step 3. If yes, set the min $t_{ij} = \infty$, and return to Step 1.

In this example the flow constraint is not violated since $a_2 = 2 < 5$.

> *Step 3.*   Add link *i-j*, setting $w_j \leftarrow 0$, readjust the constraints, and recalculate all t_{ij}. Then go back to Step 1.

Repeating the procedure for the example under study, we find that link 3-1 is the next one added, then 4-3 (connecting link 4 to link 3 already in the network), and finally 5-2. Details are left to the reader.

The final (suboptimum) network using the Prim algorithm is shown in Fig. 9-7. The successive order of connections made is again indicated by the numbers in parentheses. The total cost of connecting the 4 links indicated is readily shown to be 17—greater than the 15 units of cost for the optimum network connection of Fig. 9-5.

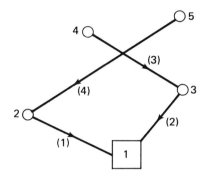

Fig. 9-7. Prim's algorithm applied to same problem as in Fig. 9-6. (Kruskal algorithm gives same result.)

Kruskal Algorithm

In this algorithm, as already noted, the least-cost links are selected, one at a time, the constraints checked, and the procedure repeated until all nodes have been connected.

Thus for the example of Fig. 9-2 again, the minimum entry in the matrix is min $c_{ij} = 3$. Since links 2-1, 3-1, and 4-3 all have this same value, a random choice must be made. Say the connection 2-1 is made. The constraint obviously checks here. Repeating for 3-1, the constraint again checks. Then for 4-3, $a_4 + a_3 = 5 \leq 5$ also checks. However, no further connections may now be made through node 3. Thus the connections 5-3 and 5-4, which are the next in order of increasing cost, cannot be made. Finally the algorithm concludes with link 5-2 being connected into the network. The resultant network is thus exactly that found using the Prim algorithm. Both results are poorer in this case than the Esau-Williams result which gave the true optimum configuration in this case.

A second example for comparison is shown in Fig. 9-8. In Fig. 9-8b we show allowable connections and costs involved. (The example and the numbers shown are taken from the Kershenbaum-Chou paper, Fig. 2. The nodes have been renumbered, however, to make them agree with the notation used here.)

The C matrix (cost matrix) for this network, corresponding to the costs shown in Fig. 9-8, is given by

node→	1	2	3	4	5	6
node ↓ 1	–	2	20	19	3	3
2	2	–	8	–	–	–
$C =$ 3	20	8	–	19	–	–
4	19	–	19	–	4	–
5	3	–	–	4	–	1
6	3	–	–	–	1	–

Connections not allowed are indicated by –.

Assume that the maximum flow in any link can again not exceed 5. Say the traffic numbers (traffic generated/unit time) at each node and destined for the central node are given by

$$a_2 = 2, \quad a_3 = 3, \quad a_4 = 1, \quad a_5 = 3, \quad a_6 = 2$$

These are indicated in Fig. 9-8a.

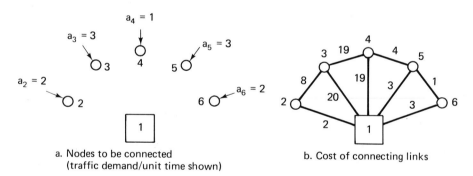

a. Nodes to be connected
(traffic demand/unit time shown)

b. Cost of connecting links

Fig. 9-8. Another example of terminals to be connected to central unit.

The minimum spanning tree for this collection of nodes is shown in Fig. 9-9. The traffic flow in each branch is also indicated alongside the appropriate arrow. Note the flow constraint is violated in branch 5-1. The cost of this tree connection is 18 units. This thus serves as a lower bound on the cost of a feasible (constrained) set of network connections.

The optimum (lowest cost) feasible network is readily found using the Chandy-Russell branch-and-bound technique previously described. We shall outline the approach here quite briefly, leaving details to the reader. Recall

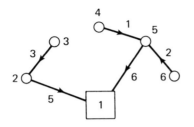

Fig. 9-9. Minimum spanning tree, flows indicated.

that links (branches) 2-1 and 5-1 in the minimum spanning tree of Fig. 9-9 that are already connected to the central unit remain connected in the optimum feasible network. For the first feasible subset AA, then, connect in any other link. Say link 3-2 is thus established. In this case the two subsets AA and AB to be investigated are defined as follows:

AA: established links 2-1, 5-1, 3-2

AB: established links 2-1, 5-1; links not allowed—3-2.

The lower bound costs on these are then found, using the minimum spanning tree procedure of Chandy-Russell described earlier, to be given by $L_{AA} = 18$, $L_{AB} = 29$. The minimum spanning tree for AA turns out to be the same as that of Fig. 9-9. In addition the flow constraints indicate that link 4-3 is not allowed since its connection into the network would violate the constraints.

Clearly the lower bound of the two subsets is $L = L_{AA} = 18$. The solutions for this bound are again infeasible. Subset AA must then be further partitioned into subsets AAA and AAB. Both have links 2-1, 5-1, 3-2 established and link 4-3 not allowed. To define AAA, connect 6-5 in. Then AAB does not allow this connection. Proceeding again as previously, the lower bounds are now found to be $L_{AAA} = 33$ and $L_{AAB} = 20$. The minimum spanning tree solution for AAB with cost 20 is shown in Fig. 9-10. It is apparent

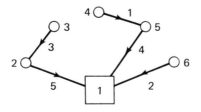

Fig. 9-10. Optimum constrained solution, flows indicated. Cost = 20. (Esau-Williams solution also.)

that this is a feasible solution. Hence this must be the optimum solution as well. The algorithm thus terminates.

The heuristic algorithms may also be applied to this problem. It is left to the reader to show that Fig. 9-10 turns out to be the Esau-Williams solution as well. The Kruskal and Prim algorithms produce the network shown in Fig. 9-11. Its cost, as indicated, is 33 units. It has already been noted that both Chandy-Russell and Kershenbaum-Chou have found through experimentation that the Esau-Williams algorithm generally performs well. Kershenbaum and Chou in particular have tested the Kruskal and Prim algorithms as well, and have found the ordering of results obtained to be given by Esau-Williams, Kruskal, Prim. Both papers quoted contain references to other heuristic algorithms as well.

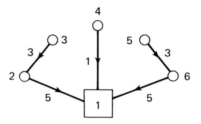

Fig. 9-11. Suboptimum solution, Kruskal and Prim algorithms. Cost = 33.

Unified Heuristic Algorithm

Kershenbaum and Chou have shown that all three heuristic algorithms described thus far, plus others quoted in the literature, may be considered special cases of a unified algorithm appropriate for solving the multipoint connection problem. The algorithm is essentially a modified form of the Kruskal algorithm where instead of successively connecting in more and more costly links, the cost less a weighting factor is used as the measure of comparison.

To be specific we shall use the notation already defined above. Thus let c_{ij} be the line cost of link i-j, connecting terminal i to j. Let w_i be the weight associated with terminal i. Then the trade-off function $t_{ij} = c_{ij} - w_i$ is the measure of comparison in this modified Kruskal-type algorithm. Different definitions of w_i produce the various algorithms already described as well as others in the literature. The table below* indicates the weighting factor w_i appropriate to each algorithm. This includes initial values as well as changes that may have to be made during the execution of the algorithm.

*Kershenbaum and Chou, "Designing Multidrop Teleprocessing Networks," Table 1, p. 1766.

TABLE OF WEIGHTS

Algorithm	Initialization	Update when i–j is brought in
Kruskal	$w_i = 0, \quad i = 1, \ldots, N$	none
Prim	$w_1 = 0$ $w_i = -\infty, \quad i = 2, \ldots, N$	$w_j \leftarrow 0$
Esau-Williams	$w_i = c_{i_1}, \quad i = 1, \ldots, N$	$w_i \leftarrow w_j$

The unified algorithm is readily described as follows:*

Step 0. Initialize the w_i for $i = 1, 2, \ldots, N$. Initialize the constraints. Set $t_{ij} \leftarrow c_{ij} - w_i$ for all i, j when c_{ij} exists and no constraints are violated with the connection i-j.

Step 1. Find $t_{i'j'} = \min_{\substack{i,j \\ i \neq j}} t_{ij}$

If $t_{i'j'} = \infty$, terminate algorithm. Otherwise go to Step 2.

Step 2. Evaluate the constraints under the connection i'-j'. If any are violated, set $t_{i'j'} = \infty$, go to Step 1. If not, go to Step 3.

Step 3. Add link i'-j'. Relabel one of the nodes to correspond to the other. (Connection is made.) Reevaluate constraints. Update w_i as in table, reevaluate t_{ij}, go to Step 1.

Note that we have essentially carried through all these steps earlier in describing the three heuristic algorithms introduced in this chapter. Kershenbaum and Chou have considered other w-rules than the three corresponding to these three algorithms. One approach suggested is to parameterize the weights w_i and then search through the various solutions obtained for different values of the parameters. As an example let c_{i_2} be the cost of connecting node i to its second nearest feasible neighbor. One rule Kershenbaum and Chou have found useful is then given by

$$w_i = a(bc_{i_1} + (1 - b)c_{i_2})$$

By choosing several values of the parameters a and b, one can generate a variety of solutions. Each choice favors a different set of links. With $a = 0$, the Kruskal algorithm is obtained. With $a = b = 1$, the Esau-Williams algorithm results, etc.

In addition to the cost of the network solution obtained (how close to optimum the solution is), the effectiveness of an algorithm depends on its computational complexity or computer running time required. In this parti-

*Ibid., p. 1765.

cular algorithm (as well as the special cases contained within it) a particularly time-consuming task is that of calculating t_{ij} for all node pairs and then searching through the list for the minimum. This has to be done over again each time a link is connected into the network and updating takes place. If there are N nodes (terminals, concentrators, etc.) to be connected together, there are potentially $N(N-1)/2$ values of t_{ij} to be examined. For large N this can be very time-consuming. In this case however it is generally unlikely that all node pairs need to be examined; many nodes may be large distances apart and obviously won't be connected together. In fact at worst one may always connect a node directly to the center. Kershenbaum and Chou have in fact found that large network problems may be handled effectively by just allowing the K-nearest neighbors ($K \leq 5$ appears a good choice experimentally) as well as the central node to be considered as feasible candidates for connection to a given node. This reduces the computational complexity considerably. The unified algorithm is then found to be bounded in the number of computations required by

$$AN^2 + BKN + CKN \log_2 K$$

Here A, B, C are arbitrary constants.

The leading N^2 term is due to the need, in the general algorithm, to update all w_i weights each time a node is connected into the network. In those cases where this is not necessary (the three algorithms described previously fit into this class), the computational complexity reduces to $BKN + CKN \log_2 K$ operations.

PROBLEMS

9.1 Refer to Fig. 9-8. For this centralized network example verify that Fig. 9-9 to 9-11 provide, respectively, the minimum spanning tree solution, the minimum cost network obeying the constraints as obtained both by the branch-and-bound technique and the Esau-Williams algorithm, and a suboptimum solution found using both the Kruskal and Prim algorithms.

9.2 Refer to the centralized network example of Problem 5.1.

(1) Find the minimum cost network if there are no constraints on traffic in any link, all line capacities are identical, and the cost of the lines is $0.50/month/mile.

(2) Find the minimum cost network if the line capacities are all 2400 bps with a cost of $0.50/mo/mile (*Hint*: Why is this now a *constrained* flow problem?)

(3) Find the minimum cost network if the line capacities are now all 4800 bps, at a cost of $0.65/mo/mile. Compare (2) and (3). Use the branch-and-bound algorithm in (2) and (3).

9.3 Repeat parts (2) and (3) of Problem 9.2 above using the three heuristic algorithms discussed in this chapter.

9.4 Refer to the seven-city centralized network discussed in Chap. 1, 3, and 5. Recall that concentrators in Chicago, Detroit, New York, Charlotte, Tallahassee, Miami, and New Orleans are to be connected to a central computer facility in Washington, D.C. Determine the least-cost network assuming all line capacities are the same and that the cost of the lines is $1.50/mo/mile. There are no constraints on the design.

9.5 Repeat Problem 9.4 if the communication costs are $1.50/mo/mile for the first 200 miles, $1.25/mo/mile for the second 200 miles, and $1.00/mo/mile for any distance greater than 400 miles.

9.6 A bank in Paris decides to establish a data network connecting terminals located in each of its nine branches in Paris and in the outlying districts to a processing facility in its central office. A multipoint connection is to be used to minimize cost. The costs in francs/month of establishing connections between the various branches and the central facility (designated as "1") are given in Table P9-1. Traffic generated at each station, in average number of bps., is shown in Table P9-2. The line capacities are all 480 bps.

(1) Use the branch-and-bound technique and a heuristic algorithm and compare results.

(2) Repeat (1) if the effective line utilization on any line is to be less than 0.5.

TABLE P9-1

CONNECTION COSTS (FRANCS/MONTH)

Branch →	1	2	3	4	5	6	7	8	9	10
Branch ↓ 1	—	50	150	200	200	100	100	200	300	200
2		—	100	180	100	250	–	–	–	–
3			—	100	200	300	–	–	–	–
4				—	250	300	–	–	–	–
5					—	50	100	200	300	–
6						—	50	150	250	–
7							—	100	200	100
8								—	100	50
9									—	100
10										—

TABLE P9-2

EXPECTED TRAFFIC (BPS), BETWEEN BRANCH AND CENTRAL

Branch →	2	3	4	5	6	7	8	9	10
	150	80	150	100	80	100	100	100	150

9.7 A data network is to be established connecting each of the 48 state capitals in the continental United States to the White House in Washington, D.C.

(1) Determine the least-cost network if cost is proportional to distance and no constraints are invoked.

(2) Any one link can handle messages from no more than three capitals. Use the branch-and-bound technique and compare results with those of (1).

(3) Use the Kruskal algorithm to find a suboptimum constrained solution and check with that of (2).

9.8 A bank in Little Rock, Ark., is setting up a data network to connect its seven branches to a CPU in Little Rock. The seven cities in which the branches are located and the cost connection matrix for them are indicated in Table P9-3. (The costs were derived by taking a proportion due to distance along with a proportion involving the total business handled by each branch of the bank. 2400 bps lines are used.)

(1) Show the minimum spanning tree solution is that of Fig. P9.8.

TABLE P9-3

COST CONNECTION MATRIX

City	Little Rock	N. Little Rock	Fort Smith	Pine Bluff	Jonesboro	Hot Springs	Fayetteville	Texarkana
Little Rock	–	2	52	13	45	15	58	59
N. Little Rock	2	–	52	14	43	16	58	62
Fort Smith	52	52	–	60	85	42	23	55
Pine Bluff	13	15	60	–	50	18	72	50
Jonesboro	45	43	85	50	–	59	81	95
Hot Springs	15	16	42	18	59	–	55	41
Fayetteville	58	58	23	72	81	55	–	78
Texarkana	59	62	55	50	95	41	78	–

Arkansas

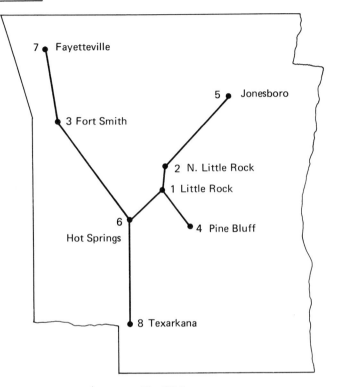

Fig. P9.8

TABLE P9-4

MESSAGES GENERATED

City	Population	Traffic (messages/min.)
Little Rock	132,483	30
N. Little Rock	60,040	14
Fort Smith	53,802	12
Pine Bluff	57,389	13
Jonesboro	30,482	6
Hot Springs	35,631	7
Fayetteville	30,729	6
Texarkana	30,840	6

(2) The traffic generated by each branch (proportional to the population of the city) is indicated, in messages/min., in Table P9-4. No more than 20 messages/min. can be handled on any one link. Use the

branch-and-bound technique to find the constrained optimum solution. Show that this consists simply of connecting node 3 in Fig. P9.8 directly to node 1. Find the average queueing delay for the network, assuming concentrators are used at each of the nodes. Assume messages average 3600 bits in length, including overhead.

Network Design

Algorithms

10

In the previous chapter we discussed the very important multipoint connection problem of network design. Recall that in that problem we were interested in determining the least-cost way of connecting terminals to a concentrator subject to traffic (time delay) and/or reliability constraints. Alternately the problem may be phrased as one of optimumly connecting concentrators in fixed, known locations in multipoint fashion to a central computer or processing facility.

That problem focuses of course on just one portion of the overall network design question. As previously stated this consists of deciding where, in a geographically-distributed network, to locate concentrators or multiplexers, how many to use, which terminals to associate with which concentrators, and, finally, how to interconnect the concentrators. It is apparent that this overall question is so complex, particularly with modern networks incorporating hundreds of terminals and tens or hundreds of concentrators, that it cannot be solved in its entirety. The approach has been rather to take one subproblem at a time, isolate it from the main problem, develop algorithms for its solution, and then combine the solutions into the solution of the overall network design problem. Even in this case resort is of necessity commonly made to heuristic algorithms, as noted in the previous chapter. Heuristics are then compared on the basis of their expected convergence to solutions "not too far" from the optimum and on their comparative computational requirements.

The validity of this piecemeal approach, aside from its absolute necessity at the present time, rests on the observation that most traffic inputs tend to cluster in small geographic regions. Large urban areas, for example, would be expected to generate more traffic than sprawling rural regions. It is thus logical to assume that hierarchies of network design should lead to fairly good solutions. For example, terminals in one area would be expected to be connected to a concentrator located centrally to that area. Concentrators in turn could be interconnected *independent* of the way in which terminals were connected to them; the summed effect of the traffic coming into a concentrator, the overall input traffic rate, is the significant parameter in determining the interconnection of concentrators. Alternately, the concentrators in a region could be connected in multipoint fashion to a "super" or regional concentrator, and the regional concentrators then in turn interconnected. This hierarchical approach has in fact been under investigation as a mode of attack for extremely large data networks with thousands of terminals interconnected.*

Centralized network design, with all messages flowing inward to a central computer, lends itself particularly to a piecemeal approach to design: first connect terminals to a particular concentrator in multipoint fashion, then connect the concentrators multipoint fashion to the central facility. The techniques of the last chapter can then be used directly in solving each one of these two subproblems, *providing*, however, that the concentrator locations are known beforehand.

In this chapter we focus on two intermediate design problems, outlining heuristics suggested for their solution. These consist of:

1. the question of where to locate concentrators, how many to use and which terminals to associate with each, in a centralized star-type network configuration.

2. the minimum cost interconnection of concentrators in a distributed-network environment.

Although these again touch only on a part of the overall design problem, the two techniques discussed, combined with the multipoint design algorithms of the last chapter, can be used to provide a viable design for an overall network. The reader is referred to the literature, where appropriate, for design approaches and algorithms that attempt this further synthesis.

*Network Analysis Corporation, Glen Cove, N.Y. First semiannual report, May 1973, ARPA Contract DAHC15-73-C-0135, Chap. 3.

TERMINAL CONNECTIONS AND CONCENTRATOR LOCATIONS IN A CENTRALIZED NETWORK

The first set of algorithms we discuss focuses again on a centralized data network. Here two levels are envisioned, however: terminals may be concentrated into a remote concentrator or connected directly to the central processor, and the remote concentrators in turn are then connected directly to the central facility. Terminal locations are assumed known, as are *possible* sites for the concentrators. A subset of these concentrators is to be selected, as is the set of terminals associated with each. Two simple algorithms, the so-called "Add" algorithm and the "Drop" algorithm, are outlined for the solution of this double hierarchy of star connections. (These will be seen to be similar in form to the Esau-Williams algorithm of the last chapter.) We follow the approach of Bahl and Tang.* The same paper also discusses a more complex algorithm for solving the same problem.

Another algorithm is described, in the context of an example, by James Martin in his book, *Systems Analysis for Data Transmission.*** Martin also provides an example of connecting concentrators in multipoint fashion to a central facility, rather than the star connection noted thus far.† Woo and Tang†† have also extended the double hierarchy of star connections to include terminals connected in multipoint fashion to concentrators, which are then connected in star connection to the central node. An improved algorithm for concentrator location is provided by D. A. Greenberg.§

The problem to be discussed in this section may be described succinctly as follows:§§ A number n of known terminals is to be connected, via concentrators, to a central facility S_0. Call the set of terminals $\{T_1, T_2, \ldots, T_n\}$. A possible set of concentrator locations $\{S_1, S_2, \ldots, S_m\}$ is available, and a subset is to be chosen, with terminals assigned to each or connected directly

---

*L. R. Bahl and D. T. Tang, "Optimization of Concentrator Locations in Teleprocessing Networks," *Proc. Symposium on Computer-Communication Networks and Teletraffic*, Polytechnic Institute of Brooklyn, New York, 1972, pp. 355–62.

**J. Martin, *Systems Analysis for Data Transmission*, Prentice-Hall, Inc., Englewood Cliffs, N.J., 1972, Chap. 42.

†Ibid., Chap. 43.

††L. S. Woo and D. T. Tang, "Optimization of Teleprocessing Networks with Concentrators," *Proc. IEEE National Telecommunications Conference*, Atlanta, Ga., Nov. 1973, pp. 37C–1 to 37C–5.

§D. A. Greenberg, "A New Approach for the Optimal Placement of Concentrators in a Remote Terminal Communications Network," *Proc. IEEE National Telecommunications Conference*, Atlanta, Ga., Nov. 1973, pp. 37D–1 to 37D–7.

§§Bahl and Tang, "Optimization of Concentrator Locations."

to S_0. (The set of concentrator locations can be chosen to be at terminal locations, if desired.)

Concentrator S_j has a fixed cost f_j consisting of fixed hardware cost and the communications cost of connecting S_j to S_0. (Higher speed lines must of course be used to accommodate the terminal traffic.) Each concentrator is assumed to have a maximum port or terminal capacity e. (This is the maximum number of terminals that may be connected to it.) For the central facility S_0 we choose $f_0 = 0$ and $e_0 \geq n$. Let c_{ij} be the cost of connecting terminal i to concentrator j ($i = 1, 2, \ldots, n; j = 1, 2, \ldots, m$). Low-speed lines are assumed used here. We can set up an explicit expression for the total cost function Z to be minimized by defining two binary connection parameters. Thus, let

$$x_{ij} = 1, \quad \text{iff } T_i \text{ is connected to } S_j$$
$$= 0, \quad \text{otherwise} \tag{10-1}$$

Call concentrator S_j *open* if it is in use, *closed* if it is not in use. Let $y_j = 1$ if S_j is open, $y_j = 0$ if S_j is closed. Then

$$y_j = 1 \quad \text{iff } \sum_{i=1}^{n} x_{ij} > 0$$
$$= 0, \quad \text{otherwise} \tag{10-2}$$

(Thus, $y_j = 1$ so long as there is at least 1 terminal connected to it.) The total cost Z to be minimized is then

$$Z = \sum_{j=0}^{m} y_j f_j + \sum_{i=1}^{n} \sum_{j=0}^{m} x_{ij} c_{ij} \tag{10-3}$$

The first term represents concentrator cost; the second, the cost of terminal-to-concentrator links.

The minimization is to be carried out subject to two constraints:

(1) $$\sum_{j=0}^{m} x_{ij} = 1 \quad (i = 1, 2, \ldots, n)$$

(This indicates a terminal i must be connected to some concentrator including the central facility S_0.)

(2) $$\sum_{i=1}^{n} x_{ij} \leq e \quad (j = 1, 2, \ldots, m)$$

(This indicates of course that no more than e terminals may be connected to concentrator j.)

The problem posed here, that of finding the set of y_j's and x_{ij}'s that minimizes Z subject to the two constraints, is a 0–1 integer programming problem. The same problem arises in other fields of engineering and in management science, and is known as the capacitated plant location problem. Exhaustive enumeration or branch-and-bound procedures have been used for the exact solution of problems of this type.* We focus here on two heuristic algorithms, however, again because of the relative complexity of data network problems.

If the choice and location of the concentrators to be used are known, i.e., the y_j's are known, the problem can be solved easily by linear programming techniques. This special case may be used as well as a starting point for heuristics.

We now describe the two heuristic algorithms in terms of a simple example. Six terminals $T_1 \ldots T_6$ are to be connected to three concentrators S_1, S_2, S_3 or to the central node S_0, as shown in Fig. 10-1. Note that concentrator

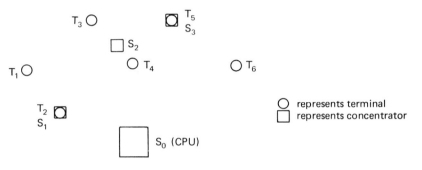

Fig. 10-1. Network example.

S_1 and terminal T_2 are at the same site, as are concentrator S_3 and terminal T_5. Assume that no more than three terminals may access any one concentrator. Hence $e = 3$. Also say the concentrator costs are all identical. Thus $f_1 = f_2 = f_3 = 2$. The terminal-concentrator link costs are given by the c_{ij} matrix of Table 10-1.

TABLE 10-1

COST MATRIX, c_{ij}

$S_j \rightarrow$	0	1	2	3
$T_i \downarrow$ 1	2	1	2	4
2	1	0	1	2
3	4	1	2	2
4	1	2	1	2
5	2	3	2	0
6	4	4	3	2

*Ibid; see references to the plant location literature.

Add Algorithm

The first algorithm to be described is the Add algorithm. Initialization consists of connecting all terminals to S_0. All concentrators are closed. Concentrators are opened one at a time, in iterative fashion, to provide a maximum decrease in cost. The algorithm is thus a steepest-descent type of algorithm. Fig. 10-2 shows the initialization step of the algorithm for the example under discussion. The total cost in this case is

$$Z = \sum_{i=1}^{6} c_{i0} = 14$$

(Note that this is the sum of the entries in column 0 in Table 10-1.)

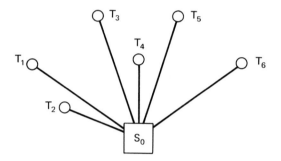

Fig. 10-2. Initialization, Add algorithm. $Z = 14$.

Iteration 1.

Each concentrator is checked, one at a time, to determine which one, if any, provides the greatest improvement over the initialization step. Thus, open S_1 up first and connect the terminals with the largest decrease in cost, $c_{i1} - c_{i0}$, to a maximum of $e = 3$. In this case terminals T_1, T_2, T_3 connected to S_1 are found to provide the greatest improvement over the initialization step. For these three terminals connected to S_1, the others remaining connected to S_0,

$$Z_1 = \sum_{i=4}^{6} c_{i0} + f_1 + \sum_{i=1}^{3} c_{i1} = 11$$

Now try opening S_2 instead. Here terminals 3 and 6 only are to be connected. (An additional terminal connected to S_2 provides no improvement over connecting to S_0 directly.) For this case it is readily found that

$$Z_2 = 13$$

Finally, with S_3 open, connecting terminals 3, 5, 6 to it provides the greatest improvement over initialization. Specifically,

$$Z_3 = 10$$

All concentrators have now been checked. Z_3 is the smallest cost, so S_3 is opened up, and iteration 1 ends. The result of this iteration is shown in Fig. 10-3.

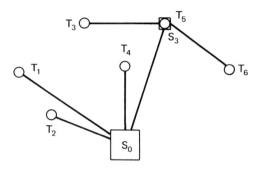

Fig. 10-3. Iteration 1, Add algorithm. $Z = 10$.

Iteration 2.

S_3 is left open, and S_1 and S_2 are checked to see if opening one or the other provides any improvement. All terminals ($i = 1, 2, \ldots, 6$) are considered, including those previously connected to S_3. Opening S_1 first, with terminals T_1, T_2, T_3 connected to it, we find we gain 3 units of cost and lose 2 for a net gain of 1. (The difference in costs, $c_{i3} - c_{i1}$ and $c_{i0} - c_{i1}$, for all terminals connected to S_3 and S_0, respectively, is evaluated to see if improvements result.) Repeating for S_2 we find no improvement possible. The iteration is thus completed with $Z = 9$, and T_1, T_2, T_3 connected to S_1, T_4 to S_0, and T_5 and T_6 to S_3. No further improvement is possible using this algorithm (i.e., all terminals and concentrators are accounted for), and iterations stop. The final Add algorithm solution is shown in Fig. 10-4.

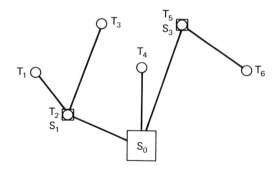

Fig. 10-4. Iteration 2, final solution, Add algorithm. $Z = 9$.

Drop Algorithm

This algorithm is, as the name indicates, very similar to the Add algorithm. It starts however with all concentrators *open* and then proceeds to close one at a time, systematically and iteratively, until no further improvement is possible.

To initialize, terminals are connected to their "nearest" (i.e., least-cost) concentrator, in order, until the maximum number are accommodated by any concentrator. Specifically, for the terminals and concentrators of Fig. 10-1, scanning through the entries of Table 10-1, row by row, we find the following connection or incidence matrix after the initialization step. (The entries represent nonzero x_{ij}'s.)

TABLE 10-2

INITIAL CONNECTION MATRIX x_{ij}

$S_j \rightarrow$	0	1	2	3
$T_i \downarrow$ 1			1	
2			1	
3			1	
4				1*	
5					1
6					1

*This entry could equally-well have been located in column 0 since the cost c_{4j} is the same in either case, from Table 10-1. We choose column 2, even though the connection will ultimately be shown to be poorer, to keep the method general.

The cost of this configuration, shown in Fig. 10-5, is readily shown to be

$$Z = 11$$

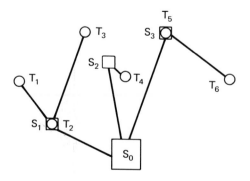

Fig. 10-5. Initialization, Drop algorithm. $Z = 11$.

For the first iteration we try closing one concentrator at a time to see if any improvement results. Thus choosing S_1 first as a possible choice for closing we find that transferring T_1 to S_0 or S_2 results in a negative gain of -1. The same is true for T_2. Transferring T_3 to S_2 or S_3 also results in a gain of -1. The *net* gain is $-3 + f_2 = -1$. So this choice is not acceptable. Closing S_2, with T_4 transferred to S_0, provides a net gain of 2. Finally, considering the closing of S_3 we find a net gain of -1. The iteration is thus completed with S_2 closed, T_4 transferred to S_0, and $Z = 9$. The resultant configuration is shown sketched in Fig. 10-6.

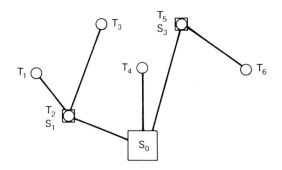

Fig. 10-6. Iteration 1, final solution, Drop algorithm. $Z = 9$.

We now repeat for the next iteration, checking to see if closing S_3 or S_1 results in a cost improvement. It turns out in this case that no improvement is possible, and the algorithm concludes with the solution shown in Fig. 10-6. Note that in this very simple example the solutions obtained by both the Add and Drop algorithms are the same.

DISTRIBUTED NETWORK DESIGN

Cut Saturation Algorithm

A variety of algorithms have appeared in the literature that focus on least-cost topological design of distributed networks. In most cases concentrator locations are assumed known. It is then required to choose the set of links, i.e., find the communications network that produces a least-cost design subject to various constraints. Among the constraints included are generally a maximum average time delay for data transmission and some specified reliability criterion. The latter quantity is often specified in terms of nodal connectivity. Two-connectivity, for example, means that every node (concentrator location) is connected to at least two other nodes. This implies at the very least alternate route capability in the event of a link failure any-where in the network. The optimum choice of link capacity is often included in the network algorithm because of the generally nonlinear relation between cost and capacity. The choice of capacity for fixed topology has already been discussed in previous chapters. It is obviously a much more complex problem to include the optimum choice of capacity in algorithms designed to find the optimum network topology.

In this introductory section we focus for simplicity's sake on a heuristic algorithm that assumes link capacity to be given and to be the same for all links in the network. The reader is referred to the literature for a discussion of algorithms that include the choice of link capacity as well.* The algorithm to be described briefly here, the so-called *cut saturation algorithm*, iteratively finds the least-cost distributed network for a specified throughput, subject to time delay and reliability constraints. The throughput represents the traffic in bits/sec (bps), generated, on the average, between any two nodes in the net-work, assumed the same for all node pairs. The time delay constraint is taken care of by a routing subroutine that finds the optimum routing of messages between all source-destination pairs after each network design iteration. Reliability is ensured by a two-connectivity constraint. The cut saturation algorithm** consists of five basic steps in any one iteration:

1. *Routing.* The optimal link flows are found, for a given network design, that minimize overall average time delay. Some optimum routing algorithms for this purpose are discussed in the next chapter.

2. *Saturated cutset determination.* Once the optimum flows are found the links are ordered according to their utilization. The links are then removed, one at a time, in order of utilization. The minimal set that discon-nects the network is called a saturated cutset. The saturated cutset for a 26-node ARPA network is shown in Fig. 10-7.†

---

*A great deal of attention has focused in the USA on the design of networks using the so-called TELPAK-tariff for high capacity links. Papers on network design that use TELPAK tariffs as a specific example include B. Rothfarb and M. C. Goldstein, "The One-Terminal TELPAK Problem," *J. of ORSA*, **19**, 1971, 156–69; D. J. Kleitman and A. Claus, "A Large-Scale Multicommodity Flow Problem: TELPAK," *Proc. Symposium on Com-puter-Communication Networks and Teletraffic*, Polytechnic Institute of Brooklyn, New York, 1972, pp. 335–38; M. C. Goldstein, "Design of Long-Distance Telecommunications Networks—The TELPAK Problem," *IEEE Trans. on Circuit Theory*, **CT-20**, 1973, 186–92; E. Hansler, "An Experimental Heuristic Procedure to Optimize A Telecommunication Network Under Nonlinear Cost Functions," *Proc. Seventh Annual Princeton Conference on Information Sciences and Systems*, New Jersey, 1973, pp. 130–37.

**M. Gerla, H. Frank, W. Chou, and J. Eckl, "A Cut Saturation Algorithm for Topological Design of Packet-Switched Communication Networks," *Proc. IEEE National Telecommunications Conference*, San Diego, Dec. 1974, pp. 1074–85.

†Network Analysis Corp., Second semi-annual report, Dec. 1973, ARPA Contract DAHC15–73–C–0135, Fig. 5, Chap. 4.

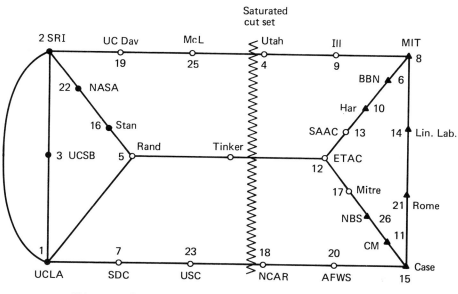

● ▲ = "Distance − 2" nodes for add-only step

Fig. 10-7. 26-node ARPA network. (Courtesy of Network Analysis Corp., second semi-annual report, Dec. 1973, ARPA Contract DAHC15-73-C-0135, Chap. 4, Fig. 5.)

3. *Add-only step.* This adds the least-cost links to the network that will divert traffic from the saturated cutset. To divert traffic effectively nodes on either side of and relatively far removed from the cutset should be linked. But the further apart the nodes are, the higher the communications cost. As a compromise a "distance 2" criterion is used: Nodes that are at least two links removed from the cutset nodes are chosen as candidates for possible linkage. Nodes satisfying this condition are shown shaded in Fig. 10-7.

4. *Delete-only operation.* This step in the algorithm eliminates links from a highly connected topology. One link at a time is removed at each iteration, the one chosen being the link that is the most expensive and least used according to the following criterion : Maximize

$$E_i = D_i \times \frac{C_i - f_i}{C_i} \qquad (10\text{-}4)$$

where D_i is the cost of link i, C_i is its capacity, and f_i, its flow.

5. *Perturbation step.* Once a desired throughput range has been attained, the network links are rearranged, using Add-only and Delete-only operations, to reduce the cost. Upper and lower bounds of about $\pm 5\%$ about the desired throughput are set, and Add-only and Delete-only operations are used

sequentially so long as the throughput remains within the bounds. If the throughput $R < R_{min}$, the lower bound, an Add-only step is used to bring the throughput up. If $R > R_{max}$, the upper bound, a Delete-only step is used to reduce the throughput.

A flow chart of the perturbation portion of the algorithm is shown sketched in Fig. 10-8.* The step marked "Is network dominated" checks to see if the perturbation method results in a *poorer* solution. A list of cost and throughput pairs (D_i, R_i) of previous possible network solutions is kept. If a new network configuration found using the perturbation method has its (D, R) pair poorer than a previous solution (i.e., the cost is higher and throughput is less), the link deleted is added back, and the iteration is continued.

It is apparent that the cut saturation algorithm operates to relieve the most heavily congested portion of the network. (This is of course the purpose of finding the saturated cutset.) Adding links in the vicinity of the saturated cutset should obviously be more effective in improving the network throughput capability than in other portions of the network. Solutions obtained for a 26-node ARPA network are shown plotted in Fig. 10-9.** They are compared there with solutions obtained using a branch exchange method for distributed network design.† Similar results were obtained for 10- and 40-node networks.†† The branch exchange method iteratively adds, deletes, or exchanges links, and computes the corresponding cost and throughput variations. If the result of a topological modification is favorable, it is accepted. The procedure is exhaustive and terminates when no more improvement is possible. The branch exchange method is much more time consuming to run than the cut saturation method. (The cut saturation method is selective rather than exhaustive in its choice of links to be added or deleted.) For this reason a suboptimum routing technique to reduce computational time is used in practice to determine the throughput after each branch exchange. At the end of the branch exchange algorithm an optimal routing algorithm must still be used to reexamine a number of possible solutions in order to improve the accuracy.

The computational complexity C of the cut saturation algorithm (or equivalently, the execution time) is found to depend approximately on the square of the number of links NA§

$$C = \delta(NA)^2 \tag{10-5}$$

*Ibid., Chap. 4, Fig. 9.
**Gerla et al., "Cut Saturation Algorithm for Topological Design," Fig. 7.
†H. Frank and W. Chou, "Topological Optimization of Computer Networks," *Proc. IEEE*, **60**, no. 11, Nov. 1972, 1385–96.
††Gerla et al., "Cut Saturation Algorithm for Topological Design."
§Ibid.

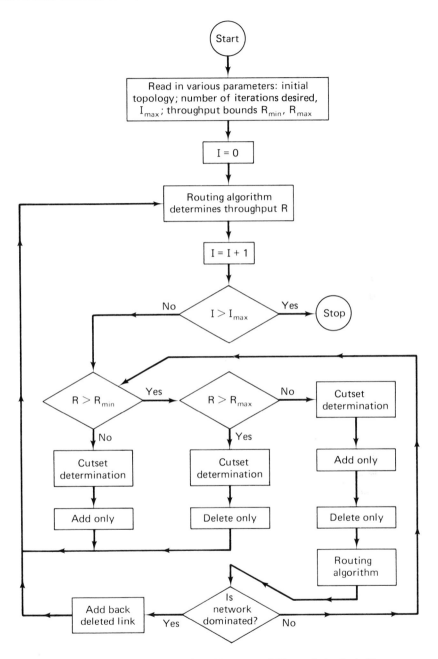

Fig. 10-8. Perturbation algorithm. (Courtesy of Network Analysis Corp., second semi-annual report, Dec. 1973, Chap. 4, Fig. 9.)

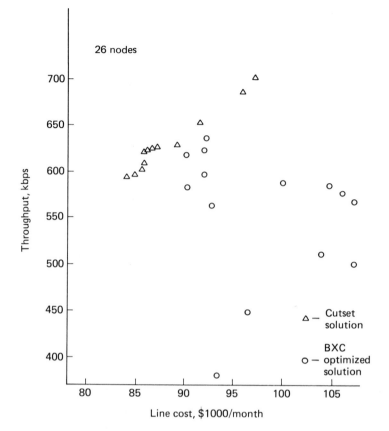

Fig. 10-9. Cutset solution, 26-node ARPA network; comparison with branch exchange. (Courtesy of M. Gerla et al., "A Cut Saturation Algorithm for Topological Design of Packet-Switched Communication Networks," *Proc. IEEE National Telecommunications Conference*, San Diego, Dec. 1974, Fig. 7.)

The two major contributors to the computations required are the routing algorithm and the cutset modification algorithms, with the routing algorithm used (a flow deviation procedure to be described in the next chapter) requiring the bulk of the execution time.

Sample computations on 10- and 26-node networks using just the Add-only and the Delete-only portions of the algorithm, indicate that these two algorithms separately provide results fairly close to the complete cut saturation algorithm. An example of such a computation on a 26-node network is shown in Fig. 10-10.* (Compare Fig. 10-9 and 10-10.) A lower bound on the

*Ibid., Fig. 3.

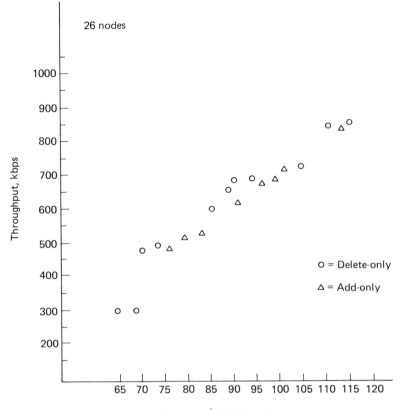

Fig. 10-10. 26-node ARPA network Delete- and Add-only portions of algorithm. (Courtesy of M. Gerla et al., "Cut Saturation Algorithm," Fig. 3.)

throughput-cost curve may be found by approximating the step function form of link cost-capacity curves by concave lower envelopes. It is found, for the cases considered in the paper under discussion, that the cut saturation solutions are within 5% and 10% of the lower bound. This is an indication that the cut saturation solutions are close to optimum. Results reported in the paper indicate that the cut saturation solutions are relatively insensitive to starting network topology. Trees, minimum spanning trees, and two-connected topologies were examined for this purpose.

An additional step in the cut saturation algorithm not mentioned above involves collapsing chains. Chains are portions of a network with a sequence of serial nodes. A network satisfying the two-connected criterion noted earlier should contain many chains. Those chains carrying predominantly transit traffic (i.e., traffic directed between nodes external to the chain and hence uniform throughout the chain) can be "collapsed" or replaced by a single link to improve the efficiency of the algorithm. The reader is referred to the paper cited for further details.

PROBLEMS

10.1 One hundred terminals are to be connected, via concentrators, to a central processing facility in New York City. The terminals are clustered into groups of 10 terminals each. A concentrator can accommodate at most 30 terminals. Five cities are to be considered as possible sites for concentrators. The cities, the fixed cost (in $/month) of locating a concentrator in each, and monthly line charges (representing the cost of leased lines to N.Y.C.) appear in Table 10-P1:

TABLE 10-P1

City	Fixed Cost ($/mo)	Line Cost ($/mo)
1. White Plains, N.Y.	$350	50
2. Poughkeepsie, N.Y.	$350	140
3. Hartford, Conn.	$350	225
4. New Haven, Conn.	$350	175
5. Bridgeport, Conn.	$350	125

Each group of terminals costs $100/terminal/month, or $1000/group/month, to connect into the network (this includes terminal rental, modem rental, and other fixed costs), plus monthly mileage charges, depending on the concentrator to which connected. The mileage charges appear in Table 10-P2.

TABLE 10-P2

MILEAGE CHARGES, $/MONTH, TERMINAL GROUP
TO CONCENTRATOR

City →	N.Y.C	1	2	3	4	5
Terminal group 1	150	100	600	1000	600	500
↓ 2	200	0	500	900	500	400
3	600	400	400	400	400	400
4	700	500	500	100	400	500
5	1000	800	600	0	400	500
6	500	300	500	400	300	200
7	800	600	700	200	200	400
8	700	500	600	400	0	200
9	500	300	600	600	200	0
10	300	250	500	600	300	200

Use both the Add and Drop algorithms to determine at which sites to establish concentrators and which terminal groups to connect to each. Compare results.

10.2 A department store chain with headquarters in Houston, Tex., has branches in the following locations:

(1) *New Mexico*—Sante Fe, Albuquerque, Gallup, Las Vegas, Roswell, Clovis, and Las Cruces.

(2) *Texas*—Amarillo, Lubbock, Wichita Falls, Dallas, Fort Worth, San Angelo, Abilene, Waco, El Paso, Austin, San Antonio, Corpus Christi, Houston, Galveston, and Laredo.

(3) *Louisiana*—Shreveport, Baton Rouge, New Orleans, and Lake Charles.

(4) *Oklahoma*—Oklahoma City, Tulsa, and Lawton.

A data communications network is to be designed connecting terminals in each of the branch stores via concentrators to a central processor in Houston. An iterated approach is to be used in carrying out the design: first determine where to locate the concentrators and which terminals to associate with each, then determine an improved connection plan for the concentrators, then choose line capacities to minimize time delay at fixed cost, then go back to the beginning to see if the concentrator location and terminal connection can be improved. Specific steps to be carried out are categorized in the following parts of the problem:

(a) The stores in Santa Fe, Albuquerque, Amarillo, Lubbock, Dallas, Fort Worth, Houston, Baton Rouge, New Orleans, and Tulsa have 10 terminals each. The others have five terminals each. The terminals are 300 bps devices. The average traffic on each consists of 1500 bit messages, transmitted twice a minute.

Concentrator locations are to be considered at the following cities: Albuquerque, Oklahoma City, Lubbock, Dallas, San Angelo, San Antonio, and Baton Rouge. Terminals from any one store will be multiplexed on one line so they must all connect to one concentrator. No concentrator can handle more than 40 terminals.

Use the Add and Drop algorithms to determine two possible sets of concentrator locations and terminals associated with each. Choose the lower cost solution. (You may of course speed up the algorithms by ruling out obvious poor connection choices.)

A typical line cost schedule for low-speed data up to 300 bps to be used for the terminal-concentrator line cost calculations appears as follows:*

Mileage	$/mo/mile
1–100	1.10
101–250	0.77
251–500	0.44
501–1000	0.33
1001–up	0.22

For simplicity's sake we ignore here significant cost savings possible in sharing wider band lines by using frequency division or time-division multiplex techniques.**

A similar table of mileage charges for voiceband data to be used in computing the concentrator—CPU line costs appears as follows:†

Mileage	$/mo/mile
1–25	3.30
26–100	2.31
101–250	1.65
251–500	1.155
501–up	0.825

In addition, monthly concentrator rental charges, service terminal charge, and modem rental charge, come to $500/month.

(b) Given the concentrator locations found in (a), use a heuristic multipoint algorithm to see if a concentrator network configuration can be found that reduces the cost.

   The lines in the concentrator network are all assumed to be of 4800 bps capcity. The line utilization on any one line is to be kept to less than 0.6. Use the concentrator line costs of (a).

(c) Repeat (a) and (b) using the following alternate rates for voiceband data transmission: $0.60/mo/mile plus $600/month service terminal and concentrator rental charge.

---

*M. Gerla, "New Line Tariffs and Their Impact on Network Design," *AFIPS Conference Proc.*, National Computer Conference, **43**, 1974, 577–82.
P. M. McGregor, "Effective Use of Data Communications Hardware," *AFIPS Conference Proc.*, National Computer Conference, **43, 1974, 565–75.
†Gerla, "New Line Tariffs."

(d) Find some improved capacity assignments if possible for the concentrator lines using the network configuration found in (c). Capacities are to be chosen to minimize the cost with the maximum average time delay from any concentrator to the central processor constrained to be below a specific value. (This thus ignores the transmission time delay incurred in transmitting messages from the terminals to the concentrators.) The three voiceband capacities available and their respective costs are:

    2400 bps $0.45/mo/mile plus $540/mo fixed charge

    4800 bps $0.60/mo/mile plus $600/mo

    9600 bps $0.90/mo/mile plus $680/mo

(e) See if it is possible to improve on the results of (b) and (c) by iteration. For example, using the configuration found in (b) develop an algorithm to determine if reassignment of terminals will improve the cost-time delay performance. Develop an algorithm that iteratively exchanges branches, trying some of the concentrator locations left out in (b) to see if improvement results. It will probably be necessary to again assume all line capacities are the same, but consider the possibility of incorporating in the algorithms a procedure that tests different line capacities as well.

10.3 Search out a realistic example of a network to be designed and carry out as much of the design as possible; examples would include data networks for businesses, hospitals, air lines, schools, etc. Examples of existing networks may be used, in which case you may want to compare your design with that adopted. Alternately, you might attempt a design for a projected application. Gather as much statistics as possible concerning number of terminals needed, terminal usage (message rate and average message length), etc. Try to determine actual costs for terminal purchase, line rental, modem purchase or rental, concentrator purchase or rental, service charge, etc. Trade journals, manufacturers or suppliers of modems, terminals, and concentrators, and communication carriers should be consulted for up-to-date cost figures.

Routing
and Flow Control

11

The various examples of networks encountered in this book have each used a different technique for routing messages from a given source to a specified destination. In the TYMNET system, described in Chap. 2, the central supervisory program establishes a route each time a user connects into the system. A least-cost routing algorithm is used, as described in Chap. 2, in determining the appropriate route.

In the SITA system a fixed routing technique is used, with routes between all source-destination pairs specified on the basis of a shortest path type of algorithm. Alternate routing is used, routes being chosen on the basis of a specified priority. These routes are changed several times a year.* Finally, in the ARPA network a local adaptive routing algorithm is used, with individual nodes making their own decisions as to which outgoing links to associate with which destinations, on the basis of messages exchanged with their nearest neighbors on the order of once a second.

Note that these three examples cover a variety of approaches to establishing routes for messages in a store-and-forward network: the routes can be established centrally (as in TYMNET and SITA) or locally (as in the ARPA case); they can be fixed and deterministic, chosen on the basis of *average* traffic statistics (as in the SITA example); they can be fixed during the entire

*G. J. Chretien, W. M. Konig, J. H. Rech, "The SITA Network, Summary Description," *Computer-Communication Networks Conference*, University of Sussex, Brighton, U.K. Sept. 1973.

message interval, although varying with demand (as in the TYMNET case); they can be adaptive, following a stochastic control strategy (as in the ARPA network).

There is obviously no unique way of establishing message routes. The comparative study of routing strategies is still in its infancy, and work is currently being carried out by many investigators in an attempt to develop the area further. In this chapter we shall first attempt to categorize various types of routing algorithms, along the lines already noted above, and then focus in more detail on some of the routing techniques suggested. Because of the complexity of the problem much of the existing comparison of strategies has been carried out by simulation. We shall, however, describe some limited analytical studies on adaptive routing in a later section.

Following that section we shall discuss fixed routing strategies designed to minimize average time delay, the same criterion used in the capacity assignment problem of the early chapters of this book. The routing algorithms used here are essentially static flow assignment strategies that distribute the flows in the network to minimize the time delay. Two algorithms will be discussed here. One of them is the algorithm to which reference was made in the last chapter on network design. The topological design of the ARPA network, involving the development of a least-cost distributed network configuration with specified time delay and reliability constraints, used this routing algorithm.

The study of fixed routing leads us naturally into shortest path routing. The simplicity of this technique has also led to its use in some network designs as well. Finally, we conclude the chapter with a discussion of flow control and techniques suggested for limiting congestion in a network. Some simple models for handling the analysis of flow control techniques are studied in this last section.

SURVEY OF ROUTING ALGORITHMS

The basic routing problem is that of establishing a continuous path, usually incorporating several links in a network, between any pair of source and destination nodes, along which messages are to be sent. The implementation of the route chosen consists of setting up at each node along the path a routing table that directs messages with a particular destination address to the appropriate outgoing link at that node. The table and associated table lookup procedures are incorporated in the memory and software of the computer at the node in question.

Various ways of classifying routing procedures have been suggested in the literature. One classification distinguishes between deterministic and stochastic (random) strategies.* Another classifies the techniques according to whether they're centrally or locally controlled.**,† (The latter is also called distributed control.) Although it is difficult to evaluate the various algorithms comparatively because of the variety of performance criteria that might be chosen, generally speaking one would like to route messages to obtain a minimum average time delay or response time. One would like the algorithm to provide a reasonable response time over a range of traffic intensities. The complexity of the calculations to be carried out, if any, the signaling capacity required for transmitting routing information, the rate at which the algorithm adapts in the case of adaptive procedures, all must be considered in the evaluation. The stability of the algorithm under load fluctuations or in the presence of error bursts is also very important.

Deterministic Techniques

Consider the deterministic class first. The algorithms in this class do not adapt to changes in traffic but may be designed to provide satisfactory performance, *on the average*, over a range of traffic intensities. Alternately they can be designed to perform very simply, requiring little, if any, calculation and very little signaling information. One example of a deterministic algorithm is a least-time delay algorithm. Here the routes for any source-destination pair are chosen to minimize the overall average time delay. This algorithm assumes the traffic matrix for the network, as discussed in earlier chapters, to be given and then finds the least-time paths. Two ways of implementing this algorithm will be discussed later in this chapter as already noted. The routing tables in this case may be updated periodically or altered when the source-destination traffic rate entries in the traffic matrix undergo significant changes. This requires a central control that continually estimates network traffic rates, carries out the routing calculation, and transmits the appropriate routing table changes to the nodes in question. Interestingly it is found that *multiple* routes provide optimum (least-time) performance in this case, with a specified fraction of entering messages at any node corresponding to a particular source-destination pair, routed over each outgoing link. The

*G. F. Fultz and L. Kleinrock, "Adaptive Routing Techniques for Store-and-Forward Computer-Communication Networks," *Proc. IEEE International Conference on Communications* Montreal, June 1971, pp. 39–1 to 39–8.

H. Rudin, "On Routing and 'Delta Routing': A Taxonomy and Performance Comparison of Techniques for Packet-Switched Networks," *IEEE Trans. on Communications*, **COM-24, no. 1, Jan. 1976, 43–59.

†J. M. McQuillan, "Adaptive Routing Algorithms for Distributed Computer Networks," Bolt, Beranek, and Newman Report No. 2831, May 1974, Chap. 3. (Also available as doctoral thesis, Division of Engineering and Applied Physics, Harvard University, 1974.)

central control in this case instantaneously knows the status of traffic everywhere in the network and can take quick action. This corresponds to a nonrealizable procedure. However, it does provide a bound on other procedures that might be investigated. Such a technique has been called an *ideal observer* technique.*

Shortest path techniques of various kinds may also be used to establish a specified route for messages between any source-destination nodal pair.** One example would simply be to send messages along the path containing the fewest number of links. This may not correspond to the least-time path, but it is more simply calculated than the latter and requires no updating unless a particular link or node fails. Alternate paths may be assigned in a hierarchical fashion to accommodate such contingencies or to account in a limited way for traffic variations. A more general version of the shortest path algorithm weights each link by a specified factor depending on link cost, length of link, link propagation delay, estimated traffic on the link, number of errors detected, etc. It is apparent that on this basis the least-time routing algorithm may be considered a generalized form of the shortest path algorithm. The TYMNET strategy involves the use of a generalized shortest path algorithm. The SITA routing strategy uses the shortest path approach as well. Shortest path algorithms will be considered further later in this chapter. It is apparent that the shortest path class of algorithms requires centralized control.

One final class of deterministic algorithms involves "flooding" the network with messages. Each node receiving a message simply retransmits it over all outgoing links, or a selected number of these following some simple rule. (For example, one selected set might be those outgoing links "generally directed" to the desired destination node.) This technique was first proposed and studied, via simulation, by a group at Rand Corporation that carried out pioneering work on computer-communication networks in the early and mid-1960s.† The technique is simple and robust, the messages always arriving at their required destination. But, as the name indicates, the network becomes flooded with multiple copies of any message. The technique is thus only appropriate under low traffic conditions. As the flooding rule becomes more selective the number of multiple messages is reduced but at the expense of increased complexity.

*Fultz and Kleinrock, "Adaptive Routing Techniques."

D. J. Silk, "Routing Doctrines and Their Implementation in Message-Switching Networks," *Proc. IEE*, London, **116, no. 10, Oct. 1969, 1631.

†B. W. Boehm and R. L. Mobley, "Adaptive Routing Techniques for Distributed Communication Systems," *IEEE Trans. on Communication Technology*, **COM-17**, no. 3, June 1969, 340–49. For more details on this technique and some random techniques discussed further on, see also Rand Corp. Memorandum RM-4781-PR, Feb. 1966, by the same authors under the same name.

Random (Stochastic) Routing

As in the deterministic case there is a variety of routing algorithms that can be subsumed under the random category. These algorithms can involve local (distributed) control or central control. They may involve fixed strategies with little or no calculations (other than a random number calculation), or more complex adaptive strategies such as the one used in the ARPA network and other networks.

The simplest type of random routing strategy involves assigning fixed decision rules as to which neighboring node to send messages. No source or destination information is required. Algorithms of this type have been analyzed by Kleinrock* and Prosser.** Consider for example the symmetric loop-type networks of Fig. 11-1. In part a. each node is shown connected to two other nodes. There is a probability p that a given message entering any node will be directed to one neighbor, a probability $1-p$ that it will be directed to the other neighbor. Similarly, in part b. each node is connected to three other nodes, and, as a special case, messages are routed randomly with equal probability to any one of the three nodes to which connected. Other examples can be constructed as well.

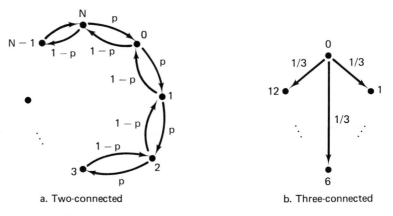

a. Two-connected   b. Three-connected

Fig. 11-1. Random fixed routing, symmetric networks.

The relative advantages and disadvantages of random fixed strategies of this type have been summarized by Kleinrock.† They are simple in concept and in realization, with no directory needed. They tend to be robust and are

*L. Kleinrock, *Communication Nets; Stochastic Message Flow and Delay*, McGraw-Hill, New York, 1964. Reprinted, Dover Publications, 1972. See Chap. 6 and Appendix D.

R. T. Prosser, "Routing Procedures in Communication Networks," *IRE Trans. on Communication Systems*, **CS-10, no. 4, 1962, "part I: Random Procedures," 322–29; "part II: Directory Procedures," 329–35.

†Kleinrock, *Communication Nets*.

relatively insensitive to changes in network structure, and they are highly stable. They are, however, highly inefficient and lead to increased time delays. (Messages are routed over relatively more links than in a fixed route case.) The random routing and consequent increase in the number of links traversed increases the internal traffic of the network as well, and may be shown to lead to an effective increase in the traffic intensity. The network thus overloads more quickly than would otherwise be the case. This class of routing techniques does not make use of any available information as to traffic patterns, desirability of certain routes, etc.

As an example, consider K-connected symmetric networks of the type of Fig. 11-1 with $N = 12$ (hence $N + 1 = 13$ nodes) and variable K. Let the probability of communicating with each of the K nodes to which a particular node is connected be $1/K$. Then p in Fig. 11-1a is $\frac{1}{2}$. The $K = 3$ case is shown in Fig. 11-1b, and a fully-connected network would have $K = 12$. Kleinrock has calculated the average number of links $\bar{n}$ traversed by a message entering at any node before reaching its destination node. Each node is assumed equally-likely to be the desired destination. The results of the calculation, as taken from Kleinrock,* p. 105, appear in Table 11-1. They are compared in

TABLE 11-1

AVERAGE NO. OF LINKS TRAVERSED

K	$\bar{n}$ (random)	$\bar{n}$ (shortest path)
2	30.3	3.5
3	14.7	2.25
4	14.0	1.67
12	12	1

the table to the average number of links traversed under a shortest path algorithm.** Note the inefficiency of the random algorithm as compared to the shortest path case. Similar calculations, verified by simulation,† show the effective traffic intensity is $\bar{n}\rho$, with $\rho = \gamma/\mu C$, γ the total message arrival rate for the network, C the total capacity of the network, and $1/\mu$ assumed the same. The network thus saturates in the vicinity of $\rho = 1/\bar{n}$, with the average time delay, assuming independent $M/M/1$ queues, becoming unbounded at that point.

As already noted several times the ARPA network uses an adaptive random routing strategy. This is one example of a whole class of such

*Ibid.
**For the shortest path algorithm, with $K = 2$ and arbitrary N, as an example,

$$\bar{n} = \frac{1}{N}\left[2\sum_{i=1}^{N/2} i\right] = \frac{1}{2}\left(\frac{N}{2} + 1\right)$$

†Ibid., pp. 102, 103.

routing algorithms in which each node carries out least-time estimates and decides, on a decentralized or locally-determined basis, which outgoing link to use to minimize the estimated time delay to a specified destination. A typical node X and its neighboring nodes are shown in Fig. 11-2. Assume that node X makes an estimate $T(X, D, L_N)$ of the time taken for a message to go from the current node X to destination node D via neighboring node N. This can be stored in a delay table as shown in Fig. 11-3a. For any given destination D the minimum entry in the delay table provides the appropriate outgoing link over which to route messages destined for D. These are shown circled. The corresponding output lines appear in the routing table of Fig. 11-3b. Three destination node entries only are specified in this example, and the network is assumed to have 10 nodes altogether.

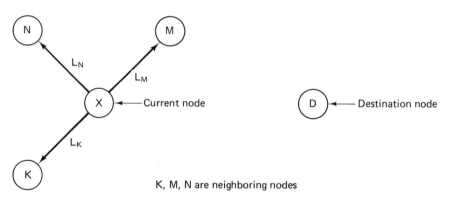

K, M, N are neighboring nodes

Fig. 11-2. Typical node in a network.

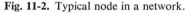

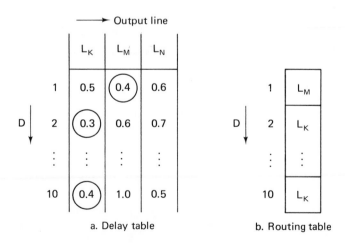

a. Delay table   b. Routing table

Fig. 11-3. Delay and routing tables for node X in 10-node network.

The minimum time delay estimate to be put into the routing table is given mathematically as

$$T(X, D)|_{min} = \min_{L_N} T(X, D, L_N) \qquad (11\text{-}1)$$

How are the time delay estimates $T(X, D, L_N)$ that go into the delay table determined? Various suggestions have been made and/or implemented. A particularly simple procedure consists of using as the time delay estimate the number of messages waiting in the queue at the particular outgoing line. This is then called the *shortest queue plus zero bias algorithm*. The time estimate here is thus the queueing delay at the node in question. Another variation is to rank the various output queues, selecting the highest ranked one that is free. If none are free the message waits until a line does become free, this latter then corresponding to the shortest queue. These schemes are all variations of the "hot potato" routing strategy developed by P. Baran as part of the Rand Corp. work noted earlier.*

Another scheme for estimating the time delay investigated by Baran and his coworkers at Rand Corp., entitled *"backward learning,"*** uses as the estimate a weighted version of the time delay incurred by messages going in the reverse direction from the destination node, considered as a source, to the node in question. The assumption then is that traffic in the two directions is symmetrical, and that elapsed time in one direction provides an estimate of time in the other direction. Specifically, the algorithm updates the previous estimate in terms of a newly-measured time by the following equation:

$$T(X, D, L_N)|_{new} = T(X, D, L_N)|_{old} + k[HN - T(X, D, L_N]/_{old} \qquad (11\text{-}2)$$

Here HN, called the *handover number*, is the current measure of the time for a message to go from D to X, coming in the *reverse* direction over link L_N. Notice that a simple first-order recursion relation is used to modify the time estimate. The words "handover number" refer to the fact that a message is assumed to carry with it a number representing time delay that is incremented appropriately at each intermediate node through which it passes. This technique was found in practice to suffer from a "ping-pong" or looping effect, in which messages sometimes return to a node from which they were previously transmitted. In addition, backwards learning was found to adapt poorly to damaged networks (those in which nodes or links become disabled).

Both the shortest queue and backwards learning techniques are sometimes called *isolated* local routing techniques, with nodes essentially making routing decisions on their own.

*P. Baran et al., "On Distributed Communications," series of 11 reports, Rand Corp., Santa Monica, Ca., August 1964.

**Ibid.; Boehm and Mobley, "Adaptive Routing Techniques for Distributed Communication Systems."

Other local routing techniques of the adaptive type have neighboring nodes transmitting information to one another in an effort to improve the time estimate of Eq. (11-1). The ARPA algorithm is such an example. Here all neighbors exchange, on a periodic basis, their own estimates of the minimum time required to reach a particular destination.[*][**] The node in question then adds its own estimate of the time required to go to each neighbor (essentially the queueing delay on the appropriate outgoing link). Specifically, node N will transmit to all its neighbors the quantity $T(N, D)|_{min}$ (as in Eq. (11-1)) that represents its estimate of the minimum time to reach destination D. Node X will add to this $T(X, L_N)$, its estimated queueing delay on link L_N. The time estimate to go from node X to destination node D via outgoing link N is then

$$T(X, D, L_N) = T(X, L_N) + T(N, D)|_{min} + D_p \qquad (11\text{-}3)$$

This delay estimate is now inserted into node X's delay table.

Note that a bias term D_p has been added to the estimate from node N. It is found necessary in practice to do this to reduce looping or ping-pong effects. This technique is thus also called the *shortest time plus bias* routing algorithm. The bias term D_p has an optimum value normally found from simulation studies. That an optimum does exist is readily demonstrated. If D_p is very small, looping occurs as already noted, with a corresponding increase in time delay. On the other hand, assume D_p is large compared to the queueing delay at each node. Each node in passing on its neighbor's estimate then essentially increments that estimate by D_p. The estimated time delay from a typical node such as X to destination D via L_N is then

$$T(X, D, L_N) \doteq MD_p \qquad (11\text{-}4)$$

where M is the estimated number of links between X and D via L_N. Equation (11-1) then gives rise to a shortest path algorithm in this special case with a time delay that must by definition be lower bounded by the shortest time delay estimate. A typical simulation curve showing the variation of average single packet delay with D_p is shown in Fig. 11-4.[†] Typically the optimum value of D_p is found to be about 60 msec.

The Swedish TIDAS data network used to control the transmission of power over the Swedish power grid has adopted an ARPA-type locally adaptive routing strategy.[††] Comparative simulation studies of the ARPA-type and related algorithms have appeared in the literature.[§]

---

*McQuillan, "Adaptive Routing Algorithms."
**Fultz and Kleinrock, "Adaptive Routing Techniques."
†Ibid.
††T. Cegrell, "A Routing Procedure for the TIDAS Message-Switching Network," *IEEE Trans. on Communications*, **COM-23**, no. 6, June 1975, 575–85.
§R. L. Pickholtz and C. McCoy, Jr., "Effects of a Priority Discipline in Routing for Packet-Switched Networks," *IEEE Trans. on Communications*, **COM-24**, no. 5, May 1976, 506–15.

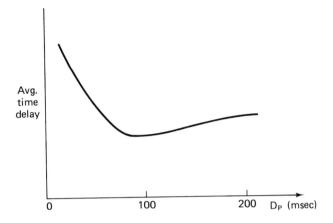

Fig. 11-4. Shortest time plus bias algorithm. Variation with bias constant.

ADAPTIVE ROUTING
IN CENTRALIZED NETWORKS

It has already been noted that the analysis of adaptive routing algorithms is extremely complex. Although various approaches have been suggested and various investigators are looking into this problem, their efforts have so far met with limited success. Simulation has been relied on almost exclusively to investigate various algorithms and to carry out comparative studies of the different strategies suggested. The basic problem of analysis is the fact that for a distributed network the study of adaptive routing involves the time-varying behavior of a set of interactive queues, work on which is still in its infancy.*

Yet it is only through analysis combined with simulation that one can hope to obtain a complete understanding of the adaptive routing problem, leading to possibly improved strategies and more efficient systems. Some analysis of a primitive form of adaptive routing, appropriate to centralized communication network, has been carried out, however, and we focus on this work in this section.**,† This work concerns itself with strategies for routing messages from a data source to the appropriate concentrator, of a number available. The routing or concentrator selection is carried out adaptively in

---

*See, for example, H. Kobayashi, "Applications of the Diffusion Approximation to Queueing Networks, part II," *J. of the ACM*, **21**, July 1974, 459–69.

**C. W. Brown and M. Schwartz, "Adaptive Routing in Centralized Computer-Communication Networks," *Proc. IEEE International Conference on Communications*, San Francisco, June 1975, 47–12 to 47–16.

†C. W. Brown, "Adaptive Routing and Resource Allocation," Ph.D. dissertation (Electrical Engineering), Polytechnic Institute of New York, June 1975.

time, using updated information, received periodically, as to the state of each of the concentrators in a fixed group. Note that although the "routing" here is of a rather primitive type, with one decision only to be made for any particular packet, the problem posed is quite practical. For all networks do have the problem of matching data sources to concentrators. In practice users may receive a telephone number to call to connect them to the appropriate concentrator. In addition the problem may be looked on as one of resource allocation, with the concentrators a set of resources to be allocated among the users (the data sources) in an efficient and cost-effective way.

Consider the example of a multisource, multiconcentrator network of Fig. 11-5. A single source example with Q concentrators is shown in Fig. 11-6.* Messages from the sources are assumed to pass through a controller (switch) or group of controllers that sets up the appropriate connection to the concentrators to which messages are to be sent. In the model to be discussed in this section we assume switch connections may be changed at regular time intervals spaced one slot apart, with a slot being the time required to transmit one packet. All messages are taken to be one packet long. The appropriate switching or routing strategy is established by the controller on the basis of information as to the states of the queues at each concentrator, transmitted by

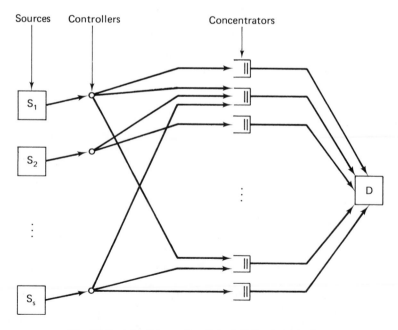

Fig. 11-5. Adaptive routing for centralized network.

*This example is used for illustrative purposes only. In a real-life single source case one would simply route single packet messages to concentrators in succession.

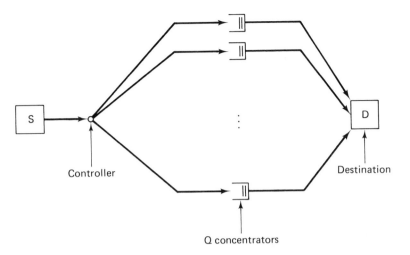

Fig. 11-6. Single source network.

each concentrator once every T slot intervals. Obviously the smaller T is, the more effective the switching strategy, but at the cost of increased signaling information and additional control calculations.

We shall discuss in this section the performance of an optimum control strategy under a specified performance criterion and compare it with some suboptimum strategies that are computationally much simpler to obtain. The performance varies of course with traffic statistics, with the update time T, with the number Q of concentrators, etc.

Figure 11-7 shows a typical timing diagram with the T-slot interval indicated. At the beginning of each such interval, queue length information from each of the Q queues is received by the controller. The controller must then determine the setting of the switches in each one of the $(T - 1)$ slots following. For simplicity's sake we assume here that there is one source only and that this source may send packets to one concentrator only in any one slot interval. (Note again that this is an artifical example used for illustrative purposes only.) The switch positions remain unchanged during this interval. (Analysis of a more general random switching strategy in which more than one concentrator may receive packets from a given source, in any one slot, on a probabilistic basis, indicates that this fixed switching strategy is quite close to optimum for the performance criterion investigated.)*

With these assumptions the routing strategy reduces to that of finding the number $v(k)$, $v = 1, 2, \ldots, Q$, for each k, representing the concentrator (queue) to which traffic is to be sent in slot k. The strategy obviously depends on the performance criterion chosen. A natural criterion is that of minimum

---

*Ibid. The more realistic case of multiple sources is considered in this work.

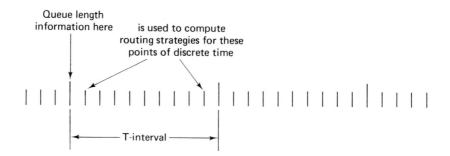

Fig. 11-7. T-intervals, $T = 10$.

expected waiting time of all packets that enter the system during a T-slot interval. A somewhat simpler and related criterion is that of minimizing the sum of the expected queue lengths for each of the Q concentrator queues and for each time slot. Both have been considered.* Again for simplicity we focus here on the second one only.

If we let $x_m^{(j)}(k + 1)$ represent the probability that m packets are waiting in queue j ($j = 1, 2, \ldots, Q$) at the end of the kth slot, the expected queue length for slot k, summed over all queues, is

$$C(k) = \sum_{j=1}^{Q} \sum_{m=0}^{L} [mx_m^{(j)}(k + 1)] \qquad (11\text{-}5)$$

Here L is the maximum queue size.

The average queue length over the entire T-slot interval that is to be minimized by the appropriate choice of the controller switch in each of the T time slots is then

$$C = \frac{1}{T} \sum_{k=0}^{T-1} C(k) \qquad (11\text{-}6)$$

To see how this cost function is related directly to the switch positions, the traffic statistics, and to the queue lengths, as received at the beginning of the T-slot interval, we write a recursive relation between $x_m^{(j)}(k + 1)$ and the probability $x_i^{(j)}(k)$ that there were i packets waiting in queue j at the end of the $(k - 1)$ slot. Thus let $p_{im}^{(j)}(k)$ be the (transition) probability that m packets are in queue j at time $(k + 1)$, given i were there at time k. This clearly depends on whether the switch is connected to concentrator j or not, so we shall henceforth write $p_{im}^{(j)}(v(k))$. It is apparent that the two x's are related by

$$x_m^{(j)}(k + 1) = \sum_{i=0}^{L} x_i^{(j)}(k)p_{im}^{(j)}(v(k)) \qquad (11\text{-}7)$$

again invoking the assumption that all buffers are limited to L packets.

*Ibid.

The transition probabilities are in turn determined by the packet arrival probabilities at each concentrator (queue) during each slot, which depend in turn on source traffic statistics and the controller routing strategy (switch positions). To evaluate the connection we consider all possible ways in which i packets at the beginning of a slot can be converted to m packets at the end. Specifically, let $r_m^{(j)}(v(k))$ be the probability that m packets arrive at queue j during slot k. Then the transition probability $p_{im}^{(j)}(v(k))$ takes on the following possible values:

(1) $\qquad\qquad\qquad m < i - 1, \qquad p_{im}^{(j)} = 0 \qquad\qquad\qquad$ (11-8)

(Recall that no more than one packet per slot may be transmitted from any one concentrator, so clearly the queue size cannot drop by more than one packet.)

(2) $\qquad\quad i > 0, \qquad i - 1 \leq m < L, \qquad p_{im}^{(j)} = r_{m-i+1}^{(j)}(v) \qquad$ (11-9)

(Since there must have been one packet transmitted, there must have been $m - i + 1$ arrivals.)

(3) $\qquad\qquad i = 0, \qquad m < L, \qquad p_{im}^{(j)} = r_m^{(j)}(v) \qquad\qquad$ (11-10)

(4) $\qquad\quad i > 0, \qquad m = L, \qquad p_{im}^{(j)} = 1 - \sum_{n=0}^{L-i} r_n^{(j)}(v) \qquad$ (11-11)

(Since the buffer can only hold L packets, and one packet was transmitted, there could have been $L - (i - 1), L - i + 2, L - i + 3, \ldots$, arrivals. All possible arrival probabilities must be summed over.)

(5) $\qquad\qquad i = 0, \qquad m = L, \qquad p_{im}^{(j)} = 1 - \sum_{n=0}^{L-1} r_n^{(j)}(v) \qquad$ (11-12)

How do the switch positions (or routing strategies, slot by slot) come in to play? Say the probability that n packets are generated in one slot interval by the source is given by r_n. For example, for Poisson statistics with λ packets/slot generated on the average, we have of course

$$r_n = \frac{\lambda^n e^{-\lambda}}{n!}, \qquad n = 0, 1, 2, \ldots \qquad (11\text{-}13)$$

Then *if* the switch is connected to concentrator j in slot k (ie., $v(k) = j$),

$$r_n^{(j)}(v) = r_n$$

Otherwise, with the switch *not* connected to concentrator j, $(v(k) \neq j)$,

$$r_n^{(j)}(v) = \delta_{n0}$$
$$= 0 \qquad n \neq 0$$
$$= 1 \qquad n = 0$$

This last condition accounts for the fact that with the concentrator disconnected from the source, the state of the concentrator queue must drop by 1 if the queue has at least one packet waiting at the beginning of the slot. (As a check, let $r_0^{(j)} = 1$ in Eq. (11-8)–(11-12).)

With the message arrival statistics known (e.g., Poisson as in Eq. (11-13)), one can ostensibly search through all possible routing sequences (all possible values of $v(k)$, $k = 0, 1, 2, \ldots, T - 1$) to find the one sequence that minimizes the cost function of Eq. (11-6). For Q concentrators there are Q^T such sequences. This becomes computationally too complex to carry out for even simple networks. As an example, if $T = 10$ and $Q = 3$, there are $3^{10} \sim$ 60,000 such sequences to test out. Clearly algorithms other than exhaustive enumeration must be invoked. In this case both branch-and-bound and dynamic programming algorithms can be utilized.[*] Using these algorithms it has been possible to evaluate the optimum routing strategy. Typical plots appear in Fig. 11-8 to 11-10.[*,**] These represent cost functions averaged out over all possible initial queue states. These curves are plotted for the case of two concentrators and one source only, but are typical of the kinds of results obtainable for other combinations as well.

All curves have been calculated for the case of $L = 10$; i.e., a maximum of 10 packets stored in each queue. Because of the finite queue size assumed

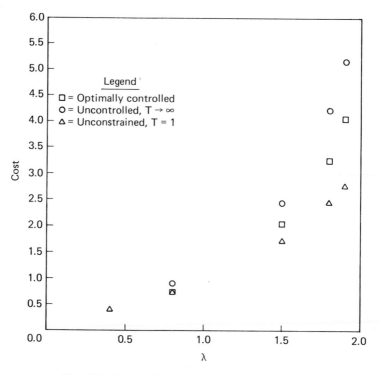

Fig. 11-8. Cost vs. λ for $L = 10$, $Q = 2$, $T = 10$.

[*]Ibid.
[**]Brown and Schwartz, "Adaptive Routing in Centralized Networks."

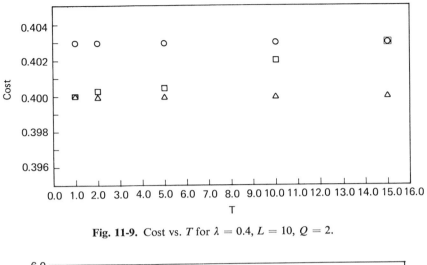

Fig. 11-9. Cost vs. T for $\lambda = 0.4$, $L = 10$, $Q = 2$.

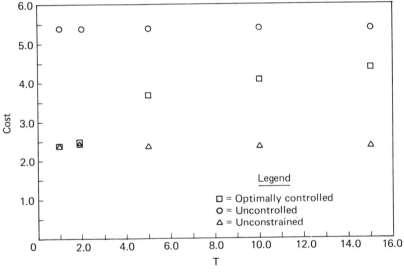

Fig. 11-10. Cost vs. T for $\lambda = 1.9$, $L = 10$, $Q = 2$.

it is possible to obtain a blocked condition and have packets turned away. This represents a penalty on the system operation that should be taken into account. One simple way used in obtaining the results of Fig. 11-8 to 11-10 was to penalize the system by an extra amount whenever the full queue state was reached. Specifically, in the cost function of Eq. (11-5), the state $m = L$ is weighted by a factor $B > L$ instead of L.itself. (For example, $B = 20$, with $L = 10$, has been used in finding the optimum routing strategies that in turn lead to the results of Fig. 11-8 to 11-10.)

Figure 11-8 shows the cost rising with increasing traffic parameter λ. Since there are two queues in the network, the maximum average message arrival rate is taken as 2. This rise in cost is of course similar to the typical increase in average queue length or time delay encountered with increasing traffic in queueing systems. Also shown in Fig. 10-8 for comparison are two other plots. The one labeled "uncontrolled" represents a system in which no controller is used, packets being routed randomly between the two concentrators. This situation is also equivalent to letting $T \longrightarrow \infty$, so that the time between receipt of signaling information as to the states of the queues becomes unbounded. The curve labeled "unconstrained" represents the case of a controller receiving queue state information *every* slot interval (i.e., $T = 1$) and updating its central strategy correspondingly. This is the best that can be done under the assumptions of the model utilized here. Note that the performance of the $T = 10$ optimal control strategy lies roughly between the two extremes of no control and control updated every slot interval.

Figures 11-9 and 11-10 show the performance of the routing algorithm as a function of update interval T, for two values of traffic parameter λ. Fig. 11-9 represents a light traffic case, and Fig. 11-10 a heavy traffic case. Note how the performance deteriorates with T, approaching the completely random routing (uncontrolled) case as $T \longrightarrow \infty$.

In Table 11-2 we show the actual optimal routing strategies obtained for the two-queue case for different values of initial queue length l_1 and l_2. Note that the optimal strategies tend to route traffic at first to the queue observed initially to be the smaller and, when the queues are roughly equalized, tend to alternate between the two queues.

TABLE 11-2

OPTIMAL ROUTING STRATEGIES, TWO-QUEUE CASE*

Initial Length		Strategy	
l_1	l_2	$\lambda = .4$	$\lambda = 1.9$
0	0	1212121212*	1212121212*
3	0	2212121212	2211212121
5	0	2222121212	2222112121
5	3	2222112121	2122112121
5	4	2222112121	2121212121
8	0	2222222121	2222121212
8	5	2222222111	2212211212
8	7	2122222111	2211122121

*An asterisk indicates that the opposite strategy ($1 \longrightarrow 2$ and $2 \longrightarrow 1$) is also optimal.

The optimal strategies shown suggest a possible suboptimum routing strategy: route all packets initially to the smallest queue. The expected lengths of the various queues as functions of time are then approximated with linear functions. The scheme is thus called a "linear estimated crossover" strategy. When the expected length of the initially smallest queue crosses that of the initially second smallest queue the traffic is split between these two (alternating traffic between them). This is continued until either all queues are equally sharing the load or the end of the T-slot interval is reached. This scheme is obviously much simpler computationally than the optimum routing scheme. The result of a performance evaluation of this scheme is shown in Fig. 11-11. Note how well it performs compared to the optimum

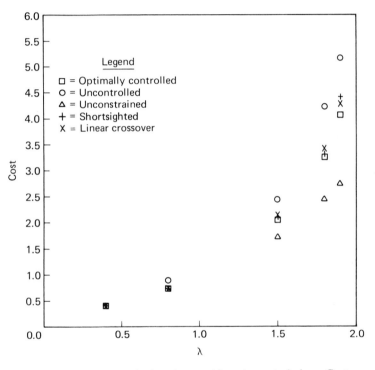

Fig. 11-11. Comparison of suboptimum with optimum technique. Cost vs. λ for $L = 10$, $Q = 2$, $T = 10$.

scheme. Also shown is the performance plot of another suboptimum routing algorithm, the so-called "shortsighted" algorithm. In this procedure computation is saved by computing the "best" strategy for the next time slot only, based on the strategy used up to that time. The procedure thus does not have to search through all possible strategies for the entire T-slot interval. Details of these algorithms appear in the references.*·**

*Brown and Schwartz, "Adaptive Routing in Centralized Networks."
**Brown, "Adaptive Routing and Resource Allocation."

OPTIMAL ROUTING IN NETWORKS—FIXED
ASSIGNMENT STRATEGIES

We have discussed thus far various techniques proposed for adaptively routing messages in a message-switched store-and-forward network. These enable decisions to be made in accordance with changes in the network—e.g., topological changes due to node and/or link failures, ever-present fluctuations in traffic, etc. They correspond to the introduction of dynamic control into the network, the control to be carried out locally, at each node, or centrally, for a group of nodes. The signaling information required to carry out the dynamic control must of course ultimately be assessed as a penalty on the network (both in terms of the cost required for implementation and in terms of the channel capacity that must be devoted to the flow of signals).

We now focus on *fixed* routing strategies. Here the routing tables at each of the nodes do not reflect the dynamic conditions on the network, but are adjusted and then left unchanged for periods of time large compared to normal traffic fluctuations in the network. The simplest example, as noted earlier, is shortest path routing. Here changes would only be made if the network topology changed. Again, as noted earlier, the shortest path routing may be modified to incorporate some measure of traffic conditions in the network by defining a path metric which is not strictly distance dependent. This then gives rise to the possibility of dynamically-varying shortest path algorithms as well. (TYMNET, as noted earlier, incorporates some of these ideas.) There is thus a continuum of possible routing algorithms, ranging from the adaptive type that changes the routes relatively rapidly in accordance with dynamically-varying estimates of traffic, to the fixed type that may be changed relatively infrequently, possibly on a monthly or annual basis.

In this section we focus on fixed routing strategies designed to minimize overall average time delay. The shortest path type of routing algorithm will be discussed further in the next section. The minimum time delay algorithms are said to be globally optimum in the sense that they produce a minimum overall time delay averaged over all nodes of the network and averaged over statistically-varying time delays due to traffic fluctuations. This is exactly the approach we took in the early parts of this book in discussing optimum capacity assignment. We found the link capacity required under *average* traffic conditions. We assumed implicitly that the averages were not changing with time or that the traffic statistics were *stationary*. We repeated this same assumption in discussing concentration and buffering and in the network topological design discussion of the last two chapters. The optimal routing strategy to be discussed in this section is thus the one that provides the best *average* time delay, providing that the underlying statistics do not change with time.

By monitoring traffic statistics and estimating the appropriate averages at each of the nodes, one could conceivably use this technique in a quasi-adaptive mode as well. However this is rather unlikely for relatively complex networks first because of the computational complexity of the algorithm, and second because of the need to transmit appropriate message arrival statistics from each of the nodes to a central control facility.* However, the technique is useful in providing a measure against which adaptive techniques, appropriately averaged, may be compared. It has also been used in the topological design of various networks (e.g., the ARPA network, as noted in previous chapters) since the optimum topology in a minimum time sense depends on the routing strategy. It could also be used to provide fixed routes, to be changed relatively infrequently in accordance with updated network and traffic information.

The routing strategy in the sense considered here assigns the appropriate paths, from source to destination, for every source-destination pair, to minimize the overall average time delay. The expression for overall average time delay will be exactly the one used many times in earlier chapters of this book in determining time delay. As we shall see shortly the problem is essentially formulated as that of a multicommodity flow problem. Interestingly, we shall find multiple routes arising quite naturally. The optimum solutions thus prescribe *several* paths over which messages from any source-destination pair are to be routed, with the fraction of the total average number of messages transmitted per unit time specified on any path.

To be specific consider a network with NN nodes and NA links or arcs connecting them. Fig. 11-12 provides a typical small network example. The lines are assumed full-duplex. For an asymmetrical network there are $NN(NN - 1)$ possible source-destination pairs. As noted in earlier chapters we must then specify an $NN \times NN$ traffic matrix with entries consisting of the average traffic arrival rates destined between the various nodes. For example, γ_{ij} messages/unit time are shown arriving at node i in Fig. 11-12 and destined for j. If the arrival rates are the same in both directions, the matrix is symmetrical and only half the entries need be specified.

For such a network with Poisson arrivals and exponential message lengths assumed, and invoking the independence assumption again, we have, as in earlier chapters, the expression for the average time to be minimized given by

$$\bar{T} = \frac{1}{\gamma} \sum_{i=1}^{NA} \left[\frac{\lambda_i/\mu}{C_i - \lambda_i/\mu} + \lambda_i T_i \right] \qquad (11\text{-}14)$$

*A related adaptive strategy using incremental delay calculations made at each node that are then passed on to neighboring nodes and that is then shown to converge asymptotically to the global optimum routing procedure discussed in this section is outlined in the paper by R. G. Gallager, "A Minimum Delay Routing Algorithm Using Distributed Computation," IEEE Trans. on Communications, *COM–25*, No. 1, Jan. 1977. See also the paper by T. E. Stern, "A Class of Decentralized Routing Algorithms Using Relaxation," *Proc. IEEE National Conference on Telecommunications*, Dallas, Dec. 1976.

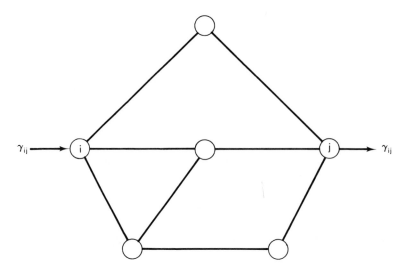

Fig. 11-12. Example network. γ_{ij} is average message rate between source i and destination j.

Here as previously, C_i is the capacity in bits/sec (bps), on link i; λ_i is the average message flow over link i; and $1/\mu$ is the average message length, assumed equal for all links. T_i can represent processing delay, propagation delay, or some other fixed delay in link i; γ is the sum of all the message flows entering the network. It is also possible to generalize $\bar{T}$ to include acknowledgement messages, if separately transmitted, and multipriority messages, although we shall not do this here.* We choose to write this expression in terms of average flow, in bps, by defining the flow in link i to be $f_i \equiv \lambda_i/\mu$. We then have

$$\bar{T} = \frac{1}{\gamma} \sum_{i=1}^{NA} \left[\frac{f_i}{C_i - f_i} + f_i T_i' \right] \tag{11-15}$$

Here $T_i' = \mu T_i$.

The routing strategy used obviously determines these flows. Specifically, say there are M source-destination pairs in the network. We then say that there are M commodities to be distributed in the network. The objective of the routing strategy is to assign paths for each of these commodities to minimize the overall average time delay. Say that the average flow in link i, in bps, due to commodity k ($k = 1, 2, \ldots, M$) is f_i^k. Then we must have the total flow in link i given by

$$f_i = \sum_{k=1}^{M} f_i^k \tag{11-16}$$

*L. Kleinrock, "Analytic and Simulation Methods in Computer Network Design," *AFIPS Conference Proc.*, Spring Joint Computer Conference, AFIPS Press, Montvale, N.J., **36**, 1970, 569–79.

The assignment of f_i^k for all commodities and for all links in the network determines the paths and hence the routes for all commodities.

Consider now a typical node l. At this node (and for every other node in the network) the message flows must be conserved, commodity by commodity. The average incoming message flow, due to commodity k, whether generated at node l, or whether coming from elsewhere in the network, must equal the average outgoing message flow of commodity k. More precisely, if we label commodities by the source-destination nodal pairs, and links by the two nodes to which connected, we have, at node l, due to commodity (i, j),

$$\sum_{k=1}^{NN} f_{kl}^{ij} - \sum_{m=1}^{NN} f_{lm}^{ij} = \begin{array}{ll} -r_{ij}, & \text{if } l = i \\ r_{ij}, & \text{if } l = j \\ 0, & \text{otherwise} \end{array} \qquad (11\text{-}17)$$

Here $r_{ij} \equiv \gamma_{ij}/\mu$ represents the average traffic in bps generated at node i and destined for node j. These parameters are shown indicated in Fig. 11-13. Such a conservation equation must be written at each node, for each commodity. For M commodities there are $M \times NN$ such equations. For an asymmetrical network, with each node communicating with every other node, $M = NN(NN - 1)$, and there are $NN^2(NN - 1)$ such equations.

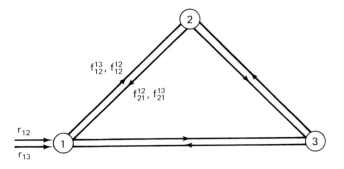

Fig. 11-13. Conservation law demonstrated.

The object of the routing strategy is to find each f_{kl}^{ij} in the network, $f_{kl}^{ij} \geq 0$, satisfying the conservation equations, such that $\bar{T}$ is minimized. (One additional obvious constraint is the capacity constraint $f_i < C_i$. This constraint is normally ignored in the various algorithms devised to find the solution to this constrained optimization problem since $\bar{T} \rightarrow \infty$ as $f_i \rightarrow C_i$. The capacity constraint serves as a penalty function on the time delay to be minimized and is automatically brought into play if f_i becomes too large. This assumes of course the prior value of f_i was a feasible one, satisfying all constraints.)

Various algorithms have been utilized for solving this constrained optimization problem. One approach suggested is to approximate the $\bar{T}$

function to be minimized by piecewise linear functions. The problem then reduces to a set of linear minimum cost flow problems with shortest route solutions. (The path metric or arc "length" in this case turns out to be the linear cost or time delay of an arc.) This approach becomes unwieldy, however, for large networks, with the number of variables and constraints used becoming quite large.*

Other algorithms use iteration to converge to the desired constrained optimum. They all rely on the fact that $\bar{T}$, the objective function to be minimized, is convex, as is the feasible set of multicommodity flows. There is thus just one global minimum to be found. One iterative technique that has been found very useful is the *Flow Deviation* (FD) *method.*** The algorithm very simply stated is as follows:

1. With $f^n = (f_1, f_2, \ldots, f_{NA})$ the vector representing the current (nth iteration) set of link flows, compute the set of derivatives $l_i \equiv \partial \bar{T}/\partial f_i$, $i = 1, 2, \ldots, NA$. Find the shortest route flow vector v, under the metric $l = (l_1, l_2, \ldots, l_{NA})$, satisfying the multicommodity constraints.

2. Set

$$f^{n+1} = (1 - \lambda)f^n + \lambda v \qquad 0 \leq \lambda \leq 1 \qquad (11\text{-}18)$$

and find an optimum λ such that $\bar{T}(f^{n+1})$ is minimized.

The statement that v is the shortest route flow vector under the metric l means simply that

$$l \cdot v^T = \sum_{i=1}^{NA} l_i v_i$$

is to be minimized. In the next section we describe one version of the shortest route algorithm.

This choice of v and the corresponding convergence of the FD algorithm is readily demonstrated. Ultimately f^{n+1} should converge to the desired f that minimizes $\bar{T}$ under the multicommodity constraints. One condition for this is to obviously choose $v = f$, if possible. Consider then that we are in the vicinity of the optimal flow solution f. For a stationary solution any variation away from f should increase $\bar{T}$. Consider a small variation δf away from f. Then

$$\bar{T}(f + \delta f) \equiv \bar{T}(f') \geq \bar{T}(f) \qquad (11\text{-}19)$$

Here $f + \delta f$ is also a feasible, multicommodity flow. To generate this, let

$$\delta f = \delta \lambda (v - f) \qquad (11\text{-}20)$$

*M. Gerla, "The Design of Store-and-Forward Networks for Computer-Communications," Ph.D. dissertation, Dept. of Computer Science, UCLA, 1973.

**L. Fratta, M. Gerla, and L. Kleinrock, "The Flow Deviation Method: An Approach to Store-and-Forward Communication Network Design," *Networks*, 3, John Wiley & Sons, Inc., New York, 1973, 97–133. See also Gerla, "Design of Store-and-Forward Networks."

Then for $\delta\lambda \ll 1$ we must have, at a stationary point,

$$\bar{T}(f') - \bar{T}(f) \equiv \delta\bar{T}(f) \doteq \sum_{i=1}^{NA} \delta f_i \frac{\partial \bar{T}}{\partial f_i} \geq 0 \qquad (11\text{-}21)^*$$

With $\delta f_i = \delta\lambda(v_i - f_i)$ and $l_i = \partial\bar{T}/\partial f_i$, we have, for all $\delta\lambda$,

$$\sum_{i=1}^{NA} l_i(v_i - f_i) \geq 0 \qquad (11\text{-}22)$$

It is apparent then that

$$\sum_{i=1}^{NA} l_i v_i \geq \sum_{i=1}^{NA} l_i f_i \qquad (11\text{-}23)$$

and at the optimum point the equality is satisfied. To have the iterated flow f^{n+1} approach the optimum flow f as best as possible, we should thus attempt to minimize $\sum_{i=1}^{NA} l_i v_i$. This is of course the shortest route solution, under the metric l.

One can actually show that such a shortest route calculation should be carried out for each commodity. For let there be a perturbation with respect to any one of the commodities, say commodity k; f must still represent a stationary solution. Repeating the approach above, we get

$$\sum_{i=1}^{NA} l_i(v_i^k - f_i^k) \geq 0 \qquad (11\text{-}24)$$

where v_i^k must satisfy the kth set of conservation equations, and f_i^k is the portion of flow f_i corresponding to commodity k.

The FD algorithm has been applied to various examples of ARPA-type (distributed) networks.** An example of a much simpler network and the optimum distribution of flows (hence the desired routing strategy) shown is sketched in Fig. 11-14. Note that multiple routing does in fact arise quite naturally here. (This network represents a simplified model of one incorporating a satellite as one of the nodes, in this case node 3. Each of the links leading to node 3 is shown with a normalized propagation delay of 0.5.)

In evaluating the effectiveness of an algorithm to solve a particular task, one is generally interested in several measures of efficiency:

   1. complexity of computations required. (The CPU execution time generally reflects this measure.)
   2. CPU storage (core) requirement.
   3. rate of convergence of iterative algorithms.

---

*Using vector notation, $\bar{T}(f') = \bar{T}(f) + \delta f \cdot \nabla\bar{T}(f)$. The components of $\nabla\bar{T}(f)$ are just $\partial\bar{T}/\partial f_i$. This gives Eq. (11-21).

**Fratta, Gerla, and Kleinrock, "Flow Deviation Method"; Gerla, "Design of Store-and-forward Networks."

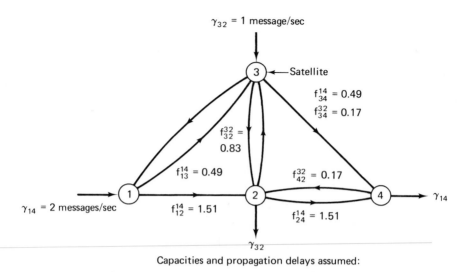

Fig. 11-14. Network example, optimum flows shown (all other flows = 0). Two commodities, 4 nodes, 8 possible flows (average message length = 1 unit).

The FD algorithm consists of two parts: shortest route computation and flow assignment. The number of operations required for the shortest route computation is proportional to $NN^2 \log_2 NN$, using a highly efficient shortest route algorithm.* The flow assignment calculation requires the order of NN^2 computations. Here $M = NN(NN - 1)/2$ commodities have been assumed. The FD technique provides the *total* flow f_i in any link i. To determine the individual commodity flows in each link, as required for routing assignments, additional bookkeeping must be carried out. One way to handle this is to update the individual commodity flows at each iteration. This requires the order of $M \cdot NA$ calculations.

The core requirement for the FD algorithm is proportional to NN^2.

The rate of convergence of the FD technique is rather slow, however.** A more recent algorithm, called the *Extremal Flows* (EF) *method*,† uses a

---

*More standard procedures to be described in the next section require the order of NN^3 computations for the shortest route calculation.

**M. Best, "Optimization of Nonlinear Performance Criteria Subject to Flow Constraints," *Proc. 18th Midwest Symposium on Circuits and Systems*, Concordia University, Quebec, Canada, Aug. 1975, pp. 438–43.

†D. G. Cantor and M. Gerla, "Optimal Routing in a Packet-Switched Computer Network," *IEEE Trans. on Computers*, C-**23**, no. 10, Oct. 1974, 1062–69.

steepest descent or gradient-type iteration to speed up the rate of convergence. Its computational complexity is comparable to that of the FD method. A third algorithm, the gradient projection technique, which uses a gradient search, modified to account for the constraints of the problem, has been used to determine optimum routes in a message-switched store-and-forward network.* Its rate of convergence is generally faster than that of the FD algorithm, and it outputs the individual commodity routes directly with no added bookkeeping required, but its computational complexity is greater than that of the FD algorithm. It appears primarily suited to routing determination in small networks or in those for which only a subset of the nodes will be expected to communicate with one another. (The number of commodities M is thus relatively small.) Other algorithms have been suggested as well.**

SHORTEST PATH ALGORITHMS

We have noted in passing several times in this chapter that shortest path algorithms play a key role in route determination in store-and-forward networks. They can either be used directly in the determination of an optimal fixed route under some cost or distance metric, or, as in the flow deviation algorithm described in the previous section, they often play a role as part of a more complex routing algorithm.

There is a long history of the use and implementation of shortest path algorithms. We refer the reader to the literature for a comparative discussion of some of the algorithms.†,††,§ The most efficient implementations of these algorithms are modifications of an algorithm originally due to Floyd.§§,¶

In this section we simply describe, by example, one of the many shortest path algorithms available. This is done for completeness to make this material as self-contained as possible. The reader is urged to refer to the literature for further discussion, if desired.

*M. Schwartz and C. K. Cheung, "The Gradient Projection Algorithm for Multiple Routing in Message-Switched Networks," *IEEE Trans. on Communications*, **COM-24**, no. 4, April 1976, 449–56.

**Best, "Optimization of Nonlinear Performance Criteria."

†L. R. Ford, Jr. and D. R. Fulkerson, *Flows in Networks*, Princeton University Press, New Jersey, 1962.

††H. Frank and I. T. Frisch, *Communication, Transmission, and Transportation Networks*, Addison-Wesley, Reading, Mass., 1971, pp. 206–10.

§L. E. Hitchner, "A Comparative Study of the Computational Efficiency of Shortest Path Algorithms," University of California, Berkeley, *Operations Research Center Report* ORC 68–25, Nov. 1968.

§§Frank and Frisch, *Communication, Transmission, and Transportation Networks*.

¶Hitchner, "Computational Efficiency of Shortest Path Algorithms."

The shortest path algorithm we shall describe is a single commodity flow, shortest path algorithm. It thus provides the shortest path in the network (under some given metric) between a specific source-destination nodal pair. No constraints are included, so that these have to be separately checked. For the multiple commodity case, as discussed in the previous section, both single commodity and multiple commodity constraints (for example, the capacity constraint) have to be checked. This specific algorithm has two parts. It first establishes the shortest distance (under the metric assumed) between the given source node and every other node in the network. Each node is then labeled with this distance as well as the node next in to the source. The algorithm then works backward from the desired destination node to the source node using the shortest distance information, and the label as to the node next in to the source. The steps in the algorithm are indicated below. Part 1 is the initialization step. Part 2 determines the shortest distance to any node from the source node and labels each node with the node next in to the source. Part 3 determines the shortest path, working backward from the destination.

Specific Algorithm

1. *Initialization.* Assign to all nodes N_i, $i = 1, 2, \ldots, NN$, labels of the form ($\bullet$, $d(i)$), where, with N_a the starting node, $d(a) = 0$, and $d(i) = \infty$, $i \neq a$. (The $\bullet$ represents temporary blanks.)

Let $l(i, j)$ be specified and known as the "length" between N_i and N_j. (*Note:* If $l(i, j)$ is undefined, N_i and N_j are not connected.)

2. *Shortest distance labeling of all nodes.* Find a branch i, j so that

$$d(i) + l(i, j) < d(j)$$

If such a branch is found, change the label on node N_j to $(N_i, d(i) + l(i, j))$. Repeat until no such branch can be found.

At the end of this part of the algorithm all nodes are labeled with their shortest distance from source node N_a and with the neighboring node next in, along the shortest path.

3. *Shortest path determination.* To identify the shortest path from source node N_a to destination node N_b,

    a. Let $i = b$.
    b. Identify N_k from the label $(N_k, d(b))$ assigned to node N_b. If N_k does not exist there *is no path* from N_a to N_b in the network.
    c. Set $i = k$. If $i = a$, then terminate. Otherwise return to Step *b*.

This part of the algorithm essentially works backward from destination node N_b, determining the shortest path to N_a.

EXAMPLE. Consider the network shown in Fig. 11-15. Nodes N_a and N_b are the source and destination nodes respectively. The numbers adjacent to the links represent the link lengths $l(i, j)$, with directions of flow indicated by the arrows.

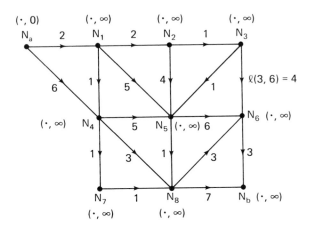

Fig. 11-15. Network example, shortest path determination. Link "lengths" are indicated; initial node labels shown.

We shall trace through, step-by-step, the shortest path determination from N_a to N_b using the algorithm just described. To initialize we label all nodes, except N_a, $d(i) = \infty$. We also have $d(a) = 0$. This is shown in Fig. 11-15 as well.

Referring to Step 2 of the algorithm note that the only branches i, j initially satisfying the inequality $d(i) + l(i, j) < d(j)$, are those connected to source node N_a. For the only $d(i) \neq \infty$ is $d(a) = 0$. The algorithm thus starts at N_a and in essence says to look at *any* node connected directly to N_a.

1. As an example, consider N_4. Since

$$d(4) = \infty > d(a) + l(a, 4) = 6$$

we replace the label $(\cdot, \infty)$ at N_4 with $(a, 6)$.

2. Consider N_1. Replace $d(1) = \infty$ by $d(a) + l(a, 1) = 2$, and label N_1 $(a, 2)$. (The algorithm could just as well have gone to N_5, N_8, or N_7 from N_4.)

3. Consider N_4 again. Since $d(1) + l(1, 4) = 3 < d(4) = 6$, we replace $d(4) = 6$ by 3, and relabel N_4 $(1, 3)$. (This is indicated in Fig. 11-16, as are all subsequent steps in this example, by lines drawn through previous labels.)

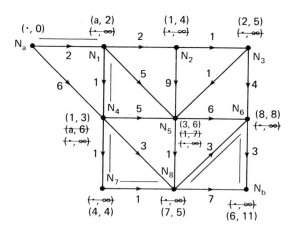

Fig. 11-16. Shortest path determination, step-by-step.

4. Consider N_2. Replace $d(2) = \infty$ by $d(1) + l(1, 2) = 4$, and label N_2 $(1, 4)$.

5. Consider node N_5. This has three neighboring nodes, with $d(2) = 4$, $d(1) = 2$, and $d(4) = 3$, respectively. Any of these three can be used to relabel N_5. Pick node 1 arbitrarily. Then $d(5) \leftarrow d(1) + l(1, 5) = 7$, and N_5 is labeled $(1, 7)$. This is shown in Fig. 11-16.

6. Consider N_3. Replace $d(3) = \infty$ by $d(2) + l(2, 3) = 5$. (From Fig. 11-16, $d(2) = 4$ and $l(2, 3) = 1$.)

7. Return to N_5. Replace $d(5) = 7$ as found in Step 5 above by $d(3) + l(3, 5) = 6$, so that N_5 is now labeled $(3, 6)$. (Hence this step finds that node 5 is closer to N_4 via node 3 than by node 1 as chosen in Step 5.)

Continuing this procedure (for example, going on to node 6 and choosing one of two alternatives, then on to N_7, N_8, with three alternatives, N_6 relabeled, and finally arriving at N_b), we get the complete set of labels shown in Fig. 11-16. No other choices will reduce the distances indicated, and this part of the algorithm terminates.

The final part of the algorithm sets up the shortest path from N_b back to N_a. The label $(6, 11)$ at N_b indicates that this shortest path is 11 units in length and that the node next in from N_b along this path is N_6. (Note that with the labels shown the shortest path distance between *any* node N_i and N_a is known, and the shortest path with N_i as a destination can readily be determined as well.) Moving to N_6 we find $(8, 8)$, indicating that N_8 is the next node in. Continuing, we get, proceeding from node to node,

$$N_b\ (6,\ 11) \longrightarrow N_6\ (8,\ 8) \longrightarrow N_8\ (7,\ 5) \longrightarrow N_7\ (4,\ 4) \longrightarrow N_4\ (1,\ 3)$$
$$\longrightarrow N_1\ (a,\ 2) \longrightarrow N_a\ (\ \cdot\ ,\ 0)$$

This shortest path is indicated by double lines in Fig. 11-16.

The shortest paths, using the metrics indicated in Fig. 11-15, between N_a in this example and all other nodes, as obtained from Fig. 11-16, are shown indicated in Fig. 11-17.

Another example of the application of this shortest path algorithm, using the same network configuration as in Fig. 11-15, but with all lengths chosen to be unity is shown in Fig. 11-18. The set of shortest paths, from N_a to all other nodes, for this network is shown sketched in Fig. 11-19. It is left to the reader to verify the solutions of Figs. 11-18 and 11-19. Note the effect of changing the network link lengths on the shortest paths obtained.

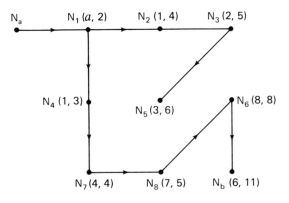

Fig. 11-17. All shortest paths, N_a to N_i, network of Fig. 11-15.

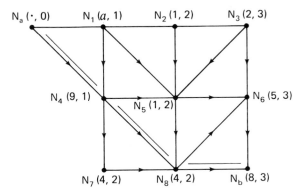

Fig. 11-18. Shortest path determination, all lengths $= 1$.

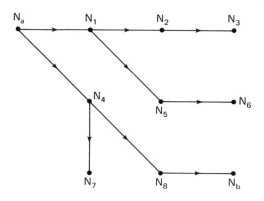

Fig. 11-19. All shortest paths, lengths $= 1$.

CONGESTION CONTROL IN NETWORKS

In previous sections we have described methods of routing messages in store-and-forward networks. These various methods, whether fixed or adaptive, local or centralized, deterministic or stochastic, attempt to direct messages from source to desitnation in as rapid a manner as possible consistent with constraints on cost. It is apparent, however, that even with the best possible routing procedure, messages will sometimes encounter congestion and be delayed in reaching their destination. This may be due to normal fluctuations in traffic above the average level for which the routing algorithm was designed; it may be due to unexpected surges at some points in the network; it may be due (in the case of an adaptive routing algorithm in particular) to traffic building up momentarily at places in the network *after* routing decisions have been made and routing tables updated. Deadlocks may even occur in the case of messages split into multiple blocks or packets, where a message cannot be reassembled and emptied out of the destination buffer because one or more packets are prevented from arriving. These latter packets may in turn be held at transit buffers because an intermediate node to which directed is full and cannot accept them, again for similar reasons. Other types of deadlock can occur as well. This was noted in Chap. 2 in discussing the ARPA network.

Various methods of easing congestion in networks or limiting it to manageable values have been suggested and, in some cases, implemented in networks. One category imposes a constraint on the rate of flow of messages of each source-destination pair. The ARPA network flow control described in Chap. 2 is one example.*,** In this case the restriction is applied directly at

*R. E. Kahn and W. R. Crowther, "Flow Control in a Resource-Sharing Computer Network," *IEEE Trans. on Communications*, **COM-20**, no. 3, part II, June 1972, 539–47.

V. G. Cerf and R. E. Kahn, "A Protocol for Packet Network Interconnection," *IEEE Trans. on Communications*, **COM-22, no. 5, May 1974, 637–48.

the source and can be called an example of an *end-to-end* control. In the same category are restrictions on the messages of the user that are applied once the messages are inside the network. These controls are referred to as *local controls*. An example is the congestion control scheme of the TYMNET system that limits the number of characters a node will buffer for any given user.*,** A second category puts a global constraint on the total number of messages (or packets) that may appear anywhere in the network. An example is the *isarithmic congestion control* proposed by D. W. Davies.†,†† Here the number of packets circulating throughout the network may not exceed a prescribed number, and a user can enter a new packet (or packets) into the network only if he is notified (by various means) that room is available for it.

In this section we first describe a quantitative model for the two control mechanisms of the first category and outline the analytic approach used to obtain trade-off curves for these mechanisms; we then describe briefly some simulation work done on the isarithmic control method. The reader is referred to the literature for a discussion of the problem of deadlock in computer networks.§

Control of Source-Destination Message Flow

We have previously noted that both end-to-end and local control techniques are used in data networks to limit congestion. We now describe one simple model for which analytical results can be obtained describing the performance of both examples of these control procedures. This analysis is abstracted from a longer paper to which the reader is referred for details.§§ Assume the routing strategy for the network is fixed. A particular user then transmits messages to some destination along a fixed path through the network. This path consists of course of a series of tandem concentrators connected by communication lines, each modeled in the usual way by a queue. We shall call this path a tandem or logical link.. An example of an M-stage link appears in Fig. 11-20. In all previous work on buffering in this book we have assumed that queues are independent, and that time delays

---

*L. R. Tymes, "TYMNET—A Terminal-Oriented Communication Network," *AFIPS Conference Proc.*, Spring Joint Computer Conference, **38**, 1971, 211–16.

M. Schwartz, R. R. Boorstyn, and R. L. Pickholtz, "Terminal-Oriented Computer-Communication Networks," *Proc. IEEE*, **60, no. 11, Nov. 1972, 1408–23.

†D. W. Davies, "The Control of Congestion in Packet-Switching Networks," *IEEE Trans. on Communications*, **COM-20**, no. 3, June 1972, 546–50.

††D. W. Davies and D. L. A. Barber, *Communication Networks for Computers*, John Wiley & Sons, Inc., London, 1973, 407–10.

§R. E. Kahn and W. R. Crowther, "Flow Control in a Resource-Sharing Computer Network."

§§M. C. Pennotti and M. Schwartz, "Congestion Control in Store-and-Forward Tandem Links," *IEEE Trans. on Communications*, **COM-23**, no. 12, Dec. 1975, 1434–43.

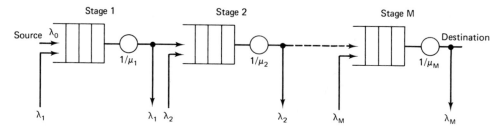

Fig. 11-20. A queueing model of a logical link.

encountered at each queue may be independently calculated. As we shall see shortly our models for congestion control no longer permit us to make this assumption. We shall thus have to consider the joint statistics of the queues comprising the link. A large literature covering this area of *queueing networks*, particularly with application to operating system analysis and distributed computer performance, has begun to appear. Although our discussion here will be self-contained the reader is referred to some of the basic papers in the field for further study and extensions.*

The messages generated by the user of the logical link of Fig. 11-20, called link messages, are assumed generated at a Poisson rate with parameter λ_0 messages/sec. As these messages proceed along the path from concentrator to concentrator they encounter messages at each buffer with which they share the logical link. These so-called external messages (each following its own logical path) may be arriving from another node in the network or may be externally inputted at the node in question. This is of course the usual picture of message transmission we have encountered throughout this book. We now make the assumption, to simplify the analysis, that external messages use any one stage of the logical link only, with new external messages entering at the next stage. External messages are thus assumed to enter a buffer along the logical link, are statistically multiplexed first-come-first-served with any link messages also entering the buffer, are transmitted to the next node along the path, and then leave the logical link. At the next buffer new external

---

*See, for example, the paper by F. Baskett, K. M. Chandy, R. R. Muntz, and F. G. Palacios, "Open, Closed, and Mixed Networks of Queues with Different Classes of Customers," *J. of the ACM*, **22**, no. 2, April 1975, 248–60. A central limit theorem approach to queueing network analysis appropriate to the heavy traffic case which appears to provide accurate results for realistic traffic statistics and is readily extended to nonstationary situations appears in H. Kobayashi, "Applications of the Diffusion Approximation to Queueing Networks," *J. of the ACM*, part I, April 1974, 316–28; part II, July 1974, 459–69. The fundamental work on queueing networks appears in the papers by J. R. Jackson, "Jobshop-like Queueing Systems," *Management Science*, **10**, no. 1, Oct. 1963, 131–42, and "Networks of Waiting Lines," *Operations Research*, Aug. 1959, 518–21.

messages are assumed to be statistically multiplexed with any link messages arriving. The link messages are thus the only ones that follow the tandem path in question from beginning to end. The external messages are also assumed to be Poisson-distributed, with parameters $\lambda_1, \lambda_2, \ldots, \lambda_M$ independently chosen at the respective nodes $1, 2, \ldots, M$. As in previous queueing analyses in this book we assume the messages are all exponentially-distributed. For analytical tractibility we must again invoke the independence assumption that all message lengths, even those of the link messages flowing along the entire logical link, are independently chosen at each node. We further assume that at any one link both types of messages, link and external, have the same average length. At node 1 along the path, the messages are $1/\mu_1$ sec long, on the average; at node 2 they are $1/\mu_2$ sec long, etc. The complete model, with all parameters indicated, appears in Fig. 11-20. (Note that we have subsumed the line capacities in the μ parameters, so that the dimensions of $1/\mu$ are average time units per message.)

How does congestion now arise with this model? As λ_0, the average link message rate, increases, more link messages appear in the buffers along the path, and the external messages at each buffer suffer a corresponding increase in time delay. It is this increased time delay that manifests itself as congestion. A flow control technique must attempt to either keep λ_0 from increasing beyond a certain prescribed rate, or must keep the number of link messages present along the link to within a prescribed limit. This then points up the control strategy trade-off we shall shortly quantify with curves: as a control mechanism is invoked, reducing the congestion by limiting the number of link messages, the link user is penalized correspondingly. His throughput is limited or, equivalently, he is blocked from entering messages until some of his previous messages have cleared the system. But each external user experiencing congestion as a result of the link user increase in traffic rate is in turn a link user himself on his own link and may in turn also produce congestion along his own path. So the control mechanism really reduces congestion throughout the network and keeps the throughout of *all* users to tolerable proportions.

Now consider the two examples of flow control mentioned earlier. We can limit the link user to a maximum of N messages anywhere along the logical link. This is of course the end-to-end control technique noted previously. Similarly we can limit the link user to no more than N_i messages at node i along the complete path ($i = 1, 2, \ldots, M$). This corresponds to a local control strategy.

Figures 11-21 and 11-22, respectively, indicate the details of these two control strategies, as seen at the first two stages of the logical link. Note that in the end-to-end control case, messages arriving when there are already N present in buffers 1 through M are blocked from entering the network and are assumed lost. (In practice they would probably be stored somewhere on an

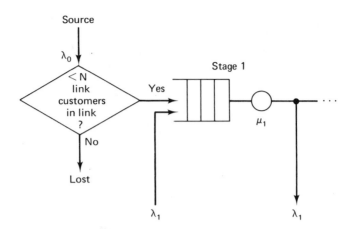

Fig. 11-21. Modification to queueing model due to end-to-end controls.

external queue, but details of that operation are not considered here.) The link user thus experiences a reduction in throughput. This is measured by the probability P_B that an arriving link message is blocked. It is this parameter that we shall calculate.

For local control, link messages arriving at the head of the ith queue when there are N_{i+1} link messages waiting at the node $i + 1$ following are blocked until one of the link messages at node $i + 1$ is transmitted. The external messages at node i continue to be transmitted, however. When the blocked condition is removed the link messages held back are immediately served. Only at the first link are link messages completely blocked from the system, as in the end-to-end case.

To evaluate and compare these two schemes we need a quantitative measure of congestion on the logical link. We have already indicated that congestion manifests itself as an increase in waiting time. We therefore choose to define congestion C precisely as the relative or fractional increase in time delay suffered by external messages due to the presence of link messages, averaged over all external messages in the link. Letting T_i be the average time delay incurred by external messages at node i, and T_{ni} the corresponding time delay when there are no link messages present, we have

$$C = \sum_{i=1}^{M} \frac{\lambda_i}{\lambda} \left(\frac{T_i - T_{ni}}{T_{ni}} \right) = \sum_{i=1}^{M} \left(\frac{\lambda_i}{\lambda} \frac{T_i}{T_{ni}} - 1 \right) \qquad (11\text{-}25)$$

with

$$\lambda = \sum_{i=1}^{M} \lambda_i$$

We can invoke Little's theorem (Chap. 6) to relate this definition of congestion to the average number of external messages waiting at each node.

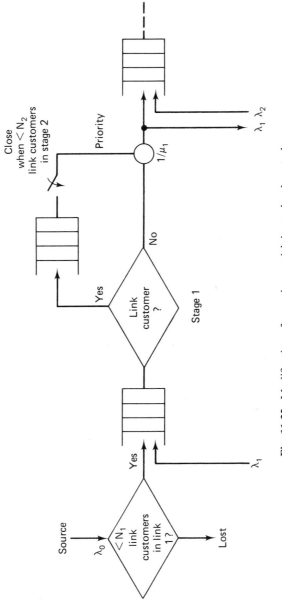

Fig. 11-22. Modification of queueing model due to local controls.

247

Thus we have immediately that

$$T_i = \frac{E(m_i)}{\lambda_i} \tag{11-26}$$

with $E(m_i)$ the average number of external messages at node i. More specifically, for the case where no link messages are present at all, we have, from our previous M/M/1 discussion of Chap. 6,

$$T_{ni} = \frac{E(m_{ni})}{\lambda_i} = \frac{1}{\mu_i - \lambda_i} \tag{11-27}$$

Introducing Eq. (11-27) and (11-26) into (11-25), we have, finally,

$$\lambda C = \sum_{i=1}^{M} [(\mu_i - \lambda_i)E(m_i) - \lambda_i] \tag{11-25a}$$

We thus need to calculate the average number of external messages at node i for the two models of Fig. 11-21 and 11-22. We shall indicate how this is done for the end-to-end case. For the local control case it turns out an approximate analysis only can be made. We shall therefore only present results for this case and refer the reader for details of analysis to the appropriate references.[*,**]

To calculate $E(m_i)$, the average number of external messages at node i, as well as the blocking probability P_B, in the end-to-end case, we must determine the equation of state of the queueing network of Fig. 11-20. Because the link messages thread throughout the network it is not obvious the queues are independent (even with the independent message length assumption), and the equation of state involving the joint statistics of all nodes must be written. Specifically, let $n_1, n_2, \ldots, n_M$ represent the link messages at nodes 1 through M, respectively. (Then $\sum_{i=1}^{M} n_i \leq N$ for the end-to-end strategy.) We also have $m_1, m_2, \ldots, m_M$ as the external messages waiting respectively at each of the nodes. Let $\mathbf{n}$ and $\mathbf{m}$ be the vectors representing the M link and external message numbers (states), respectively, at each of the nodes. Then we must find $P(\mathbf{n}, \mathbf{m})$, the probability of having state $(\mathbf{n}, \mathbf{m})$ for the system, for all possible system states.

To do this we assume statistical equilibrium prevails (i.e., stationary statistics) and set up balance equations equating the stationary probability $P_L(\mathbf{n}, \mathbf{m})$ of *leaving* state $(\mathbf{n}, \mathbf{m})$ to the probability $P_E(\mathbf{n}, \mathbf{m})$ of *entering* that state. This is a standard procedure invoked in many branches of statistics (it is used quite often in statistical physics, for example). Its first application to queueing networks goes back to the work of Jackson, referenced earlier. As an example, consider a single M/M/1 queue with external messages only. Let

*M. C. Pennotti and M. Schwartz, "Congestion Control in Tandem Links."
**M. C. Pennotti, "The Control of Congestion in Message-Switched Networks," Ph.D. thesis, Polytechnic Institute of New York, June 1974.

$P(m)$ be the probability (to be found) that there are m messages in the queue. The probability of leaving this state is then

$$P_L(m) = (\lambda + \mu)P(m) \qquad (11\text{-}28)$$

since an arrival *or* a departure changes the state.* Similarly, the probability of entering state m must be given by

$$P_E(m) = \lambda P(m - 1) + \mu P(m + 1) \qquad (11\text{-}29)$$

Equating Eq. (11-29) and (11-28), we get

$$(\lambda + \mu)P(m) = \lambda P(m - 1) + \mu P(m + 1) \qquad (11\text{-}30)$$

just the governing Eq. (6-10), in Chap. 6, for the M/M/1 queue.

We now extend this approach to the more general tandem queueing link of Fig. 11-20. The probability (actually, *rate*) of *leaving* state $(\mathbf{n}, \mathbf{m})$ is given by

$$P_L(\mathbf{n}, \mathbf{m}) = \left(\lambda_0 + \sum_{i=1}^{M} \lambda_i + \sum_{i=1}^{M} \mu_i\right)P(\mathbf{n}, \mathbf{m}) \qquad (11\text{-}31)$$

extending Eq. (11-28). The quantity within parentheses represents all the possible ways of leaving state $(\mathbf{n}, \mathbf{m})$. For the end-to-end control strategy, Eq. (11-31) assumes $\sum_{i=1}^{M} n_i < N$ (otherwise $\lambda_0 = 0$), as well as n_i and $m_i > 0$ (otherwise $\mu_i = 0$, since no departure can take place from an empty queue).

The evaluation of the probability $P_E(\mathbf{n}, \mathbf{m})$ of *entering* state $(\mathbf{n}, \mathbf{m})$ is somewhat more complicated. One must enumerate all possible ways of arriving at state $(\mathbf{n}, \mathbf{m})$ from other states of the system. It is left to the reader to show that this probability is given by

$$P_E(\mathbf{n}, \mathbf{m}) = \lambda_0 P(n_1 - 1, n_2, \ldots, n_M, \mathbf{m})$$

$$+ \sum_{i=1}^{M} \lambda_i P(\mathbf{n}, m_1, m_2, \ldots, m_i - 1, \ldots, m_M)$$

$$+ \sum_{i=1}^{M-1} \frac{n_i + 1}{n_i + 1 + m_i} \mu_i P(n_1, n_2, \ldots, n_i + 1, n_{i+1} - 1, \ldots, n_M, \mathbf{m})$$

$$+ \frac{n_M + 1}{n_M + 1 + m_M} \mu_M P(n_1, n_2, \ldots, n_M + 1, \mathbf{m})$$

$$+ \sum_{i=1}^{M} \frac{m_i + 1}{n_i + m_i + 1} \mu_i P(\mathbf{n}, m_1, m_2, \ldots, m_i + 1, \ldots, m_M) \qquad (11\text{-}32)$$

Note that if a link message leaves node i it must appear at node $i + 1$, except for the final node. Similarly, if an external message leaves link i, it exits from the system. Use has been made of these conditions in writing Eq.

---

*This equation actually represents the *rate* of leaving state m. We would have to multiply through by Δt to obtain the probability of leaving the state in time Δt. There will be an equivalent Δt in the equation for $P_E(m)$, so it can be dropped. Alternately, it suffices to equate the *rates* of leaving and entering states. We shall actually deal with rates, suppressing the Δt factor, but shall use the word probability for ease in terminology.

(11-32). Note also that a link message will depart only if it is in service. For n_i link messages and m_i external messages at node i, the probability that a link message is in service is $n_i/(n_i + m_i)$, assuming messages randomly arriving $\left(\sum_{i=1}^{M} n_i < N \right)$ and being served in the order first-come-first-served. A similar expression obviously holds true for the probability that an external message is in service at link i, and so appears in Eq. (11-32).

The equation of state for the tandem link is now given by equating Eq. (11-31) and (11-32). It is then again left to the reader to show by substitution that the solution to this resultant equation is given by

$$P(\mathbf{n}, \mathbf{m}) = P(\mathbf{0}, \mathbf{0}) \prod_{i=1}^{M} \left(\frac{\lambda_0}{\mu_i} \right)^{n_i} \left(\frac{\lambda_i}{\mu_i} \right)^{m_i} \frac{(n_i + m_i)!}{n_i! \, m_i!} \qquad (11\text{-}33)$$

This result is a special case of one obtained by Baskett and Muntz for more general queueing networks.*

To find the unknown constant $P(\mathbf{0}, \mathbf{0})$ we must of course sum $P(\mathbf{n}, \mathbf{m})$ over all possible states, setting the sum equal to 1. It is at this point that we have to invoke the end-to-end control condition that $\sum_{i=1}^{M} n_i \leq N$. Specifically then,

$$\frac{1}{P(\mathbf{0}, \mathbf{0})} = \sum_{n} \sum_{m_1=0}^{\infty} \sum_{m_2=0}^{\infty} \cdots \sum_{m_M=0}^{\infty} \prod_{i=1}^{M} \left(\frac{\lambda_0}{\mu_i} \right)^{n_i} \left(\frac{\lambda_i}{\mu_i} \right)^{m_i} \frac{(n_i + m_i)!}{n_i! \, m_i!} \qquad (11\text{-}34)$$

Here the symbol $\sum_{n}$ is a shorthand term representing the fact that we are summing over all possible partitions of the vector $\mathbf{n}$ such that $n = \sum_{i=1}^{M} n_i \leq N$. (For example, if $N = 2$ and $M = 2$, the possible values of $\mathbf{n}$ that we must sum over are $(0, 0)$, $(1, 0)$, $(0, 1)$, $(1, 1)$.) The evaluation of Eq. (11-34) is readily carried out by interchanging the order of $\sum_{m_i}$ and $\prod_{i}$. For then it is easy to see that Eq. (11-34) is equally-well given by

$$\frac{1}{P(\mathbf{0}, \mathbf{0})} = \sum_{n} \prod_{i=1}^{M} \left(\frac{\lambda_0}{\mu_i} \right)^{n_i} \frac{1}{n_i!} \sum_{m_i=0}^{\infty} \frac{(n_i + m_i)!}{m_i!} \left(\frac{\lambda_i}{\mu_i} \right)^{m_i} \qquad (11\text{-}34a)$$

Letting ρ_i represent λ_i/μ_i, the summation over m_i in Eq. (11-34a) is easily evaluated by first introducing a standard identity:

$$\sum_{m_i=0}^{\infty} \frac{(n_i + m_i)!}{m_i!} \rho_i^{m_i} = \sum_{m_i=0}^{\infty} \frac{d^{n_i}}{d\rho_i^{n_i}} \rho_i^{n_i + m_i} \qquad (11\text{-}35)$$

Then, interchanging summation and differentiation, evaluating the sum and differentiating, we have

$$\frac{1}{P(\mathbf{0}, \mathbf{0})} = \sum_{n} \prod_{i=1}^{M} \frac{[\lambda_0/(\mu_i - \lambda_i)]^{n_i}}{1 - \rho_i} \qquad (11\text{-}36)$$

---

*F. Baskett and R. R. Muntz, "Queueing Network Models with Different Classes of Customers," *Proc. IEEE Computer Conference*, San Francisco, Sept. 1972. See also Baskett et al., "Open, Closed, and Mixed Networks of Queues."

The desired solution for $P(\mathbf{n}, \mathbf{m})$, with $P(\mathbf{0}, \mathbf{0})$ evaluated, can thus be seen to be given by

$$P(\mathbf{n}, \mathbf{m}) = \frac{1}{Z_M^N} \prod_{i=1}^{M} \left(\frac{\lambda_0}{\mu_i}\right)^{n_i} \rho_i^{m_i} (1 - \rho_i) \frac{(n_i + m_i)!}{n_i! \, m_i!} \tag{11-37}$$

where

$$Z_M^N = \sum_n \prod_{i=1}^{M} \left(\frac{\lambda_0}{\mu_i - \lambda_i}\right)^{n_i} \tag{11-38}$$

As we shall shortly show, all desired statistical parameters of the tandem link (average number of messages waiting, congestion, blocking probability) are obtainable from this function Z_M^N just defined. An observant reader will note that this is related to the partition function of statistical physics from which equations of state and significant physical parameters are usually found. A few brief comments are in order, however. First note that if the link messages are set equal to zero ($n_i = 0$, $\lambda_0 = 0$), Eq. (11-37) reduces simply to that for M independent M/M/1 queues. If $\lambda_i = 0$ and $m_i = 0$ now, the case of zero external messages, we get for the distribution of link messages

$$P(\mathbf{n}, \mathbf{0}) = \frac{1}{Z_M^N} \prod_{i=1}^{M} \left(\frac{\lambda_0}{\mu_i}\right)^{n_j} \tag{11-39}$$

with Z_M^N appropriately modified by setting all $\lambda_i = 0$, $i = 1, 2, \ldots, M$. In the more general case with external messages present, the distribution of link messages is found by summing Eq. (11-37) over all possible values of $\mathbf{m}$. This gives

$$P(\mathbf{n}) = \frac{1}{Z_M^N} \prod_{i=1}^{M} \left(\frac{\lambda_0}{\mu_i - \lambda_i}\right)^{n_i} \tag{11-40}$$

This is the same expression as in Eq. (11-39) with μ_i replaced by $\mu_i - \lambda_i$. (See Eq. (11-38) also.) The interpretation of this is that the effect of the external messages on the link messages is equivalent to that of reducing the service rate at each node by the corresponding external arrival rate. Since, as already noted and as we shall see below, all statistical parameters of interest for the *general* end-to-end control model depend solely on Z_M^N, which from Eq. (11-38) depends on $(\mu_i - \lambda_i)$, the tandem link model of Fig. 11-20 can be sketched in equivalent form by leaving out all external message arrivals and departures and simply replacing all service parameters μ_i by $(\mu_i - \lambda_i)$.

Consider first the blocking probability P_B for end-to-end control. This is just the probability that $\sum_{i=1}^{M} n_i = N$; i.e., the probability that there are N link messages present in the tandem link, so that new link messages arriving are turned away. This turn out to be given by

$$P_B = 1 - \frac{Z_M^{N-1}}{Z_M^N} \tag{11-41}$$

This is proven quite simply by noting that

$$P_B = \sum_{n=N} P(\mathbf{n}, \mathbf{m}) = \sum_{n \leq N} P(\mathbf{n}, \mathbf{m}) - \sum_{n \leq N-1} P(\mathbf{n}, \mathbf{m}) \qquad (11\text{-}42)$$

where the shorthand notation $\sum_{n \leq N}$ is used to represent the sum over all states $(\mathbf{n}, \mathbf{m})$ such that $\sum_{i=1}^{M} n_i \leq N$. The first sum in the right-hand side of Eq. (11-42) is just 1. It is left for the reader to show that the second sum over $n \leq N - 1$ gives just Z_M^{N-1}/Z_M^N.

The average number of link messages at node i is just

$$E(n_i) = \sum_{\text{all } (\mathbf{n}, \mathbf{m})} n_i P(\mathbf{n}, \mathbf{m}) \qquad (11\text{-}43)$$

We shall show below that this sum is readily evaluated by differentiating Z_M^N:

$$E(n_i) = \frac{x_i}{Z_M^N} \frac{d}{dx_i} Z_M^N \qquad x_i \equiv \frac{\lambda_0}{\mu_i - \lambda_i} \qquad (11\text{-}44)$$

Similarly, the average number of external messages at node i, needed to evaluate the congestion parameter C (Eq. (11-25a)) is found to be given by

$$E(m_i) = \sum_{\text{all } (\mathbf{n}, \mathbf{m})} m_i P(\mathbf{n}, \mathbf{m}) = \frac{\lambda_i}{\mu_i - \lambda_i}[1 + E(n_i)] \qquad (11\text{-}45)$$

If $E(n_i) = 0$, as would be the case if there were no link messages, $E(m_i)$ is just the M/M/1 queue result. Eq. (11-45) thus indicates that the effect of link messages on $E(m_i)$ is just to increase it by the factor $1 + E(n_i)$ from what it would be if no link customers were present.

The congestion parameter as defined by Eq. (11-25a) simplifies considerably by the use of Eq. (11-45) for it now becomes

$$\lambda C = \sum_{i=1}^{M} \lambda_i E(n_i) \qquad (11\text{-}46)$$

with

$$E(n_i) = \frac{x_i}{Z_M^N} \frac{d}{dx_i} Z_M^N$$

as in Eq. (11-44) above. Note that the congestion, initially defined to be the relative increase in delay time suffered by external messages, turns out to be given by the weighted sum of average link messages. As pointed out previously, both the blocking probability P_B and the congestion C can be obtained analytically from the function Z_M^N.

The derivations of Eq. (11-44) and (11-45) follow directly from introducing moment-generating functions. Thus, define the $2M$-dimensional moment-generating function (see Chap. 6 for the one-dimensional counterpart)

$$G(\mathbf{v}, \mathbf{w}) \equiv E(v_1^{n_1} \ldots v_M^{n_M} w_1^{m_1} \ldots w_M^{n_M})$$

$$= \sum_{\text{all states}} \prod_{i=1}^{M} v_i^{n_i} w_i^{m_i} P(\mathbf{n}, \mathbf{m}) \qquad (11\text{-}47)$$

$P(\mathbf{n}, \mathbf{m})$ is given by Eq. (11-37). Substituting this equation in Eq. (11-47) and then noting that the sum over all states of the resulting expression is similar to the one given by Eq. (11-34), one can simplify by the use of Eq. (11-36) to obtain

$$Z_M^N G(\mathbf{v}, \mathbf{w}) = \prod_{i=1} \left(\frac{1 - \rho_i}{1 - \rho_i w_i} \right) \sum_n \prod_{i=1}^M \left(\frac{v_i \lambda_0}{\mu_i - \lambda_i w_i} \right)^{n_i} \tag{11-48}$$

Note by comparing the second product in Eq. (11-48) with Eq. (11-38) for Z_M^N how $G(\mathbf{v}, \mathbf{w})$ and Z_M^N are related. (As a check, $G(\mathbf{1}, \mathbf{1}) = 1$, as required.)

From the moment-generating property of $G(\mathbf{v}, \mathbf{w})$ we now have

$$E(n_i) = \frac{\partial G(\mathbf{v}, \mathbf{w})}{\partial v_i}\bigg|_{\mathbf{v}, \mathbf{w}=1} = \frac{x_i}{Z_M^N} \frac{dZ_M^N}{dx_i} \tag{11-49}$$

from Eq. (11-48). Here, as already noted, $x_i \equiv \lambda_0 / (\mu_i - \lambda_i)$. Similarly, upon differentiating $G(\mathbf{v}, \mathbf{w})$ with respect to w_i, and setting $\mathbf{v}, \mathbf{w} = \mathbf{1}$, we get $E(m_i)$. Eq. (11-45) again follows from Eq. (11-48).

Using Eq. (11-38) to find Z_M^N for various tandem link examples with traffic on each link specified, one may now find the congestion parameter C and the blocking probability P_B from Eq. (11-44) and (11-46), and Eq. (11-41), respectively, for the same examples, and evaluate the effect of end-to-end congestion control. As an example, consider a three-stage uniform tandem link for which all external average message rates are the same, and all message lengths are on the average the same. We thus have $\lambda_1 = \lambda_2 = \lambda_3 = \lambda$ and $\mu_1 = \mu_2 = \mu_3 = \mu$. Fig. 11-23 shows a plot of the resultant congestion

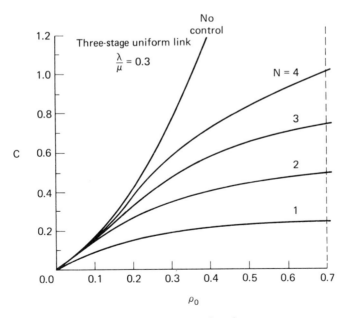

Fig. 11-23. End-to-end control performance.

parameter C versus the link message traffic intensity $\rho_0 \equiv \lambda_0/\mu$. (Recall again that the line speeds or capacities in bps have been subsumed in the reciprocal message length parameter μ.) The external message traffic intensity has been taken to be $\lambda/\mu = 0.3$. The curve labeled "no control" is the one for which $N \longrightarrow \infty$; i.e., the case for which any number of link messages is allowed in the system. The congestion parameter for this case displays the typical queueing delay characteristic, rising beyond bound as the link traffic increases, with ρ_0 approaching 0.7. Now if the end-to-end control is invoked, with $N = 4$ (i.e., no more than four link messages are allowed anywhere in this example of three links in tandem), the congestion parameter levels off to a fixed value independent of ρ_0. If the number of link messages allowed on the link is reduced to $N = 3$, the congestion is reduced still more. Maximum reduction is of course obtained for $N = 1$. The price paid for introducing congestion control is a reduced link message throughput. This has of course been noted previously. This throughput is given specifically, in terms of the blocking probability, by $\lambda_0(1 - P_B)$. As the congestion control is invoked and becomes more stringent (with successive reductions of N), the blocking probability increases and the throughput decreases. Fig. 11-24 shows a plot of the resul-

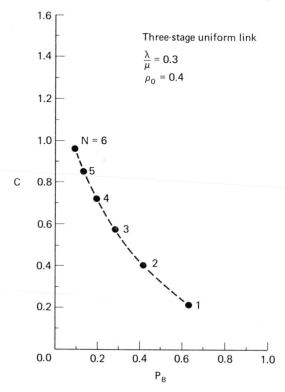

Fig. 11-24. End-to-end control: congestion vs. blocking probability.

tant trade-off curve, C versus P_B, for the same three-stage uniform link example of Fig. 11-23, but calculated for the specific link traffic intensity $\rho_0 = 0.4$. Note that the congestion parameter is reduced from $C = 1$ with $N = 6$ to $C = 0.2$ with $N = 1$, but with blocking probability rising from less than 0.1 to 0.6. The effective link message throughput in turn is reduced from $0.9\lambda_0$ to $0.4\lambda_0$. Similar curves could be obtained for other values of ρ_0 and λ/μ, as well as for uniform and nonuniform links of various sizes.*

As pointed out previously local congestion control can only be analyzed approximately. Details appear in the references.** A typical performance curve for a three-stage tandem link using local control appears in Fig. 11-25. There are more control variations possible with local control since the maximum number of link messages allowed at each node can be independently varied. (Recall that no more than N_i link messages are allowed at node i. See Fig. 11-22.) Fig. 11-25 has been sketched for the special case of $N_1 = N_2 = N_3$. Similar curves may be obtained for different combinations of N_i.† It is

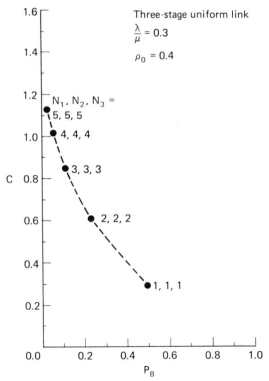

Fig. 11-25. Local control: congestion vs. blocking probability.

*Pennotti, "Control of Congestion in Message-Switched Networks."
**Ibid.; also Pennotti and Schwartz, "Congestion Control in Tandem Links."
†Pennotti, "Control of Congestion in Message-Switched Networks."

apparent that local control performance is similar to that of end-to-end control. This is shown specifically in Fig. 11-26 with the curves of Figs. 11-24 and 11-26 overlaid on one another. For this example the two control schemes

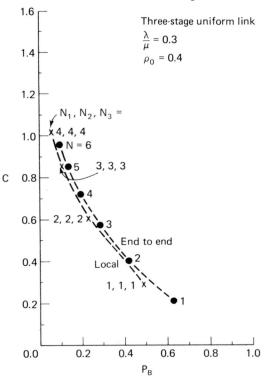

Fig. 11-26. Comparison of control schemes.

behave in similar fashion. Similar results have been demonstrated for other examples including nonuniform links.* This means that factors other than the amount of congestion control desired will dictate the choice of which one of these two schemes will be used. These factors may include implementation complexity, the buffer size (memory capacity) required at each node, etc. Whichever scheme is used, however, curves such as those of Figs. 11-24 to 11-26 can be used to determine the necessary trade-off between congestion control and throughput. Although these curves are based on a rather simplified and possibly artificial model of flow control in a network, they should provide a first approach to a designer interested in implementing flow control in a network.

*Ibid.

Global Control: Isarithmic Method

We have discussed thus far simple models for two types of congestion control used in practice: end-to-end control in which the number of messages per user (or equivalent packets) allowed in the network is limited, and local control in which individual nodes limit the number of messages they will accept from any one user. We now outline briefly a third approach to congestion control, in which the *total number* of packets allowed in the system is fixed. New packets can thus be entered only if the total number circulating is less than the maximum allowed, or as a replacement for a packet exiting at its destination. Some proposed loop systems use this approach: messages waiting in buffers at control points around a loop can only be read out onto the line constituting the loop when a circulating fixed-length frame reaches their particular control point, and then only if the frame is not fully occupied.[*,**] (Note the analogy to a bus circulating around a prescribed route and stopping to pick up passengers at specified control points.) The control in this case is obviously decentralized. Centralized global control methods are possible as well, although due account has to be taken of the network capacity required to transmit signal and control messages.

Another global technique suggested for topologically more complex distributed networks is the so-called *isarithmic* method for congestion control.[†,††] In this technique a constant number of "permits" circulates throughout a given network. In order for a packet to enter the network it must acquire one of the permits. Several mechanisms are possible. As one possibility a packet on reaching its destination releases its permit, and this is immediately picked up by a waiting packet. If there is no packet waiting the permit is then circulated randomly over the network. It is then picked up at the first node it reaches at which a packet is waiting. Alternately a small pool of packets may be set aside at each nodal entry point to reduce the delay experienced by packets in waiting for a randomly-circulating permit to arrive. Note that the isarithmic method has elements of similarity to the loop control method described earlier, although there the frame circulated continuously around the loop, while here the permits circulate randomly.

The National Physical Laboratory of Great Britain has carried out simulation studies of the isarithmic method.[§] One of the studies showed that

*J. F. Hayes and D. N. Sherman, "Traffic Analysis of a Ring-Switched Data Transmission Service," *Bell Systems Technical Journal*, **50**, Nov. 1971, 2947–78.

J. R. Pierce, "How Far Can Data Loops Go?," *IEEE Trans. on Communications*, **COM-20, no. 3, June 1972, 527–30.

†D. W. Davies, "The Control of Congestion in Packet-Switching Networks."

††Davies and Barber, *Communication Networks for Computers*.

§Ibid.

by optimumly choosing the permit pool size at each node, the admission delay experienced by packets in waiting to receive a permit was reduced to negligible values. The study was carried out for an 18-node network capable of handling about 8000 packets/sec before congestion sets in. For maximum queue size of 6 at each node and 90 permits total for the system (these were found to provide maximum throughput), the optimum permit pool size was found to be between 2 and 3. This meant that about half the permits were free to circulate, while the other half were assigned to pools at specific nodes. For this allocation of permits the admission delay was negligible (much less than 0.1 msec), even at a throughput of 6300 packets/sec (80% of saturation). For no fixed permit pool (all permits free to circulate) the admission delay rose to 0.3 msec, while with all permits assigned to pools the delay was 0.8 msec.

Permits of course utilize a part of the system capacity. This may be minimized, as is often done with acknowledgement messages, by embedding them in data messages.* Where no data messages are being transmitted, special permit messages must still be transmitted.

PROBLEMS

11.1   The centralized adaptive routing strategy discussed in this chapter is to be analyzed for the case of one source and two concentrators. Queue length information from each of the concentrators is sent to the controller at intervals of $T = 2$ slots. The optimum switch position (i.e., routing strategy) in each of the two slot intervals is to be found that minimizes the expected average queue length

$$C = \frac{1}{T} \sum_{k=0}^{T-1} C(k)$$

$$C(k) = \sum_{j=1}^{Q} \sum_{m=0}^{L} m x_m^{(j)}(k+1)$$

(L is the maximum queue length at each of the Q concentrators.)

(1) The maximum queue length is $L = 2$ packets. Single packet messages arrive at the source at an average Poisson rate of λ messages/slot interval. Each concentrator has an output trunk capacity of one packet/slot interval.

*Ibid., p. 407.

Find the optimum strategy for $\lambda = 0.5$, and $\lambda = 1$. For both cases queue 1 has two packets initially and queue 2 is empty. Can you explain the results?

(2) Why would the optimum strategy be to route alternately, first to one queue, then to the other, if *any* of the following initial conditions were to exist?

$$x_0^{(1)}(0) = x_0^{(2)}(0) = 1; \; x_0^{(1)}(0) = 1, \; x_1^{(2)}(0) = 1;$$
$$x_1^{(1)}(0) = 1, \; x_0^{(2)}(0) = 1; \; x_1^{(1)}(0) = x_1^{(2)}(0) = 1$$

11.2   Consider the network shown in Fig. 11-14. Use any one of the optimum routing algorithms discussed in this chapter to verify that the flows shown do provide minimum average time delay. Reading of the references cited (e.g., the papers by L. Fratta, M. Gerla, and L. Kleinrock; D. G. Cantor and M. Gerla; M. Schwartz and C. K. Cheung) may be useful in pinning down the details of the algorithms well enough to enable programming them on a computer.

11.3   Repeat Problem 11.2 using one of the examples cited in the references on optimum routing.

11.4   Refer to Problem 4.1. All line capacities are 1200 bps. Find the optimum routes for all source-destination pairs that minimize the average time delay. Compare the average time delay found with that obtained using shortest path (least number of links) routing. The comments made in Problem 11.2 are appropriate here as well.

11.5   Refer to the network example of Fig. 11-15 for shortest path determination. Show that if the costs (link "lengths") are all unity, the set of shortest paths from N_a to all other nodes is that shown sketched in Fig. 11-19.

11.6   Consider the data network shown in Fig. P11.6. Both land lines and satellite links are available as indicated. Find the shortest paths between Seattle and all the other cities in the network for interactive and batch users under the following conditions:

(1) 2400 bps land lines are weighted 1 for all users; 4800 bps lines are weighted 1 for batch users and 3 for interactive users.

(2) Satellite links are weighted 1 for batch users and 6 for interactive users.

Repeat the calculations if the earth station at New York is taken out of commission temporarily for repairs. Repeat if the Houston-Atlanta line is down temporarily.

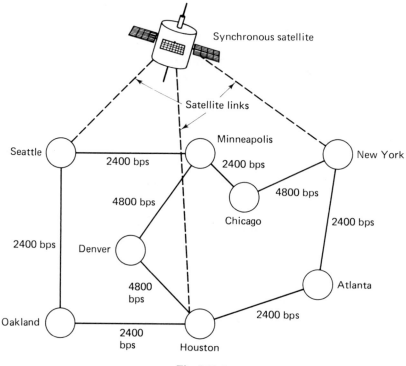

Fig. P11.6

11.7   An international wire service with headquarters in Brussels operates a worldwide data network incorporating concentrators in 10 cities as shown in Fig. P11.7.

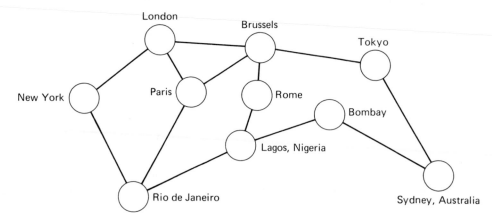

Fig. P11.7

Determine the routing strategy to be used for messages going from Brussels to each of the other cities if the criterion chosen is the least number of links. Find the best alternate strategy as well.

11.8 Consider a tandem link with M nodes. Show the probability (actually rate) of entering state $(\mathbf{n}, \mathbf{m})$ is given by Eq. (11-32).

11.9 Verify Eq. (11-33) which gives the stationary probability of being in state $(\mathbf{n}, \mathbf{m})$ of the tandem link with M nodes.

11.10 Starting with Eq. (11-37) and (11-38) for the probability of state of the M node tandem link, show

(1) the blocking probability P_B is given by Eq. (11-41)

(2) the average number of link messages at node i is given by Eq. (11-44)

(3) the average number of external messages at node i is given by Eq. (11-45).

In doing parts (2) and (3), derive Eq. (11-48) for the moment-generating function first.

11.11 End-to-end control is to be applied to a three-stage tandem link. Assume a uniform system with $\mu_i = \mu$, $\lambda_i = \lambda$.

(1) One link message only is allowed in the link. Show that congestion C and blocking probability P_B are related simply by $C = P_B/3$. (*Hint:* $Z_3^{(1)} = 1 + x_1 + x_2 + x_3$.)

(2) Two messages are now allowed in. ($N = 2$.) Let $\rho = \lambda/\mu = 0.3$. Plot both congestion C and blocking probability P_B as a function of the link message intensity $\rho_0 = \lambda_0/\mu$. (*Hint:* Show

$$Z_3^{(2)} = 1 + x_1^2 + x_2^2 + x_3^2 + x_1 x_2 + x_1 x_3 + x_2 x_3 + x_1 + x_2 + x_3$$

Then $P_B = \dfrac{6x^2}{1 + 3x + 6x^2}$ and $C = \dfrac{x + 4x^2}{1 + 3x + 6x^2}$.)

11.12 Consider a tandem link of M stages. If $N = 1$ link message is allowed in the link, show $C = P_B/M$.

Polling

in Networks

12

Polling techniques have been widely implemented in many of the existing data networks. Inquiry-response systems in particular have made use of polling procedures. The NASDAQ over-the-counter stock quotation system* and various banking networks, for example, use polling procedures for interrogating terminals in the networks. The IBM PARS (Programmed Airlines Reservations System) airline reservation system which has been widely adopted in the airline industry and which we shall describe in detail in this chapter, uses polling techniques to deliver messages waiting at possibly widely-dispersed concentrators to a centralized data processing center. Multidrop networks described in Chap. 9 use polling techniques quite commonly to maintain order among the various terminals attempting to access the central computer.

Various polling disciplines are in use (and many more could equally well be conjured up) but all require a controller to either initiate or to carry out the polling. This controller can be either a concentrator or, at a higher level, a central processor in a centralized network. For the case of terminals and other data sources connected to a concentrator, polling techniques provide an alternative access method to the interrupt or scanning mechanisms mentioned briefly in Chap. 7 in connection with asynchronous or statistical multiplexing. Lines or ports feeding into a concentrator may thus be shared

---

*M. Schwartz, R. R. Boorstyn, and R. L. Pickholtz, "Terminal-Oriented Computer-Communication Networks," *Proc. IEEE*, **60**, no. 11, Nov. 1972, 1415–18.

among a group of terminals and data sources. The question of then connecting the terminals in a cost-effective manner thus leads exactly to the multi-point design discussion of Chap. 9. In the next chapter we shall discuss random access techniques as additional alternative procedures for inputting messages into a network. These latter techniques are particularly appropriate for handling bursty traffic, with the data sources idle most of the time. We shall in fact compare polling with a random access scheme for some simple examples at the end of the next chapter.

As already noted polling is also used in some centralized networks in feeding messages from concentrators to a central system serving as the controller. The IBM PARS system to be discussed in the next section provides one example. Examples of the various topologies that might be encountered in either of these cases—terminals accessing a concentrator, or concentrators accessing a central computer—are shown in Fig. 12-1. Fig. 12-1a and 12-1b portray the tree (or multipoint) and star structures already discussed at length in previous chapters. Fig. 12-1c demonstrates a third structure, that of a loop topology. Loop connections have been widely used in many applications. They provide a simple way of connecting users together and to a central facility. The line in this case is shared by all users. In a virtual sense, as we shall see, all centralized topologies using polling can be visualized as being stretched into a loop.

Control disciplines other than polling may be envisioned for such a loop structure, and some have been adopted in practice. These control strategies have been suggested to handle the same access problem noted above: having messages from a multiplicity of sources attempt to use the same communications facility or enter the same concentration facility simultaneously. Synchronous time-division techniques have been proposed and implemented for such loop structures. Frequency-division multiplexing is possible as well. These techniques, however, suffer from the usual synchronous or line-switched network problem that time slots or frequency bands must be *dedicated* to the different users. For users with relatively infrequent bursts of short messages this means inefficient use of the communications resource.

Loop disciplines of the asynchronous or statistical multiplexing type have been proposed, analyzed, and implemented as well.* As an example, a

---

*There are a host of papers on this subject. As a representative sample see, for example, the following: Pierce, "How Far Can Data Loops Go," p. 527; West, "Loop Transmission Control Structures," p. 531; Spragins, "Loop Transmission Systems—Mean Value Analysis," p. 592; Chu and Konheim, "On the Analysis and Modeling of a Class of Computer-Communication Systems," p. 645; all in the *IEEE Trans. on Communications*, **COM-20**, no. 3, June 1972, part II. Also Hayes and Sherman, "Traffic Analysis of a Ring-Switched Data Transmission System," *Bell Systems Technical Journal*, Nov. 1971, p. 2947. See also papers by Yuen et al., A. R. Kaye, J. D. Spragins and A. G. Konheim in *Proc. Symposium on Computer-Communications and Teletraffic*, Polytechnic Institute of Brooklyn, New York, 1972.

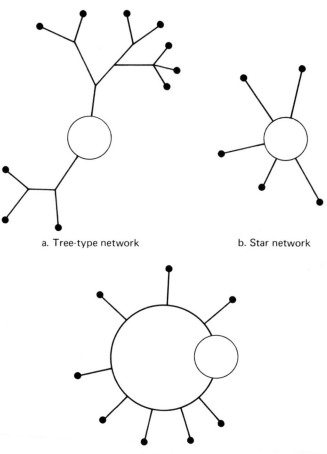

a. Tree-type network   b. Star network

c. Loop system

Fig. 12-1. Different network configurations encountered in polling.

fixed length time frame may be allocated at specified times to all users in the loop. In one version, which introduces priority into the system, the source closest to the controller is allowed to utilize as much of the frame capacity as it needs. If any capacity remains, the second source in the loop is allowed to access the frame and enter its waiting data. If the first source needs more than one frame to complete its data readout it has first priority on the next frame, etc. In an alternate system proposed the frame rotates continuously around the loop, emptying messages at terminals to which addressed and taking on messages waiting at terminals if vacancies exist at time of arrival. In this application the loop is a decentralized network with the controller serving as a flow expeditor rather than as a central processing facility to which all messages flow. Finally, as already noted, some of the random access techniques to be described in the next chapter could be adopted for the loop structure as well as the other topologies of Fig. 12-1.

Polling procedures represent the most common form of control discipline, however, for centralized structures such as those of Fig. 12-1. We shall therefore devote the remainder of this chapter to a discussion of polling in detail. As already noted we shall compare polling techniques with random access methods for some simple examples at the end of the next chapter.

Two types of polling discipline have been most commonly adopted in practice, and we shall focus on these two procedures throughout this chapter. In the roll-call or bus polling system each message source is in turn interrogated by the central source. On the arrival of a polling message the source polled transmits all messages waiting to the central system. On completion of the message transmission, polling of the next source is initiated.

In the hub or distributed control polling discipline the central source initiates polling by interrogating the message source at the end of the loop. This source transmits its waiting data and then signals the next source in line to begin transmitting. At the completion of the cycle, with all sources connected into the loop interrogated, the central source regains control.

Examples of these two polling systems are shown in Fig. 12-2, using the IBM PARS to be discussed in the next section as an example. In Fig. 12-2a we indicate a typical roll-call polling setup. In Fig. 12-2b a hub polling system is shown. In the hub polling scheme the message source furthest away is interrogated first. This source in turn polls the source next down the line, etc. The two figures point up the relative difference between the schemes. In the hub polling case an added data set is needed at each source to accept polling messages from the previous source up the line. However, the total time required for polling messages is less since these messages flow once around the loop only. In the roll-call case successive poll and poll-acknowledged messages must flow back and forth between central source and the different sources. The system response time is thus longer in the roll-call case. One would thus expect the hub polling techniques to be used in systems covering a larger geographic area, with roll-call polling restricted to smaller geographic regions, as indicated in the examples of Fig. 12-2. In practice this is not always the case because of other considerations. As an example, long distance multipoint lines leased from the telephone company in the United States are normally 4-wire configurations. Bridges are provided at the appropriate drops at which data stations (terminals or terminal controllers) are to be connected. Stations at the various drops cannot hear one another unless special expensive bridges are used, and so hub polling is generally not used for this type of configuration. Roll-call polling, with its attendant increased time delay, is often used instead. In fact most current polling applications in the United States use the roll-call approach. Hub polling for this same reason turns out to be easier to implement on loops or on groups of closely spaced

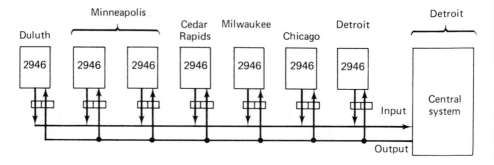

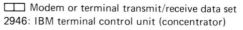

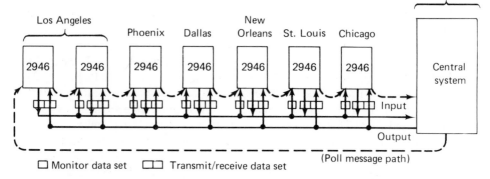

Modem or terminal transmit/receive data set
2946: IBM terminal control unit (concentrator)

a. Roll-call polling system

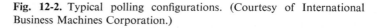

☐ Monitor data set   ☐☐ Transmit/receive data set   (Poll message path)

b. Hub polling system (Courtesy of International Business Machines Corporation
IBM 2946 Terminal Control Subsystem Component Description and
Operating Guide, 1971, Fig. 4).

Fig. 12-2. Typical polling configurations. (Courtesy of International
Business Machines Corporation.)

data stations, where two-wire lines are readily available. In those situations,
however, where response time is a critical parameter or where connections
between stations are leased individually as point-to-point lines rather than
multipoint, hub polling would presumably be used for larger distance configurations.

In the material following we shall focus on response time calculations
and shall assume that the connections made are such as to allow either roll-
call or hub polling to be used. This will enable us to compare the two techniques quantitatively in the context of some examples.

As already noted polling techniques are not restricted to large network
use only. The message sources could just as well be individual terminals. The

central source would then be a concentrator which itself might in turn be part of a larger polled network. In this case polling would be the procedure chosen for concentrating or combining the data a group of terminals.

The polling systems of Fig. 12-1 show concentrators being polled. The individual data terminals are not shown but are assumed connected to their respective concentrators, with messages being combined at the concentrator using polling, statistical multiplexing, or some other technique. In the next section of this chapter we discuss as an example of an actual polling system, the IBM PARS system. In the section following we then discuss some quantitative approaches to polling analysis. We focus, as already noted, on a response time comparison of hub and roll-call polling techniques, and on some queueing analysis of polling systems from which system response times can be obtained.

POLLING EXAMPLE

Airline Reservation Systems, IBM PARS*

The IBM PARS in its up-to-date version is an outgrowth of the original American Airlines Sabre system of 1961. The same keyboard printer and terminal interchange equipment (concentrators) were used for Delta and Pan Am systems introduced in 1964, as well as in the later PARS system, until 1969. New terminals and concentrators were introduced in the PARS system of 1969. Since the latest system is compatible with the earlier ones and uses essentially the same line control procedures, code, and message format, we shall briefly describe the older system first, then focus on the newer version. The system is designed to have a less than three sec response time.

PRE-1969 SYSTEM. The older system used an IBM 1006 Terminal Interchange Unit in conjunction with Model 1977 Terminal Units.** The terminal interchanges in a typical network might be connected as in the networks of Fig. 12-1. Polling messages from the central system, as well as information-bearing or central messages, are sent out to the terminal interchanges over a 2000 bits per sec (bps) full-duplex line. This is the main line shown in Fig. 12-2. Focusing on a typical terminal interchange unit in the larger network, as well as its associated terminals, we have the diagram of Fig. 12-3. Up to 30 terminals at speeds of 74, 148, or 207 bps, may access

---

*J. R. Knight, "A Case Study: Airline Reservation Systems," *Proc. IEEE,* **60,** Nov. 1972, p. 1423; J. P. Gray, "Line Control Procedures," *Proc. IEEE,* **60,** Nov. 1972, p. 1301; plus *IBM Reference Manuals.*

**IBM *Reference Manual,* A22–6640–1, 9000 Series Airline Reservation Systems, Remote Equipment.

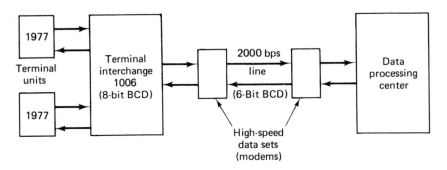

Fig. 12-3. Original PARS system (Pre-1969).

the terminal interchange simultaneously. A 6-bit BCD code is used for message transmission throughout the network. For the link between terminal and terminal interchange, however, start and stop bits, plus a BCD parity check bit, are appended so that 9-bit characters flow over that link.

The terminal interchange stores up to 4000 8-bit characters. (These are the terminal link 9-bit characters with the start bit deleted. They thus consist of a 6-bit BCD character, parity and stop bits.) Thirty-nine 100-character sections are used for storing data and one 100-character section is provided for controls. Of the 100 characters in a buffer section 98 can be used for data for a complete message or for the first segment of a long message. The interchange adds two characters—a terminal address and end of message (EOM) character. If the message is long (greater than 100 characters) additional segments are stored in other buffer sections. For these the buffer capacity is 97 characters, since a segment identifier character is added to link message segments.

Buffers are assigned on demand. Each buffer section is ready to be emptied as soon as filled or as soon as a message of less than 100 characters is completed. (This is denoted by an EOM character.) Messages are therefore transmitted in blocks, with longer messages requiring more than one block.

There are four modes of data flow in an interchange corresponding to data flowing to and from the low-speed terminals, and data flowing to and from the high-speed line to the central processing facility. The buffers store messages going both to and from the central processor. A message going to the center (*inbound* direction) is fed out at the 2000 bps rate when the terminal interchange is polled; (a go-ahead message is received). If a message is going to a terminal set it is fed out of the buffer at the appropriate rate when a message is completed (*or* a buffer section is filled), and the terminal is available for receiving.

In the receive, low-speed mode all terminal lines are scanned very rapidly and cyclically. All bits on all lines are scanned many times during the period they are on the line. Randomly occurring inputs from all terminals are thus effectively accepted simultaneously and are dumped "instantaneously" into a buffer, first-come-first-served. Nine serial bits per character appear, as noted earlier. The character is shifted bit by bit into a character register. When the stop bit is received, eight bits, excluding the start bit, are transferred into storage. A buffer is assigned and its address placed in the control word at the start of the message.

In the send high-speed mode an EOM character is added when the buffer is filled with up to 98 message characters. (The actual end of a message is signaled by the agent at the terminal by pressing the ENTER button which generates an EOM-complete character. When the message segment in a buffer is less than 98 characters long and completes the message, the EOM-complete character replaces the interchange-added EOM. Several kinds of EOM characters are available in this system.) As the buffer is filled the message contained is assigned to the inbound high-speed line control. As other messages are completed they are similarly assigned. Transmission begins when the go-ahead message is received. As each message is transmitted the buffer containing that message is made available for other messages. When all messages waiting have been transmitted the interchange initiates a go-ahead message. In the hub polling mode this is a signal to the next interchange to initiate transmission. In the roll-call mode this is a signal to the central processor to poll the next interchange.

The message format for the high-speed data (inbound and outbound, to and from the central processor) is shown in Fig. 12-4. The first synchroniza-

Sync 1 char.	Sync 2 char.	Interchange address	Terminal address (stored in buffer)	Segment identification (stored in buffer)	Body of message (stored in buffer)	End of message (stored in buffer)	Check char.
111111	111110	1 char.	1 char.	1 char.	As many as 98 characters	1 char.	1 char.

Fig. 12-4. High-speed data message format, pre-1969 PARS, 6-bit BCD characters. (Courtesy of International Business Machines Corporation, *IBM 9000 Series Airlines Reservation Systems Remote Equipment Reference Manual,* 1961, Fig. 21.)

tion character (S1) is called the bit synchronization group. The second (S2) is called the character synchronization group. These characters are added to the *first* inbound message of a sequence outputted by an interchange after receiving the go-ahead. They are dropped from outbound messages, on receipt. The check character is added before an inbound message moves to the high-speed data set.

The go-ahead or polling message formats are indicated in Fig. 12-5. Note that they consist essentially of a standard 6-bit go-ahead character and

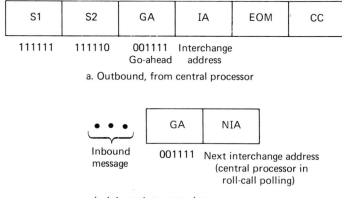

| S1 | S2 | GA | IA | EOM | CC |

111111   111110   001111   Interchange
                  Go-ahead   address

a. Outbound, from central processor

| GA | NIA |

Inbound   001111   Next interchange address
message   (central processor in
                        roll-call polling)

b. Inbound, to central processor

Fig. 12-5. Go-ahead (polling) message formats, pre-1969 PARS.

the next interchange address. Outbound go-ahead messages, from the central processor to the interchange, have standard synchronization, EOM, and check characters appended. (Compare with the data message format of Fig. 12-4.) Inbound go-ahead messages, signaling the completion of message transmission, appear at the end of a sequence of messages as in Fig. 12-5, and so do not require the additional control characters. (When the interchange has nothing to transmit, the additional characters are appended.) The NIA character in Fig. 12-5b is the next interchange address in hub polling. The go-ahead message in this case then serves as the polling message. In roll-call polling the central processor address is used, and this signals the central processor to poll the next interchange (using the format of Fig. 12-5a).

Outbound messages, from the central computer to the interchange and from there to the appropriate terminal, are acknowledged by the interchange if incomplete (more to come) or unsolicited. Such messages are recognized by special EOM characters. If the message is received correctly a special 4-character acknowledgement (ACK) is sent back to the central data center. The format of this ACK is shown in Fig. 12-6. When a message is received from the data center a buffer is assigned to it at the outbound high-speed line. The interchange adds a parity check bit and stop bit to each character received. The resultant 8-bit character is then transferred to the buffer. The interchange at the same time accumulates the check character. At the end of the message the check is compared with the check character received. If the

| IA | TA | EOM-incomplete | CC |

Fig. 12-6. ACK format, pre-1969 PARS.

two do not agree the incorrect message is discarded, and the buffer is released. The data center receiving no acknowledgement repeats the message.

No acknowledgement is generated for messages that are complete. If checking deems them incorrect they are also dropped from the buffer. The agent at the appropriate terminal requests a repeat by pressing a REPEAT button after receiving no reply. There is thus no automatic repeat in this case.

*CURRENT PARS.** In 1969 a modernized PARS was introduced by IBM. The 1006 Terminal Interchange Unit was replaced by the IBM 2946 Terminal Control Unit (TCU). The new system is compatible with both Sabre line control and the previous PARS systems. Associated with the 2946 TCU are two types of terminals—a 4505 keyboard and video display, and a 1980 printer.

The 2946 is a microprogrammed control unit. The control program is stored on a disk and loaded when desired. Adapters provide the interface with the communications system and the terminal units. There are various models of the 2946. The No. 1 model provides 16,384 bytes of storage and can accommodate eight 4505 terminals and eight 1980 printers. The No. 2 model provides 32,768 bytes and can accommodate sixteen 4505s, four 1980s plus eight 4505s *or* four 1980s. The No. 4 model has 32,768 bytes of storage, expandable to 49,152 bytes. It can accommodate sixteen 4505s, plus sixteen 4505s and four 1980s, *or* sixteen 1980s.

High-speed communications are again carried out in either the roll-call or hub polling modes. In either case a 6-bit BCD code is used over full-duplex, 4-wire synchronous transmission facilities. Both modes may be operated at 2000, 2400, or 4800 bps.

In the roll-call (or direct polling) mode the central system again sends a go-ahead message to an addressed TCU. A typical system configuration appeared in Fig. 12-2a. The TCU responds by sending any stored inbound messages. End of transmission to the central system is again indicated by a go-ahead (GA) character, followed by a next interchange address (NIA) character. In this case of roll-call polling the NIA is the central address. The various message formats are shown in Fig. 12-7. Note how similar they are to the formats discussed previously (Figs. 12-4 and 12-5). Note the concatenation of messages from any one TCU in the inbound direction. As previously, only one set of S1, S2 (beginning) and GA NIA (end; continue polling) characters is used. Cyclic checking is used here as in the earlier system. The 6-bit cyclic check character is formed by using the generator polynomial $g(x) = x^6 + x^5 + 1$.

Four types of end of message characters are used in this system: message complete, message incomplete, message from terminal push-button, and

IBM 2946 Terminal Control Subsystem Component Description and Operating Guide, IBM Systems Development Division, June 1971.

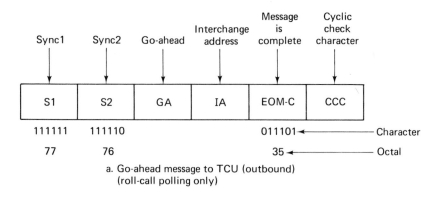

a. Go-ahead message to TCU (outbound)
(roll-call polling only)

Beginning
of message

S1 S2 IA TA Text EOM CCC IA TA Text CCC ... IA TA Text EOM CCC GA NIA

Terminal
address

End

b. TCU response (inbound, if more than 1 message stored)
(roll-call or hub polling)

S1 S2 GA NIA

c. TCU response (inbound) — no message to send

Fig. 12-7. Message formats, IBM PARS (6-bit BCD).

unsolicited output message. The code for each of these is indicated, in binary and octal form, in Fig. 12-8.

	Message	Binary	Octal
(1) Complete	EOM-C	011101	35
(2) Incomplete	EOM-I	001101	15
(3) Push button	EOM-PB	111101	75
(4) Unsolicited	EOM-U	101101	55

Fig. 12-8. End-of-Message Character Formats, IBM PARS.

As already mentioned previously, in the hub polling mode the central system starts the polling sequence by sending a go-ahead message to the most remote TCU in the network. A typical example appeared in Fig. 12-2b. This TCU responds by sending out, over the inbound line, any queued messages destined for the central system. These are preceded, as shown in Fig. 12-7b, by two synchronization characters. They are followed by a go-ahead message addressed to the next TCU on the inbound line. This message consists, as previously noted, of the go-ahead character GA and the address of the next TCU, previously denoted by NIA. All TCUs down line from the one currently sending its queued messages synchronize on the two synchronization characters. All of them also look for the go-ahead character. This alerts them to the address character following. The one addressed responds by repeating the procedure: it again starts with the two synchronization characters, follows with control characters and text, as in Fig. 12-7b, and concludes with a go-ahead character and the address of the next TCU down line. All this is necessary because the different poll message data sets on the inbound line run asynchronously. The two synchronization characters must thus always be inserted on the inbound lines. On the outbound line all data sets are controlled by the CPU. (Carrier is always on, so synchronization can always be maintained by the CPU.) The last TCU on the inbound line (the one closest to the central processor) uses the central system address for NIA. If no messages are waiting a TCU simply changes the NIA character. The complete inbound sequence of characters then appears exactly as in Fig. 12-7—the format is identical (except for the NIA character used) to that already discussed for the roll-call mode.

The only difference between the message formats in the two cases then is that, in the hub polling case, the NIA character is changed at each successive TCU. In the roll-call case it is always the address of the central system. As already noted in the discussion of Fig. 12-2b, two data sets are required at each TCU for hub polling. One is the normal modem (transmitting/receiving set) for message transmission and receiving, the other is a monitor receiving set used on the inbound line to detect go-ahead messages or polling messages directed to its particular TCU.

In the next section we shall be discussing response time and polling interval estimates for polling systems. It is apparent that these are statistical parameters and that even though the system may be designed to provide, *on the average*, reasonable time intervals for polling, there is a chance that the polling interval—the time between successive polls of a TCU—may become excessive. This is of course quite possible under heavy traffic conditions, with the central system then possibly clogged with queued messages. The IBM PARS provides a timeout feature to ease this situation. When a predetermined polling interval at a TCU is exceeded, a timeout occurs locking all keyboards attached to that TCU, preventing messages from being added to the inbound queue. The interval used is specified during installation: it is at most 22 sec and should of course be larger than the time between polls under normal loading conditions. (In the next section some typical calculations indicate the normal polling interval for 10–20 TCUs is the order of 0.5

to 1 sec.) A minimum timeout interval should also allow for the transmission of one full screen of data in this system. As an example, say a screen contains 960 characters arranged in 15 double-spaced display lines. At a line speed of 4800 bps, it would take $960 \times \frac{6}{4800} = 1.2$ sec to transmit these 960 6-bit characters. For line speeds of 2400 and 2000 bps, the transmission times are 2.4 and 2.9 sec, respectively. If a single-spaced display screen is used 1920 characters can appear on the 30-line display. The time required to transmit the 1920 characters in this case, and hence the minimum system timeout, is of course twice the time of the double-spaced screen.

In addition to the timeout feature the PARS system is provided with a fail mode procedure. The CPU maintains control at all times and can, on command, change the addressing sequence. For example, if an error is detected (an interchange fails to respond), the CPU begins polling all units, starting with the one closest in, to locate the one that failed. A new addressing sequence is then set up that skips the failed unit. The system also has a slow poll capacity. It can return to the unit that failed, on a slower basis, to check if the unit is still out.

The outbound message format (from central system to a TCU and then to a terminal) used in this PARS system is similar, except for the CRT terminals, to that of the previous system (Fig. 12-4).* There are two synchronization characters, followed by IA (interchange address), TA (terminal address), then text or central data, EOM, and CCC, a cyclic check character. If a message is a printer message and is accepted it is acknowledged *unless* it ends in EOM-C. There is then no acknowledgement. The acknowledgement message is again the 4-character IA TA EOM-I CCC.

ANALYSIS OF POLLING SYSTEMS**

We have spent some time in the preceding section discussing the details of one polling system in current use. We propose in this section to summarize some published work that analyzes the statistical behavior of polling systems.

---

*In the CRT case the interchanges and terminal address characters are followed by two added command characters. The first is for write or erase-write. The second indicates where and how to write.

A. R. Kaye and T. G. Richardson, "A Performance Criterion and Traffic Analysis for Polling Systems," *INFOR*, **11, no. 2, June 1973, 93; W. W. Chu and A. G. Konheim, "On the Analysis and Modeling of a Class of Computer-Communication Systems," *IEEE Trans. on Communications*, **COM-20**, no. 3, June 1972, part II, 645–60; J. F. Hayes and D. N. Sherman, "A Study of Data Multiplexing Techniques and Delay Performance," *Bell Systems Technical Journal*, Nov. 1972, p. 1983. See also papers by A. R. Kaye, Yuen et al., in the *Proc. Symposium on Computer-Communications and Teletraffic*, Polytechnic Institute of Brooklyn, New York, 1972.

This work focuses on the statistics of polling intervals or *scan times*, the time between successive polls or scans of a specific concentrator (or terminals if that is the unit being polled), and *response time*. Both are useful measures of performance, although response time is more directly related to user needs. Focusing on these two measures of performance we can extract design information useful in the design of various polling schemes.

It is apparent that scan time and response time are related: longer scan times must obviously correspond to longer response times. It is not as obvious, however, that one of the critical parameters in the determination of both is the so-called *walk-time** or fixed portion of the scan time attributable to polling messages, propagation delay, modem synchronization time, and other necessary overhead. It is this irreducible scan time component, particularly the polling message portion, that makes polling schemes differ in their time response characteristics from other multiplexing schemes, including those of the loop type. One can show very simply that it is this parameter that plays the key role in establishing the scan time and response time. Reducing this parameter reduces both time measures correspondingly. Hence one may profitably compare polling schemes on the basis of their respective walk-times.**

Specifically, assume N polled message sources are connected in a loop, as shown in Fig. 12-9.† Associated with each message source is an irreducible

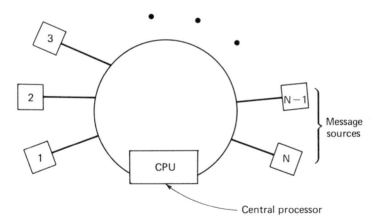

Fig. 12-9. Model of polling system.

---

*The term comes from the Operations Research literature involving the analysis of inspection and repair schemes, on a periodic basis, of large numbers of machines.

**Kaye and Richardson, "Performance Criterion and Traffic Analysis for Polling Systems."

†As noted earlier all topologies in a centralized system may be visualized as stretched into a virtual loop so far as polling is concerned. The loop of Fig. 12-9 thus represents all the topologies of Fig. 12-1.

walk-time $\bar{w}$ (in theory this can be statistically varying, but we shall assume throughout that this is a fixed time interval). The actual value of $\bar{w}$, to be discussed below, depends on the particular polling scheme to be used. The overall walk-time or fixed time per scan is thus*

$$L = N\bar{w}$$

Assume the traffic at each message source is the same, on the average, and represent the traffic intensity at each source by the usual parameter ρ. (This is then, in the previous queueing theory notation, $\rho = \lambda/\mu$, with λ the average Poisson message arrival rate at the source, and $1/\mu$ the average service time or message length, in units of time. The traffic parameter ρ may be adjusted to include both inbound and outbound messages.)

The average scan time is then readily shown to be

$$\bar{t}_c = \frac{N\bar{w}}{1 - N\rho} = \frac{L}{1 - N\rho} \tag{12-1}$$

This has the common queueing theory form, with the overall effective traffic intensity of the system given, as expected, by $N\rho$. Note that the scan time is directly proportional to the total walk-time $L = N\bar{w}$. For very low traffic ($N\rho \ll 1$), the average scan time reduces, as expected, to the irreducible value L. It may be somewhat surprising to have the scan time *always* proportional to L, at all traffic rates. It is thus apparent that for fixed traffic one can only reduce the scan time by reducing the walk-time. We shall therefore compare hub and roll-call polling schemes, in the paragraphs following, specifically on the basis of their respective walk-times. The average response time expression to be discussed later is more complex, but for low traffic the average response time approaches $\bar{t}_c/2$; i.e., one half the average scan time. It, too, is therefore reduced by reducing the system walk-time.

The derivation of Eq. (12-1) is very simply carried out. Let $\bar{n}$ be the average number of messages waiting at a message source when the poll message arrives. Then $\bar{n}/\lambda$ must be the number of messages arriving in $\bar{t}_c$ units of time, since all messages are assumed to be outputted on the arrival of a poll message. If we let $\bar{s}$ represent the average time required to transmit or serve $N\bar{n}$ messages (this is then the number served in an average scan or polling interval), we have

$$\bar{t}_c = \frac{\bar{n}}{\lambda} = N\bar{w} + \bar{s} \tag{12-2}$$

Thus the scan time is just the sum of the total walk-time plus the message service time.

---

*There is no common set of symbols to represent the different parameters in polling analyses. We have chosen to use the notation of the Hayes-Sherman paper cited, in most of the discussion that follows. Where necessary we introduce other authors' notation as well.

The average time required to serve all $N\bar{n}$ messages is however just $N\bar{n}/\mu = N\lambda\bar{t}_c/\mu = N\rho\bar{t}_c$, with $1/\mu$ the average message length. (Note again that we are assuming for simplicity in this model that all sources have identical statistics.) Thus,

$$\bar{s} = N\rho\bar{t}_c \qquad (12\text{-}3)$$

Combining Eqs. (12-2) and (12-3), then

$$\bar{t}_c(1 - N\rho) = N\bar{w} \qquad (12\text{-}2\text{a})$$

and Eq. (12-1) follows.

Time Delay Comparison of Hub and Roll-Call Polling*

We have already noted in the first section of this chapter that roll-call polling introduces longer time delays than hub polling because of the additional number of polling messages, inbound and outbound, used, as well as the resultant increase in propagation delay. We can quantify these remarks and in the process discuss ways of reducing time delay by appropriate system design, by focusing on the average walk-time in both cases of hub and roll-call polling. As pointed out earlier, we emphasize time delay for simplicity in comparing polling schemes, and ignore the additional (often overriding) factors such as: modem costs, line connections available from the carrier (whether 2-wire or 4-wire, multipoint or sequence of point-to-point connections), bridges available at the drops, different logic required for the two polling schemes, etc. The time delay calculation is particularly significant for very long lines, possibly thousands of miles in length.

Recall that in the IBM PARS system a two-character go-ahead message consisting of the GA and NIA characters appears at the end of a composite message. These have to be read, recognized, and new ones added at the end of a composite message in the polling systems used. A delay is incurred at each terminal in carrying out these operations. Modem synchronization time adds additional delay. Say the total delay incurred per message source is C characters, or NC characters for the system of N sources. In addition let Y, in characters, be the round-trip propagation delay for the loop encompassing the system (see Fig. 12-9). The total fixed delay, or total walk-time, for the hub polling case is just the sum of the two types of delay:

$$L|_{\text{hub}} = NC + Y \qquad (12\text{-}4)$$

In the roll-call mode the central controller polls a message source by sending a poll message P characters long. (In the IBM PARS system this is

---

*Kaye and Richardson, "Performance Criterion and Traffic Analysis for Polling Systems."

the outbound 6-character poll messages S1 S2 GA IA EOM-C CCC, with IA the address of the particular TCU being polled.) For N sources there is thus an additional time delay of NP characters incurred by the roll-call mode as compared to hub polling. The total walk-time in the roll-call case is thus

$$L|_{\text{roll}} = NP + NC + Y' \qquad (12\text{-}5)$$

with Y' the total propagation delay incurred. Note that the C character delay per source is common to both modes of polling.

The overall propagation delay Y' depends on the geometry of the roll-call system. It is generally greater than Y, the loop propagation delay. It is the presence of the additional poll message delay NP plus the higher propagation delay that accounts for the increased time delay of roll-call polling systems.

As an example of the calculation of the propagation delay factor Y' in roll-call polling assume N terminals are uniformly distributed around a loop as shown in Fig. 12-9. It is apparent that the minimum propagation delay is incurred if the first $N/2$ terminals are polled clockwise (assuming N even), while the remaining $N/2$ terminals are polled counterclockwise. Note that this corresponds to the system of Fig. 12-10a, with the controller (central system) located at the center of a two-way transmission bus facility. Each set of poll messages results in a two-way (round–trip) propagation delay. The propagation delay of the configuration in Fig. 12-10a is then

$$Y' = 2\left(\frac{Y}{N} + \frac{2Y}{N} + \ldots + \frac{N}{2}\frac{Y}{N}\right) = \frac{Y}{2}\left(1 + \frac{N}{2}\right) \qquad (12\text{-}6)$$

if the terminals are all spaced the same distance apart, with the central facility included. Here Y is the *total* round-trip propagation delay already mentioned.

Now consider the configuration of Fig. 12-10b. The terminals here are strung out in a multipoint connection from the central facility. This corresponds to the configuration of Fig. 12-2. With terminals again equally spaced from one another and from the central facility we have as the propagation delay in this case

$$Y' = \left(\frac{Y}{N} + \frac{2Y}{N} + \ldots + \frac{NY}{N}\right) = \frac{Y}{2}(1 + N) \qquad (12\text{-}7)$$

This indicates the increased time delay incurred in placing the central facility at the end of the multipoint connection rather than at the center. (Of course considerations other than time delay may dictate the particular choice of geometry used. Most commonly the central controller would be located at a central processing facility which is fixed in its location. Polling connections to concentrators are then made from this point outward. The two cases of Fig. 12-10 do indicate the improvement in time delay that might be obtained were the system designer free to move central facility and terminals about at will. Multipoint *cost* calculations would also have to be made to determine,

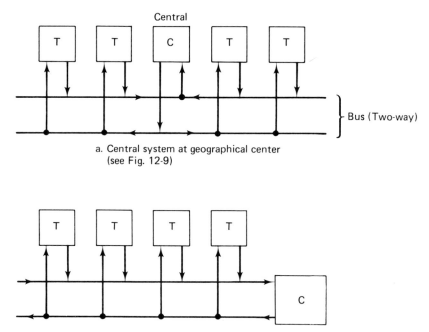

a. Central system at geographical center
(see Fig. 12-9)

b. Central system at one end

Fig. 12-10. Polling system configurations.

costwise, a particularly desirable configuration. In addition, the delay may be dominated by modem turn-on time and line turnaround time (on 2-wire lines). This is particularly true for multipoint links and for relatively small line lengths. In this case decreasing the propagation delay would not affect matters much.)

Some typical numbers, again using PARS as an example, serve to clarify these points.

Assume a modem synchronization time of 8.5 msec. Let this correspond to the symbol C (in equivalent characters) previously introduced. Say a typical propagation delay is 4 msec/100 miles.* Consider a polling network with 10 terminals spaced 200 miles apart. Assume 2400 bps lines are used, and 6-bit characters are transmitted. (Then $C \equiv 3.4$ char.) For the configuration of Fig. 12-10a, with the processor at the center of the network, the roll-call walk-time, in msec, is

$$L|_{\text{roll}} = 10(8.5 + 15) + 80(6) = 710 \text{ msec}$$

(The round-trip propagation delay term Y in msec here corresponds to

*Knight, "Case Study: Airline Reservations Systems." This is a conservative estimate for propagation delays on terrestrial links.

4000 miles of coverage, or 160 msec delay.) The corresponding hub poll walk-time, in msec, is

$$L|_{\text{hub}} = 10(8.5) + 160 = 245 \text{ msec}$$

For the configuration of Fig. 12-10b the roll-call walk-time is, using Eq. (12-7),

$$L|_{\text{roll}} = 235 + 80(11) = 1115 \text{ msec} = 1.1 \text{ sec}$$

For system traffic intensity $N\rho < 0.1$ the average scan times are the same as the walk-time. As traffic intensity increases, however, the scan times increase following the familiar queueing relation of Eq. (12-1). As an example, if $N\rho = 0.5$ (then $\rho = 0.05$ for 10 terminals), the average scan times are double the walk-times calculated above.

Now let 4800 bps be used in the roll-call mode. The only change in the calculation above involves the 6-character poll message (assuming the modem synchronization time remains at 8.5 msec.) This now corresponds to 7.5 msec/message. The two roll-call walk-times then become 640 msec for the configuration of Fig. 12-10a, and 1.04 sec for that of Fig. 12-10b. The average scan times are also reduced somewhat in the same proportion.

Response Time Calculations

As already noted the system performance measure more suitable for user interests is the average response time. As previously defined in this book this would be the average time for the system to respond to the user's message, including the time required to transmit the user's own message, on the average. There are basically three contributions to the average delay incurred in responding to a user message:

1. inbound delay due to buffering of messages at the message source. (Recall that these wait for the source to be polled. Only then are waiting messages transmitted to the central processor.)

2. message processing delay at the processor itself.

3. outbound delay due to buffering of messages at the central processor waiting to be transmitted to the appropriate message source.

In addition there is message propagation delay which can often be neglected in geographically-constrained systems. (In the previous section propagation delay was taken into account, particularly in roll-call systems where the cumulative propagation delay of a multiplicity of poll messages increased the single message delay considerably, because of its direct effect on average walk-time and hence scan time. A message source at a distance of 2000 miles from the central facility has a round-trip propagation delay of roughly 160 msec. This must be added to the normal buffering response time. For response times of 1 sec or more the *direct* propagation delay is clearly negligible. It still enters indirectly through the walk and scan times, however.)

In this section we shall focus, for simplicity's sake, on the inbound time delay only. Some of the papers referenced do consider the outbound time delay as well. As already noted this may be readily taken into account if it is assumed that for each inbound message there is an outbound counterpart of known average length.

Various calculations have been carried out to determine the average response time of polling systems—some have assumed fixed-length messages, others the common M/M/1 queue model with exponentially-distributed message lengths, some with the possibly more realistic geometric message length distributions. In some cases single unit buffers have been assumed, in others, infinite buffers. The reader is referred to the papers cited at the beginning of this section for details. The calculation of the statistics of polling systems, except for the average scan time or polling interval already calculated (Eq. 12-1), is inherently difficult because of the interdependence of the status of messages waiting at the various message sources. The problem of analysis is therefore one of calculating the joint statistics of an interconnected network of queues, always a difficult problem, except in certain specialized cases.

Konheim and Meister have carried out the analysis of a polling system retaining the interdependent relations between the queues polled and have developed explicit expressions for the various statistics of scan and inbound response times.* Chu and Konheim, among the papers cited previously, summarize the results of this analysis as well.

The assumptions made in the analysis are those of independent Poisson arrival processes at each message source, with geometric message lengths, and infinite buffers at each source. Complete symmetry is assumed to prevail with all sources having the same equilibrium statistics. As in Konheim's work on the concentrator problem (cited previously in Chap. 7), synchronous transmission is assumed, once a polling message has been received at a source: 1 data unit is removed from the buffer every Δ sec so long as the buffer is not empty.

The results of the analysis are as follows: Let p be the average number of data units arriving in Δ sec at a given terminal or message source. (As noted in Chap. 7, for an average Poisson arrival rate of λ messages/sec, with each message geometrically-distributed with an average number of $1/p$ of data units, $\rho = \lambda\Delta/p < 1$. ρ is of course equivalent to the traffic parameter ρ previously used in this section.) They then find the average scan time $\bar{t}_c$ to be given by Eq. (12-1), previously derived using a very simple approach.

*A. G. Konheim and B. Meister, "Waiting Lines and Times in a System with Polling," *J. of the ACM*, **21**, no. 3, July 1974, 470–90.

The variance of the scan time t_c, $V(t_c)$, is in turn found to be given by

$$V(t_c) = \frac{N\sigma^2 \bar{t}_c \Delta}{(1-\rho)(1-N\rho)} \qquad (12\text{-}8)^*$$

Here σ^2 is the variance of the number of data units arriving in Δ sec (see Chap. 7). $\bar{t}_c$ is assumed to be in units of seconds, consistent with Δ. For the special case of fixed length messages and Poisson arrivals, $\sigma^2 = \rho = \lambda\Delta$.

The average message delay time, in seconds, *excluding average message length* (which can simply be added to get the inbound component of the message response time), is then found to be given, in data unit intervals, by

$$E(D) = \frac{\overline{t_c^2}}{2\bar{t}_c}(1-\rho) + \left(\frac{1-\rho}{2}\right)\Delta$$

$$= \frac{\bar{t}_c}{2}(1-\rho) + \frac{N\sigma^2\Delta}{2}\frac{1}{(1-N\rho)} + \left(\frac{1-\rho}{2}\right)\Delta \qquad (12\text{-}9)$$

Here $\overline{t_c^2} = V(t_c) + \bar{t}_c^2$ is the second moment of the scan time. Equation (12-8) has been used in going from the first line to the second in Eq. (12-9).

Note how the message response time depends on the average scan time, which in turn depends directly on the walk-time discussed in detail earlier. Note also that the leading term in the expression for average response time is just one half the average scan time. In particular, for $N\rho \ll 1$, the low traffic case, the average inbound response time is half the scan time, or, from previous considerations half the total walk-time. It is thus apparent that polling schemes that reduce the walk-time reduce the message response time as well.

Finally, Konheim and Meister have carried out calculations for the average buffer occupancy, as well as the probability that the buffer occupancy will exceed a specified number of data units. For small probability ($<10^{-3}$), this is the same as the probability of buffer overflow or blocking in the finite buffer case. (See the related discussion in Chap. 7.) This thus enables the designer to determine the buffer size required for a given probability of blocking.

The average buffer occupancy $E(W)$ (in data units) is found to be given by

$$E(W) = \frac{1}{2}\frac{\sigma^2}{1-N\rho} + \frac{1}{2}\frac{L\rho(1-\rho)}{1-N\rho}$$

$$= \frac{1}{2}\frac{\sigma^2}{1-N\rho} + \frac{1}{2}\bar{t}_c\rho(1-\rho) \qquad (12\text{-}10)$$

Some numerical examples are of interest: Assume $N = 10$ message sources, with a system traffic intensity $N\rho = 0.5$. Assume 300 characters/sec

---

*The walk-time has again been assumed to be constant. For statistically variable walk-times, another term, proportional to the walk-time variance, appears. (Konheim and Meister, "Waiting Lines and Times in a System with Polling," p. 487.)

lines are used. The basic data unit is then assumed to be a character, and $\Delta = 3.3$ msec/character.

Case 1. Fixed Message Length, $\sigma^2 = \rho = 0.05$

Then the average scan time, average inbound message delay time (excluding message transmission time), and the average buffer occupancy are given, as a function of the walk-time per message source, by the entries in Table 12-1. Equations (12-1), (12-9), and (12-10) were used to calculate the respective entries.

TABLE 12-1

$N = 10$, $N\rho = 0.5$, $\sigma^2 = \rho = 0.05$

$\bar{w}$ (walk-time)		Total system walk-time $(N\bar{w})$	$\bar{t}_c$ (avg. scan time)		$E(D)$ (avg. delay time)		$E(W)$
char.	msec	sec	char.	sec	char.	sec	char.
1	3.3	0.033	20	0.066	10.5	0.035	0.53
2	6.6	0.066	40	0.132	20	0.066	1.0
5	16.5	0.165	100	0.33	48.5	0.16	2.4
10	33	0.33	200	0.66	96	0.32	4.8
20	66	0.66					
100	330	3.3	2000	6.6			

Note that even with $N\rho = 0.5$, a rather sizeable traffic situation, $E(D) \sim \bar{t}_c/2$. For with $N = 10$, $\rho = 0.05 \ll 1$, and from Eq. (12-9), all terms except the leading term are negligible.

Case 2. Average Message Length $= 2$ characters

$$\left(\frac{1}{\rho} = 2, \quad \sigma^2 = 3\rho, \quad \rho = 2\lambda\Delta \right)$$

TABLE 12-2

$N = 10$, $N\rho = 0.5$, $\sigma^2 = 3\rho$

$\bar{w}$ (walk-time)		Total walk-time	$E(D)$ (avg. delay time)		$E(W)$
char.	msec	sec	char.	sec	char.
1	3.3	0.033	11.5	0.038	0.6
2	6.6	0.066	21	0.069	1.1
5	16.5	0.165	49.5	0.163	2.5
10	33	0.33	97	0.32	4.9
20	66	0.66			

Note that although the average message length has doubled in this case, the average arrival rate λ has been halved to keep the traffic parameter Np the same as in Case 1. Thus although the variance of the message length σ has tripled, its effect on response time is negligible. (See Eq. (12-9).) The average delay time, inbound, is still approximately one half the average scan time. The buffer occupancy as well has not changed very much.

Case 3. Average Message Length = 5 characters

$$\left(\frac{1}{p} = 5, \quad \sigma^2 = 9p, \quad p = 5\lambda\Delta\right)$$

TABLE 12-3

$\bar{w}$ (walk-time)		Total walk-time	$E(D)$ (avg. delay time)		$E(W)$
char.	msec	sec	char.	sec	char.
1	3.3	0.033	14.5		0.925
2	6.6	0.066	24		1.4
5	16.5	0.165	52.5		2.8
10	33	0.33	100	0.33	5.2
20	66	0.66			

Again the increase in message length has negligible effect on average response time and average buffer occupancy. Note how this differs from results previously found for statistical multiplexers (Chap. 7). Here, in the polling case, it is the *walk-time* that plays the key role in determining these *average* system parameters.

These results will be used in some example problems at the end of the next chapter. A time delay comparison will then be made, for these examples, between both roll-call and hub polling and a simple random access scheme.

PROBLEMS

12.1 Ten concentrators spaced 300 miles apart are connected multidrop fashion to a central processor. Calculate the overall walk-time, the average scan time, and the average message delay time, inbound, for both hub and roll-call polling for the following cases:

(1) modem synchronization time = 50 msec; propagation delay = 4 msec/100 miles; query (polling) message = six 8-bit characters.

(2) modem synchronization time = 10 msec; propagation delay = 1 msec/100 miles; polling message = six 8-bit characters.

2400 bps lines are used, data messages inbound are all 20 characters long. Each concentrator has 30 terminals connected to it, and the average message generation rate of each terminal is 1.5 messages/min.

12.2 Terminals located in London, Amsterdam, Brussels, Paris, Munich, Zurich, Milan, and Rome are connected by full-duplex lines in a string, as indicated, to a polling concentrator in Rome. Determine the average scan time and average inbound message delay time for both hub and roll-call polling, and compare. In the case of hub polling London would be interrogated first. The modem synchronization time is 150 msec at each of the terminals; 300 bps terminals and lines are used; the poll message is six 8-bit characters long; messages are all 50 8-bit characters long; and the average message arrival rate at each terminal is 1 message/20 sec. Take the propagation delay to be 2 msec/100 km.

12.3 A number of agent terminals used primarily for making and confirming airline reservations are located within a radius of 50 miles from a polling concentrator in New York City to which they are all connected. The terminals are all 150 bps devices, modem synchronization times are 100 msec, and the polling message is six 8-bit characters long. Propagation delay is 4 msec/100 miles.

(1) Determine the total system walk-time if roll-call polling is used and there are 10, 20, and 50 terminals connected. Make any reasonable assumptions about the location of the terminals with respect to the concentrator.

(2) Determine the average message inbound delay for the three cases of (1) if messages are all 10 characters (80 bits) long, and 150 bps lines are used. Each terminal generates on the average of 1 message/min. Find the average terminal buffer occupancy for the same three cases.

(3) Repeat (2) if messages are geometrically-distributed, at multiples of 5 characters, the average message being 10 characters long.

(4) Repeat (2) if 300 bps terminals and lines are used.

Random Access Techniques 13

We have already pointed out in several places in this book that there exist a variety of ways of concentrating messages in a message-switched network. A common technique discussed in detail in Chaps. 7 and 8 is that of statistical or asynchronous multiplexing. In that case terminals or other data sources access ports feeding directly into concentrators. Messages are transmitted directly on arrival to the concentrator buffers, using some form of interrupt or scanning mechanism. Polling techniques discussed in the previous chapter are commonly used to effect data transmission in centralized multipoint networks of the type discussed in Chap. 9. Contention techniques are also used in such networks with data sources requesting permission to transmit from the processor designated as "master". Both contention and polling can be used in a loop or ring topology as well. The basic point here is that with data sources connected effectively in series and with no concentration used, only one source at a time can transmit. Polling and contention techniques are used to maintain order, to prevent messages from different data sources from being transmitted simultaneously, garbling each other's transmission. The price paid, however, is increased time delay due to the polling mechanism or to the request to transmit a message in a contention scheme.

In those applications involving bursty messages, in which a given data source duty cycle is very low, (i.e., messages may be short and transmitted infrequently as in a time-shared application or in an inquiry-response system), it may still be appropriate to have all terminals transmit randomly, at will.

Because of the statistical nature of the data generation process and the bursty character of the messages, it may turn out that the chance of two or more sources attempting to transmit simultaneously is quite low. This technique in which a multiplicity of data sources transmit at will and randomly to a central destination has been labeled a *random access* technique. The prime applications thus far have been to packet radio and satellite communications in which the terminals must transmit by radio.* If they all use the same frequency channel the problem of having this group of users access the same receiver (at the central destination) is identical to that of terminal access using multipoint or loop connections noted earlier. The Aloha system of the University of Hawaii has pioneered in the use of random access techniques to connect by radio a large number of geographically-distributed users to a central computer.**

We shall discuss in this chapter a variety of random access techniques developing out of the work on the Aloha system. These include pure Aloha, slotted Aloha, and a number of reservation-type Aloha techniques. (Some of the reservation schemes are related to the contention schemes noted earlier.) We shall summarize some of the analysis carried out to determine the time delay throughput characteristics of the various techniques. This allows comparisons to be made with other access techniques such as polling.

PURE ALOHA CHANNEL

Assume k data sources are each transmitting independently at a Poisson rate of λ messages/sec. Messages are assumed to be fixed length packets, each τ sec long.† The maximum possible throughput of such a channel, obtained only if one user were allowed to access the channel and transmit packets continuously with no gaps in the transmission, would obviously be $1/\tau$ packets/sec. This is thus the capacity of the channel. By allowing a multiplicity of users to access the same channel randomly, the possibility of simultaneous transmission arises. The actual throughput must thus be considerably less than the maximum possible. The Aloha random access scheme relies on the bursty characteristic of the messages transmitted by any one user: it

---

*A wire application is described in R. M. Metcalfe and D. R. Boggs, "Ethernet: Distributed Packet-Switching for Local Computer Networks," *Communications of the ACM*, **19**, no. 7, July 1976, 395–404.

**See N. Abramson, "The Aloha System," N. Abramson and F. Kuo, eds., *Computer Networks*, Prentice-Hall, Inc., Englewood Cliffs, N.J., 1973, Chap. 14.

†Multipacket messages may also be carried but we choose to focus on the simpler case of single packet messages in this introductory treatment. A simple example of a multipacket situation is considered in the discussion of Reservation Aloha later in this chapter.

assumes $\lambda\tau \ll 1$. As in statistical multiplexing a group of users can thus share the channel and use it much more efficiently than one bursty user alone. The price paid, however, as we shall see, is that the maximum allowable throughput drops considerably below the channel capacity. One user could thus potentially use the channel much more efficiently than the group of users, but only if he were transmitting *continuously*. If his transmission is bursty the random access mode enables a great many more users to share the channel.

With k users the effective utilization of the channel (relative to the maximum rate of transmission of $1/\tau$ packets/sec) is

$$S \equiv k\lambda\tau < 1 \tag{13-1}$$

The parameter S thus plays the role of the traffic intensity or utilization parameter ρ used previously in this book. We shall henceforth call S the channel throughput, measured in average number of packets transmitted in an interval τ sec long. For the pure Aloha system with a large number of identical users it will turn out that there exists a maximum throughput given by

$$S_{max} = \frac{1}{2e} \doteq 0.18 \tag{13-2}$$

The pure Aloha random access scheme thus allows at most 18 % of the capacity to be utilized. This may be quite satisfactory in practice, however. As an example say a 24 kbits/sec (kbps) channel is available. Packets are 1000 bits long so that $\tau = \frac{1}{24}$ sec = 42 msec. A single user could thus transmit as many as 24 packets/sec over this channel. Say the average user only transmits on the average one message/minute, however. The pure Aloha random access technique thus allows a maximum of $k = (1/2e\lambda\tau) = 265$ users to transmit at will. This is obviously a sizeable number. The average number of 4400 bps is far less than the maximum possible capacity 24,000 bps, but the random access technique used to accommodate this number is simple and requires a limited control mechanism.

To demonstrate that the capacity of the pure Aloha scheme is given by Eq. (13-2) we first describe the transmission strategy in more detail. A user on transmitting awaits an acknowledgement message from the central system (receiver). (This is transmitted in a broadcast mode over a separate channel to all users.) If after an appropriate timeout he receives no acknowledgement (this timeout is at least the two-way propagation delay of the system), he repeats the original single packet message. With the random access strategy, however, the lack of acknowledgement is presumably due to two or more users attempting to access the system simultaneously, resulting in a garbled message or a so-called "collision" detected at the receiver. To prevent this from recurring the retransmissions must be staggered. The simplest technique is to have the users affected transmit at some random time after the timeout.

The effect of collisions is to reduce the actual system throughput. Alternately the channel traffic consists both of newly-generated packets (at an average rate of S packets per τ-sec time interval) and retransmitted packets. As the number of newly-generated packets increases (either by increasing the number of users k, or by increasing the message arrival rate λ), the chance of a collision increases. This in turn increases the number of retransmissions, which in turn increases the chance of a collision, and a runaway effect occurs; the channel becomes unstable. It is this effect that produces a limit on the system throughput. The system throughput characteristic which provides the maximum value of S is easily derived. Call G the average channel traffic per τ sec interval. Then

$$G = S + \text{avg. no. of retransmissions in a } \tau \text{ sec interval}$$

A retransmission occurs due to at least one collision. Since messages are one packet or τ-sec long, a collision with a given user's message will take place if any other user decides to transmit in an interval $\pm\tau$ about the time of initiation of a given message. We assume now that the *total channel traffic*, consisting of newly-generated packets plus retransmitted packets, obeys *Poisson statistics*, with parameter G. This is obviously not true since retransmissions do not correspond to a Poisson process. Studies indicate, however, that with the random retransmitted strategy chosen, particularly with the random time delay becoming very large, the Poisson assumption does become valid.* The probability that at least one collision will take place (due to other packets generated within a 2τ-sec interval about any packet initiation) is then $1 - e^{-2G}$. The average number of retransmissions is $G(1 - e^{-2G})$, and

$$G = S + G(1 - e^{-2G}) \tag{13-3}$$

Hence we have, very simply,

$$S = Ge^{-2G} \tag{13-4}$$

This is the desired throughput equation for a pure Aloha system operating under stable equilibrium conditions. Equation (13-4) is shown sketched in Fig. 13-1. Note that S approaches a maximum value of $1/2e = 0.18$. This is also readily shown by differentiating Eq. (13-4) with respect to G.

Equation (13-4) is easily derived in an alternate fashion by noting that G is the total average channel traffic while S is the portion of G corresponding to newly-generated packets. Then S/G, the fraction of packets actually transmitted that corresponds to a successful transmission, must equal the probability of success on an initial try. This is just the probability that no collision will take place, just e^{-2G} for Poisson statistics.

Note also that the average number of transmission attempts per packet generated is just $1 + E = G/S = e^{2G}$. This is a measure of the time delay (exclusive of propagation delay) in the system. Here E is the average number

*S. S. Lam, "Packet Switching in a Multi-Access Broadcast Channel with Application to Satellite Communication in a Computer Network," Ph.D. dissertation, Dept. of Computer Science, UCLA, April 1974.

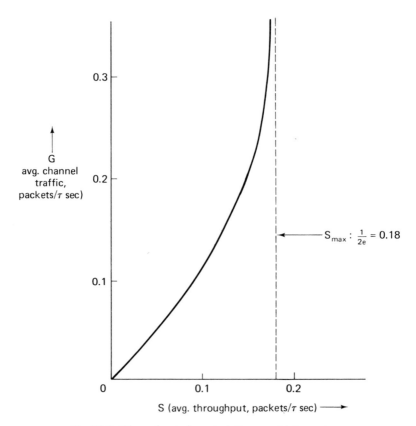

Fig. 13-1. Throughput characteristic, pure Aloha system.

of retransmissions per packet. So as the throughput increases approaching the maximum value of 0.18, the delay goes up correspondingly. The time delay-throughput characteristic will be explored more specifically in the next section. As a *lower bound* on time delay, however, assume that propagation delay is negligible and that packets are immediately retransmitted, with just a one slot-τ-sec delay, if no acknowledgement is received in the next time interval. Then the minimum average time delay D_{min}, in units of τ-sec intervals, is just

$$D_{min} = e^{2G} \tag{13-5}*$$

This is shown sketched as the lower curve in Fig. 13-2. Now let the two-way

---

*Actually, as shown in the next section, this is not quite valid, since with no randomization in the retransmission, messages having once collided will always collide again. The expression for the average number of retransmission attempts per packet generated on which Eq. (13-5) is based, $E = e^{2G} - 1$, turns out to be true for the average (randomized) delay very large. This is discussed in the next section.

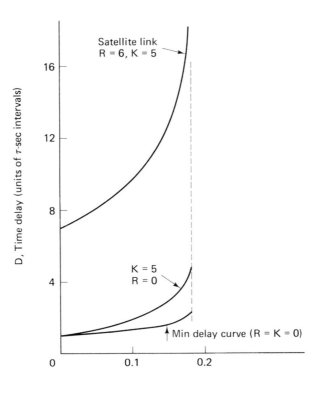

Fig. 13-2. Time delay-throughput characteristic, pure Aloha system.

propagation delay in the system be R τ-sec time intervals. This is then the minimum time (exclusive of processing delay at the receiver) required to receive an acknowledgement. Say that the random time delay factor introduced before retransmission of a packet is uniformly-distributed from 1 to K τ-sec intervals. The *average* time delay due to this retransmission staggering is then $(1 + K)/2$ time intervals. The average round-trip time delay in the system is then

$$D = R + 1 + E\left(R + \frac{K+1}{2}\right) \qquad (13\text{-}6)$$

with $E = e^{2G} - 1$.

Figure 13-2 shows two additional curves relating time delay and throughput. One curve represents a system with negligible propagation delay, but with an average retransmission delay of five time units. The other curve represents a system involving satellite communication. The round-trip time delay is 0.27 sec, or approximately six 42 msec time intervals. The minimum round-trip time delay is then seven time intervals, as shown in the figure.

As noted previously in connection with Eq. (13-5), Eq. (13-6) and the curves of Fig. 13-2 are only gross approximations since the throughput Eq. (13-4) assumes retransmission to be delayed many time intervals after a collision. Yet that equation is used in Eq. (13-6) in determining the round-trip time delay D, with the average number of time intervals $(K + 1)/2$ finite. A more detailed discussion of the time delay-throughput characteristic will be given in the next section on *slotted Aloha*. It is found that there exists an *optimum* average retransmission delay interval in the sense of minimizing the time delay D for a given throughput S. That this is to be expected may be seen intuitively: the shorter the randomized retransmission interval the greater the chance that retransmitted packets will again collide. So one wants to make this interval (or K in Eq. (13-6)) larger. But if the interval is larger, the time delay is increased. So there appears to be an optimum randomized delay. An analysis of this retransmission delay for pure Aloha for both fixed and randomized delay appears in a paper by Hayes and Sherman.* As noted above this point will be taken up again in discussing the slotted Aloha characteristic. It will be shown there that the optimum is quite broad, and the choice of the parameter K not critical.

SLOTTED ALOHA

The pure Aloha scheme provides a maximum utilization of $1/2e = 0.18$. This is due to collisions with other packets possibly transmitted within a $\pm\tau$ or 2τ-sec (packet) interval about the one under consideration. Consider now a system in which all users are synchronized to one common clock (presumably located at the common receiver). Let the time scale now be divided into specified packet intervals or *slots* τ-sec long. An example is shown in Fig. 13-3. Users are constrained to transmit in these time slots only (as referenced to the common receiver time). It is apparent that "collisions" will now occur only if two or more packets arrive at the receiver during the same time interval. Since there can be no overlap of packets from adjacent intervals the capacity of this scheme is exactly twice that of the pure Aloha system. In particular, it is apparent that the system throughput S (in packets/slots) obeys the equation

$$S = Ge^{-G} \tag{13-7}$$

and

$$S_{\max} = \frac{1}{e} = 0.368 \tag{13-8}$$

Here G is again the average channel traffic (new packets plus retransmissions)

*J. F. Hayes and D. N. Sherman, "A Study of Data Multiplexing Techniques and Delay Performance," *Bell Systems Technical Journal*, **51**, no. 9, Nov. 1972, 1983–2011.

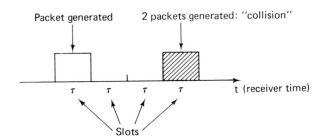

Fig. 13-3. Time slots in slotted Aloha.

in packets/slot. Poisson statistics have again been assumed for both the newly-arriving and retransmitted packets.

Slotted Aloha thus provides a substantial improvement in allowable throughput over the pure Aloha technique but at a cost in complexity: all transmitting terminals must be synchronized to the receiver. This may pose no problem for a network, whether wire or radio, covering a small geographic area. But for small mobile users dispersed over a large area or for a satellite communications system, the introduction of slotted Aloha techniques poses additional problems of implementation.

What is the time delay-throughput characteristic of slotted Aloha? This is obviously important in establishing the performance of slotted Aloha systems and in comparing random access schemes with other access schemes such as polling and statistical multiplexing. We outline here an approach due to Lam and Kleinrock. Details may be found in the references cited.[*,**,†]

The time delay characteristic depends on the method of handling the retransmission of packets having undergone a "collision". For this analysis assume that if a packet is not acknowledged after a fixed delay of R slots (this is generally the round-trip propagation delay as noted in the previous section under pure Aloha), it is retransmitted j slots later, with j chosen from a uniformly-distributed length distribution K slots long. This is the same randomization procedure discussed in the last section, but cued now to the receiver time scale in slots. The average time delay is then again D slots, but with D modified slightly from that of Eq. (13-6) to account for packets arriving anytime before a slot interval begins:

$$D = R + 1.5 + E\left(R + \frac{1}{2} + \frac{K+1}{2}\right) \qquad (13\text{-}6a)$$

*L. Kleinrock and S. S. Lam, "Packet-Switching in a Slotted Satellite Channel," *AFIPS Conference Proc.*, National Computer Conference, **42**, 1973, 703–10.

L. Kleinrock and S. S. Lam, "Packet-Switching in a Multi-Access Broadcast Channel: Performance Evaluation," *IEEE Trans. on Communications*, **COM-23, April 1975, 410–23.

†Lam, "Packet Switching in a Multi–Access Broadcast Channel."

Here E is the average number of retransmissions required per packet generated. As previously, E is related under equilibrium conditions to S, the system throughput, and G, the channel traffic:

$$1 + E = \frac{G}{S} \qquad (13\text{-}9)$$

We shall indicate how to evaluate the retransmission parameter E, G, S, and D as a function of K, the maximum number of slots a retransmission attempt is delayed. Poisson statistics will again be assumed. G, S, and D will be found to depend in a complex way on each other and on K. In particular, an optimum K will be found to exist that minimizes D with the throughput S fixed. This point has already been noted earlier. As $K \longrightarrow \infty$ the throughput characteristic of Eq. (13-7) will be found to hold. For $K > 4$, however, the throughput will be found to be close to that given by Eq. (13-7), so the choice of K is not too critical.

To find E and hence S/G and D we proceed as follows: Let $q_n =$ the probability of a successful transmission, given a new packet has been generated, and $q_t =$ the probability of a successful transmission, given a retransmitted packet is transmitted. The probability p_i that a given packet requires exactly i retransmissions to be successfully received is then

$$p_i = (1 - q_n)(1 - q_t)^{i-1}q_t \qquad i \geq 1 \qquad (13\text{-}10)$$

The average number of retransmissions is then

$$E = \sum_{i=1}^{\infty} ip_i = \frac{1 - q_n}{q_t} \qquad (13\text{-}11)$$

using Eq. (13-10).

Now how does one find q_n and q_t? Consider q_t first. This is the probability of a successful retransmission. Without loss of generality say the collision requiring this retransmission took place in the jth slot previous (Fig. 13-4). To have a successful retransmission, three conditions must be satisfied:

1. No other packet from the jth slot, involved in the transmission, should be retransmitted in the current slot (call the probability of this event q_c)

2. Packets possibly retransmitted from the previous $(K - 1)$ slots other

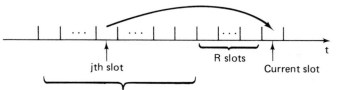

Fig. 13-4. Retransmission of packet with collision in jth slot.

than the jth one shouldn't be retransmitted in this slot (the joint probability here is called q_0^{K-1})

3. No *new* packet should be generated in the *current* slot (the probability of this event is e^{-S}).

Putting all of these together, assuming all of these events independent, the probability q_t of a successful retransmission is just

$$q_t = e^{-S} q_c q_0^{K-1} \tag{13-12}$$

Consider now q_c, the probability that no other packet from the jth slot was retransmitted in the current slot. This may be written

$$q_c = \sum_{l=1}^{\infty} q_c(l)$$

with $q_c(l)$ the probability that l packets other than the packet under consideration were generated in slot j causing the collision and that none of these overlap in the current slot. This is of course conditioned on the fact that $l \geq 1$ in order to have had a collision in the first place. It is then left for the reader to show that

$$q_c = \sum_{l=1}^{\infty} \frac{G^l e^{-G}}{l!} \frac{\left(1 - \dfrac{1}{K}\right)^l}{1 - e^{-G}} \tag{13-13}$$

$$= \frac{e^{-G/K} - e^{-G}}{1 - e^{-G}}$$

after some manipulation. As a check note that $q_c \to 1$ as $K \to \infty$, for with K slots to choose from, the probability becomes zero as $K \to \infty$ that the other packets involved in the collision will be retransmitted in the current slot.

Similarly, q_0 is the probability that no packet from one of the other $(K - 1)$ slots, excluding the jth one, (say the nth slot) that could be involved in a retransmission in the current slot is actually retransmitted in that slot. There are two possibilities: either none or one packet was generated in slot n, in which case there would have been no collision and hence no retransmission; or two or more packets were generated, in which case a collision with a resultant retransmission would have occurred. In this latter case we have to include the probability that the retransmitted packet is *not* transmitted in the current slot. Summing the probabilities of these possibilities we have

$$q_0 = \sum_{i=2}^{\infty} \frac{G^i e^{-G}}{i!} \left(1 - \frac{1}{K}\right)^i + G e^{-G} + e^{-G} \tag{13-14}$$

$$= e^{-G/K} + \frac{G}{K} e^{-G}$$

It is left for the reader to show that as $K \to \infty$, $q_0^{K-1} \to e^{S-G}$. Using Eq.

(13-13) and (13-14) in (13-12), q_t is then found as a function of S, G, and K. In particular, as $K \longrightarrow \infty$, $q_t \longrightarrow e^{-G}$.

In a similar manner it is left for the reader to show that q_n, the other probability required in the evaluation of E, the average number of retransmissions (Eq. (13-11)), is given by

$$q_n = q^K e^{-S} \qquad (13\text{-}15)$$

Again, as $K \longrightarrow \infty$, $q_n \longrightarrow e^{-G} = q_t$. Hence in the limit of large K (i.e., the random retransmission delay is the order of many slots), $E \longrightarrow e^G - 1$, and $S/G = 1/(1+E) \longrightarrow e^{-G}$, exactly as in Eq. (13-7).

For finite K, Eq. (13-6), (13-9), and (13-11) must be solved simultaneously, using Eq. (13-12) to (13-15) to find the desired throughput and time delay-throughput curves. Lam has carried out the required analysis and calculations.* He finds that an optimum K does exist in the sense of minimizing time delay for a given throughput S. For example, for very small S (approaching zero),

$$E \cong \frac{KS}{K-1} \qquad S \text{ small} \qquad (13\text{-}16)$$

and

$$D \cong R + 1.5 + \frac{KS}{K-1}\left[R + \frac{K+1}{2} \right] \qquad S \text{ small} \qquad (13\text{-}17)$$

The optimum value of K that minimizes D in Eq. (13-17) is then given by the largest integer such that $K^2 - 3K - 2R \leq 0$. As an example, with $R = 0$, this is just $K = 3$. For $R = 6$, it is $K = 5$, and $R = 12$, $K = 6$.

An example of a time delay-throughput plot taken from Lam's work appears as Fig. 13-5. Here $R = 12$. (The calculations were carried out for a 50 kbps satellite channel with a 0.27 sec round-trip propagation delay and 1125 bit packets, so that the slot interval $\tau = 22.5$ msec, and $R = 0.27$ sec/22.5 msec = 12 slots.) For this case the optimum K is 6 for small S, but notice from Fig. 13-5 that this value is close to optimum over almost the entire range of throughput S. Note also that the actual value of K to be used is not critical. Over much of the curve values of K from 2 to 40 do not change the results very much.

Figure 13-6, also taken from Lam, shows the throughput characteristic and how it varies with K. For $K > 5$ the throughput is almost at the $K \longrightarrow \infty$ throughput value given by $S/G = e^{-G}$.

The fact that the delay-throughput characteristic is not very sensitive to the precise value of K is also readily demonstrated in the extreme case of zero propagation delay. Setting $R = 0$ in Eq. (13-6a) and noting that $E = G/S - 1$ from Eq. (13-9), we can find the average time delay D in terms of packet slots for various values of K and compare. Figure 13-7 shows three curves, for

*Ibid.

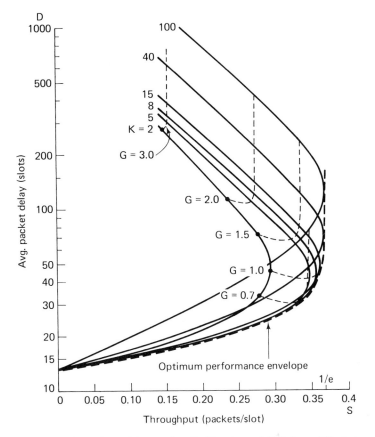

Fig. 13-5. Throughout-delay trade-off. (Courtesy of S.S. Lam, "Packet-Switching in a Multi-access Broadcast Channel with Application to Satellite Communication in a Computer Network," Ph. D. dissertation, Dept. of Computer Science, UCLA, April 1974, Fig. 3-4.)

$K = 2$, 5, and 15. Note again the relative insensitivity to K over most of the throughput range. For even at $K = 5$ the throughput S is close to the $K \longrightarrow \infty$ value of Ge^{-G} so that E in Eq. (13-6) does not change very much with K. It is only when G approaches 1 and the number of retransmissions E becomes significant that the average number of slots $(K + 1)/2$ in the random delay strategy begins to make a difference in the average delay D.

Hayes and Sherman[*] in analyzing a pure Aloha system with a random retransmission strategy come to similar conclusions. They assume a random timeout interval exponentially-distributed with mean $1/\alpha$. This is thus comparable to the average timeout interval $(K + 1)/2$ used here, assuming a

[*]Hayes and Sherman, "Study of Data Multiplexing Techniques," p. 2004.

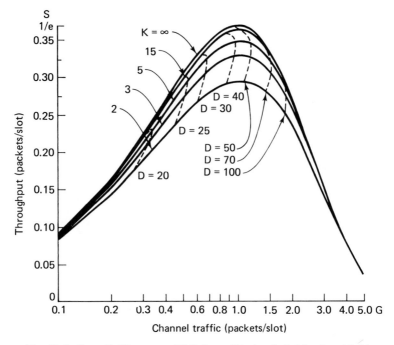

Fig. 13-6. S vs. G. (Courtesy of S.S. Lam, "Packet-Switching in a Multi-access Broadcast Channel," Fig. 3-3.)

uniformly-distributed timeout interval. Their calculations also indicate that an optimum timeout interval, in the sense of minimum average delay, exists, and they find by trial and error that the optimum average timeout interval is given approximately by $1/\alpha \doteq 1/k\lambda$, with k again the number of users ($k > 10$), and λ the average packet arrival rate of each. As an example, if $S = k\lambda\tau = 0.18$, the maximum possible for the pure Aloha system, $1/\alpha \doteq \tau/0.18 \equiv 5$ slots or so. If $S = 0.1$, $1/\alpha \doteq 10$ slots. These numbers appear comparable to those obtained by Lam for the slotted Aloha case, using a very different model and method of analysis.

Note that beyond the point of maximum throughput in Fig. 13-5 and 13-6 the curves indicate a drop in throughput and a concurrent rapid rise in time delay. This is ostensibly due to the rapid increase in collisions and hence additional retransmitted packets. Closer analysis indicates that the Aloha system can exhibit instabilities in the vicinity of the maximum throughput value. The equilibrium results in that region turn out to be valid only for a finite interval of time, with the system then moving to a new operating point, corresponding to increased time delay and decreased throughput.* In general,

*Lam, "Packet-Switching in a Multi-Access Broadcast Channel." Also Kleinrock and Lam, "Packet-Switching in a Multi-Access Broadcast Channel: Performance Evaluation."

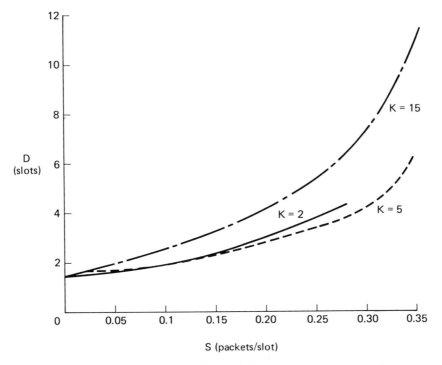

Fig. 13-7. Delay-throughput characteristic, zero propagation delay $(R = 0)$.

reducing the number of users accessing the channel or increasing the random retransmission time delay K can render an unstable channel stable. Dynamic control procedures have also been investigated for maintaining potentially unstable channels stable.*

HIGHER CAPACITY ALOHA SYSTEMS

As noted in the previous section the maximum possible throughput of a slotted Aloha channel is 0.368, although instabilities may arise in the vicinity of this throughput value. Considerable thought has been given to the possibility of improving the throughput characteristic of Aloha systems, and a variety of schemes have been proposed in the literature. These include several reservation Aloha schemes in which users request slots in advance of transmission (note that these schemes are then similar to contention-type accessing

*Ibid. Also, S. S. Lam and L. Kleinrock, "Packet-Switching in a Multi-Access Broadcast Channel: Dynamic Control Procedures," *IEEE Trans. on Communications,* **COM-23,** no. 9, Sept. 1975, 891–904.

schemes), and carrier-sense Aloha in which users monitor other users' transmissions and only transmit when they sense no other transmissions are taking place.* The former schemes of course trade off increased throughput for increased time delay. (The reservation request requires an additional two-way propagation delay.) The latter schemes have been shown in theory capable of exceeding a throughput figure of 0.8. The requirement here, however, is that user stations be close enough together so that the delay involved in listening to all other transmissions is a small fraction of a slot interval. As the propagation delay increases, the throughput improvement deteriorates.

We shall discuss in this chapter one particular reservation-Aloha scheme proposed in the literature. Details of other schemes suggested for improving the random access throughput characteristic appear in the literature cited. Before proceeding to discuss the reservation Aloha scheme, however, it is of interest to consider some simple slotted Aloha configurations in which throughputs greater than the maximum value of 0.368 arise. These configurations thus demonstrate so-called "excess" or higher capacity. This is not a contradiction of the discussion of the previous section. Recall we initiated the discussion in this chapter by indicating that one user alone should attain a capacity of 1; i.e., by continuously transmitting packets at the rate of one per slot he uses the channel capacity most efficiently. However, the point of using random access techniques is precisely the one of *sharing* the channel among a group of users who individually transmit relatively infrequently and at random. The slotted Aloha throughput maximum of $1/e = 0.368$ implicitly assumes a very large number of such users, so that the Poisson assumption can be considered valid.**

We shall now focus on a random access slotted Aloha system with a finite number k of users. In this model we assume user i has a known probability S_i of transmitting a packet and a probability $1 - S_i$ of not transmitting a packet in any slot interval. We then demonstrate that such a system has excess capacity. In particular, if one user is a "large" user, with a desired high throughput, and all the others are small users, it is possible for the large user to transmit at a throughput approaching 1 (the ultimate capacity), at the

*L. Kleinrock and F. A. Tobagi, "Packet-Switching in Radio Channels: Part I— Carrier Sense Multiple-Access Modes and Their Throughput-Delay Characteristics," *IEEE Trans. on Communications*, **COM-23**, no. 12, Dec. 1975, 1400–16.

**The Poisson assumption is of course valid if each user transmits at a Poisson rate. This was the assumption *explicitly* made in the past two sections. However, as will be demonstrated shortly, the Poisson statistics also arise naturally out of another model in which many users independently transmit or don't transmit packets with specified probabilities in each slot interval. This is nothing more than the well-known observation of probability theory that the sum of independent Bernoulli variables approaches a Poisson random variable. This model of a finite number of users is the one used by Lam and Kleinrock in the papers cited previously to discuss the stability of a slotted Aloha system.

expense of course of the small users. It is only when all the users are "small", with $k \longrightarrow \infty$, that the Poisson-limited throughput of $1/e = 0.368$ is attained. This model and the analysis following are due to Abramson.[*]

Consider k users then, user i having a probability S_i of generating a new packet and a probability $G_i > S_i$ that a new packet *or* a retransmission is generated in each slot. The probability that a packet generated by user j will encounter no collision is then simply

$$\prod_{\substack{i=1 \\ i \neq j}}^{k} (1 - G_i)$$

and the user j throughput is then given by

$$S_j = G_j \prod_{\substack{i=1 \\ i \neq j}}^{k} (1 - G_i) \tag{13-18}$$

Consider, as an example, two classes of users, with k_1 users in class 1, k_2 users in class 2. Then $k_1 + k_2 = k$. Let the respective message throughput and traffic rates be $S_1, G_1 ; S_2, G_2$. From Eq. (13-18) then,

$$S_1 = G_1(1 - G_1)^{k_1-1}(1 - G_2)^{k_2} \tag{13-19}$$

and

$$S_2 = G_2(1 - G_2)^{k_2-1}(1 - G_1)^{k_1} \tag{13-20}$$

Equations (13-19) and (13-20) are parametric equations defining possible values of S_1, S_2 in the (S_1, S_2) plane. The maximum possible traffic rates, defining boundaries in this plane, are of course given by the condition $k_1 G_1 + k_2 G_2 = 1$; i.e., the total traffic cannot exceed one packet per slot.

As a special case let $k_1 = k_2 = 1$. There are thus two users in the system. Then it is apparent that the two parametric equations become

$$S_1 = G_1(1 - G_2) \qquad S_2 = G_2(1 - G_1)$$

or, using $G_1 + G_2 = 1$ to determine the *maximum* throughputs,

$$S_1 = G_1^2 \qquad S_2 = (1 - G_1)^2$$

The maximum throughput pairs for this case are shown sketched in Fig. 13-8. Note, as expected, that either user can exceed the slotted Aloha capacity and in fact approach a throughput of 1 if the other user reduces his packet throughput rate accordingly.

Let the number of users now get very large ($k \longrightarrow \infty$), with equal packet generation and retransmission rates $S_i = S/k$ and $G_i = G/k$, respectively. S and G are thus the channel throughput and traffic, respectively. Then from

---

[*]N. Abramson, "Packet-Switching with Satellites," *AFIPS Conference Proc.*, National Computer Conference, **42**, June 1973, 695–702.

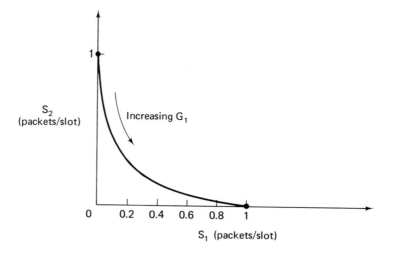

Fig. 13-8. Maximum throughputs, two-user case.

Eq. (13-18),

$$S = \lim_{k \to \infty} G\left(1 - \frac{G}{k}\right)^{k-1} = Ge^{-G} \tag{13-21}$$

just the slotted Aloha equilibrium Eq. (13-7). So the slotted Aloha result previously derived on the basis of Poisson statistics also arises from this model of a large number of users, each of which has a small probability S/k of generating a packet in any slot interval. As noted earlier in a footnote this is as to be expected since Poisson statistics are obtained when a large number of Bernoulli random variables are summed.

Finally, consider the case of one large user and a large number of small users accessing the channel. This is modeled by letting $k = 1$ and $k_2 \to \infty$ in Eq. (13-19) and (13-20). Letting $G_2 = G/k_2$ and $S_2 = S/k_2$, as in the example above, we have, in the limit, as $k_2 \to \infty$,

$$S = Ge^{-G}(1 - G_1) \tag{13-22}$$

and

$$S_1 = G_1 e^{-G} \tag{13-23}$$

It is apparent that these throughput relations are also obtained for the case of a Poisson user class generating an average of S new packets/slot, and a single user with a probability S_1 of generating a packet, both randomly accessing the same channel. The maximum throughput curve for this case appears as Fig. 13-9. (The maximum number of packets/slot transmitted over the channel is of course again given by $G + G_1 = 1$.) Note again, as expected, that the single user can transmit at rates much greater than $1/e = 0.368$, but only at the expense of the large number of small users, of course.

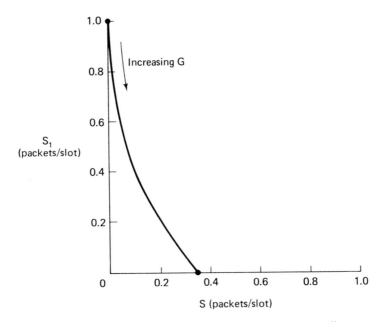

Fig. 13-9. Maximum throughputs, one large user plus many small ones.

RESERVATION ALOHA

It was noted earlier at the beginning of the previous section, that there exist other, less obvious, ways of increasing the useful throughput of a slotted Aloha channel. Reservation Aloha schemes in particular represent ingenious techniques in which the throughput of the channel can be increased above the slotted Aloha maximum at the cost of added time delay. Several such schemes have been suggested, with some limited analysis and simulation conducted to verify their ability to improve the system throughput. We shall summarize some of their distinguishing characteristics briefly and focus on the analysis of one such scheme in more detail. In one suggested procedure* slots are organized into frames with at least R slots. (R is again the round-trip propagation delay.) If a user (station) has had a successful packet transmission in the previous frame he gets to keep the slot. He loses the slot if he has nothing to transmit. Empty slots, including those involved in collision in the previous frame, are available to all users on a random access basis. So in this reservation scheme the reservation is obtained by first transmitting a packet successfully. This improves on the slotted Aloha technique in those cases where

*W. Crowther, et al., "A System for Broadcast Communication: Reservation Aloha," *Proc. Hawaii Sixth International Conference on System Science*, Jan. 1973.

stations have long messages to transmit, or transmit continuously. It adds in effect a line-switching capability to the normal packet-switching mode of the Aloha scheme. The channel throughput rate of this scheme can approach 1, at the expense of long packet delays. For a given throughout, packet delays increase as the number of stations increases. It is essentially limited to a number of stations in the order of R, the round-trip delay in slots.

A second reservation scheme has been proposed by R. Binder.* This scheme combines time-division multiplexing with dynamic allocation of unused message slots. Specifically, each user in the network is assigned one slot per frame. All unused assigned slots, as well as any unassigned slots per frame, are then available to the network as a pool on a first-come-first-served basis. A user can retrieve his assigned slot, if previously occupied by another user, by simply transmitting a packet, thereby generating a collision. The next frame time he simply transmits his desired packet. This scheme is obviously useful for short duration interactive traffic and makes available to each user almost the entire capacity of the network when the other users are either not transmitting or transmitting infrequently. Simulation results have indicated an improved delay-throughput characteristic over conventional time-division multiplexing.**

A third scheme which we shall describe in more detail and whose analysis provides a good application of both the slotted Aloha technique and the $M/G/1$ queueing analysis of Chap. 6 is the reservation Aloha procedure suggested by Roberts.† There are two states of the system proposed—an Aloha state and a Reserved state. In the Reserved state a time frame is set up consisting of $M + 1$ slots. The first M of these are allocated to users on a reserved basis; the last slot per frame is partitioned into V smaller slots, each available for transmitting small reservation-request packets. This is indicated in Fig. 13-10a. A user wishing to transmit a message consisting of one or more fixed size packets first transmits a request to the central system for a reservation for the desired number of packets, using one of the V smaller slots at the end of the frame for this purpose. Requests are transmitted using the slotted Aloha random access technique. Upon receipt of an acknowledgement transmitted in a broadcast mode by the control system, the actual message to be transmitted is queued up waiting for the appropriate reserved slot or slots over which transmission can take place. All users listen for acknowledgement broadcasts, and all update their reservation queue counters on receipt of any acknowledgement. A user then knows the particular slot or slots allocated to his own

*R. Binder, "A Dynamic Packet-Switching System for Satellite Broadcast Channels," *Proc. IEEE International Conference on Communications*, San Francisco, June 1975, pp. 41–1 to 41–5.

**Ibid.

†L. G. Roberts, "Dynamic Allocation of Satellite Capacity Through Packet Reservation," *AFIPS Conference Proc.*, National Computer Conference, **42**, June 1973, 711–16.

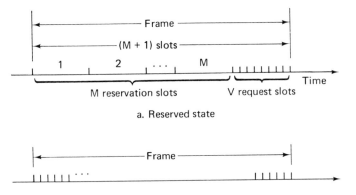

a. Reserved state

b. Aloha state: all request slots

Fig. 13-10. Robert's Reservation-Aloha scheme.

message. Should the reservation-request packet be garbled during transmission because of a collision or error in transmission, the normal slotted Aloha procedure is followed: no acknowledgement is transmitted by the central system; the user in question, not receiving an acknowledgement after an appropriate timeout interval, retransmits the request packet in one of the V slots allocated in another frame, with appropriate randomization in retransmission to reduce the possibility of further collision.

Whenever the reservation queue goes to zero, indicating there are no messages in the network waiting to be transmitted, the system reverts to the Aloha state (Fig. 13-10b) with all $(M + 1)$ slots per frame sectioned into V small slots each and available for reservation requests. As soon as such a request is correctly acknowledged the system moves to the reservation state.

We shall show below, using some simple analysis,* that this reservation scheme results in a substantial improvement in throughput over the slotted Aloha scheme (the throughput can approach a maximum value of $M/(M + 1)$ relative to 1, in contrast to $1/e = 0.368$ of the slotted Aloha scheme) at the cost, of course, of increased time delay in the low throughput region. For the minimum time delay in the light load region consists of two roundtrip delays (request packet delay *and* message delay) plus transmission time, contrasted with the simple round-trip delay plus transmission time for the slotted Aloha system.

Specifically, assume we again have k users, each transmitting at a rate of λ messages/sec. Let Z be the channel capacity in large (message) packets/sec. (This is just $1/\tau$, with τ the packet size, in seconds, as used previously.) Then the small slot (request packet) utilization in the Aloha state is just S_1

*Ibid.

$= k\lambda/ZV$; the small slot channel utilization in the Reserved state is S_2 $= k\lambda(M + 1)/ZV$, since the effective capacity for the request packets in this state is $ZV/(M + 1)$; and the channel utilization for messages queued up and then transmitted using the reserved slots is $S_3 = Bk\lambda(M + 1)/MZ$. Here B is the average message length, in packets. Both S_1 and S_2 must be less than $1/e = 0.368$, while $S_3 < 1$, since the latter represents the traffic intensity for an $M/G/1$ queue, with effective trunk capacity $MZ/(M + 1)$.

The actual channel utilization or traffic intensity ρ for the system is

$$\rho = \frac{Bk\lambda}{Z} \tag{13-24}$$

since this represents the ratio of packets/sec introduced into the system to the capacity Z, in slots or packets/sec. It is apparent from the definition of S_3 that ρ can also be written $\rho = MS_3/(M + 1)$, and hence

$$\rho < \frac{M}{M + 1} \tag{13-24a}$$

By making M, the number of slots per frame allocated to reservations, larger we effectively increase the system utilization. It is this fact that enables the system to be taken to higher utilizations than the normal Aloha system. However, there is a limit to which we can increase M since the number of reservations accepted must also satisfy the maximum rate of request packet acceptance dictated by a slotted Aloha limitation. Specifically, we also have

$$S_2 = \frac{MS_3}{BV} \le \frac{1}{e}$$

and hence

$$M \le \frac{BV}{e} \tag{13-25}$$

As an example, say all messages are one packet long. Let $V = 6$ (i.e., there are 6 request slots per frame). Then $M \le 2$, and $\rho < \frac{2}{3}$. If, as another example, we have messages uniformly distributed in length from one to eight packets, $B = 4.5$. With $V = 6$ again, $M \le 9$, and $\rho < 0.9$. So there is a critical interplay between the various parameters of the system. We shall follow Roberts' procedure in choosing V initially. (He does this on the basis of determining the minimum request packet size and number of request packet repetitions, or request packet redundancy, required to attain a specified detectability in noise.) It then turns out there is an optimum M (below the maximum given by Eq. (13-25)) for each value of ρ to minimize the average time delay. This is similar to the result found in the slotted Aloha case that there is an optimum retransmission interval K to minimize time delay. As was the case there, we shall show here, by example, that the actual choice of M is not critical, the time delay characteristic being rather broad as a function of M.

To determine the time delay characteristic we note that the time delay is the summed effect of round-trip propagation time plus two time delay terms: the Aloha-type time delay incurred in making reservations, and an $M/G/1$ queueing delay incurred by messages waiting for their reserved time slot to arrive. Recall from Chap. 6 [Eq. (6-61) and (6-62)] that the queueing delay for an $M/G/1$ queue can be written as the transmission time $1/\mu$ plus the average waiting time $E(W) = E(t^2)/2(1 - \rho)$, with $E(t^2)$ the second moment of the message length, in sec; λ the effective message arrival rate in messages/sec; and ρ the traffic intensity. In the system under study here we have already indicated that the effective arrival rate is $k\lambda$; the traffic intensity, so far as the message queueing delay portion of the system is concerned, is $S_3 = Bk\lambda(M + 1)/MZ$; the effective line capacity, in slots per second, is $MZ/(M + 1)$. Let the second moment of the message length, in units of packets squared, be $\overline{B^2}$. This is converted to units of seconds squared by dividing by the square of $MZ/(M + 1)$. The transmission time, in seconds, is also $B(M + 1)/MZ$. Putting all of this together the $M/G/1$ queueing delay D_q is readily found to be given by

$$D_q = \frac{B(M + 1)}{MZ} + \frac{YS_3(M + 1)}{2MZ(1 - S_3)} \qquad (13\text{-}26)$$

with $Y \equiv \overline{B^2}/B$.

The overall time delay is then

$$D_r = D_s + D_q + \frac{R}{Z} \qquad (13\text{-}27)$$

with D_s the request-packet or reservation delay, and R the round-trip propagation delay in packets.

The request-packet delay D_s is found by noting that this is just a random access Aloha-type delay incurred by the request packets with the system in either the Reserved or Aloha states. Let the delay in the Aloha state be D_1, with a probability $(1 - S_3)$, since S_3, the message or large slot utilization, is by definition the fraction of time message packets are being transmitted, or just the probability the system is in the Reserved state. Similarly, let the request-packet time delay in the Reserved state be D_2, with probability S_3. The overall request-packet delay is then

$$D_s = D_1(1 - S_3) + D_2 S_3 \qquad (13\text{-}28)$$

What are the Aloha time delays D_1 and D_2? Consider D_1 first. With the system in the Aloha state each large message slot is divided into V reservation-request slots. It is then apparent that D_1, in units of message packets or larger slots, is just

$$D_1\big|_{\text{slots}} = R + \frac{1.5}{V} + E_1\left[R + \frac{0.5}{V} + \frac{K + 1}{2V}\right] \qquad (13\text{-}29)$$

This is just Eq. (13-6a) reinterpreted for this system. D_1, in seconds, is obtained simply by dividing through by Z, the number of message slots transmitted per second.* Here the number of retransmissions $E_1 = G_1/S_1 - 1$, as noted earlier in this chapter, with G_1 the total Aloha traffic made up of newly-generated and retransmitted request packets. We shall assume $G_1/S_1 = e^{G_1}$ for simplicity. (Recall that this implies K very large, but is already a good approximation for $K > 4$ or 5.)

The request-packet delay D_2 in the Reserved state is similarly found except that now one must take into account the availability of request-packet slots at the end of each frame only (Fig. 13-10a). This adds an additional time delay of $M/2$ message slots for requests arriving, on the average, in the middle of a frame. Retransmitted requests may also have to be delayed until the next frame or the ones beyond that, depending on the relative values of the round-trip propagation time R, M, the randomized delay parameter K (in units of small or request slots), and V. For the specified case where $R > (M + 1)$ and $K \leq V$, it is readily shown that D_2, in units of message slots, is given by

$$D_2 |_{\text{slots}} = R + \frac{M}{2} + \frac{1.5}{V} + E_2 \left[R + \frac{M}{2} + \frac{K + 1}{2V} \right] \qquad (13\text{-}30)$$

Here again, $E_2 = G_2/S_2 - 1$, with E_2 the average number of retransmissions per request-packet generated. We shall also assume that S_2 and G_2, the newly-generated plus retransmitted packet intensity, are related by $G_2/S_2 = e^{G_2}$. D_2, in seconds, is again found by dividing by Z.

It is now a simple matter to combine Eq. (13-26) to (13-30) to determine the total delay-throughput characteristic, D_r vs. ρ, for this reservation scheme. This has been done for two cases, using an example similar to that worked out by Roberts.** Results appear in Fig. 13-11 and 13-12. A satellite system has been assumed, with 10 user stations located on the ground, transmitting to the satellite via a 50 kbps channel. In the first case all messages are assumed one packet long, a packet being 1350 bits. For this example, $Z = 37$ slots/sec and $R = 0.27Z = 10$ slots. Both K and V have been taken equal to 6. In the second case the messages are either one packet long (1350 bits) or 8 packets long, each assumed to be generated randomly 50% of the time. It is then readily shown that $B = 4.5$ and $Y = \overline{B^2}/B = 7.2$ for this case. Fig. 13-11 shows the resultant delay-throughput curve for the first case for the reservation Aloha system, using a fixed value of $M = 2$. (Two of these slots are then allocated to actual message transmission, on a reserved basis.) The maximum throughput or traffic intensity for this example is $\rho = \frac{2}{3}$. Superimposed on the

---

*Roberts in his analysis, Ibid., also includes an M/G/1-type waiting time term for request packets generated, waiting to be transmitted. For the number of users k very large, this turns out to be negligible since the throughput *per user* is $S_1/k \ll 1$, in order to keep $S_1 < 0.368$.
   **Ibid.

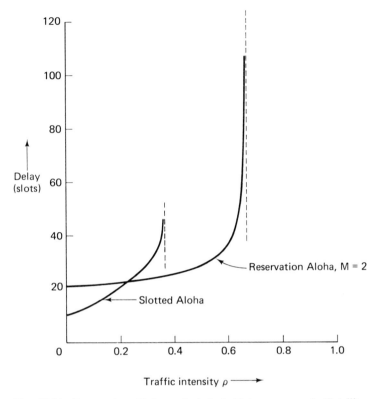

Fig. 13-11. Reservation Aloha and slotted Aloha compared. (Satellite link, 10 user stations, 50 kbps channel, 1350-bit packets.)

same figure is the equivalent curve for a slotted Aloha system. Note, as expected, that the initial reservation time delay for low intensity is greater than that for the slotted Aloha system because of the necessity to undergo two round-trip time delays. This is of course the dominant time delay ($2R = 20$ slots, in this example). Even with $M = 2$, the reservation system can operate considerably beyond the maximum slotted Aloha utilization of 0.368. By choosing larger values of M as ρ increases (in this example $M = 2$ is the only possibility at low values of ρ), one can increase the reservation Aloha throughput range, approaching 1.

Figure 13-12 is a similar curve drawn for case 2. Here the effect of varying M is shown. Note that for $\rho = 0$ values of M from 2 to 6 provide almost the same time delay value—this is of course due to the relatively large double round-trip time delay ($2R = 20$ slots) that dominates this satellite example. For $\rho = 0.5$ the time delays for $M = 4$ to 8 are all very close together ($M = 5$ provides the actual minimum), while for $\rho = 0.8$, $M = 9$ provides the minimum time delay.

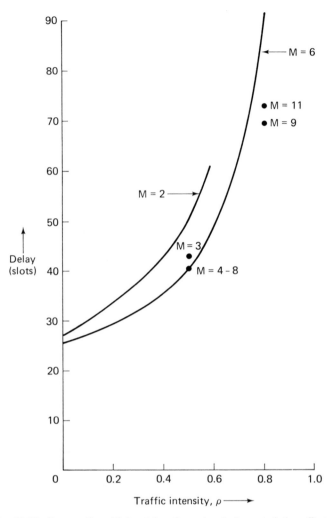

Fig. 13-12. Reservation Aloha delay-throughput characteristic: effect of varying M (messages of varying length).

RANDOM ACCESS AND POLLING COMPARED

Considerable time has been devoted in this chapter to an analysis of various types of random access schemes, all as an outgrowth of the basic work on the Aloha system of the University of Hawaii. As already noted, other schemes have been suggested and analyzed as well, and these are left for the reader to explore further.*

*See for example the discussion on carrier-sense multiple-access modes, by Kleinrock and Tobagi, "Packet-Switching in Radio Channels."

It is apparent that random access techniques provide a viable alternative to other access or multiplexing techniques for large numbers of data sources, *operating in a bursty mode*, attempting to access a central computer facility. This facility could be a communications concentrator or processor, serving as one node of a distributed network, or it could be the central system for the network itself. Although the principal applications of Aloha-type techniques suggested have been to packet radio or satellite communications, it is apparent that the techniques are applicable as well to existing land data communication systems. In particular, they could be adopted for use with multipoint networks of the type discussed in Chap. 9, loop-type systems to which reference was made in Chap. 12,* or provide the first step of concentration for a statistical multiplexer.

It is thus of considerable interest to provide a quantitative comparison between random access and other multiplexing techniques in current use. One such comparison has appeared in the literature.** In this work a random access technique of the pure Aloha-type is compared with roll-call polling and a third technique, a loop system in which users share the same line, and newly-generated messages are entered only when gaps appear in the line traffic. The comparison in this work is made on the basis of round-trip message delay. It is found, for the examples developed in this paper, that the random access system does in fact provide a lower average delay than the other systems investigated over most of the range of parameters considered. Particular attention is given in this paper to the allocation of channel capacity to the transmission of overhead information, such as polling messages and acknowledgement traffic. It is found, as was noted in Chap. 12 on polling, that the polling system performance is particularly sensitive to receiver synchronization time, as reflected in the walk-time parameter for the system.

In this final section of this chapter on random access techniques we carry out a similar calculation, comparing a slotted Aloha random access scheme with roll-call and hub polling for three different examples. The comparison here is on the basis of *message forward or inbound delay* only. We ignore here the cost of implementing the various access schemes. This may actually turn out to be the critical parameter, however. For example, in a satellite system, one of the examples considered below, a polling strategy requires the ground stations to be linked in some manner. The cost of doing this— whether through common carrier facilities or through private radio links, for example—has not been considered here. We use for this purpose Eq. (12-10) of Chap. 12 and Eq. (13-6a) of this chapter. The first two examples, depicted in Fig. 13-13a, assume the user stations are dispersed equally about the central system they are accessing, and are connected by land lines to the central sys-

---

*Ethernet is an example of such an application. See Metcalfe and Boggs, "Ethernet: Distributed Packet-Switching."
**Hayes and Sherman, "A Study of Data Multiplexing Techniques."

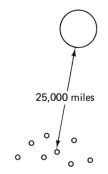

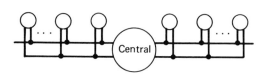

a. 100 – and 1000 – mile land networks

b. Satellite system; ground terminals within 1000 – mile region

Fig. 13-13. Examples used in comparing random access and polling techniques.

tem. Propagation delay in this case is taken *conservatively* as 4 msec/100 miles. In the first example the k stations are all taken to be within 50 miles of the central system, with a total line length of 100 miles. The loop propagation delay (Chap. 12) is then $Y = 4$ msec. In the second example the k stations are all within 500 miles of the central system, with a total line length of 1000 miles. The loop propagation delay is then 40 msec. Roll-call polling is assumed to be the polling scheme adopted for both examples, so that the propagation delay factor in the calculation of the polling system walk-time is

$$Y' = \frac{Y}{2}\left(1 + \frac{k}{2}\right) \tag{13-31}$$

(See Eq. (12-6), Chap. 12.)

In the third example, depicted in Fig. 13-13b, the k user stations, all located within a 1000-mile circuit on the earth, access a processor located on a synchronous satellite 25,000 miles above the earth. The round-trip propagation delay is then 0.27 sec. Hub polling is taken as the polling mode in this example because of the large distance involved. The satellite thus interrogates one of the ground stations, which in turn polls a neighboring ground station, and so on. The total round-trip propagation delay for the polling system of 0.31 sec then is dominated by the 0.27 sec satellite-ground link delay.

For all three examples we assume the message channel to have a capacity of 4800 bps. Fixed length messages or packets of 100 8-bit characters, including overhead, are transmitted in all cases. The roll-call polling messages are taken to be 6 characters long (these are assumed embedded as overhead characters in the 100-character packets in the hub polling case), including one user station address character. This thus limits the number of stations to $2^7 = 128$ in these examples. The receiver synchronization (modem turn-on) time in the roll-call case is taken as 10 msec (six characters) and in the hub polling case as 20 msec. Both roll-call and hub systems thus assess each user station 20 msec for the synchronization and polling message portions of the walk-time. Table 13-1 summarizes the resultant walk-times for the various examples for three values of k, using Eq. (13-31) to determine the propagation delay for the roll-call examples, and taking 0.31 sec to be the total propagation delay for the hub polling examples.

TABLE 13-1

SYSTEM WALK-TIMES (SEC)

$k \rightarrow$	10	50	100
100-mile circuit (roll call)	0.212	1.05	2.1
1000-mile circuit (roll call)	0.320	1.52	3.02
satellite circuit (hub polling)	0.51	1.31	2.31

These walk-times are critical in determining the inbound message delay for the polling systems, as noted in Chap. 12. In particular, from Eq. (12-1) we have the average poll scan time given by

$$\bar{t}_c = \frac{L}{1 - k\rho} \tag{13-32}$$

with L the system walk-time, and ρ the traffic intensity at each user station. The inbound message delay time for the polling systems (excluding time required to acknowledge the message) is then given by

$$D = \frac{\bar{t}_c}{2}(1 - \rho) + \frac{k\sigma^2 \Delta}{2(1 - k\rho)} + \frac{(1 - \rho)\Delta}{2} + \Delta \tag{13-33}$$

This equation is the same as Eq. (12-9) of Chap. 12, with the message transmission time Δ added. As in previous chapters Δ represents the time required to output a data unit. In these examples, with fixed length 100-character packets, Δ is the same as the packet slot time and is just 0.167 sec for a 4800 bps channel. For fixed length packets we also have $\sigma^2 = \rho = \lambda\Delta$, with λ the average message (packet) arrival rate per station.

Using the walk-times shown in Table 13-1, plus Eq. (13-32) and (13-33), the inbound message delay times for the polling systems in the three examples of Fig. 13-13 have been calculated. These are shown plotted as a function of the number of user stations k in the polling curves of Fig. 13-14 to 13-17. As indicated in the figures two message arrival rates, one message/min. and two messages/min., have been assumed. Note again that the inbound delays for the polling cases do not include time required to acknowledge correct receipt of a message. In the satellite case in particular, this includes an additional round-trip delay of 0.27 sec plus computer processing time.

Also shown plotted in Fig. 13-14 to 13-17 are curves of inbound message time delay for a slotted Aloha random access system. In the case of the 100- and 1000-mile networks the propagation delay has been neglected (note again how this differs from the polling case) so that the inbound delay expression for these networks is given by

$$D = 1.5\Delta + E\Delta\left(1 + \frac{K}{2}\right) \tag{13-34}$$

from Eq. (13-6a). The packet length or slot interval Δ is again taken as 0.167 sec in calculating the curves. Two sets of curves are shown plotted, one for

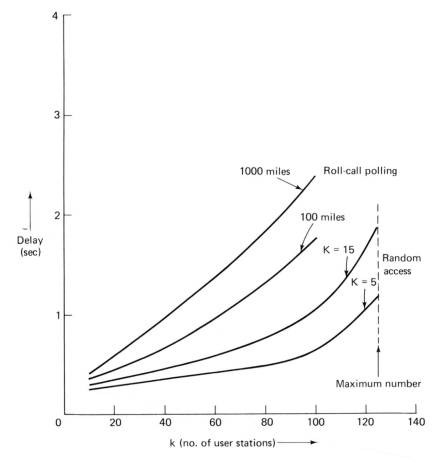

Fig. 13-14. Random access vs. roll-call polling, 100–and 1000–mile networks ($\lambda = 1$ message/min.).

$K = 5$, the other for $K = 15$. Figure 13-6 was used to calculate the retransmission parameter $E = G/S - 1$ for the two values of K, although it is apparent that, except for the values of throughput S approaching the maximum allowable, E doesn't vary much with K.

For the satellite example the only propagation term used for the random access calculations was the round-trip earth-satellite propagation delay of 0.27 sec. In this example, with $\Delta = 0.167$ sec, the round-trip delay in slots is $R = 1.6$, so that the delay expression in seconds becomes

$$\frac{D}{\Delta} = 3.1 + E\left(2.6 + \frac{K}{2}\right) \tag{13-35}$$

with Δ again taken as 0.167 sec.

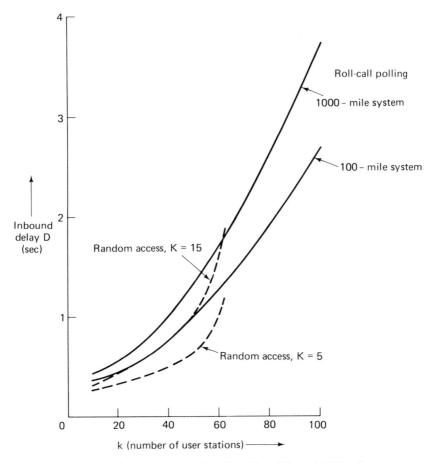

Fig. 13-15. Random access vs. roll-call polling, 100- and 1000-mile networks ($\lambda = 2$ messages/min.).

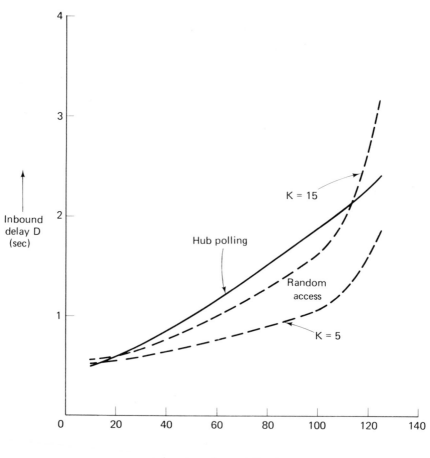

Fig. 13-16. Satellite example: hub polling vs. random access ($\lambda = 1$ message/min.).

Figure 13-14 to 13-17 indicate, in agreement with Hayes and Sherman,* that random access techniques appear to offer an advantage over polling if the number of stations in the network is not too large or if the message arrival rate per station is low enough. Polling techniques can obviously handle more user stations, however, since the slotted Aloha technique limits at $S = 0.368$. (Recall also that for stability reasons one might want to operate at S considerably below this maximum value unless some control mechanism were invoked to keep the system stable.) Doubling the message arrival rate per station from one to two messages/min. appears for these examples to affect

*Ibid.

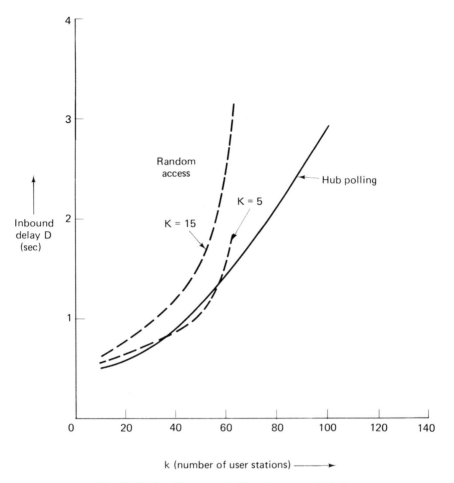

Fig. 13-17. Satellite example ($\lambda = 2$ messages/min.).

the random access scheme more since the throughput S doubles as well bringing the system that much closer to the maximum allowable throughput of 0.368. The polling schemes are affected much less in these examples since the maximum allowable throughput is 1. At the point of maximum allowable throughput for the random access scheme the polling schemes are still relatively unaffected by the throughput limitation, and their performance is dominated, as pointed out in Chap. 12, by the walk-times rather than throughput.

But note again that a word of caution is necessary in using results such as these. The comparison here has been made strictly on the basis of time delay. Cost considerations have not been included. In the case of the satellite example in particular, as noted earlier, the ground terminals must be linked in some manner, and the cost of doing this has not at all been considered here.

PROBLEMS

13.1 A group of terminals uses a pure Aloha accessing technique to communicate with a remote concentrator over a 4800 bps channel. Packets are 100 bits long. Terminals transmit, on the average, one message every two minutes. What is the maximum number of terminals that may use the channel? Repeat for a slotted Aloha system. What if packets are 200 bits long? What if terminals transmit once every 30 sec, on the average?

13.2 Ten earth stations use a slotted Aloha technique to access a communications satellite located 25,000 miles above the earth's surface. Assume the number of stations is large enough so that the Poisson statistics model used in discussing the slotted Aloha performance is valid. Each earth station transmits 1000-bit packets using a 56 kbps channel. The average transmission rate of an earth station is one packet/sec. Packets undergoing a collision are retransmitted using a uniformly-distributed length distribution of $K = 6$ packet slots. Determine the average time delay to the time of packet acknowledgement.

13.3 Repeat Problem 13.2 if the average transmission rate is increased to 1.5 packets/sec. What would the result be if 15 earth stations each transmitted one packet/sec, on the average? What would the result be if the packet length were increased to 1500 bits, with the same 10 stations transmitting at a rate of one packet/sec, on the average?

13.4 Compare the result of Problem 13.2 to that using a hub polling scheme. All 10 stations are connected by land lines, and the satellite initiates the polling cycle by interrogating one of the earth stations. Assume the earth-satellite propagation delay dominates. Modem synchronization times are 10 msec. What would the result be if this number were 50 msec.? Compare the polling and Aloha implementations required. (Note that the polling procedure requires the use of land lines.)

13.5 Consider Problem 13.2 with 30 ground stations accessing the satellite. Show the slotted Aloha technique is no longer feasible. What changes would have to be made to allow a slotted Aloha access technique to be used? Consider hub polling as in Problem 13.4. Show this is feasible and calculate the time delay as in Problem 13.4. (Note again, however, that the polling technique would require terrestrial links for its implementation.)

13.6 100 mobile 1200 bps data terminals are deployed within a radius of 20 miles from a central system with which they communicate. All terminals communicate on the same assigned frequency. Terminals transmit, on the average, one 200-bit message every two minutes.

(1) Investigate the feasibility of using a pure Aloha random access scheme. Show the average time delay to receipt of an acknowledgement message is approximately 0.5 sec if a uniformly-distributed retransmission delay of from 1 to $K = 6$ packet intervals is used, and 0.78 sec if $K = 12$.

How sensitive are these results to the assumption of one message transmitted every two minutes? How much could this average rate be increased? Discuss some mechanisms for ensuring a tolerable *average* rate is not exceeded. Could a larger number of mobile units be accommodated?

(2) Investigate the use of a roll-call polling scheme. Show that the average location of a data terminal is 13.3 miles from the central system if the mobile units are assumed uniformly-distributed within a circle of 20 miles radius from the center. Calculate the two-way average propagation delay for the roll-call mode from this number. Pick some reasonable receiver synchronization times and a reasonable length polling message. (Note that the address portion has to be long enough to address 100 units.) Calculate the average inbound delay time and compare with that of the random access scheme of (1). How sensitive is your result to the choice of synchronization time and polling message length? Determine the effect of increasing the number of mobile units. Could a hub polling scheme be used? If so, how? How would such a system perform in this example?

13.7 Refer to the analysis in this chapter of retransmission in the slotted Aloha system. Show that the probability q_t of a successful transmission conditioned on a retransmitted packet generated is given by Eq. (13-12). Verify Eq. (13-13) and (13-14). Show that as $K \longrightarrow \infty$, $q_t \longrightarrow e^{-G}$. Show similarly that the probability q_n of a successful retransmission conditioned on a new packet generated is given by Eq. (13-15). Show that in the limit of large K, $E \longrightarrow e^G - 1$.

13.8 A 4800 bps data channel is to be accessed using slotted Aloha techniques. Packets are 1000 bits long. Two users vie for the channel. User 1 has a probability p_1 of transmitting a packet in any slot interval; user 2's probability is p_2. Find and sketch the maximum average throughput characteristic (packet/slot) of each user as p_2 is varied from 0 to 1.

13.9 Refer to the discussion in the text concerning the Reservation Aloha system leading to the curves of Fig. 13-11 and 13-12. Recall that the example assumes 10 earth stations transmitting on a 50 kbps channel to a satellite. In one case the messages are all one packet long of 1350 bits. In the Aloha state the message slot is divided into $V = 6$ request slots. $K = 6$ as well.

In the second case the messages are equally likely to be one packet or eight packets long. Calculate the delay-throughput characteristics for these two cases, verifying the Reservation Aloha curves of Fig. 13-11 and 13-12.

Line Control

Procedures 14

IIIIIIIIIIIIIIIIIIIIIIIIIIIIIIIIIIIIIIIIIIIIIIIIIIIIIIIIIIIIIIIIIIIIIIIIIIIIIIIIIIIIIIIIIIIIIIIIIIIIIIIIIIIIIIIIIIIIIIIIIIIIIIIIIIIIIIIIIIIIIIIIIIIIIIIIIIIIIIIIIIIIIIIIIIIIIIIIIIIIIIIIIIIIIIIII

In our study of data networks thus far we have focused on the overall design concepts. We have assumed messages transmitted between nodes of a network to be made up of packets or blocks of multibit characters without worrying too much about the actual structure of the message blocks transmitted. Only in discussing examples of networks, or polling disciplines used in practice, did we indicate that there is much more to message transmission than the transmission of an arbitrary sequence of data bits.

Obviously it is not sufficient to just start transmitting a desired sequence of data symbols from one nodal concentrator or terminal to another. The receiving concentrator must sense the arrival of a new message, it must be synchronized properly to the bits as they arrive and to bits grouped as characters, in order to properly decode the message received. These communication functions and others to be described shortly—all necessary to establish a connection between the two ends of a link in a network, to disconnect when ready, to handle contingencies when they arise—are subsumed under the title line control procedures or data communication control procedures. They are part of a larger class of protocols or rules that have to be established to ensure that messages flow smoothly and accurately between any two terminals or terminal-computer pairs wanting to communicate in a network.

Each of the network examples described in Chap. 2 had a line control procedure specified. In discussing the formatting of message blocks, the provision of synchronization characters, the delineation of header and data characters, the specification of error detection and acknowledgement procedures, etc., we were implicitly focusing on the line control procedure for the network in question. In discussing the IBM PARS system in Chap. 12 we similarly outlined the line control procedure used to establish, maintain, and terminate communication between the central processor and the concentrators. In this chapter we pursue the line control question more specifically and more systematically. We first outline the requirements of a line control procedure. We then provide examples of standard line control procedures (some of the networks discussed use variations of these), and then conclude the chapter with a brief discussion of a new line control procedure that attempts to come to grips with problems that have arisen over the years with previous standards. Throughout the chapter we focus on line control procedures only. Readers interested in information on higher-order protocols and high-level network concepts, such as the IBM System Network Architecture, SNA, (which uses the IBM SDLC line control to be discussed at the end of the chapter) and the Digital Equipment Corporation's DECNET and Digital Network Architecture, DNA, are referred to the literature for discussions of these.*

Some of the many references to work in the field of line control procedures to which we shall have occasion to refer in the material following appear in the footnote.**

LINE CONTROL REQUIREMENTS

As already noted earlier an appropriate line control must provide for rules or procedures that enable communication between two ends of a link to be established, that enable synchronism to be established and maintained so that messages can be properly delivered, and that terminate message transmission when completed. The control must provide for the formatting and

---

*SNA is described in a series of papers in a special issue of the *IBM Systems Journal*, **15**, no. 1, 1976, 2–80. See for example, J. H. McFayden, "Systems Network Architecture: An Overview," pp. 4–23.

For a discussion of DECNET and DNA see S. Wecker, "The Design of DECNET—A General Purpose Network Base," *IEEE Electro 76*, Boston, Mass., 1976; G. E. Conant and S. Wecker, "DNA: An Architecture for Heterogeneous Computer Networks," *Proc. 1976 International Conference on Computer-Communications*, Toronto, Canada, Aug. 1976.

B. W. Stutzman, "Data Communication Control Procedures," *Computing Surveys*, **4, Dec. 1972, 197–220; J. P. Gray, "Line Control Procedures," *Proc. IEEE*, **60**, Nov. 1972, no. 11, 1301–12; R. A. Donnan and J. R. Kersey, "Synchronous Data Link Control: A Perspective," *IBM Systems J.*, **13**, no. 2, 1974, 140–62; J. L. Eisenbies, "Conventions for Digital Data Communication Link Design," *IBM Systems J.*, **6**, no. 4, 1967, 269–302; A. J. Neumann et al., "A Technical Guide to Computer-Communication Interface Standards," *NBS Technical Note 843*, Aug. 1974; D. E. Carlson, "ADCCP—A Computer-Oriented Data Link Control," *IEEE Compcon 75*, pp. 110–13.

checking of messages; it must have an acknowledgement procedure to indicate messages received correctly or incorrectly; it must have a procedure defined that must be followed if the data received were declared to be in error. Enlarging on this latter point procedures must also be established for detecting the existence of all possible contingencies and for such contingencies to be systematically dealt with.

In implementing these rules data codes are normally established. These codes generally include special characters or identifiers that can be used to handle all the requirements noted above. Since the transmission of these special characters constitutes overhead that reduces transmission efficiency, a major problem in protocol and code design is that of providing for all contingencies in establishing and maintaining communication between two nodes, with a minimum of overhead and cost. For standardization purposes and because of changes in network design and configuration that inevitably occur, the protocol and accompanying code should also be capable of adjustment to different modes of communication—half-duplex or duplex, polled or nonpolled—and to different network configurations—centralized or distributed networks, loop or multipoint connection, etc. It is apparent that the establishment of a protocol, even on a link (node-to-node) basis, and the code to go with it, is a far from trivial task.

Consider the following example that typifies some of the problems raised above.* Assume half-duplex transmission is available. Ten control characters are available to establish and maintain transmission. These are described below. (They are similar to some of the ASCII or ISO characters to be discussed later.)

1. SYN. Used to indicate start of a message and to establish synchronism.

2. ENQ. An inquiry symbol to see if receiver is ready or available to receive messages.

3. ACK. and 4. NAK. Positive and negative acknowledgement messages.

5. STX. Start of text. Denotes data following.

6. ETX. End of text.

7. ETB. End of block. This indicates that more text is yet to come; the message is not concluded.

8. US. Unit separator. This also indicates that more text is to follow. The message may be broken up or a series of messages may be grouped together with US denoting the separations.

*P. G. Stein, "Communications Protocol: The Search for SYNC," *Datamation*, April 1973, pp. 55–57.

    9. EOT. End of transmission.

   10. BCC. Parity check character for detecting errors.

A typical conversation might go as follows:

$\longrightarrow$ To receiver $\longleftarrow$ From receiver

1. SYN SYN ENQ
   (This establishes transmission)

                                          SYN SYN ACK 1.
               (The receiver indicates it is ready to receive)

2. SYN SYN STX (data) US BCC (data) ETB BCC
   (More data to come; message not complete)

                                          SYN SYN ACK 2.

$\longrightarrow$ To receiver $\longleftarrow$ From receiver

3. SYN SYN STX (data) . . .

                                          SYN SYN ACK 3.
   If the receiver detects an error in the line 3. characters above, it transmits a NAK message:

                                          SYN SYN NAK 3'.
   The transmitter then repeats the line 3. sequence.

4. SYN SYN STX (data) US BCC (data) ETX BCC.
   (The data transmission is now complete)

                                          SYN SYN ACK 4.

5. SYN SYN EOT
   (Signoff. An ENQ message is then needed to start up again.)

    Note from this simple example how the control characters were used, in a well-defined fashion, to establish and maintain communication. It is apparent that other rules could have been established as well. (Recall the examples already considered in this book. Others will be considered later in this chapter.) For example, for more efficient transmission, particularly if data messages are flowing in both directions, the ACK message might be embedded in a reverse outgoing message. (This is done, for example, in the TYMNET and ARPA networks.) The NAK might be dispensed with, the lack of receipt of an ACK after a specified timeout denoting the need to retransmit the message. Are two SYN characters needed or could one be used to establish synchronism and denote the start of a message? How are the control characters to be chosen? The SYN character, particularly, must be selected so that it is not confused with text characters. How many bits long should the control characters be? (The longer they are, the more control characters that can be defined. But the protocol may then become less efficient.) These and other questions will be considered further.

It is apparent that there are three phases to the process of message transmission:*

1. The establishment phase in which, depending on the type of network or transmission to take place, a station may be selected to receive a transmission, permission may be requested to send a transmission, or notification may be given that a message is forthcoming.

2. The message transfer phase.

3. The termination phase. This terminates the logical connection and returns the system to the initial state.

A communications protocol must be capable of guiding the system from one phase to another. To be useful in a wide variety of situations it must be capable of handling or adapting to various types of network connection and transmission. Figure 14-1 portrays the three phases of transmission, with particular reference to networks that include polling or selection strategies.** The message transfer can be point-to-point, one node (or terminal) communicating with another in either half-duplex (alternate one-way) or duplex

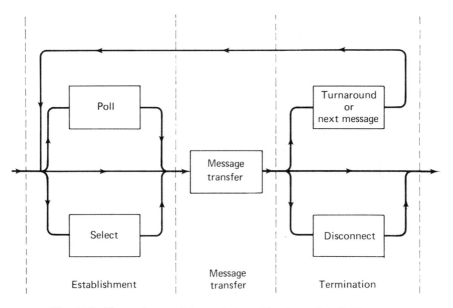

Fig. 14-1. Three phases of transmission. (Courtesy of A.J. Neumann, B.G. Lucas, J.C. Walker, and D.W. Fite, *NBS Technical Note* **843**, Aug. 1974, p. 74, Fig. 4-4.)

*In line-switched networks as well as those using virtual circuits two additional signaling phases are generally required to establish a connection and then to disconnect.

**Neumann et al., "Computer-Communication Interface Standards," p. 74, Fig. 4-4.

transmission; or it can take place in a multipoint environment. In this last case polling strategies of various kinds can be used, with transmission taking place to and from a central node, or transmission can be one-way only, with the central node selecting nodes or terminals to which it wants to transmit messages. A standard protocol and its accompanying data code should be capable of handling these situations, as well as other possible network categories.

Consider point-to-point transmission as a specific example. The pattern of data flow with time, in terms of the phases of transmission indicated, may be diagrammed as shown in Fig. 14-2.* (Note that the simple example given earlier may be diagrammed in this form, as may the data flow from node-to-

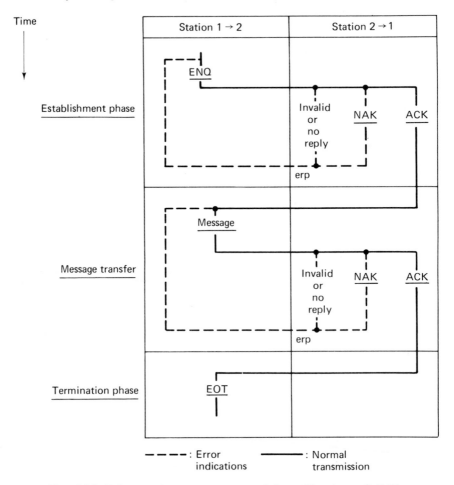

Fig. 14-2. Point-to-point message transmission. (Courtesy of B.W. Stutzman, "Data Communication Control Procedures," *Computing Surveys*, **4**, no. 4, Dec. 1972.)

*Stutzman, "Data Communication Control Procedures."

node in some of the network examples considered in earlier chapters.) The diagram also indicates *direction* of flow, with station 1 shown as the transmitter or initiator of the transmission, and station 2 the receiver. (In duplex transmission a similar diagram would be used, with directions reversed, to show messages flowing from 2 to 1.) As already noted earlier ENQ represents an inquiry data sequence (this was given as SYN SYN ENQ in the simple example provided earlier) indicating station 1 is ready to transmit.* Station 2 replies with an acknowledgement or a negative acknowledgement. The NAK sequence is sent by station 2 when it is not ready to receive or has received the message incorrectly. (In some protocols these two categories are distinguished, and different reply sentences are returned.) The NAK sequence, no reply, or an invalid reply provide error indications to the transmitting station, and the ENQ sentence is then repeated. More generally, on an invalid reply, no reply, or if repeated NAKs are sent, the system goes into a predetermined error recovery procedure. (This is denoted by erp in Fig. 14-2.)

A similar diagram may be sketched for nodes or stations communicating in polled or selection modes.** Within the broad confines of the three phases of message transmission shown in Fig. 14-2, the link protocol and data code that implements it must further provide for synchronization at the bit and character level, provision must be made for framing messages, for error checking and error recovery procedures, and for abort procedures if necessary. (The control is then passed on to a "higher level authority.") The code itself, in addition to providing for these necessary functions, should also enable control symbols to be readily distinguished from data symbols, and it should provide for the transmission of various kinds of control messages. (In addition to ACK and NAK symbols, framing symbols, polling or selection symbols, status messages, address of sender and receiver, data message and acknowledge message counts, among others, may be needed.) Provision for the transmission of transparent text (that is, text not grouped into the usual 8-bit character format) is a highly desirable feature. Finally, a code should have provision for an expandable control character set to allow additional conditions and requirements to be handled or additional capability to be added, as desired.

In the section following we discuss several existing communications control disciplines, and their accompanying character sets. Ways in which some of the various requirements listed above are met will be noted in the context of our discussion.

---

*Recall that in some existing systems there is no formal inquiry sentence. Station 1 simply transmits its message preceded by a header that effectively represents the establishment phase. This is common in distributed-type networks with duplex transmission. The fast select mode available in some of the protocols described in the next section also allows the transmitter to move directly from the establishment to the message transfer phase without waiting for an acknowledgement.

**Ibid.

EXAMPLES OF LINK CONTROL PROCEDURES

ANSI Data Link Control*

ANSI Data Link Control is the U.S. standard based on the 7-bit ASCII code (American Standard Code for Information Interchange). ASCII is compatible with the International Standard code ISO R646. Of the 128 possible 7-bit characters, 32 are set aside as control characters. Of these, 10 are reserved as line control characters. The ASCII code is shown described completely in Fig. 14-3. The 10 line control characters are tabulated as follows:

SOH. Start of heading. This always appears at the beginning of a sequence of characters comprising a heading and containing address, routing, and other control information.

$b_4 b_3 b_2 b_1$ / Row	$0\,0\,0$ — 0	$0\,0\,1$ — 1	$0\,1\,0$ — 2	$0\,1\,1$ — 3	$1\,0\,0$ — 4	$1\,0\,1$ — 5	$1\,1\,0$ — 6	$1\,1\,1$ — 7
0 0 0 0 0	NUL	DLE	SP	0	@	P	`	p
0 0 0 1 1	SOH	DC1	!	1	A	Q	a	q
0 0 1 0 2	STX	DC2	"	2	B	R	b	r
0 0 1 1 3	ETX	DC3	#	3	C	S	c	s
0 1 0 0 4	EOT	DC4	$	4	D	T	d	t
0 1 0 1 5	ENQ	NAK	%	5	E	U	e	u
0 1 1 0 6	ACK	SYN	&	6	F	V	f	v
0 1 1 1 7	BEL	ETB	'	7	G	W	g	w
1 0 0 0 8	BS	CAN	(	8	H	X	h	x
1 0 0 1 9	HT	EM	)	9	I	Y	i	y
1 0 1 0 10	LF	SUB	*	:	J	Z	j	z
1 0 1 1 11	VT	ESC	+	;	K	[	k	{
1 1 0 0 12	FF	FS	,	<	L	\	l	|
1 1 0 1 13	CR	GS	−	=	M	]	m	}
1 1 1 0 14	SO	RS	.	>	N	^	n	~
1 1 1 1 15	SI	US	/	?	O	___	o	DEL

Fig. 14-3. ASCII code table, source: ANSI X3.4-1968.

*Ibid. Also, Gray, "Line Control Procedures;" Neumann et al., "Computer-Communication Interface Standards." This last paper provides some history of the ANSI procedure, discusses possible extensions, and provides a bibliography of standards documents. It also discusses the International Standard code ISO R646, of which the ASCII code is the American version. Further discussion of ISO appears in D. W. Davies and D. L. A. Barber, *Communication Networks for Computers*, Wiley, London, 1973. ANSI stands for American National Standards Institute; ISO for International Standards Organization.

STX. Start of text. This terminates the heading, if any, and precedes the text portion of message or message block.

ETX. End of text. This terminates the sequence of characters (text) begun with STX.

ETB. End of transmission block (heading or text), indicating this is not the end of the text. (The final message block, with concluding text, would then be followed by an ETX.)

EOT. Terminates transmission.

ENQ. Enquiry. This character, preceded by some prefix characters to be agreed on by all stations in the network (e.g., two SYN characters), initiates transmission. It represents a request for a response from a remote station. It may also be used to request station identification and status.

ACK. Acknowledgement character, from receiver to sender.

NAK. Negative acknowledgement.

SYN. Synchronous idle. This appears at the beginning of all transmitted character sequences and may be inserted in a long sequence of characters to maintain synchronization. (The ANSI protocol provides for the transmission of at least two SYN characters between successive blocks to maintain synchronization.) Note then that the SYN characters provide the necessary bit and character synchronization in this line control procedure. To ensure that the SYN bit sequence is unique in any message block those characters that, combined with a left or right shift of the SYN pattern, will produce an erroneous SYN pattern, are precluded from appearing, respectively, after or before the SYN.*

DLE. Data Link Escape. This changes the meaning of a string of characters immediately following. It can thus be used to allow new control functions to be added. Examples of such extended control sequences include

DLE EOT = DEOT, a mandatory disconnection

DLE 0 = ACK 0, and

DLE 1 = ACK 1, used as alternating acknowledgements

in those cases where numbered acknowledgements are needed.

In addition to these 10 line control characters a block check character (BCC) is used in those ANSI link configuration categories where checking, in addition to normal character parity check, is carried out. The check character is obtained by forming the exclusive OR of each bit position in the characters

*Gray, "Line Control Procedures."

following the first SOH or STX. (The STX is included if the SOH appears in a transmission block.) Internal SYNs are excluded. The BCC then follows the ETB or ETX of a transmission block. A message consisting of one block would then appear as follows:

SOH (Heading) STX (Text) ETX BCC

A multiblock message would appear as follows:

SOH (Heading) STX (Text) ETB BCC

SOH (Heading) STX (Text) ETX BCC

In a more advanced version of ANSI, cyclic redundancy checking with two check characters used is carried out.

The ANSI data link protocol was developed primarily for centralized multipoint networks or point-to-point links utilizing alternate two-way transmission. The standardized procedures set up for establishing and terminating a link connection reflect this emphasis on one-way or alternate two-way transmission. Proposed new standards provide for two-way simultaneous or conversational transmission. Examples of link configuration categories for which link establishment and termination procedures have been established include the following:*

1. One-way only transmission from a control station (master) to tributaries (slaves) connected in centralized, multipoint fashion. The establishment of the link to the appropriate receiving tributaries is made via a selection procedure—a prefix sequence followed by ENQ. The prefix sequence includes the tributary addresses plus other characters whose format and content are not provided for in the ANSI standard. They must be agreed upon by the network users. The link is terminated on the transmission of EOT by the Control Station.

2. Two-way alternate point-to-point transmission. Here either station, at either end of the link, contends for master status. The station wishing to transmit sends ENQ with no prefix. The receiving station responds with either ACK or ACK 0, or with NAK. (An optional prefix may be used in either case.) In the latter case the transmitting station repeats ENQ. Transmission terminates with the transmission of EOT or DEOT by the master.

3. Two-way alternate centralized multipoint transmission. Here the control station may serve as master, or it may assign that role to a tributary, becoming in turn a slave for the period of that transmission. The first category corresponds to the selection mode of 1. above with transmission established through the issuance of a prefix plus ENQ. The second category corresponds to a polling mode (see Fig. 14-1). An appropriate prefix followed by ENQ

*Neumann et al., "Computer-Communication Interface Standards." pp. 69–76.

establishes this mode. The tributary to which the polling message is addressed immediately assumes master status if ready to transmit a message. If not ready it responds with EOT. Transmission is terminated in either category when the current master issues an EOT. The control station then takes over control again.

Various other link configuration categories are provided for: two-way multipoint centralized with a first select procedure (the master transmits a selection prefix immediately followed by a message), two-way point-to-point nonswitched, etc. All in all, there are seven classes of establishment-termination procedures and message transfer procedures, for a total of 30 possible control procedures that are standardized.* This obviously leads to problems. Some of these are apparent in the three examples given above: the establishment and termination procedures differ somewhat in the different categories; prefixes are optional and not standardized; some control characters change from one category to another. (As an example, the DEOT sometimes means "disconnect the link" and sometimes terminates a transmission without breaking the connection.) Basically the ANSI standard is a list of alternative procedures some of which are not consistent with one another. It has "multiple dialects" because of the various categories defined and because of the various details left to the user for definition or implementation. There are a multiplicity of versions, limiting the protocol's usefulness as a standard.** Other problems noted include a lack of standardized procedures for error recovery actions and the fact that most control characters are not subject to block checking.† (As an example, the prefix-ENQ sequence is not covered.) Burst errors can introduce undetected errors in control sequences, complicating error recovery procedures. (Individual users must thus define their recovery procedures or change the error checking strategy.)

IBM Binary Synchronous Communication (BSC) Protocol††

This protocol is similar to the ANSI link control procedure just described and is used extensively by U.S. industry. It was developed by IBM prior to the adoption of the ANSI standard, and the latter retains many of the BSC features. BSC protocol has been implemented in three code sets: ASCII, EBCDIC, and the IBM 6-bit transcode. It was originally developed to replace a multiplicity of special purpose procedures and codes, each developed for a particular system. It allows alternate transmission only and applies to two link

---

*Ibid, p. 73, Table 4-3.
**Gray, "Line Control Procedures."
†Ibid.
††Eisenbies, "Digital Data Communication Link Design." Neumann et al., "Computer-Communication Interface Standards," pp. 79–81.

configurations only—two-way alternate centralized multipoint and point-to-point transmission with either station contending for master status.

The basic conventions of this protocol cover (as in the ANSI case): transmission codes, transmission initialization, message delineation and blocking, error detection and correction, ACK signals, and termination of transmission. Its basic set of control characters is similar to that of ANSI. However, it includes in addition an ITB character that indicates the end of intermediate text or heading block (this is followed immediately by a block check character, (BCC)), a WACK character that provides an "affirmative acknowledgement but wait" reply, plus other special characters.

The conventions established provide for encoding of data, synchronization procedures, operational control functions (procedures for sending messages and coordinating the operation of stations comprising the link), information formats, timeouts for initiating repeat or recovery procedures, and error control. Note that these are again the necessary functions of any link protocol, already mentioned several times previously in this chapter.

BSC has a transparent mode feature. In the transmission of transparent text (i.e., data not following a standard character format), all control signals are preceded by DLE. A DLE character is similarly inserted at the transmitter following any DLE character occurring within the text. At the receiver, then, any character following a DLE that is neither a DLE nor a control character is then treated as an error. The DLE STX two-character sequence indicates start of transparent test; DLE ETX indicates the end of this text.

Some typical formats in the various phases of transmission will indicate the similarities and differences between the BSC and ANSI protocols.* (Ø represents a prescribed synchronization pattern, and "A" an address of at most six, or in the case of polling, seven noncontrol characters.)

MESSAGE ESTABLISHMENT PHASE

1. *Point-to-point contention mode*

   Ø ENQ
   Ø ACK 0   This is the basic acknowledgement message.
   Ø NAK
   Ø WACK

2. *Multipoint transmission: supervised mode*

   a. *selection mode*

      Ø A ENQ
      Ø A STX text. . .   This provides fast selection, eliminating the ENQ and ACK sequence.
      Ø A DLE STX transparent text. . .

*Eisenbies, "Digital Data Communication Link Design," p. 282.

Ø A SOH heading.	This provides fast selection for heading transmission.

Replies in this mode are essentially the same as in the contention mode case.

b. *polling*

Ø A ENQ	This is the polling address sequence.
Ø EOT	This is a negative reply, ending transmission.
Ø STX text . . .	This is an affirmative reply followed by text.
Ø DLE STX text . . .	
Ø SOH heading . . .	

Note that the polling and selection replies are different. In particular EOT is used to indicate a negative reply in polling, NAK in the selection mode. Note also that either text or a heading or a combination of both may be sent. The STX or SOH characters terminate the establishment phase in the fast selection case. Fast selection assumes the receiving station is ready to receive. Any reply must then be to the entire block, not to the selection sequence. The fast selection feature saves a reply plus the time required to change the direction of transmission twice. This can provide a sizeable saving in time over long communication links and improves the throughput. It is particularly useful with short messages, requiring only one or two blocks per transmission.

MESSAGE TRANSFER PHASE.*   Here text information only or header plus text, can be transmitted. Messages can be transmitted in transparent text by using DLE STX as previously. We indicate the heading-text combination only. Note how similar this is to previous examples considered.

Ø SOH heading STX text ETX BCC	
Ø SOH heading ENQ.	This indicates the block is to be disregarded. The ENQ character is thus used for terminating transmission. It is a signal to the receiver that there may be a malfunction at the transmitter. (The ENQ calls for a NAK reply, indicating the receiver is waiting for a repetition.) ENQ following text serves the same purpose.

*Ibid., p. 284.

Ø SOH heading ETB BCC.   This indicates there is only one
                                     heading block.

Ø SOH heading ITB BCC STX text . . . This is an intermediate head-
                                     ing block followed by a text
                                     block.

Various other format combinations are possible.

The message transfer phase is entered in this protocol when the starting
characters STX, DLE STX, or SOH are transmitted. This state is maintained
until an end-of-transmission signal is sent returning the link to the original
control state. (See Figs. 14-1 and 14-2.) The starting character initiates block
checking; the ending character signals the end of a block and immediately
precedes the block checking character. The ETB and ETX characters call for
a change of direction of transmission immediately following BCC. The ITB
character does not. The ITB is used to overcome extensive turnaround
delays. The use of the ITB enables long messages to be broken into shorter
transmission blocks. It is only these shorter blocks that need to be retransmitted in the event of an error.

BIT-ORIENTED OR TRANSPARENT LINK CONTROL PROCEDURES

The specific data link protocols described up to this point have their
difficulties in implementation, as already noted; various versions exist for
different applications, they require special provision for the transmission of
transparent text, different formats are used in the transmission of different
kinds of messages, etc. The American National Standards Institute (ANSI)
and the International Standards Organization (ISO) have under development
new standards which will simplify the line protocol problem and provide for
the transmission of transparent text. The ANSI standard is called the
Advanced Data Communication Control Procedure (ADCCP) while the ISO
standard is called *High-Level Data Link Control* (HDLC). Both of these line
control procedures are very similar. IBM has announced a new *Synchronous
Data Link Control* (SDLC), similar in concept to these two standards.
Other computer companies have begun to adopt bit-oriented protocols as
well.

All three protocols utilize the concept of a common frame structure for
the transmission of all types of messages, for various modes of transmission.
The frame is delimited or set off by two identical 8-bit flag characters, one at
the beginning of the frame, the other at the end. We shall summarize some of
the properties of these protocols in this section. Details appear in the refer-

ences.* Recall again some of the requirements of a link control procedure: it must signal the desire to establish transmission; it must provide a means of identifying the sender and prospective receiver(s) from among a group connected on a multipoint facility; it must provide a means of detecting errors and initiating corrective action. It should be applicable to a variety of applications:**

1. *conversational traffic*, consisting of fairly short messages. The data link control overhead should thus be as short as possible. Relatively fast response time is also wanted here.

2. *inquiry-response systems*, with short input and normally long output messages. Duplex transmission is necessary here.

3. *batch transmission*. Large quantities of data are transmitted. Half-duplex transmission can be used on point-to-point lines to half-duplex terminals.

4. *satellite communications*, with attendant large propagation delays. Two-way simultaneous control capability is needed in the line protocol, as well as extended block numbering, since additional blocks will be transmitted while waiting for an ACK message.

The protocol should be applicable to different kinds of polling, including hub polling; it should allow for contention and/or interrupt transmission by stations connected in multilink or loop fashion, etc.

These new protocols attempt to accommodate these applications and requirements. Each link (whether point-to-point, multipoint, hub, loop, etc.) has one station designated permanently as a primary station. This station initiates or authorizes transmission, is responsible for traffic management or the control and organization of data flow, and error recovery. In the ADCCP protocol, as an example, two generic types of configurations, replacing the multiplicity of configurations described under the ANSI protocol, are defined. The primary/primary link corresponds to point-to-point links. Here one station is designated as the primary station in each direction of transmission, serving as the secondary station in the reverse direction. The primary/secondary link configuration consists of one designated primary station and

---

*A description of the ADCCP proposal appears in Carlson, "ADCCP—A Computer-Oriented Data Link Control," and Neuman et al., "Computer-Communication Interface Standards," pp. 83–92. Included in the latter is a brief comparison with HDLC and the IBM SDLC. The HDLC proposal is described briefly in Davies and Barber, *Communication Networks for Computers*, pp. 234, 235. The IBM SDLC is described in detail in Donnan and Kersey, "Synchronous Data Link Control," pp. 140–162. An earlier discussion of ADCCP and SDLC appears in Gray, "Line Control Procedures," pp. 1301–12.

**Donnan and Kersey, "Synchronous Data Link Control."

one or more secondary stations. It includes two-way simultaneous (duplex) transmission, alternate transmission, and multipoint transmission.

All three protocols use a similar standardized frame to support the line control procedures. This frame is shown in Fig. 14-4. All fields, except for the information field whose length is unspecified, are required in all transmissions. The 8-bit flag sequence beginning and ending the transmission of a frame is given by

$$F = 0\ 111\ 111\ 0$$

Flag 0 111 111 0	Address	Control	Information	Block check	Flag 0 111 111 0
8 Bits	·8 Bits	8 Bits		16 Bits	8 Bits

Fig. 14-4. Frame format, bit-oriented procedures.

This flag sequence is used to establish and maintain synchronization. All stations on the link hunt for this sequence. They then check for their address. Bit stuffing is used to ensure that the flag is the only such data field appearing in a frame. Thus a 0 is inserted at the transmitter any time five 1's appear consecutively anywhere in the frame outside of the flag fields. At the receiver, after frame reception has begun, the bit following five consecutive 1's is deleted if it is a 0. If it is a 1 and is in turn followed by a 0 the frame is declared ended. If the sixth 1 is followed by another 1 the frame must be in error and is rejected.

With the frame delimited by the two flags and bit stuffing used to prevent the occurrence of a flag sequence in the data to be transmitted, the information field in Fig. 14-4 becomes transparent to the choice of data transmission. Any sequence of bits is acceptable. These line control procedures are for this reason called bit-oriented.

The 8-bit address field shown in Fig. 14-4 refers to secondary station addresses only. A total of 256 stations or groups of stations may thus be addressed. Both ADCCP and HDLC protocols allow address field extension, in multiples of 8 bits (an octet). In this mode of operation the first bit in an 8-bit address field, with another such field following, is set equal to 0. The first bit in the last address field is set at 1. The control field may also be extended beyond the eight bits shown, if desired. (The basic mode of eight bits provides for modulo 8 sequence numbering of messages; the extended mode provides for mod 128 frame sequence numbering.)

Three types of frames are utilized in these link protocols to transmit data, to send supervisory and control signals and responses to these, and to regulate traffic flow. These three modes of operation are called the Information Transfer (I) mode, the Supervisory (S) mode, and the Unnumbered Control (U) mode. The IBM SDLC terminology for this last frame type is Non-Sequenced (NS) mode. There is no information field present in either the S or U modes. The control field of Fig. 14-4 identifies which of the three frame formats is being transmitted. A 0 in the first bit position of this field represents the I mode, a 10 in the first two bits represents the S mode, and a 11 combination the U mode. The three formats are indicated in Fig. 14-5.* The P/F or poll/final bit is used by the primary station to instruct the secondary station addressed to transmit. It is used by a secondary station to indicate the transmission of the final frame.

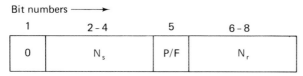

Bit numbers ⟶

1	2 - 4	5	6 - 8
0	N_s	P/F	N_r

a. Information transfer (I) format

Bit numbers ⟶

1	2	3	4	5	6 - 8
1	0	S	S	P/F	N_r

b. Supervisory (S) format

Bit numbers ⟶

1	2	3	4	5	6	7	8
1	1	M	M	P/F	M	M	M

c. Unnumbered (U) format

Fig. 14-5. Control field formats, bit-oriented data link protocols.

The 3-bit send sequence count Ns in the I format indicates the sequence number of this current frame. A primary station maintains such a count, accumulated modulo 8, for each secondary station or group of secondaries (denoted by the address) with which it is currently communicating. The secondary station of course has only one such count, since it addresses the

*Ibid.; Carlson, "ADCCP—A Computer-Oriented Data Link Control."

primary only. As many as eight such frames can thus be outstanding at any one time. (Note that the various data networks described in Chap. 2 used similar sequence count procedures to speed up information flow and increase the network throughput.) The 3-bit receive sequence count Nr is used to acknowledge error-free reception of frames. (It is thus similar to the embedded ACK procedures used in the TYMNET and ARPANET systems described in Chap. 2.) This count indicates to the receiving station to which the frame is being transmitted that all frames through Nr — 1 from that station have been received correctly, and that frame Nr is now expected. This count is incremented for each valid, in-sequence, error-free, I-format frame received. After completing a frame the transmitting station increments its send sequence count Ns by one. The receiving station compares the received Ns count with its internal Nr count. If the two counts agree and the error check indicates the frame is error-free, the frame is accepted. The receiving station then increments its Nr count by one and uses the Nr count of the received frame to determine which of its own transmitted frames were received correctly. These can then be released from their buffers, completing the acknowledgement procedure.

The S format is used to control information flow. Since it contains no information field a sequence count is not needed. In its place two supervisory (S) bits are transmitted, providing four supervisory functions: 00 denotes ready to receive (RR); 10 is used for not ready to receive (RNR); 01 or REJ (reject) is used to signal rejection of all frames received from Nr on, with retransmission requested; and 11 is used for a selective reject (SREJ) function, in which frame Nr only is rejected.* The SREJ thus serves as a negative acknowledgement for the frame specified. This function is used to reduce retransmission time in recovering from an error condition.** With this selective NAK feature there is no need to retransmit a set of frames that may have been received error-free.

The U format (or NS format in the SDLC notation) has five modifier function bits (Fig. 14-5) that allow 32 commands, and responses to them in the case of secondary stations, to be established. It is in defining the various commands and responses for this format that the three protocols differ. ASCCP, for example, defines 10 Unnumbered Commands and seven Unnumbered Responses.† Commands include mode setting, polling of secondary stations without affecting sequence numbers, exchanging station identification, and logically terminating a connection. The responses include acknowledgement of a mode setting function, rejection of an invalid command, and request

---

*This function does not appear in the SDLC protcol. See the *IBM Manual*, "IBM Synchronous Data Line Control," General Information, GA 27–3093–0, March 1974.

**Carlson, "ADCCP—A Computer-Oriented Data Link Control."

†Ibid.

for initialization. The IBM SDLC protocol specifies various commands and/or responses in its NS format.* These include, among others, transmission of information without sequence numbering (used in transmitting group or broadcast messages); placing addressed secondary stations in one of several operational modes (normal response mode, in which a secondary initiates transmission only on reception of a poll-type frame from primary, asynchronous response mode in which a secondary may begin transmission without prior receipt of a poll-type frame—this could be used in long systems or in hub polling, and an initialization mode); exchange of identification information, etc. Secondary stations can use the Ns mode to acknowledge nonsequenced commands and to request certain initialization procedures from the primary. It can be used as well for diagnostic related responses, to reject a command from the primary, etc. (In this last case the reason for the reject is included in the information field following the control field.)

The 16-bit block check sequence uses polynomial checking on the address, control, and information fields only. The two flag sequences are not included in the checking, since the entire frame is rejected if either one of these two fields is found to have an error. Note that because of the frame delimiting there is no need to specify the size of the information field. This is the transparent feature noted earlier. The block check sequence always begins 16 bits prior to the last 8-bit flag received (Fig. 14-4). (The use of 16 bits for checking is wasteful of transmission efficiency if the information field is lacking or small in size. The use of a single format and a single error-checking algorithm simplifies the protocol considerably, however.) All three protocols use the same generator polynomial $g(x) = x^{16} + x^{12} + x^5 + 1$. This is the polynomial specified as an international standard for 16-bit check fields in the CCITT recommendation V.41. In actual implementation it is suggested that the initial remainder of the division be preset to all 1's before division by the generator polynomial is carried out. The 16-bit check sequence of Fig. 14-4 is then transmitted, with the coefficient of the highest term first, as the complement of the resultant remainder term. This results in a nonzero remainder at the receiver when the inverse operation of checking is carried out. This procedure provides protection against possible obliteration of the F flags.

*Donnan and Kersey, "Synchronous Data Link Control," and *IBM manual*, "IBM Synchronous Data Line Control."

Elements of

Point–to–Point

Data

Communication   **APPENDIX**

|||||||||||||||||||||||||||||||||||||||||||||||||||||||||||||||||||||||||||||||||||||||||||||||||||||||||||||||||||||||||||||||||||||||||||||||

Throughout this book the reader is assumed to have some familiarity with the types of communication facilities and devices used in modern point-to-point data communications. For those readers not familiar with this information we offer this brief summary. This material, read in conjunction with Chap. 2 which discusses examples of large-scale networks incorporating the communication facilities described here, should provide the reader with the necessary background to pursue the detailed quantitative discussions provided in the rest of the book. A much more detailed description of current data communication practice, types of facilities available, modems, terminals, and multiplexers used, appears in the book *Teleprocessing Network Organization* by James Martin.* This book, plus references provided in this appendix as well as in other chapters, should be consulted for additional information.

The material in this appendix is presented in two sections. The first describes briefly the types of communication lines and methods of transmission used in current data communications. It should provide the reader with an understanding of the terminology used in Chap. 2 and elsewhere in the book. The second section describes two examples of typical data transmission configurations. These serve to reinforce the terminology of the first section. Calculations of the cost of providing these facilities also provide a simple introduction into the use of realistic tariffs and the cost trade-

*J. Martin, *Teleprocessing Network Organization*, Prentice-Hall, Inc., Englewood Cliffs, N.J., 1970.

offs between alternative methods of providing the desired transmission capability.

SUMMARY OF TERMINOLOGY

Communication lines are often designated by the carrier from whom leased or by whom they are operated in terms of the transmission speed or capacity, in bits/sec (bps), they are capable of accommodating. For example, in the U.S. line speeds commonly available are 0 to 150 bps, 300, 600, 1200 bps, all in the low-speed range; 2400–9600 bps, medium-speed, most commonly over voice-grade circuits; and the higher speeds such as 48 kbps, 56 kbps, 240 kbps, etc. Most of these lines have been designed to carry analog signals. (Voice-grade circuits, for example, are the same circuits that are used for normal telephone transmission with a usable bandwidth extending roughly from 300 Hz to 3400 Hz.) Modulator-demodulator combinations, called *modems* for short, are thus required at each end of a given circuit, at the data terminal-circuit interface, to convert the data stream to the appropriate analog signals and then back again.* Some all-digital facilities are becoming available, however, and this trend is expected to continue. (The Bell System DDS network and the Datapac Network of the Trans-Canada Telephone System are typical examples.) In such cases modems are not needed. (The user can then provide his own interface circuitry for connection to the digital network, or this can be provided by the carrier.)

Full-duplex lines are those capable of transmitting in both directions simultaneously. Half-duplex lines are capable of transmission in either direction, but can be used in only one direction at a time. The actual physical embodiments of these lines consist of local loops from the data source to the common carrier central exchange and then trunks between exchanges. These trunks themselves can be frequency or time-slotted channels on open-wire lines, coaxial cable, microwave links, satellite links, etc. Most private networks lease their communication lines from the common carriers (e.g., ATT or Western Union in the U.S.). Leasing charges usually have a fixed monthly cost which depends on the number of data terminals connected, plus a monthly mileage charge. Typical costs as specified in legal documents called tariffs, are provided in the next section as well as in some of the problems at the end of the various chapters in this book. Two useful papers discussing facilities available and tariffs for their use are referenced.**,†

*J. R. Davey, "Modems," *Proc. IEEE*, **60**, no. 11, Nov. 1972, 1284–92.

M. Gerla, "New Line Tariffs and Their Impact on Network Design," *AFIPS Conference Proc.*, National Computer Conference, **43, 1974, 577–82.

†P. McGregor, "Effective Use of Data Communications Hardware," *AFIPS Conference Proc.*, National Computer Conference, **43**, 1974, 565–75.

Data transmission is carried out asynchronously or synchronously. In asynchronous transmission each data character is transmitted independently and must thus carry its own start and stop information. Low-speed data terminals (teletypewriters and other keyboard devices are typical examples) are generally asynchronous, with each character transmitted as it is generated. Chap. 2 refers to a number of such terminals. In the U.S. many asynchronous terminals use the ASCII 8-bit data code (see Chap. 14 for details of the ASCII code). A character then consists of eight data bits plus two additional bits appended for start and stop: the first bit is generally 0, denoting start; the last bit is a 1, denoting stop. A 75 bps teletype is thus capable of transmitting a maximum of 7.5 characters/sec. A 150 bps teletype can transmit 15 char./sec, at most. With human operators three char./sec *data* rates, each character transmitted at the teletype bit rate, are more common.

Higher-speed devices (e.g., 2400 bps and higher) commonly use synchronous transmission. In this case characters are transmitted one after the other at the given bit rate. A complete message block consisting of a number of characters must thus have its beginning and end designated. Known synchronization characters (patterns of bits) are used to designate the beginning of the block. Examples of methods of handling synchronous transmission appear in Chap. 2 and 14. (The synchronous device can, for example, be a remote job entry terminal or a nodal concentrator in a network transmitting to another node.) Obviously the speed of the device must be matched to the communication line to which it is connected.

It is often advantageous to multiplex or combine several low-speed transmissions into one higher-speed transmission to save cost. Examples appear in various chapters in the book. As noted in several places we stress concentration or statistical multiplexing in this book because of its inherent flexibility and because, with the advent of microcomputer technology, the trend would appear to be moving in that direction. At present most applications requiring the multiplexing of just a few data streams use frequency-division (FDM) or time-division (TDM) multiplexing instead, because of the considerably lower costs involved. This trade-off may be expected to change as concentrator costs are reduced. (An example used in the next section describes an application in which a microcomputer concentrator turns out to be cheaper to use than a time-division multiplexer.) As the name indicates FDM divides the bandwidth of a communications facility into separate channels, allowing each data terminal to use its own channel. As an example, six 150 bps terminals might be multiplexed over one voice-grade line, with considerable saving in cost over the use of six separate low-speed lines.*

Frequency-division multiplexing, although relatively inexpensive, is rather wasteful of bandwidth both because of the modulation technique in

---

*Ibid., for some typical calculations. Similar calculations for TDM, taken from McGregor, appear in the next section.

use for low-speed transmission (generally frequency-shift keying) and the need for guard bands between the channels. As a result a maximum bit rate of 2000 bps can be accommodated over a voice-grade line. Modern modems allow the transmission of 9600 bps over conditioned voice-grade lines.* (Conditioned lines are those available for lease from the carrier that provide certain levels of guaranteed specification limits on attenuation and delay as a function of frequency, as well as noise.) Time-division multiplexing (TDM) allows essentially all of this capacity to be used and is therefore much more efficient in bandwidth than FDM. As the name indicates, TDM allocates a time slot to each data terminal connected, converting multiple low-speed inputs to one high-speed output, or reverse.** As an example, eight 1200 bps terminals could be combined into one 9600 bps data stream by sequentially sampling each terminal in order. Time-division multiplexers are at present more costly than frequency-division multiplexers. They become cost-effective when larger numbers of terminals are to be multiplexed onto one line. In many applications combinations of various multiplexing techniques are often used. For example, several remote terminals might be frequency-division multiplexed and the resultant combined signal transmitted over a higher-speed line to a remote concentrator for combining with other signals. The Datran system described briefly in Chaps. 1 and 2 used a hierarchy of time-division multiplexers to synchronously combine large numbers of data sources of varying rates while it was in operation.

EXAMPLES AND TYPICAL COST CALCULATIONS

In this section we provide two simple examples of the interconnection of data terminals, modems, multiplexers, and lines to provide complete point-to-point communications between terminals and a computer or between pairs of terminals geographically separated. For each example we carry out some typical cost calculations that compare various ways of providing the necessary communication capability. This should provide an introduction to the cost calculations carried out throughout the book. Because of the assumed use of statistical multiplexers in much of the network discussion in this book, message time delay due primarily to concentrator buffering is shown to play an important role in assessing network performance. Where multiplexers are used, however, there is no time delay. (In some design situations in such cases the time required to connect a source with a destination is used as the equivalent criterion.) We thus focus on the calculation of cost only in these introductory examples.

A word of caution is advisable at this point, however. The calculations

*Davey, "Modems."
**McGregor, "Effective Use of Data Communications Hardware."

carried out in the two examples following depend on typical costs available at the time of calculation. These costs may change dramatically, invalidating conclusions that might be drawn from the results. The calculations are presented as simple tutorial exercises only. A reader faced with similar design calculations should consult the up-to-date tariffs of the common carrier from whom the facilities are to be leased, as well as the manufacturers of the devices to be rented or purchased. The reader is cautioned to treat the specific cost calculations here and in fact in the rest of the book, with care. They are given as examples only.

EXAMPLE 1.* Six 1200 bps terminals, with three located at each of two sites, are to be connected to a central processor at a third site. The general picture is shown sketched in Fig. A-1a. First assume they are individually connected, by full-duplex point-to-point voice-grade lines, to the processor at location A. With analog carrier facilities available each data set must be connected by a 1200 bps modem by local loop to the nearest carrier central office, and then by a voice-grade line to the carrier central office at site A nearest to the processor. Local loops then carry each signal to the central processor site, at which point six 1200 bps modems are needed to demodulate the signals for processing by the CPU. The resultant network configuration, showing the modems, voice-grade lines, and central offices, appears in Fig. A-1b. The cost of this configuration is readily calculated by using the following typical lease charges:**

1. line cost, leased voice-grade line (full-duplex)

	miles	$/mo/mile
First 25 miles	1–25	3.30
Next 75 miles	26–100	2.31
Next 150 miles	101–125	1.65

In addition the first drop or station (terminal in this case) at an exchange or central office costs $13.75/mo, while additional stations at the same exchange cost $8.25/mo each.

2. 1200 bps modem rental cost is $25/mo. Using these figures the 100-mile lines are readily found to cost $251.75/mo each, the 60-mile lines $163.35 each, the 12 drops (three each at exchanges B and C, six at exchange A) $117/mo, and the 12 modems required (see Fig. A-1b) $300/mo. The total cost turns out to be $1674/mo.

---

*McGregor, "Effective Use of Data Communications Hardware."
**Ibid. Full-duplex costs are generally 10% higher than half-duplex costs.

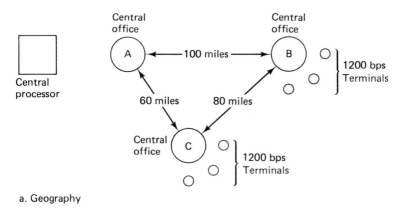

a. Geography

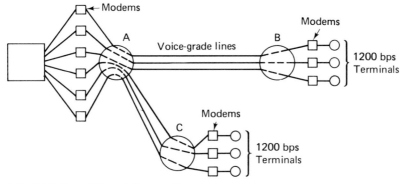

b. Individual, point-to-point connections

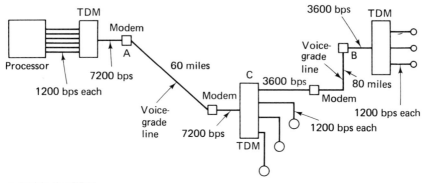

c. Multipoint TDM

Fig. A-1. Example of a multipoint TDM connection.

Now consider the possibility of using a multipoint connection and time-division multiplexing to save line costs. A possible configuration is shown in Fig. A-1c. The number of lines is reduced considerably, as is the number of modems required. But three multiplexers are now needed, as shown in the figure. The lease of 3600 bps modems costs about $100/mo, while the 7200 bps modems rent for about $150/mo. A typical TDM rents for $50/mo plus $10/channel/mo. Note that the TDM at site A has six channels connected, that at site B has three channels, and the one at C has four channels. A simple calculation then shows the total system cost to be $1207/mo, considerably less than the $1674/mo required for the six individual connections of Fig. A-1b.

*EXAMPLE 2.**   In this next example we compare the use of time-division multiplexers and microcomputer concentrators. In this example, shown in Fig. A-2a, two 110 bps, four 300 bps, and two 1200 bsp asynchronous terminals, plus two 4800 bps synchronous data sources are to be connected from Chicago to New York. In the first case two TDMs are used, connected as shown, to multiplex the eight asynchronous sources onto a voice-grade line using a 4800 bps modem. The two 4800 bps synchronous sources are accommodated by a 9600 bps modem, the data again to be transmitted over a voice-grade line. Modem rentals run $115/mo each for the 9600 bps modems. The TDMs with eight channels connected, as shown, have a leasing cost of $133/mo. The two lines together turn out to cost $1609/mo. (The two costs are not quite equal since the line carrying 4800 bps traffic doesn't have to be conditioned as well as the one carrying 9600 bps traffic.) The total cost comes to $2475/mo. Now consider the alternative of using concentration or statistical multiplexing instead. The assumption made is that all the terminals may be accommodated using one concentrator and a 7200 bps line. This of course depends on the traffic characteristics of the individual sources, as pointed out in various chapters of the book. Data compression is used in this concentrator, as well as statistical multiplexing, to reduce the overall traffic throughput. The modems rent for $150/mo each, the concentrators $390/mo each, and the line rental comes to $785/mo. The total cost comes to $1865/mo, $610/mo less than the TDM cost. But note again that time delay has not been included here. The assumption is that the number of bits per second to be transmitted on the average is so small compared to the line capacity as to make concentrator buffering delay negligible. Other, minicomputer, concentrators cost considerably more and would turn the cost figures the other way. For example the use of minicomputer concentrators renting for $800/mo would show the TDM solution to be cheaper. (This ignores the increased flexibility made possible with concentrators, details of which are noted in Chap. 2 and in other places in the book.)

---

*Codex Corp. Application Notes, "Codex 6000 Intelligent Network Processors," Mewton, Mass., 1976.

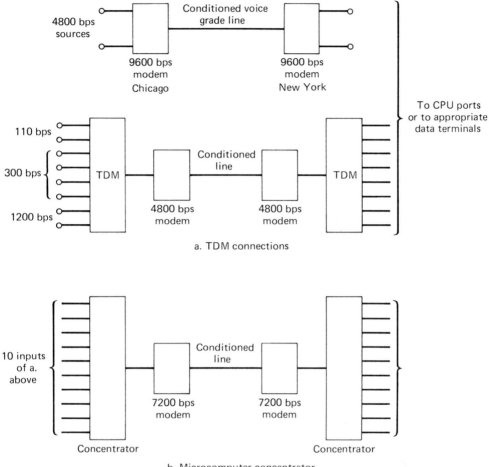

a. TDM connections

b. Microcomputer concentrator

Fig. A-2. Another example, TDM vs. concentration.

References*

||||||||||||||||||||||||||||||||||||||||||||||||||||||||||||||||||||||||||||||||||||||||||||||||||||||||||||||||||||||||||||||||||||||||||||||||||||||||||||||||||||

ABRAMSON, N., "The Aloha System," N. Abramson and F. Kuo, eds., *Computer Networks*, Prentice-Hall, Inc., Englewood Cliffs, N.J., 1973, Chap. 14.

ABRAMSON, N., "Packet-Switching with Satellites," *AFIPS Conference Proc.*, National Computer Conference, **42**, June 1973, 695–702.

BAHL, L. R. and D. T. TANG, "Optimization of Concentrator Locations in Tele-processing Networks," *Proc. Symposium on Computer-Communication Networks and Teletraffic*, Polytechnic Institute of Brooklyn, New York, 1972, pp. 355–62.

BARAN, P. et al., "On Distributed Communications," series of 11 reports, Rand. Corp., Santa Monica, Ca., Aug. 1964.

BARTLETT, K., R. SCANTLEBURY, and P. WILKINSON, "A Note on Reliable Full-Duplex Transmission Over Half-Duplex Links," *Communications of the ACM*, **12**, no. 5, May 1969, 260–61.

BASKETT, F., K. M. CHANDY, R. R. MUNTZ, and F. G. PALACIOS, "Open, Closed, and Mixed Networks of Queues with Different Classes of Customers," *J. of the ACM*, **22**, no. 2, April 1975, 248–60.

*Some of these references are reprinted in books of selected reprints on computer-communications:

P. E. GREEN, JR. and R. W. LUCKY, eds., *Computer Communications*, IEEE Press, New York, 1975.

W. W. CHU, ed., *Advances in Computer Communications*, Artech House, Dedham, Mass., 1974.

BASKETT, F. and R. R. MUNTZ, "Queueing Network Models with Different Classes of Customers," *Proc. IEEE Computer Conference*, San Francisco, Sept. 1972.

BEST, M., "Optimization of Nonlinear Performance Criteria Subject to Flow Constraints," *Proc. 18th Midwest Symposium on Circuits and Systems*, Concordia University, Quebec, Canada, Aug. 1975, pp. 438–43.

BINDER, R., "A Dynamic Packet-Switching System for Satellite Broadcast Channels," *Proc. IEEE International Conference on Communications*, San Francisco, June 1975, pp. 41–4 to 41–5.

BOEHM, B. W. and R. L. MOBLEY, "Adaptive Routing Techniques for Distributed Communication Systems," *IEEE Trans. on Communications Technology*, **COM-17**, no. 3, June 1969, 340–49.

BRANDT, G. J. and G. J. CHRETIEN, "Methods to Control and Operate a Message-Switching Network," *Proc. Symposium on Computer-Communications Networks and Teletraffic*, Polytechnic Institute of Brooklyn, New York, 1972, pp. 263–76.

BROWN, C. W., "Adaptive Routing and Resource Allocation," Ph.D. dissertation, (Electrical Engineering), Polytechnic Institute of New York, June 1975.

BROWN, C. W. and M. SCHWARTZ, "Adaptive Routing in Centralized Computer-Communication Networks," *Proc. IEEE International Conference on Communications*, San Francisco, June 1975, pp. 47–12 to 47–16.

BUTTERFIELD, S., R. RETTBERG, and D. WALDEN, "The Satellite IMP for the ARPA Network," Computer Nets Supplement, *Proc. Seventh Hawaii International Conference on System Sciences*, Jan. 1974.

CANTOR, D. G. and M. GERLA, "Optimal Routing in a Packet-Switched Computer Network," *IEEE Trans. on Computers*, **C-23**, no. 10, Oct. 1974, 1062–69.

CARLSON, D. E., "ADCCP—A Computer-Oriented Data Link Control," *IEEE Compcon 75*, pp. 110–13.

CEGRELL, T., "A Routing Procedure for the TIDAS Message-Switching Network," *IEEE Trans. on Communications*, **COM-23**, no. 6, June 1975, 575–85.

CERF, V. G. and R. E. KAHN, "A Protocol for Packet Network Interconnection," *IEEE Trans. on Communications*, **COM-22**, no. 5, May 1974, 637–48.

CHANDY, K. M. and R. A. RUSSELL, "The Design of Multipoint Linkages in a Teleprocessing Tree Network," *IEEE Trans. on Computers*, **C-21**, no. 10, Oct. 1972, 1062–66.

CHANG, J. H., "An Analysis of Buffering Techniques in Teleprocessing Systems," *IEEE Trans. on Communications*, **COM-20**, no. 3, part II, June 1972, 619–29.

CHEN, F. T., H. D. CHADWICK, and R. M. PENN, "The DATRAN Network: System Description," *Proc. IEEE National Telecommunications Conference*, New Orleans, Dec. 1975.

CHEN, F. T. et al., "Digital Multiplexing Hierarchy for an Integrated Data Transmission and Switching System," *Proc. IEEE National Telecommunications Conference*, New Orleans, Dec. 1975.

CHRETIEN, G. J., W. M. KONIG, and J. H. RECH, "The SITA Network, Summary Description," *Computer-Communication Networks Conference*, University of Sussex, Brighton, U.K., Sept. 1973.

CHU, W. W., "Buffer Behavior for Batch Poisson Arrivals and Single Constant Output," *IEEE Trans. on Communications Technology*, **COM-18**, no. 5, Oct. 1970, 613–18.

CHU, W. W., "A Study of Asynchronous TDM for Time-Sharing Computer Systems," *AFIPS Conference Proc.*, Fall Joint Computer Conference, **35**, 1969, 669–78.

CHU, W. W. and A. G. KONHEIM, "On the Analysis and Modeling of a Class of Computer-Communication Systems," *IEEE Trans. on Communications*, **COM-20**, no. 3, part II, June 1972, 645–60.

CONANT, G. E. and S. WECKER, "DNA: An Architecture for Heterogeneous Computer Networks," *Proc. 1976 International Conference on Computer-Communications*, Toronto, Canada, Aug. 1976.

Codex Corp. Application Notes, "Codex 6000 Intelligent Network Processors," Newton, Mass., 1976.

COX, D. R. and H. D. MILLER, *The Theory of Stochastic Processes*, Methuen & Co., London, 1965.

COX, D. R. and W. L. SMITH, *Queues*, Chapman and Hall, London, 1961.

CROWTHER, W. et al., "A System for Broadcast Communication: Reservation Aloha," *Proc. Sixth Hawaii International Conference on System Sciences*, Jan. 1973.

DAVEY, J. R., "Modems," *Proc. IEEE*, **60**, no. 11, Nov. 1972, 1284–92.

DAVIES, D. W., "The Control of Congestion in Packet-Switching Networks," *IEEE Trans. on Communications*, **COM-20**, no. 3, June 1972, 546–50.

DAVIES, D. W. and D. L. A. BARBER, *Communication Networks for Computers*, John Wiley & Sons, Inc., London, 1973.

DOLL, D. R., "Efficient Allocation of Resources in Centralized Computer-Communication Network Design," University of Michigan, Systems Engineering Laboratory, Nov. 1969.

DOLL, D. R., "Multiplexing and Concentration," *Proc. IEEE*, **60**, no. 11, Nov. 1972, 1313–21.

DONNAN, R. A. and J. R. Kersey, "Synchronous Data Link Control: A Perspective," *IBM Systems J.*, **13**, no. 2, 1974, 140–62.

DUDICK, A. L. et al., "Data Traffic Measurements for Inquiry-Response Computer-Communication Systems," Information Processing 71, *Proc. IFIP*, Ljubljana, Yugoslavia, Aug. 1971, North-Holland Publishing Co., pp. 634–41.

EISENBIES, J. L., "Conventions for Digital Data Communications Link Design," *IBM Systems J.*, **6**, no. 4, 1967, 269–302.

ESAU, L. R. and K. C. WILLIAMS, "A Method for Approximating the Optimal Network," *IBM Systems J.*, **5**, no. 3, 1966, 142–47.

FELLER, W., *An Introduction to Probability Theory and its Applications*, **II**, second edition, John Wiley & Sons, Inc., New York, 1971, pp. 47, 48.

FISCHER, M. J. and T. C. Harris, "A Model for Evaluating the Performance of an Integrated Circuit- and Packet-Switched Multiplex Structure," *IEEE Trans. on Communications*, **COM-24**, no. 2, Feb. 1976, 195–202.

FORD, L. R., JR. and D. R. FULKERSON, *Flows in Networks*, Princeton University Press, New Jersey, 1962.

FRANK, H. and W. S. CHOU, "Network Properties of the ARPA Computer Network," *Networks*, **4**, 1974, John Wiley & Sons, Inc., New York, 213–39.

FRANK, H. and W. S. CHOU, "Topological Optimization of Computer Networks," *Proc. IEEE*, **60**, no. 11, Nov. 1972, 1385–96.

FRANK, H. and I. T. FRISCH, *Communication, Transmission, and Transportation Networks*, Addison-Wesley, Reading, Mass., 1971, pp. 206–10.

FRANK, H., I. T. FRISCH, and W. S. CHOU, "Topological Considerations in the Design of the ARPA Computer Network," *AFIPS Conference Proc.,* Spring Joint Computer Conference, **36**, June 1970, 581–87.

FRANK, H., I. T. FRISCH, R. VAN SLYKE, and W. S. CHOU, "Optimal Design of Centralized Computer Networks," *Networks*, **1**, no. 1, John Wiley & Sons, Inc., New York, 1971, 43–58.

FRATTA, L., M. GERLA, and L. KLEINROCK, "The Flow Deviation Method: An Approach to Store-and-Forward Communication Network Design," *Networks*, **3**, John Wiley & Sons, Inc., New York, 1973, 97–133.

FUCHS, E. and P. E. JACKSON, "Estimates of Distributions of Random Variables for Certain Computer-Communication Traffic Models," *Communications of the ACM*, **13**, no. 12, Dec. 1970, 752–57.

FULTZ, G. F. and L. KLEINROCK, "Adaptive Routing Techniques for Store-and-Forward Computer-Communication Networks," *Proc. IEEE International Conference on Communications*, Montreal, June 1971, pp. 39–1 to 39–8.

GALLAGER, R. G., unpublished manuscript "A Minimum Delay Algorithm Using Distributed Computation," *IEEE Trans. on Communication,* **COM-25**, no. 1, Jan. 1977.

GAVER, D. P., JR. and P. A. W. LEWIS, "Probability Models for Buffer Storage Allocation Problems," *J. of the ACM*, **18**, no. 2, April 1971, 186–98.

GERLA, M., "The Design of Store-and-Forward Networks for Computer-Communications," Ph.D. dissertation, Dept. of Computer Science, UCLA, 1973.

GERLA, M., "New Line Tariffs and Their Impact on Network Design," *AFIPS Conference Proc.*, National Computer Conference, **43**, 1974, 577–82.

GERLA, M., H. FRANK, W.S. CHOU, and J. ECKL, "A Cut Saturation Algorithm for Topological Design of Packet-Switched Communication Networks, *Proc. IEEE National Telecommunications Conference*, San Diego, Dec. 1974, pp. 1074–85.

GOLDSTEIN, M. C., "Design of Long-Distance Telecommunications Networks—The TELPAK Problem," *IEEE Trans. on Circuit Theory*, **CT-20**, 1973, 186–92.

GRAY, J. P., "Line Control Procedures," *Proc. IEEE*, **60**, no. 11, Nov. 1972, 1301–12.

GREENBERG, D. A., "A New Approach for the Optimal Placement of Concentrators in a Remote Terminal Communications Network," *Proc. IEEE National Telecommunications Conference*, Atlanta, Ga., Nov. 1973, pp. 37D–1 to 37D–7.

HANSLER, E., "An Experimental Heuristic Procedure to Optimize a Telecommunication Network Under Nonlinear Cost Functions," *Proc. Seventh Annual Princeton Conference on Information Sciences and Systems*, New Jersey, 1973, pp. 130–37.

HARCHARIK, J. R., "TYMNET, Present and Future," *IEEE Eascon Meeting*, Washington, D.C., Sept. 30, 1975.

HAYES, J. F. and D. N. SHERMAN, "A Study of Data Multiplexing Techniques and Delay Performance," *Bell Systems Technical Journal*, **51**, no. 9, Nov. 1972, 1983–2011.

HAYES, J. F. and D. N. SHERMAN, "Traffic Analysis of a Ring-Switched Data Transmission System," *Bell Systems Technical Journal*, **50**, Nov. 1971, 2947–78.

HEART, F. G., R. E. KAHN, S. M. ORNSTEIN, W. R. CROWTHER, and D. C. WALDEN, "The Interface Message Processor for the ARPA Computer Network," *AFIPS Conference Proc.*, Spring Joint Computer Conference, **36**, June 1970, 551–67.

HITCHNER, L. E., "A Comparative Study of the Computational Efficiency of Shortest Path Algorithms," *Operations Research Center Report*, **ORC 68-25**, University of California, Berkeley, Nov. 1968.

HU, T. C., *Integer Programming and Network Flows*, Addison-Wesley, Reading, Mass., 1969, pp. 122–23.

IBM 2946 Terminal Control Subsystem Component Description and Operating Guide, IBM Systems Development Division, June 1971.

IBM Manual, "IBM Synchronous Data Line Control," General Information, GA 27-3093-0, March 1974.

IBM Reference Manual, A22-6640-1, 9000 Series Airline Reservation Systems, Remote Equipment.

IBM Systems Journal, **15**, no. 1, 1976, 2–80.

JACKSON, J. R., "Jobshop-like Queueing Systems," *Management Science*, **10**, no. 1, Oct. 1963, 131–42.

JACKSON, J. R., "Networks of Waiting Lines," *Operations Research*, Aug. 1959, pp. 518–21.

KAHN, R. E. and W. R. CROWTHER, "Flow Control in a Resource-Sharing Computer Network," *IEEE Trans. on Communications*, **COM-20**, no. 3, part II, June 1972, 539–47.

KAYE, A. R., "Analysis of a Distributed Control Loop for Data Transmission," *Proc. Symposium on Computer-Communications Networks and Teletraffic*, Polytechnic Institute of Brooklyn, New York, 1972, pp. 47–58.

KAYE, A. R. and T. G. RICHARDSON, "A Performance Criterion and Traffic Analysis for Polling Systems," *INFOR*, **11**, no. 2, June 1973, 93.

KERSHENBAUM, A. and W. S. CHOU, "A Unified Algorithm for Designing Multidrop Teleprocessing Networks," *IEEE Trans. on Communications*, **COM-22**, no. 11, Nov. 1974, 1762–72.

KLEINROCK, L., "Analytic and Simulation Methods in Computer Network Design," *AFIPS Conference Proc.* Spring Joint Computer Conference, **36**, 1970, 569–79.

KLEINROCK, L., *Communication Nets; Stochastic Message Flow and Delay*, McGraw-Hill, New York, 1964. Reprinted, Dover Publications, 1972.

KLEINROCK, L., *Queueing Systems*, **1**, 1975; **2**, 1976, Wiley-Interscience, New York.

KLEINROCK, L., "Models for Computer Networks," *Proc. IEEE International Conference on Communications* June 1969, pp. 21.9 to 21.16.

KLEINROCK, L. and S. S. Lam, "Packet-Switching in a Multi-Access Broadcast Channel: Performance evaluation," *IEEE Trans. on Communications*, **COM-23**, No. 4, April 1975, 410–23.

KLEINROCK, L. and S. S. LAM, "Packet-Switching in a Slotted Satellite Channel," *AFIPS Conference Proc.*, National Computer Conference, **42**, 1973, 703–10.

KLEINROCK, L. and W. E. NAYLOR, "On Measured Behavior of the ARPA Network," *AFIPS Conference Proc.*, National Computer Conference, **43**, May 1974, 767–80.

KLEINROCK, L., W. E. Naylor, and H. Opderbeck, "A Study of Line Overhead in the ARPANET," *Communications of the ACM*, **19**, no. 1, Jan. 1976, 3–13.

KLEINROCK, L. and F. A. TOBAGI, "Packet-Switching in Radio Channels: Part I—Carrier Sense Multiple-Access Modes and Their Throughput-Delay Characteristics," *IEEE Trans. on Communications*, COM-23, no. 12, Dec. 1975, 1400–16.

KLEITMAN, D. J. and A. CLAUS, "A Large-Scale Multicommodity Flow Problem: TELPAK," *Proc. Symposium on Computer-Communication Networks and Teletraffic*, Polytechnic Institute of Brooklyn, New York, 1972, pp. 335–38.

KNIGHT, J. R., "A Case Study: Airline Reservation Systems," *Proc. IEEE*, **60**, no. 11, Nov. 1972, 1423.

KOBAYASHI, H., "Applications of the Diffusion Approximation to Queueing Networks," *J. of the ACM*, **21**, part I, April 1974, 316–28; **21**, part II, July 1974, 459–69.

KONHEIM, A. G., "Service Epochs in a Loop System," *Proc. Symposium on Computer-Communications Networks and Teletraffic*, Polytechnic Institute of Brooklyn, New York, 1972, pp. 125–44.

KONHEIM, A. G. and B. MEISTER, "Waiting Lines and Times in a System with Polling," *J. of the ACM*, **21**, no. 3, July 1974, 470–90.

KRUSKAL, J. G., "On the Shortest Spanning Subtree of a Graph and the Traveling Salesman Problems," *Proc. American Mathematics Society*, **7**, 1956, 48–50.

KUMMERLE, K., "Multiplexor Performance for Integrated Line- and Packet-Switched Traffic, *Proc. 1974 International Conference on Computer-Communications*, Stockholm, Sweden, Aug. 1974.

LAM, S. S., "Packet-Switching in a Multi-Access Broadcast Channel with Application to Satellite Communication in a Computer Network," Ph.D. dissertation, Dept. of Computer Science, UCLA, April 1974.

LAM, S. S. and L. KLEINROCK, "Packet Switching in a Multi-Access Broadcast Channel: Dynamic Control Procedures," *IEEE Trans. on Communications*, **COM-23**, no. 9, Sept. 1975, 891–904.

LITTLE, D. C., "A Proof of the Queueing Formula: $L = \lambda W$," *Operations Research*, **9**, 1961, 383–87.

McFAYDEN, J. H., "Systems Network Architecture: An Overview," *IBM Systems J.* **15**, no. 1, 1976, 4–23.

McGREGOR, P. M., "Effective Use of Data Communications Hardware," *AFIPS Conference Proc.*, National Computer Conference, **43**, 1974, 565–75.

McQUILLAN, J. M., "Adaptive Routing Algorithms for Distributed Computer Networks," Bolt, Beranek, and Newman Report No. 2831, May 1974 (Harvard Ph.D. thesis); available from National Technical Information Service, AD 781467.

McQUILLAN, J. M., "The Evolution of Message Processing Techniques in the ARPA Network," *Infotech International State of the Art Report, Network Systems and Software*, 1975, pp. 541–78.

McQUILLAN, J. M., W. R. CROWTHER, B. P. COSELL, D. C. WALDEN, and F. G. HEART, "Improvements in the Design and Performance of the ARPA Network," *AFIPS Conference Proc.*, Fall Joint Computer Conference, **41**, Dec. 1972, 741–54.

MARTIN, J., *Systems Analysis for Data Transmission*, Prentice-Hall, Inc., Englewood Cliffs, N.J., 1972, Chap. 42.

MARTIN, J., *Teleprocessing Network Organization*, Prentice-Hall, Inc., Englewood Cliffs, N.J., 1970.

MAUCERI, L. J., "Control of an Expanding Network—An Operational Nightmare," *Networks*, **4**, John Wiley & Sons, Inc., New York, 1974, 287–97.

MEISTER, B., H. R. MUELLER, and H. R. RUDIN, JR., "New Optimization Criteria for Message-Switching Networks," *IEEE Trans. on Communications Technology*, **COM-19**, no. 3, June 1971, 256–60.

MEISTER, B., H. R. MUELLER, and H. R. RUDIN, JR., "On the Optimization of Message-Switching Networks," *IEEE Trans. on Communications*, **COM-20**, no. 1, Feb. 1972, 8–14.

METCALFE, R. M. and D. R. BOGGS, "Ethernet: Distributed Packet Switching for Local Computer Networks," *Communications of the ACM*, **19**, no. 7, July 1976, 395–404.

MILLS, D. L., "Communication Software," *Proc. IEEE*, **60**, no. 11, Nov. 1972, 1333–41.

Network Analysis Corp., Glen Cove, N.Y., First semi-annual report, May 1973, ARPA Contract DAHC15-73-C-0135, Chap. 3.

Network Analysis Corp., Glen Cove, N.Y., Second semi-annual report, Dec. 1973, ARPA Contract DAHC15-73-C-0135, Chap. 4.

NEUMAN, A. J. et al., "A Technical Guide to Computer-Communication Interface Standards," *NBS Technical Note 843*, Aug. 1974.

NEWPORT, C. B. and J. RYZLAK, "Communication Processors," *Proc. IEEE*, **60**, no. 11, Nov. 1972, 1321–32.

ORNSTEIN, S. M. and D. C. WALDEN, "The Evolution of a High Performance Modular Packet-Switch," *Proc. IEEE International Conference on Communications*, San Francisco, June 1975, pp. 6–17 to 6–21.

ORNSTEIN, S. M. et al., "Pluribus—A Reliable Multiprocessor," *AFIPS Conference Proc.*, National Computer Conference, **44**, 1975, 551–59.

OSSANNA, J. F., "Identifying Terminals in Terminal-Oriented Systems," *IEEE Trans. on Communications*, **COM-20**, June 1972, 565–68.

PEDERSEN, R. D. and J. C. SHAH, "Multiserver Queue Storage Requirements with Unpacked Messages," *IEEE Trans. on Communications*, **COM-20**, no. 3, part I, June 1972, 462–65.

PENNOTTI, M. C., "The Control of Congestion in Message-Switched Networks," Ph.D. dissertation (Electrical Engineering), Polytechnic Institute of New York, June 1974.

PENNOTTI, M. C. and M. SCHWARTZ, "Congestion Control in Store-and-Forward Tandem Links," *IEEE Trans. on Communications*, **COM-23**, no. 12, Dec. 1975, 1434–43.

PICKHOLTZ, R. L. and C. McCoy, JR., "Effects of a Priority Discipline in Routing for Packet-Switched Networks," *IEEE Trans. on Communications*, **COM-24**, no. 5, May 1976, 506–15.

PIERCE, J. R., "How Far Can Data Loops Go?" *IEEE Trans. on Communications*, **COM-20**, no. 3, June 1972, 527–30.

PRIM, R. C., "Shortest Connection Networks and Some Generalizations," *Bell Systems Technical Journal*, **36**, Nov. 1957, 1389–1401.

PROSSER, R. T., "Routing Procedures in Communication Networks, part I: Random Procedures; part II: Directory Procedures," *IRE Trans. on Communication Systems*, **CS-10**, no. 4, 1962, 323–35.

RANDALL, T., J. EDWARDS, and P. WALLINGFORD, "DATRAN's Time-Division Data Switching System," *Proc. IEEE National Telecommunications Conference*, New Orleans, Dec. 1975.

RICH, M. and M. SCHWARTZ, "Buffer Sharing in Computer-Communication Nodes," *Proc. IEEE International Conference on Communications*, San Francisco, June 1975, pp. 33–17 to 33–21.

ROBERTS, L. G., "Dynamic Allocation of Satellite Capacity Through Packet Reservation," *AFIPS Conference Proc.*, National Computer Conference, **42**, June 1973, 711–16.

ROTHFARB, B. and M. C. GOLDSTEIN, "The One-Terminal TELPAK Problem," *J. of the ORSA*, **19**, 1971, 156–69.

RUBIN, I., "Communication Networks: Message Path-Delays," *IEEE Trans. Information Theory*, **IT-20**, Nov. 1974, 733–45.

RUBIN, I., "Message Path-Delays in Packet-Switching Communication Networks," *IEEE Trans. on Communications*, **COM-23**, no. 2, Feb. 1975, 186–92.

RUDIN, H., "On Routing and 'Delta Routing': A Taxonomy and Performance Comparison of Techniques for Packet-Switched Networks," *IEEE Trans. on Communications*, **COM-24**, no. 1, Jan. 1976, 43–59.

RUDIN, H., "Performance of Simple Multiplexor-Concentrators for Data Communications," *IEEE Trans. on Communications Technology*, **COM-19**, no. 2, April 1971, 178–87.

SAATY, T., *Elements of Queueing Theory*, McGraw-Hill, New York, 1961.

SCHULTZ, G. D., "A Stochastic Model for Message Assembly Buffering with a Comparison of Block Assignment Strategies," *J. of the ACM*, **19**, no. 3, July 1972, 483.

SCHWARTZ, M., R. R. BOORSTYN, and R. L. PICKHOLTZ," Terminal-Oriented Computer-Communication Networks," *Proc. IEEE*, **60**, no. 11, Nov. 1972, 1408–23.

SCHWARTZ, M. and C. K. CHEUNG, "The Gradient Projection Algorithm for Multiple Routing in Message-Switched Networks," *IEEE Trans. on Communications*, **COM-24**, no. 4, April 1976, 449–56.

SHIMASAKI, N. and T. KOHASHI, "A Compatible Multiplexing Technique for Anisochronous and Isochronous Digital Data Traffic," *Data Networks: Analysis and Design, Third Data Communications Symposium*, St. Petersburg, Fla., Nov. 1973, pp. 59–67.

SILK, D. J., "Routing Doctrines and Their Implementation in Message-Switching Networks," *Proc. IEE* (London), **116**, no. 10, Oct. 1969, 1631.

SPRAGINS, J. D., "Loop Transmission Systems—Mean Value Analysis," *IEEE Trans. on Communications*, **COM-20**, no. 3, part II, June 1972, 592–602.

SPRAGINS, J. D., "Loops Used for Data Collection," *Proc. Symposium on Computer-Communications Networks and Teletraffic*, Polytechnic Institute of Brooklyn, New York, 1972, pp. 59–76.

STEIN, P. G., "Communications Protocol: The Search for SYNC," *Datamation*, April 1973, pp. 55–57.

STERN, T. E., "A Class of Decentralized Routing Algorithms Using Relaxation," *Proc. IEEE National Conference on Telecommunications,* Dallas, Dec. 1976.

STUTZMAN, B. W., "Data Communication Control Procedures," *Computing Surveys*, **4**, Dec. 1972, 197–220.

TYMES, L., "TYMNET—A Terminal-Oriented Communication Network," *AFIPS Conference Proc.*, Spring Joint Computer Conference, **38**, 1971, 211–16.

WALDEN, D. C., "Experiences in Building, Operating, and Using the ARPA Network," *Second USA-Japan Computer Conference*, Tokyo, Aug. 1975.

WECKER, S., "The Design of DECNET—A General Purpose Network Base," *IEEE Electro 76*, Boston, Mass., May 1976.

WEST, L. P., "Loop-Transmission Control Structures," *IEEE Trans. on Communications*, **COM-20**, no. 3, part II, June 1972, 531–39.

WILKOV, R. S., "Analysis and Design of Reliable Computer Networks," *IEEE Trans. on Communications*, **COM-20**, no. 3, part II, June 1972, 660–78.

WOO, L. S. and D. T. Tang, "Optimization of Teleprocessing Networks with Concentrators," *Proc. IEEE National Telecommunications Conference*, Atlanta, Ga., Nov. 1973, pp. 37C–1 to 37C–5.

YUEN, M. L. T. et al., "Traffic Flow in a Distributed Loop Switching System," *Proc. Symposium on Computer-Communications Networks and Teletraffic*, Polytechnic Institute of Brooklyn, New York, 1972, pp. 29–46.

Index

||||||||||||||||||||||||||||||||||||||||||||||||||||||||||||||||||||||||||||||||||||||||||||||||||||||||||||||||||||||||||||||||||||||||||||||||||||||||||||

A

Acknowledgement procedure (ACK), 14, 323, 324, 327
  ANSI link control, 328, 329
  ARPA network, 46, 49, 50
  bit-oriented protocols, 338
  GE network, 21
  IBM PARS, 270, 274
  TYMNET, 32
Adaptive routing, 217-220
  ARPA network, 48, 220
  in centralized networks, 221-223
ADCCP, 334-336, 338 (*see also* Line control, bit-oriented protocols)
Add algorithm, 198, 199
Airline reservation networks, 13
  IBM PARS, 267, 268, 271
  SITA network, 36
Algorithms:
  adaptive routing, 219, 220
  capacity assignment, centralized network, 87-91
  concentrator location:
    Add algorithm, 198, 199
    Drop algorithm, 200, 201

Algorithms (*cont.*):
  distributed network design:
    branch exchange algorithm, 204
    cut saturation algorithm, 202-204
  fixed routing, 234, 236, 237
    flow deviation, 234-236
    shortest path, 238
  Kruskal, minimum spanning tree, 173, 174
    with constraints, 183
  multipoint design:
    Esau-Williams, 180, 181
    Prim, 182, 183
    optimum, 179
    unified heuristic, 187
  shortest path, 238
Aloha system (*see* Random access techniques)
ANSI line control, 328-331
ARPA network, 9, 13, 41-46
  communications software, 51-54
  cutset design solutions for, 206, 207
  design criteria, 50
  error control, 45, 46, 49, 50
  flow control, 47
  network maps, 43, 44
  routing algorithm, 47, 48, 220
  sequence control, 48, 49
  traffic data, 54, 55
Arrival process:
  binomial arrivals, 155
  Poisson arrivals, 105, 106
Arrival rate, of messages, 62
ASCII code, 328, 329
  in GE network, 20
  in TYMNET, 31
Asynchronous multiplexing, 6 (*see also* Statistical multiplexing)
Asynchronous terminals and lines, 17, 25, 38, 267, 268, 342
Asynchronous transmission, 342

B

Backward learning, routing algorithm, 219
BCD code, in IBM PARS, 268, 269, 271, 272
Bernoulli distribution, 133
Binomial distribution, 133

Birth-death process, 115
Bit stuffing, bit-oriented protocols, 336
Block checking:
  ANSI protocol, 329, 330
  ARPA network, 45
  bit-oriented protocols, 339
  GE network, 20, 21
  IBM BSC protocol, 332-334
  TYMNET, 32
Blocking probability:
  in end-to-end congestion control, 251, 254
  finite $M/M/1$ queue, 114
  local congestion control, 246, 255
Branch-and-bound algorithm, in multipoint design, 174-179
Buffer allocation:
  ARPA network, 51, 53
  GE network, 17, 23, 24
  IBM PARS, pre-1969, 268
Buffer analysis:
  average buffer occupancy, 143, 145
    block storage, 162, 163, 168
    design curves, 150, 159, 161
    in polling, 282
  finite buffer analysis, 155, 156
    comparison with $M/M/1$ analysis, 158
  $M/M/1$ models for, 111, 113, 114
  probability of overflow, 148, 149, 157, 158
  queueing models, 60-62, 104, 137, 138
  synchronous output analysis, 139-143, 148-150
    comparison with $M/M/1$ results, 145, 150, 151
  time delay, 62, 112, 124, 146
  typical design calculations, 15, 152, 160, 161
  waiting time formula, 125
Bus polling (*see* Roll-call polling)

C

Capacitated plant location problem, 196
Capacity (*see* Line capacity)
Circuit switching (*see* Line switching)
Communication cost:
  calculations, typical, 344-347
  and line capacity, 59, 65
    calculations, examples, 65, 68, 92, 93

Communication cost (*cont.*):
  line cost, examples, 209-211, 345, 346
  tariffs, 85, 209, 210
Communications processor (*see* Programmable concentrators)
Communications protocol (*see* Line control)
Communications software, ARPA network, 51-54
Computer network, 1, 2 (*see also* ARPA network)
Concentration in networks, 4-7, 14
Concentration process, 136-138
Concentrator (*see* Programmable concentrators)
Concentrator assignment, in adaptive routing, 221-229
Concentrator interconnection:
  centralized network, multipoint, 179, 180, 187, 195
  distributed network, 201, 202
Concentrator location, in network design, 194-196
Conditioned lines, 343
Congestion, defined, 246, 252
Congestion control (*see* Flow control)
Contention procedure, 286
  IBM BSC protocol, 332
Cut saturation algorithm, 202-204
Cyclic checking:
  bit-oriented protocols, 339
  IBM PARS, 271

D

Data communication control (*see* Line control)
Data compression, in concentration, 347
Data link control (*see* Line control)
DATRAN, 1, 2, 15
Deadlock, 47, 242, 243
DECNET, 322
Distributed topology, 4
  ARPA and TYMNET as examples, 9, 26, 42, 43
Drop algorithm, 200, 201
Dynamic buffering, 163, 164

E

Error control, 14, 324, 327
  ANSI protocol, 329, 330
  ARPA network, 45, 46, 49
  GE network, 21

Error control (*cont.*):
  IBM PARS, 270, 271
  TYMNET, 32
Esau-Williams algorithm, 180, 181
Exponential distribution, 106, 107
External flows algorithm, for routing, 236

F

Flag sequence, bit-oriented protocols, 336
Flow control, 4, 242, 243
  ARPA network, 46, 47
  end-to-end, 242, 243, 245, 246
    analysis, 248-253
    performance, 253, 254, 256
  GE network, 21, 24
  isarithmic control, 243, 257
  local control, 243, 245-247
    performance, 255, 256
  TYMNET, 30
Flow deviation algorithm, for routing, 234-236
Format (*see* Message format; Packet)
Frame, in bit-oriented protocols, 336
Frequency-division multiplexing, 5, 342, 343
Full-duplex lines, 341

G

Gamma distribution, 134
Generator polynomial, for error detection:
  CCITT standard, 339
  IBM PARS, 271
GE network, 9, 16
  access procedure, 19
  computer systems, 19
  concentrators, 17
    line queueing, 22, 23
  error detection, 21
  load balancing, 19, 24
  message formats, 20-22
  response time, 24
  sequence numbering, 21
  transmission scheduling, 22, 23
  user characteristics, 24

Geometric distribution, 133
  as message length model, 141, 142
Gradient projection algorithm, for routing, 237

H

Half-duplex lines, 341
HDLC, 334, 335(*fn.*), 336, 339 (*see also* Line control, bit-oriented protocols)
Host computers, 13
  ARPA network, 44
  GE network, 19
  TYMNET, 26
Hot potato routing, 219
Hub polling, 265, 266 (*see also* Polling)

I

IBM BSC protocol, 331-334
IBM PARS, 267-274
  current version, 271
    message formats, 272
  pre-1969, 267
    data flow, 265, 269
    message formats, 269, 270
IMP, in ARPA network, 42, 56
  software considerations, 51-54
Independence assumption, for queueing networks, 66
Integrated network, 3
Interrupt, 136
Isarithmic congestion control, 257, 258
ISO code, 328 (*see also* ASCII code)
  in SITA network, 37

K

Kendall queueing notation, 108
Kruskal algorithm, 173, 174, 183

L

Line capacity, 3, 341
  algorithm for assignment, centralized networks, 87-91
  ARPA network, 42
  and buffer design, 161

Line capacity (*cont.*):
  calculations, examples, 65, 68, 76, 91-97
  cost of, examples, 209-211, 345, 346
  delay-cost tradeoff, 97
  equal assignment strategy, 76, 77
  GE network, 17
  to minimize maximum time delay, 86
  and minimum weighted time delay, 78-80
    min-max assignment, 79, 80
  proportional assignment strategy, 76, 77
  SITA, 36, 37
  square root assignment strategy, 59, 62-64
  tariffs for, 85, 341
  TYMNET, 26
Line control, 11, 321-323, 325-327, 335
  ANSI link control, 328-331
  bit-oriented protocols, 334-336
    block checking, 339
    differences between protocols, 338, 339
    frame format, 336
    modes of operation, 336, 337
  GE network, 21-23
  IBM BSC protocol, 331-334
  IBM PARS, 269-274
  message transmission phases, 325-327
  SITA, 37, 38
  TYMNET, 31-33
Line costs, examples, 209-211, 345, 346
Line speed (*see* Line capacity)
Line switching, 2, 3, 14, 15, 325 (*fn.*)
  and message switching, combined, 3
Line tariffs, 85, 209, 210, 341
    TELPAK, 202
Little's formula, 112, 126, 146, 207, 248
Logical link, 23, 243
Logical record, in TYMNET, 31, 32
Loop network, 8, 263-265

M

M/D/1 queue, 108, 121, 124
Message block storage, 162, 163
Message concentrator (*see* Programmable concentrators)

Message format:
  ANSI protocol, 330
  bit-oriented protocols, 336
  GE network, 19-22
  IBM BSC protocol, 333, 334
  IBM PARS, 269-272
  TYMNET, 31-33
Message length:
  ARPA network, 45, 54
  exponential model, 62, 107
    independence assumption, 66
    weighted, 74
  geometric model, 141, 142
  SITA network, 37
  TYMNET, 34
Message switching, 2, 3, 42
  and line switching, combined, 3
Message transmission, phases in, 325-327
  ANSI link control, 331
M/G/1 queue, 10, 108
  delay time, average, 124
    preemptive priority, 134
  message occupancy, average, 123, 124
  moment-generating function, 123
  waiting time, average, 125
    nonpreemptive priority, 127
Microcomputer concentrator, 345, 347
Minicomputer concentrators, 17, 26, 34, 38, 42, 56
Minimum spanning tree, 173-176, 184, 185
M/M/1 queue, 10, 108
  comparison with finite buffer analysis, 158
  comparison with synchronous output analysis, 145, 146, 151
  finite buffer, 113-115
    blocking probability, 114
  occupancy, average, 111
  state probabilities, 111
  stationary state equation, 109
  tandem network analysis, 249-251
  time delay, 62, 112, 145
    nonpreemptive priority, 127, 128
Modem, 341
Moment-generating function, 118, 252, 253
  examples, 133
  M/G/1 queue, 123

Multidrop (multipoint) connection, 11, 172
   heuristic algorithms, with flow constraints, 180, 187
   optimum algorithm, with flow constraint, 179
   polling, 262, 263
   with TDM, 344
Multiple routing, 231
Multiplexing in networks, 4-7, 14, 15

N

NAK (negative acknowledgement), 323, 327, 329, 332
NASDAQ network, 262
Network design, 3, 171, 193 (*see also* Line capacity; Topological design)
   concentrator location, 194-196
      Add algorithm, 198, 199
      Drop algorithm, 200, 201
   distributed network:
      branch exchange algorithm, 204
      cut saturation algorithm, 202
   hierarchical approach, 194
   line capacity allocation, 62-65, 78-80, 87-91
   multipoint connection, 172
      heuristic algorithms, 180, 187
      optimum algorithm, 179
Network operation:
  ARPA network, 54, 55
  GE network, 24
  SITA network, 40, 41
  TYMNET, 33, 34
Networks of queues, 244
Network topology:
  ARPA network, 43
  examples, 4, 8
  GE network, 16
  loop, 8, 263-265
  SITA network, 36
  star and tree compared, 99, 100
  TYMNET, 26, 28, 29

O

Offered load, 64, 74
Overflow probability, in buffers, 148, 149, 157, 158

P

Packet, 14
  ARPA network, 42, 45, 46, 56, 57
    length, 45, 54
Packet processing, ARPA network, 52-54
Packet switching, 2
  ARPA network, 42
Performance characteristics (*see* Network operation)
Performance criteria, 4, 7, 8
  ARPA network, 50
  capacity assignment, 63, 78, 79, 86
  DATRAN network, 15
  distributed network design, 201, 202
  GE network, 24
  multipoint design, 172
  routing, 214
    centralized network, 223, 224
  SITA network, 37
Poisson distribution, 106, 133
Poisson process, 105, 106
Pollaczek-Khinchine formula, 124, 125
Polling, 265, 266
  analysis, 281-284
  ANSI Line control, 330
  bit-oriented protocols, 337-339
  comparison with slotted Aloha, 311, 312, 314-317
  IBM BSC protocol, 333
  IBM PARS, 269-271, 273
  response time, 280
  scan time, 276, 277, 282
  SITA network, 38
  walk-time, 276
    roll-call and hub polling, compared, 277-280
Prim algorithm, 182, 183
Priority queueing:
  nonpreemptive priority, 134
  preemptive priority, 134
Programmable concentrators, 2, 13, 14 (*see also* Buffer analysis)
  ARPA network, 42, 56
    communications software, 51-54
  Codex processor, 345, 347
  GE network, 17, 23
    line queueing, 22, 23

Programmable concentrators (*cont.*):
  IBM PARS, 271
  polling with, 7, 38
  queuing models, 61, 62, 104, 137, 138
  SITA network, 38
  statistical multiplexing, 6, 60, 61
    analysis, 147
  TYMNET, 26, 34, 35
Propagation delay, 278, 279

Q

Queueing:
  arrival process, 105
  balance equations, 248, 249
  finite buffer analysis, 155, 156
  in GE network concentrator, 22, 23
  Kendall notation, 108
  messages buffered, generating function for, 120
  M/G/1 queue, 122 (*see also* M/G/1 queue)
  M/M/1 queue, 108 (*see also* M/M/1 queue)
  model of, in communication processor, 137, 138
  multiple servers, 116
  priority disciplines, 125, 134
  queue with discouragement, 117
  service-time distribution, 107, 118
  synchronous output analysis, 139-143, 148-150
  tandem queue analysis, 249-251
Queueing delay, in concentrator, 62 (*see also* Time delay)
Queueing networks, 244, 250
  tandem queue analysis, 249-251

R

Random access techniques, 287
  carrier-sense Aloha, 300
  comparison with polling, 311, 312, 314-317
  pure Aloha, 288
    time delay-throughput analysis, 289-292
  reservation Aloha, 303-305
    analysis, 307, 308
  slotted Aloha, 292
    excess capacity schemes, 301, 302
    time delay-throughput analysis, 293-296

Random access techniques (*cont.*):
   slotted Aloha and reservation Aloha, compared, 309
   stability, 298
Reassembly lockup, 47
Reliability in networks, 9
   duplicate lines, 17
   SITA network, 41
   two-connectivity design, ARPA network, 50
   TYMNET, 33
Remote concentrator, 2 (*see also* Programmable concentrators)
   in GE network, 16, 17
Response time:
   ARPA network, 54
   DATRAN network, 15
   GE network, 24
   IBM PARS, 267
   message-switched networks, 15
   polling systems, 280, 281
   SITA network, 37, 40
Roll-call polling, 265, 266 (*see also* Polling)
Routing 3, 14, 212, 213
   adaptive strategies, 217-220, 231 (*fn.*)
      ARPA algorithm, 220
      centralized network, 221-223
      isolated local routing, 219
   ARPA network, 48, 220
   fixed strategies, 230
      minimum time delay, 231-233
      shortest path algorithm, 238
   flooding rule, 215
   performance criteria, 214, 231
   random fixed rule, 216, 217
   shortest path, 73, 83, 215
      algorithm, 238
   SITA network, 38, 212
   TYMNET, 27, 30

S

Satellite links:
   ARPA network, 42, 56
   GE network, 16
   TYMNET, 26
Scanning, 136, 268, 269
SDLC, 334, 335 (*fn.*), 337 (*see also* Line control, bit-oriented protocols)

Selection procedure, 325, 327
   ANSI line control, 330
   IBM BSC line control, 332, 333
Sequence control:
   ARPA network, 48, 49
   bit-oriented protocols, 337, 338
   GE network, 21
Service-time distribution, in queueing, 105, 106
   exponential distribution, 107
   gamma distribution, 134
   general distribution, 118
Shortest path routing, 215, 235
   algorithm, 238
   examples, 73, 83
   TYMNET, 27
Shortest queue routing, 219
SITA network, 9, 35, 36
   concentrators, 38
   message characteristics, 36, 37, 129
   message path, 39
   network map, 36
   operating statistics, 40, 41
   routing, 212
   time delay calculations, 129, 130, 134
SNA (IBM System Network Architecture), 322
Star topology, 8
   concentrator location, 194-196
   GE network, 16
   line capacity calculation, examples, 60, 64, 65, 99
   and tree network, comparison, 99, 100
Statistical multiplexing, 6
   buffering calculations, examples, 151, 152, 160, 161
   loop topologies, 263, 264
   queueing models, 60, 61, 147
Store-and-forward operation, 2, 14, 27, 41, 42
   time delay analysis, 61-63
Synchronization, 20, 31
   ANSI protocol, 329
   IBM PARS, 269, 273
Synchronous terminals and lines, 16, 17, 25, 35, 38, 342
Synchronous transmission, 342

T

Tandem link, congestion control, 253-256

Tariffs, 85, 210, 341
  TELPAK tariffs, 202
Terminal-oriented networks, 2, 16, 25, 35, 36
TIDAS network, 220
Time delay:
  Aloha systems, 291, 293
    Reservation Aloha, 307, 308
  centralized network, 86
  -cost tradeoff, 97
  and line capacity, 62
  M/G/1 queue, 124
    preemptive priority, 134
  M/M/1 queue, 62, 112
    nonpreemptive priority, 127
  network, 63
    minimum average, 63
    min-max, 80-82
    weighted average, 78, 79
  polling, inbound, 282, 284
  snychronous output analysis, 146
  TYMNET, 34
Time delay analysis:
  concentrator, 61-63
    synchronous output, 146
  polling, 282-284
  SITA network, 129, 130, 134
Time-division multiplexing (TDM), 5, 6, 15, 343-346
Timeout for acknowledgement, 21, 50
Time-sharing networks, 13
TIP, in ARPA network, 42
Topological design, 3, 171 (*see also* Network design)
  ARPA network, 50
  multidrop networks, 172, 173
    heuristic algorithms, 180, 187
    optimum algorithm, 179
  star and tree topologies compared, 99, 100
Topology (*see* Network topology)
Traffic data:
  ARPA network, 54, 55
  GE network, 24
  models, 7
  SITA network, 40
  TYMNET, 33, 34
Traffic intensity, 62, 110, 140, 144 (*see also* Traffic utilization)

Traffic matrix, 72
Traffic models, 141
Traffic utilization (*see also* Traffic intensity):
   Aloha systems, 288, 306
   ARPA network, 55
   SITA, 40
   TYMNET, 34
Transmission circuits, 14 (*see also* Line capacity)
Transmission line speed (*see* Line capacity)
Transparent text, 327
   bit-oriented protocols, 336, 339
   IBM BSC protocol, 332
Tree topology, 8
   delay-cost tradeoff, 97
   line capacity calculation, examples, 65-68, 91-98
   multipoint connection, 172
   and star network, comparison, 99, 100
Trunk speed (*see* Line capacity)
Two-connectivity, 9
   in ARPA network, 50
TYMNET, 9, 25
   access procedure, 30, 31
   concentrators, 26, 34
   flow control, 30
   general characteristics, 25, 26, 33, 34
   message format, 31, 32
   network map, 28, 29
   routing algorithm, 27
   supervisory control, 26, 27, 34
   terminals handled, 25, 31

V

Virtual circuit, 325 (*fn.*)
   TYMNET, 27, 30
Voice-grade lines, 36, 341
   costs, examples, 210, 211

W

Waiting time, 125
   with priority queueing, 127
Walktime, in polling, 275, 277, 278
   calculation, examples, 279, 280, 313